⚖ NOLO Products & Services

⇨ Books & Software

Get in-depth information. Nolo publishes hundreds of great books and software programs for consumers and business owners. Order a copy—or download an ebook version instantly—at Nolo.com.

⇨ Legal Encyclopedia

Free at Nolo.com. Here are more than 1,400 free articles and answers to common questions about everyday legal issues including wills, bankruptcy, small business formation, divorce, patents, employment and much more.

⇨ Plain-English Legal Dictionary

Free at Nolo.com. Stumped by jargon? Look it up in America's most up-to-date source for definitions of legal terms.

⇨ Online Legal Documents

Create documents at your computer. Go to Nolo.com to make a will or living trust, form an LLC or corporation or obtain a trademark or provisional patent. For simpler matters, download one of our hundreds of high-quality legal forms, including bills of sale, promissory notes, nondisclosure agreements and many more.

⇨ Lawyer Directory

Find an attorney at Nolo.com. Nolo's consumer-friendly lawyer directory provides in-depth profiles of lawyers all over America. From fees and experience to legal philosophy, education and special expertise, you'll find all the information you need to pick the right lawyer. Every lawyer listed has pledged to work diligently and respectfully with clients.

⇨ Free Legal Updates

Keep up to date. Check for free updates at Nolo.com. Under "Products," find this book and click "Legal Updates." You can also sign up for our free e-newsletters at Nolo.com/newsletters.

4th Edition

The New Bankruptcy

Will It Work for You?

Attorney Stephen Elias

Fourth Edition	MAY 2011
Editor	KATHLEEN MICHON
Cover Design	SUSAN PUTNEY
Production	MARGARET LIVINGSTON
Proofreading	ROBERT WELLS
Index	VICTORIA BAKER
Printing	DELTA PRINTING SOLUTIONS, INC.

Elias, Stephen.
 The new bankruptcy : will it work for you? / By Stephen Elias. — 4th ed.
     p. cm.
 Includes index.
 Summary: "A guide to the most common types of consumer bankruptcy: Chapter 7 and Chapter 13. It provides information and strategies for making the right decisions about debt. The 4th edition includes updated exemption tables plus information on how Supreme Court cases have interpreted the laws"—Provided by publisher.
 ISBN-13: 978-1-4133-1391-8 (pbk.)
 ISBN-10: 1-4133-1391-4 (pbk.)
 ISBN-13: 978-1-4133-1500-4 (epub e-book)
 1. Bankruptcy—United States—Popular works. I. Title.
 KF1524.85.E43 2011
 346.7307'8—dc22
                     2010052793

Please note

We believe accurate, plain-English legal information should help you solve many of your own legal problems. But this text is not a substitute for personalized advice from a knowledgeable lawyer. If you want the help of a trained professional—and we'll always point out situations in which we think that's a good idea—consult an attorney licensed to practice in your state.

Dedication

To my son Rubin, who faithfully reminds me of what bankruptcy is all about.

Acknowledgments

Thanks to Robin Leonard, the original, superlative author of this book's predecessor; Lisa Guerin, Nolo editor extraordinaire, who did such a great job helping me get this book into the world in a timely manner; Janet Portman, who edited the third edition; and Kathleen Michon, editor of the fourth edition. I'm perpetually grateful for my many friends at Nolo.

To immerse myself in the new law, I attended two wonderful conferences sponsored by the National Association of Consumer Bankruptcy Attorneys. Thanks to Henry Sommer and the NACBA crew for doing such a great job.

Many thanks to Sandy McCarthy and Herb Gura, both bankruptcy petition preparers, who read the manuscript and found that it played in Peoria.

Thanks also to the thousands of bankruptcy debtors whom I've counseled over the years and who have, in return, schooled me on the various issues commonly encountered in the real world.

I couldn't have written the book without the support and love I received from my wife, coauthor, and partner in life, Catherine Elias-Jermany.

Table of Contents

Introduction

The New Bankruptcy Law: A Work in Progress

On October 18, 2005, a new law took effect that substantially changed the bankruptcy system. Shortly afterwards, *The New Bankruptcy* hit the bookshelves. Now, five years later, the fledgling law is no longer new, and I've substantially modified this fourth edition to account for the many court interpretations and rules that have put the 2005 law into effect—including several U.S. Supreme Court decisions decided in 2010. During that five-year period, I have counseled numerous bankruptcy filers on their rights and duties in Chapter 7 and Chapter 13 bankruptcies. This edition reflects the advice and information I've provided to my clients regarding how bankruptcy works and which type of bankruptcy is best for each individual client.

More specifically, this book explains how eligibility for Chapter 7 and Chapter 13 bankruptcy is determined, what debts are cancelled (discharged), what happens to your home, car, and other property, what complications might occur, what paperwork is involved, and where you can find help with your bankruptcy. Taken together, this information will help you decide whether it makes sense to handle your debt problems through bankruptcy and, if so, which type of bankruptcy is the best choice for you.

Although it provides valuable guidance for consumers who are considering bankruptcy, this book isn't intended as an authoritative reference on every detail of bankruptcy law. Nor should it be viewed as a guide on how to handle your own bankruptcy. For that task, Nolo's more detailed "do-it-yourself" bankruptcy books (*How to File for Chapter 7 Bankruptcy, Bankruptcy for Small Business Owners: How to File for Chapter 7*, and *Chapter 13 Bankruptcy: Keep Your Property & Repay Debts Over Time*) are the books to use.

Despite the five-plus years that have passed since the new law took effect, courts throughout the country are still weighing in on a number of key issues, regularly publishing opinions that are contradictory. Because only the U.S. Supreme Court can ultimately resolve these conflicts—which can take years—those of us in the bankruptcy field must live with some degree of uncertainty. Fortunately, for most readers, these contentious issues will never arise should you decide to file for bankruptcy. Still, when you run across language like, "Some courts say this while other courts say that," you'll want to do your best to learn how the courts in your area have ruled, if at all, in the unlikely event that the issue rears its head in your case. You can find out by using the resources described in Chapter 11, or by finding a public-spirited bankruptcy attorney who is willing to share this information without demanding an arm or a leg in return. ●

What Is Bankruptcy?

If you've picked up this book, you probably have more debt than you can handle. Most likely, your debt mushroomed because of circumstances beyond your control—job loss, divorce, business failure, illness, accident, or perhaps the result of a car repossession, a home foreclosure, or even your use of too many credit cards that came your way, whether you asked for them or not.

You may feel overwhelmed by your financial situation and uncertain about what to do next. Maybe a friend, relative, or even a lawyer suggested bankruptcy, describing it as the best thing in the world for you. Someone else may have said the opposite—that bankruptcy is a huge mistake and will ruin your life.

This book will help you sort through your options and choose the best strategy for dealing with your economic plight. It explains:

- how bankruptcy works
- how filing for bankruptcy under Chapter 7 or Chapter 13 (the two bankruptcy options for consumers) will affect your debts, property, home, and credit
- the procedures you'll have to follow (and paperwork you'll have to complete) to file for bankruptcy
- some common mistakes people make before, during, and after bankruptcy, and how to avoid them, and
- some alternative ways to handle your debt problems, outside of the bankruptcy system.

Armed with this information, you'll be ready to decide whether you qualify for Chapter 7 or Chapter 13 bankruptcy and, if so, which Chapter makes the most sense.

As you consider the strategies available to you, keep in mind that you're not alone. During each of the first five years of the new millennium, more than 1.5 million Americans filed for bankruptcy. So did thousands of companies. Although filings dropped dramatically just after the new law took effect in 2005, filings have once again mushroomed in these difficult times. Bankruptcy remains a necessary and pervasive part of our economic system.

And bankruptcy may be just the ticket for you. You can stop creditor collection actions (such as foreclosures, wage garnishments, and bank account levies) and:

- wipe out all or most of your debts in a Chapter 7 bankruptcy while hanging on to your home, car, and other necessary items, or
- use Chapter 13 bankruptcy to pay back a portion of your debts over three to five years and discharge the rest.

Bankruptcy may, in fact, seem like a magic wand, but it also has its drawbacks. And, because everyone's situation is a little bit different, there is no one-size-fits-all formula that will tell you whether you absolutely should or should not file. For many, the need for and advantage of bankruptcy will be obvious. Others will be able to reach a decision only after closely examining their property, debts, income, and recent financial transactions—and how persistent their creditors are. For some, simple nonbankruptcy options might do the trick—these are explained in Ch. 12 of this book.

This chapter provides some basic background information about the two types of bankruptcies most often filed by individuals: Chapter 7 and Chapter 13. In the chapters that follow, you'll find more detailed information on the issues you are likely to be interested in, including:

- whether you are eligible to file
- which debts will and will not be cancelled
- what will happen to your home, car, and other essential property items
- how your postbankruptcy credit will be affected
- how bankruptcy will affect your personal life, and
- whether you need to be represented by a lawyer or can represent yourself, perhaps with some outside help.

Types of Bankruptcy

Consumers and small business owners can choose from among several types of bankruptcy "chapters," including Chapter 7, Chapter 11, Chapter 12, and Chapter 13. Let's look at each one quickly—more about Chapters 7 and 13 just below.

Chapter 7. Chapter 7 bankruptcy is by far the most popular. In Chapter 7 bankruptcy, you fully disclose your property, debts, and financial activities over the past several years. Three months later you receive a discharge (cancellation) of most types of debts and emerge with all or most of the property you owned going in—luxury items and investment real estate (in which you have equity) commonly excepted.

Chapter 11. Chapter 11 bankruptcy helps a business stay afloat by encouraging negotiation and compromise by all concerned, so that the business can keep going and at least pay the creditors something (as opposed to a Chapter 7 liquidation, in which creditors frequently get nothing). While individuals may file under

Chapter 11, the process is unaffordable for most primarily because attorney fees can easily surpass $100,000. Even a business that starts off in Chapter 11 will typically end up in Chapter 7, where the business is liquidated. Having run out of money trying to reorganize in Chapter 11, the business can't propose a feasible plan that will pass muster under Chapter 11 guidelines. Because this book is intended primarily for individual consumers, I don't discuss Chapter 11 further (except briefly in Ch. 12).

Chapters 12 and 13. Chapter 12 and Chapter 13 are reorganization programs designed for individuals, except that Chapter 12 is especially designed for owners of family farms, while Chapter 13 is designed for everybody else, including farmers if they wish. Here I discuss only Chapter 13. As used in Chapter 13, the term "individual" includes sole proprietors and independent contractors, but not business entities such as corporations or limited liability companies (LLCs).

In a Chapter 13 bankruptcy, you prepare and file the same basic forms as you do in a Chapter 7 bankruptcy. However, you also propose a three- or five-year plan under which you typically must repay certain types of debt in full (such as back child support) and usually some portion of your unsecured debt (from 1% upwards) even though some judges will approve of plans that pay 0% of unsecured debt. Chapter 13 provides some remedies that aren't available in Chapter 7—such as the opportunity to pay off missed mortgage payments over the life of the plan—but usually isn't the bankruptcy of choice because of the extra legal fees it entails, and because people would rather get their fresh start in three months instead of three or five years. However, 10% to 15% of the people who file under Chapter 7 are required by the bankruptcy court to convert to Chapter 13, because they have sufficient income to fund a Chapter 13 plan.

Chapter 7 Bankruptcy

As I mentioned just above, Chapter 7 is a three-month process that usually only requires the filing of some paperwork and one brief appearance before the bankruptcy trustee, the official appointed to handle the case for the court. You may have to make additional brief appearances before a bankruptcy judge if you seek to waive the bankruptcy filing fee or seek approval of a reaffirmation agreement you signed in order to keep a car or other property you are making monthly payments on.

Prefiling Credit Counseling Requirement

Before you can file your papers, you must have completed a two-hour credit counseling session from a nonprofit agency, which typically costs about $50 or less, depending on your income. The agency provides a certificate of completion that you file with your other papers. There are a couple of exceptions to this prefiling counseling requirement, discussed in Ch. 2. The counselor is available online, over the telephone, and through the mail.

The Automatic Stay

After completing the credit counseling, your next step is to obtain a bankruptcy filing number. You can do this by filing what's known as a

skeleton or emergency petition, or by filing all the required paperwork at the same time. Either way, once you have a filing number, you have a powerful shield—called the automatic stay—against any efforts by your creditors to collect their debts. All you have to do if a creditor calls you after you file is to produce your case number, the date of filing, and the name of the court in which you filed. The creditor will immediately back off. All proceedings to garnish wages, repossess cars, and foreclose homes will also grind to a halt.

There are a few exceptions to the automatic stay, as you might guess. Collection of child support and alimony and certain enforcement actions by the IRS can proceed, and the stay may expire sooner than you would want if you have had a bankruptcy case dismissed in the previous year. Still, as a general rule, filing for bankruptcy will give you almost total relief from your creditors while the bankruptcy is pending. For more information about the automatic stay, see "How Bankruptcy Stops Collection Efforts" later in this chapter.

Lifting the Stay

In some situations, creditors can successfully request that the court remove (lift) the stay as to their particular situation. For instance, if the automatic stay derailed a foreclosure action, the mortgage owner can request permission from the bankruptcy judge to proceed with the foreclosure. Other common reasons for lifting the stay are car repossessions and evictions of month-to-month tenants.

The Skeleton Petition

Sometimes it's important to obtain a filing number pronto. For instance, if you're faced with an imminent foreclosure or car repossession, you'll need the automatic stay to keep things as they are so you can figure out a way to keep your house or car. But a complete bankruptcy filing involves a lot of forms and disclosure of information, and you may not have the time to prepare them all. Fortunately, you can file a skeleton petition, which requires just a few forms, and file the rest of your paperwork within 15 days. The required forms in a skeleton filing are:

- the petition (three pages plus exhibits)
- a mailing list of your creditors
- a form showing your complete Social Security number, and
- the certificate showing you've completed your credit counseling.

A Brief Description of the Chapter 7 Paperwork

Ch. 9 gives you a more detailed look at these and other official forms, and in Appendix C you'll find a sample of the paperwork involved in a typical Chapter 7 case. The text that follows is just an overview.

In addition to the paperwork required for a Chapter 7 skeleton petition, you'll need to file forms that:

- describe all your personal property and real estate, including where it is located and its approximate value
- provide information about your debts and creditors
- describe certain economic and financial transactions that occurred within the previous several years, such as property you sold or gave away within the previous two years
- state how you want to handle debts concerning cars and other property that is collateral for a loan (called secured debts)
- disclose your monthly income and monthly expenses
- state whether you want to keep any leases and contracts you have in effect or cancel them, and
- summarize your assets and liabilities.

In addition, you'll need to complete a form in which you provide your average monthly gross income for the six months prior to the month in which you plan to file. As I explain in Ch. 2, that income figure will be your starting point for deciding whether you are eligible to file a Chapter 7 bankruptcy or whether you'll have to use Chapter 13. This form is popularly known as the "means test" and must be filed in every Chapter 7 case.

The Creditors' Meeting

About 30 days after you file your bankruptcy papers, you will be required to attend a hearing known either as the "creditors' meeting" or the "341 hearing." You and your spouse (if your spouse is filing with you) are required to attend. You both must bring photo identification and official proof of a Social Security number. This event is held in a hearing room in the courthouse or federal building, but not in the bankruptcy court itself. A bankruptcy trustee, the official appointed to handle your case for the court, conducts the meeting. Another official known as the U.S. Trustee may also attend your meeting

The Big Choice: Use a Lawyer or Handle Your Own Case?

When you file your bankruptcy, your case will automatically fall within one of two categories:

- You will be represented by a lawyer who will sign your petition as your representative.
- You will be representing yourself (that is, you'll be acting as your own lawyer).

If you are represented by a lawyer, the lawyer's responsibility is to help you get the right information in your forms and make the choices that will be most appropriate for your situation. If, on the other hand, you are acting as your own lawyer, you will be responsible for these same tasks. While print and online resources will give you the information you need to make informed decisions and properly complete the paperwork, you will be solely responsible for the outcome of your case.

The court wants to make sure you understand these duties. It requires you to sign a form that explains:

- the different types of bankruptcies (discussed earlier)
- the services available from credit counseling agencies
- the penalties for knowingly and fraudulently concealing assets or making a false statement under penalty of perjury, and
- the fact that all information you supply is subject to examination by the employees of the U.S. Department of Justice.

and may ask you questions that bear on your possible ineligibility for Chapter 7 because of your income level (see "The Bankruptcy Trustee" later in this chapter).

The primary purpose of the creditors' meeting is to have you affirm under oath that the papers you filed were honest, complete, and accurate to the best of your ability. The trustee may also question you about property you've described in your paperwork, to see whether you gave it a proper value and whether you have equity that could be used to make some payment toward your unsecured debt (debt that isn't attached to collateral). In addition, the trustee may inquire further about:

- anticipated tax refunds
- recent large payments you made to creditors or relatives, if applicable
- methods you used to arrive at the value of big-ticket property items you are claiming as exempt, such as a house or car
- whether you should be required to proceed under Chapter 13 rather than Chapter 7
- your failure to file any of the required documents, if applicable
- inconsistencies in information you provided that might indicate you are being less than honest, and
- if you didn't have a lawyer prepare your papers, how you got the information necessary to make certain choices, such as which property is exempt (your answer would typically be the Internet, a Nolo book, or a telephone advice lawyer).

If you've done a good job on your paperwork, your income and expenses clearly qualify you for filing under Chapter 7, and you filed all required documents, your particular "moment of truth" in the creditors' meeting will likely be brief. Creditors rarely show up at these meetings, and the bankruptcy trustee is typically the only one asking the questions. The trustee may simply ask whether all the information in your papers is 100% correct and end the meeting if you say, "Yes."

The Role of Lawyers in Creditors' Meetings

Many people hire lawyers to represent them because they don't want to attend the creditors' meeting on their own. This fear is based on a misunderstanding of how the creditors' meeting works. When the trustee questions you, you—not your lawyer—must answer the questions. That's because you are required to cooperate with the trustee and are expected to be knowledgeable about the information you provided in your papers. Rarely does the lawyer do anything except sit there like a potted plant and maybe take some notes if the trustee requires additional information to be submitted after the meeting.

Because the creditors' meeting is typically the only personal appearance you need to make in a Chapter 7 bankruptcy, hiring a lawyer just to be represented at this meeting may be a waste of money. You'd do better by bringing paper and a pencil and taking your own notes, in case the trustee wants additional documentation.

Which Debts Are Discharged

In approximately 60 to 90 days after the creditors' meeting, you will receive a discharge order from the court. The discharge order won't refer to your specific debts, but instead will say that all legally dischargeable debts are discharged in your case. In a Chapter 7 bankruptcy, absent a successful objection by a creditor (which is rare), most credit card, medical, and legal debts are discharged, as are court judgments, deficiencies owed because of a foreclosure or repossession, and personal loans. For many filers, this means that all of their debts are discharged.

Some types of debts are not discharged in Chapter 7 bankruptcy. The most common of these are:

- debts incurred to pay nondischargeable taxes (see Ch. 3)
- court-imposed fines and restitution
- back child support and alimony
- debts owed to an ex-spouse as a result of a divorce or separation
- loans owed to a retirement plan, such as a 401(k) (because you are the creditor as well as the debtor in this situation, bankruptcy doesn't discharge the debt)
- student loans (unless you can show that repaying the loans would be an undue hardship, which is tougher than you might think and requires a separate trial in the bankruptcy court)
- federal and state taxes that first became due less than three years before your bankruptcy filing date (for example, taxes due on April 15, 2008, for tax year 2007 will not qualify for discharge until April 16, 2011), and

- debts for personal injuries or death resulting from your drunk driving.

Some types of debt will survive your bankruptcy, but only when the creditor seeks and obtains an order from the bankruptcy court excluding the debt from your bankruptcy. These are: debts arising from your fraudulent actions, recent credit card charges for luxuries, and willful and malicious acts causing personal injury or property damages. (For more on which debts are and are not discharged in a Chapter 7 bankruptcy, see Ch. 3.)

What Happens to Your Property?

With few major exceptions, as of your filing date all the property you own or are entitled to receive becomes part of your bankruptcy estate and is technically owned by the bankruptcy trustee. In addition, property you unloaded within the previous two years for significantly less than its value, and certain types of property you have come to own within the six-month period after you file, are also considered part of your bankruptcy estate. Marital property in community property states is also part of the bankruptcy estate, even if only one spouse files. There are other categories of property that may belong in your estate, but these are the main ones. See Ch. 4 for more on what property belongs in your bankruptcy estate.

What does the bankruptcy trustee do with the bankruptcy estate? He or she is looking for any property that, when sold, will generate a profit that can be used to pay your creditors. In fact, that's how these trustees earn a living—from commissions on property from the bankruptcy estate that they sell to benefit creditors. For this reason, the trustee has no interest in property that you legally own but that lacks equity. That's because property without equity won't produce any proceeds for your creditors. For example, if you owe more on your house or car than it's worth, you have no equity and the trustee won't be interested in selling them because proceeds from the sale would, by law, all go to the lender. On the other hand, if you have equity in your house or car (or any other property, for that matter), the trustee will evaluate the property's worth and consider selling it for the benefit of the creditors (and the trustee).

How Exemptions Help You Keep Your Property

Fortunately, all states have laws that allow you to keep a substantial portion of your property when you file for Chapter 7 bankruptcy. This is accomplished through laws—called exemptions—that let you protect the equity you have in various property items from being used by the trustee to benefit your creditors. In some instances, property is exempted regardless of its equity value. For instance, under one of the two California exemption systems, your furniture is exempt regardless of what it's worth. In the other California exemption system, furniture is only exempt up to $550 per item (as are appliances, animals, musical instruments, personal effects, and clothing). You can keep up to $50,000 worth of equity in your home in New York, and up to $500,000 in Massachusetts.

Most people who file for bankruptcy use the exemptions in the state where they file. But if you haven't been residing in that state for at least two years, you may have to use the exemptions from the state from which you came.

In 15 states, you have a choice of exemptions —you may use your state's exemptions or a list of federal exemptions. To find out whether your state gives you this choice, turn to the exemption chart for your state in Appendix A and look at the entry just below your state's name. It will say either that federal exemptions are allowed or (in most cases) that they are not. If your state allows the federal exemptions, you can find those exemptions after Wyoming in Appendix A. In California, you have a choice of two state exemption systems—System 1 and System 2. If you are using the California exemptions, check out the two California charts in the appendix.

Houses and Cars

People often ask whether they can keep their home and car in a Chapter 7 bankruptcy. The answer is yes in the following circumstances:

- You are current on your mortgage or car note.
- You have no significant nonexempt equity in the house or car.

Mortgages

In many cases these days, people are upside down (or underwater) on their primary residence and, therefore, have no nonexempt equity in the house. Because there is no nonexempt equity, the trustee won't be interested in selling the house, which means you can keep it—unless you are behind on your mortgage payments. If you're behind, although the trustee won't be interested in selling the house, your mortgage lender may initiate foreclosure proceedings and will probably be able to get permission from your bankruptcy judge to proceed.

What Happens If You Have Nonexempt Equity in Property?

If your equity in property is worth significantly more than an applicable exemption allows, the trustee can:

- seize and sell the property at auction
- pay any lender in the picture the amount that's owed on the property, if any
- give you the amount you are entitled to under the exemption system you are using
- distribute what remains to your unsecured creditors, and
- put in for a commission on the sale.

Frequently, before selling property with nonexempt equity, the trustee will give you an opportunity to buy it back at whatever amount you can agree upon. For instance, if you have a motorcycle that could be sold for $8,000 and you only have $3,000 worth of exemption (meaning $5,000 is nonexempt), the trustee might let you buy it back for the amount the trustee would end up with after a sale. Since sales of personal property cost time and money, the trustee might let you buy the motorcycle back for as little as $2,500–$3,000.

If you have a second mortgage and are so upside down that the value of the house doesn't even cover the first mortgage, you'll probably be able to keep your house even if you aren't current on your second mortgage (but you must be current on the first mortgage). The reason is that if there is no equity available to pay off the second mortgage, the second mortgage holder will have no economic incentive to attempt a foreclosure.

Car Loans

Cars and car notes work pretty much the same way as houses. If you have no nonexempt equity in your car, you can keep it as long as you are current on the note, but if you are behind, the lender will attempt to get permission from the judge to proceed with repossession.

Your Car or Home After Bankruptcy

If you've met the requirements for keeping your home or car as described just above, you can't assume that your bankruptcy will end your obligation to the mortgage holder or bank. To understand what happens next, let's back up a little bit.

When you take out a mortgage or car loan, you are actually doing two things:

- signing a promissory note for the amount of the loan, and
- agreeing that if you default on the loan the lender can foreclose or repossess.

When the mortgage is recorded at your local land records office, it becomes a lien (a claim) against the house. Similarly, when you take out a car loan, you are signing a promissory note and a "security agreement" that allows the car to be repossessed in case you default. When the seller records the security agreement, it becomes a lien against the car (unless you agree to reaffirm the debt—see Ch. 6).

When you file for bankruptcy, the promissory note part of a secured debt is cancelled. However, the lien securing your payment remains like the fabled smile of the Cheshire Cat. For example, if you owe $400,000 on your house when you file, the $400,000 promissory note is cancelled. However, that doesn't mean that you can stop paying on your mortgage. If you default, the mortgage lender still has the lien—which hasn't been affected by your bankruptcy—and can foreclose on the lien. Similarly, for secured debts involving a car, your Chapter 7 bankruptcy will cancel the amount you owe on the promissory note but it won't affect the lien—which means the lender can repossess the car if you default.

Especially in the case of car notes, many lenders don't like the idea of your not owing anything after bankruptcy. Their right to repossess the car in case of nonpayment isn't enough for them. They want you on the hook for the underlying debt so you don't, at some point in the future, give the car back and walk away from the whole thing. Fortunately for the lender class, bankruptcy gives them the option of requiring you to sign an agreement reaffirming the underlying promissory note, so you can't just walk away from the debt after bankruptcy.

EXAMPLE: Marisol owes $25,000 on her GMC Denali when she files for Chapter 7 bankruptcy. If she doesn't reaffirm the debt, the bankruptcy will cancel the $25,000 debt and just leave the lender with the lien— which means she'll still have to make her payments under power of the lien but won't owe the actual debt. If, after her bankruptcy, Marisol decides to turn in the car, she won't owe a cent on it. On the other hand, if Marisol reaffirms the debt, she will continue to be liable under the underlying debt after bankruptcy. Clearly, Marisol is better off not owing the money (that is not reaffirming), but the lender will be better off having her owe the money to prevent her from escaping scot-free if the car is repossessed or she gives it back.

See Ch. 6 for more on reaffirmation agreements and how secured debts are treated in Chapter 7 bankruptcy.

As for houses, reaffirmation is rare. Instead, the lenders have historically relied on foreclosure as their enforcement remedy and haven't worried about your walking way from the house. This may all be changing as more and more people decide to pack in their mortgages and let the foreclosure happen. See Ch. 5 for more about houses in bankruptcy.

RELATED TOPIC

Later chapters include detailed information on exemptions. Ch. 4 covers exemptions in general, Ch. 5 explains exemptions for a home, and Ch. 6 covers cars and other property that secures a loan.

Costs and Fees

The filing fee for a Chapter 7 bankruptcy is $299. If you can't afford the fee, you can apply for a fee waiver or permission to pay in installments. You'll have to file an Application for Waiver (or payment in installments) when you file your bankruptcy papers. The court clerk will set a hearing date for you to appear before the judge—who will decide whether you qualify for the waiver. The form, rules, and eligibility guidelines for getting a fee waiver are available at www.uscourts.gov/bankruptcycourts/resources.

html. If you want to be represented by a lawyer, you will likely have to pay an additional $1,500 to $2,000 in attorneys' fees.

If you decide to handle your own case, you will probably want to buy some outside help. This will typically consist of one or more of the following:

- one or more do-it-yourself books on bankruptcy (roughly $30 a pop)
- telephonic legal advice from a lawyer (roughly $100 an hour, although many lawyers provide free consultation as a marketing device), and
- clerical assistance with your forms from a bankruptcy petition preparer (between $100 and $200).

See Ch. 11 for more on resources you can use to file for bankruptcy.

Issues That Must Be Decided by a Judge

Chapter 7 bankruptcy is designed to run on automatic, and very few bankruptcies require a decision by an actual judge. Instead, the bankruptcy trustee runs the show for the most part. However, you and your attorney (if you have one) will have to appear before a judge if:

- your income appears to make you ineligible for Chapter 7 bankruptcy and you want to argue that an exception should be made in your case
- a creditor contests your right to file for Chapter 7 bankruptcy or discharge a particular debt (which is rare)
- you want the judge to rule that you are entitled to discharge a particular type of debt (such as taxes or student loans—see

Ch. 3 for more information on debts that can be discharged in Chapter 7 bankruptcy only with the judge's approval)

- you want to eliminate a lien on your property that will survive bankruptcy if the judge doesn't remove it (see Ch. 10), or
- you are handling your own case, are making payments on a car or other personal property, and want to keep the property and continue the contract after bankruptcy. This is called "reaffirming" the contract. (See Ch. 6 for more on reaffirmation agreements.)

See Ch. 10 for more on these and other types of issues that require action by a judge.

How a Chapter 7 Case Ends

Chapter 7 bankruptcy ends with a discharge of all the debts you are entitled to discharge. (For information on which debts can be discharged in Chapter 7, see Ch. 3.) When a debt is discharged, the creditor is forever barred from trying to collect it from you or reporting it to a credit bureau. Government entities may not discriminate against you simply because you've received a bankruptcy discharge, but private companies can and do in some circumstances. (See Ch. 9 for more on the consequences of receiving a bankruptcy discharge.)

Mandatory Budget Counseling

In addition to the requirement that you obtain credit counseling before you file for bankruptcy, you must also participate in a two-hour course on budget management before you can get your discharge. Most filers use the same agency for the budget counseling as they used for the prefiling credit counseling. See Ch. 2 for more information about this requirement.

Changing Your Mind

If you file for Chapter 7 bankruptcy and then change your mind, you can ask the court to dismiss your case. As a general rule, the court will do so unless it would not be in the best interests of your creditors. For example, your request to dismiss might be denied if you have significant nonexempt assets that the trustee could sell to raise money to pay your creditors.

EXAMPLE: Jake files for Chapter 7 bankruptcy, thinking all of his property is exempt. Shortly after he files, Jake's mother tells him that he is on the deed for a 20-acre ranchette that he, his sister, and his mother inherited from his father. Under the exemption laws applicable to Jake's bankruptcy, his share of the ranchette is not exempt which means the trustee can sell the property and distribute Jake's share to his unsecured creditors. Jake wants to hold on to the property, and so requests that his case be dismissed. His request is denied because it would not be in the best interest of Jake's creditors. The moral? Don't file Chapter 7 unless and until you know what property you own and what will happen to it in bankruptcy.

If you do dismiss your case, you can file again later, although in some circumstances you may have to wait 180 days and pay a new filing fee. Instead of dismissing your Chapter 7 case, you can always convert it to another type of bankruptcy for which you qualify (typically Chapter 13 for consumers). In Jake's case, for example, he could convert to a Chapter 13 bankruptcy in order to save the Ranchette. However, in his plan, Jake would have to pay his unsecured creditors at least as much as they would have received had Jake filed under Chapter 7—essentially, the market value of his share of the Ranchette, less sale costs and the trustee's commission. (See below, to learn more about the Chapter 13 Repayment Plan.)

Chapter 13 Bankruptcy

Chapter 13 bankruptcy works quite differently from Chapter 7 bankruptcy. In Chapter 13, you use a portion of your income to pay some or all of what you owe to your creditors over time (anywhere from three to five years, depending on your income and how much of your debt you can afford to repay). The trick to successfully using Chapter 13 to get out of debt is to make sure you have enough income to meet all of your payment obligations under the Chapter 13 laws. (See Ch. 2 to learn about the eligibility requirements for filing under Chapter 13.)

How a Chapter 13 Case Begins

To file a Chapter 13 bankruptcy, first you must complete a credit counseling course, then fill out and file a packet of forms—mostly the same forms as you would use in a Chapter 7 bankruptcy, and also provide the court with:

- a feasible plan to repay some or all of your debts over the plan period (either three or five years, depending on your income and Chapter 13 legal requirements)
- proof that you've filed your federal and state income tax returns for the previous four years, and
- a copy of your most recently filed IRS income tax return (or transcript). (See Ch. 10 for more on Chapter 13 paperwork.)

The Repayment Plan

Under a Chapter 13 repayment plan, you make payments, usually monthly, to the bankruptcy trustee, the official who oversees your case. The trustee uses that money to pay the creditors covered by your plan and to pay his or her own statutory fee (usually 10% of the amount distributed under your plan).

Under Chapter 13, you are required to devote all of your "projected disposable income" to your plan (essentially, the amount left over after paying your expenses). Your repayment period may be as short as three years if your gross average income over the six months before you file is below your state's median income, and five years if it is above. (See Ch. 2 for more on making this calculation.) In some cases, the filer needs a five-year plan to make all required payments regardless of whether his or her income is above or below the median income.

Postconfirmation Increases in Income

If your repayment plan is based on an income level that increases after the court confirms your plan, the trustee can request the court to order a jump in your monthly payments due to your new ability to pay this extra amount. The basic idea in Chapter 13 is that you have to devote all your disposable income to your plan payments.

In Chapter 13, some creditors are entitled to receive 100% of what you owe them, while others may receive a much smaller percentage or even nothing at all. For example, a Chapter 13 plan must propose that any child support you owe to a spouse or child (as opposed to a government agency) will be paid in full over the life of your plan; otherwise, the judge will not approve it. On the other hand, the judge legally could approve a plan that doesn't repay any portion of your credit card debts if you won't have any projected disposable income left after paying your back child support obligations and other obligations that must be paid in full under the Chapter 13 laws.

To have your debts fully discharged under Chapter 13, you must usually make all payments required by your plan and:

- remain current on your federal and state income taxes
- remain current on any child support or alimony obligations

Why File a Chapter 13 Bankruptcy?

Most people who have a choice between Chapters 13 and 7 choose Chapter 7. After all, it lasts three months instead of three to five years, it's easy to do yourself and much cheaper than Chapter 13 if you do hire a lawyer, and you don't have to pay down any of your debt. So, why would you choose to file a Chapter 13 bankruptcy? Here is a brief list of some reasons (all of these are discussed in more detail throughout the book):

- In Chapter 13 you can get rid of a second mortgage lien on your real estate—called a lien strip-off—if the market value of the house is less than the amount owed on the first mortgage.
- Chapter 13 sometimes provides a way to reduce your secured debts to the value of the collateral (for instance, reducing a $10,000 car note on a $5,000 car to $5,000, which lowers the payments).
- Chapter 13 lets you make up for missed payments on a house, car, or other collateral over a three- to five-year period.
- Chapter 13 gets rid of certain types of debts that aren't discharged in Chapter 7 (for instance debts owed because of divorce or a separation agreement).
- Chapter 13 allows you to operate a business while you are in bankruptcy (unlike Chapter 7, which may require that you close the business).

See Ch. 7 for a mock conversation between a bankruptcy lawyer and client in which they discuss whether the client should file a Chapter 7 or Chapter 13 bankruptcy.

Not All Disposable Incomes Are Equal

One of the oddities of the Chapter 13 law is that your projected disposable income may be different than your actual disposable income. Your projected disposable income is initially based on your average gross income over the six-month period prior to your filing date. For example, if your income was $8,000 a month for the first three months of that period and $4,000 for the second three months, your projected monthly disposable income will be $6,000—the six-month average—even though your actual income through the life of your plan will only be $4,000. (Ch. 2 explains projected disposable income in more detail, as well as how these figures and requirements might be juggled to come up with a workable repayment plan that a judge will approve.)

Chapter 13 Plan Must Pay Unsecured Creditors as Much as They Would Receive in a Chapter 7 Bankruptcy

People sometimes choose to avoid Chapter 7 bankruptcy because they stand to lose certain property that isn't exempt. Chapter 13 bankruptcy initially looks like a good alternative, because in Chapter 13 you don't have to give up any property. Rather, your obligations under your plan are based on your disposable income.

Not so fast. Even though Chapter 13 won't take your property, it does require that you pay your unsecured creditors the value of what they would have received in Chapter 7. For example, if you have $50,000 equity in your home that isn't protected by an exemption, you wouldn't lose the home in Chapter 13 bankruptcy, but you would have to propose a plan that pays your creditors at least $50,000 less sale costs and the trustee's commission. This rule often makes it difficult to propose a feasible Chapter 13 plan, due to the size of the required payment.

- annually file your federal income tax return or transcript of the return with the court, and
- annually file an income and expense statement with the court.

You also have to provide your creditors with copies of the income tax returns or transcripts you file with the court, if they request it.

Which Debts Are Discharged

If your Chapter 13 bankruptcy pays your unsecured debts in full, then you will receive a complete discharge of those debts no matter what type they are. If your plan pays less than 100%, the balance will be discharged unless they are the type of debts that aren't discharged in Chapter 13 bankruptcy.

As a general rule, most credit card, medical, and legal debts are discharged, as are most court judgments, deficiencies from a foreclosure or repossession, and personal loans. Debts that have to be fully paid in a Chapter 13 bankruptcy are:

- court-imposed fines and restitution
- back child support and alimony owed to an ex-spouse or child
- student loans
- recent back taxes
- unfiled taxes, and
- debts you owe because of a civil judgment arising out of your willful or malicious acts or for personal injuries or death caused by your drunk driving.

Debts arising from your fraudulent actions or recent credit card charges for luxuries will not be discharged if the creditor gets a court order to that effect. Ch. 3 explains which debts are discharged in a Chapter 13 bankruptcy.

Which Property Is at Risk in Chapter 13 Bankruptcy

As mentioned, you are not required to give up any property you own when you file your Chapter 13 bankruptcy case. In Chapter 13, your income is used to pay off some portion of your debt, not your nonexempt property. However, as mentioned earlier, the value of your nonexempt property can be the determining factor regarding your ability to propose a valid repayment plan.

Houses and Cars

Filing for Chapter 13 bankruptcy lets you keep your house and car as long as you stay current on the payments. You can also pay off arrearages you owe when you file. For instance, if you are $5,000 behind on your mortgage payments, you can pay an extra amount into your plan to pay it off in a reasonable amount of time. That's why Chapter 13 has typically been the remedy of choice for people facing foreclosure. (See Ch. 5 for more on what happens to your home when you file for either type of bankruptcy.)

Costs and Fees

The filing fee for a Chapter 13 bankruptcy is $274. If you can't afford the fee, you can apply for a fee waiver. If you want to be represented by a lawyer, you will probably have to pay $2,500 to $4,000 in legal fees, some of which can be paid through your plan.

If you decide to handle your own case (as some do), you will want to buy some outside help. This will typically consist of one or both of the following:

- one or more self-help law books on Chapter 13 bankruptcy (roughly $40 a pop), and
- telephonic legal advice from a lawyer (roughly $100 an hour).

Unlike the situation in Chapter 7, bankruptcy petition preparers are seldom, if ever, willing to handle Chapter 13 cases. See Ch. 11 for more on resources you can use to file for bankruptcy.

The Meeting of Creditors

When you file your Chapter 13 bankruptcy petition, the court schedules a "meeting of creditors" (usually within about a month), and sends an official notice of the bankruptcy filing and the meeting to you and all of your creditors.

You (and your spouse, if you have filed jointly) are required to attend. You'll need to bring two forms of identification—a picture ID and proof of your Social Security number.

A typical creditors' meeting in a Chapter 13 case lasts less than 15 minutes. The trustee will briefly go over your paperwork with you. No judge will be present. The trustee is likely to be most interested in whether your repayment plan meets all legal requirements and whether you will be able to make the payments you have proposed. (See Ch. 2 for more on Chapter 13 requirements.) The trustee has a vested interest in helping you successfully navigate the Chapter 13 process because the trustee gets paid a percentage of all payments doled out under your plan.

The trustee will also make sure you have filed your tax returns for all taxable periods during the four prior years. If not, the trustee will continue the creditors' meeting to give you a chance to file these returns or provide proof of filing if you've already done so. You cannot proceed with a Chapter 13 bankruptcy unless and until you bring your tax filings up to date.

When the trustee is finished asking questions, any creditors who show up will have a chance to question you. Secured creditors often come, especially if they have any objections to the plan you have proposed as part of your Chapter 13 filing. They may claim, for example, that your plan isn't feasible, that you're giving yourself too much time to pay your arrears on your car note or mortgage, or that your plan proposes to pay less on a secured debt than the replacement value of the collateral property. (See Ch. 6 for more information on collateral and other property that secures a loan.)

An unsecured creditor who is scheduled to receive very little under your plan might show

up, too, if that creditor thinks you should cut your living expenses and thereby increase your disposable income (the amount from which unsecured creditors are paid).

Come to the meeting prepared to negotiate with disgruntled creditors. If you agree to make changes to accommodate their objections, you must submit a modified plan and have it served on all of your creditors. While any objections raised by creditors won't be ruled on during the creditors' meeting (because the judge won't be there), the trustee may raise these objections on behalf of the creditors at your confirmation hearing before the judge, which will be scheduled for a couple of weeks later.

The Confirmation Hearing

Unlike Chapter 7, Chapter 13 bankruptcy requires at least one appearance in court. At this appearance, called the confirmation hearing, the judge either confirms (approves of) your proposed plan or sends you back to the drawing board for various reasons—usually because your plan doesn't meet Chapter 13 requirements in one or more particulars. For example, a judge might reject your plan because you don't have enough projected disposable income to at least pay your priority creditors in full and stay current on your secured debts—such as a car note or mortgage. For more information on Chapter 13 confirmation hearings, see Ch. 10.

You are entitled to amend your proposed plan until you get it right, or the judge decides that it's hopeless. Each amendment requires a new confirmation hearing and appropriate written notice to your creditors.

> ## Challenging the Legality of a Mortgage in Chapter 13 Bankruptcy
>
> When you file Chapter 13 bankruptcy, creditors are supposed to file a proof of claim setting out how much they think you owe. This proof of claim will determine how much they get paid as part of your Chapter 13 plan. If a secured creditor fails to file a proof of claim, you can file one on their behalf.
>
> In recent months some bankruptcy judges have found serious legal deficiencies in some mortgage lenders' claims and have refused to approve them. In theory, if the court does not approve the claim, you might get out from under the mortgage entirely. In practice, it's much more likely that legal defects in lenders' claims will result in negotiated settlements reducing the amount of your mortgage principal and interest. This area of Chapter 13 bankruptcy law is changing daily. To stay current, be sure to check for Legal Updates to this book on Nolo's website (at www.nolo.com/update) as well as periodically check Nolo's Bankruptcy and Foreclosure Blog (also found on Nolo's website).

Other Common Reasons to Go to Court

In addition to attending the confirmation hearing, you may need to go to court to:

- amend your plan after it has been confirmed (if necessary)
- value an asset (if your plan proposes to pay less for a car or other property than the creditor thinks it's worth)
- respond to requests by a creditor or the trustee to dismiss your case or amend your plan
- respond to a creditor who opposes your right to discharge a particular debt (perhaps because you engaged in fraud when incurring the debt)
- discharge a type of debt that can be discharged only if the judge decides that it should be (such as discharging a student loan because of hardship)
- eliminate a lien on your property that will survive your Chapter 13 bankruptcy unless the judge removes it, or
- oppose a secured or unsecured claim filed by a creditor.

These procedures are described in Ch. 10.

How a Chapter 13 Case Ends

If you complete your full three- or five-year repayment plan, are current on your income tax returns and your child support or alimony payments, and complete a budget management course approved by the U.S. Trustee, the remaining unpaid balance on any of your debts that qualify for discharge will be wiped out. If any balance remains on a debt that doesn't qualify for discharge, you will continue to owe the unpaid amount. (The debts that qualify for discharge in a Chapter 13 bankruptcy are explained in Ch. 3.)

Modifying the Plan and Alternatives to Full Discharge

If you can't complete your Chapter 13 plan as written, you can ask the court to modify it. As long as it's clear that you're acting in good faith, the court is likely to approve your request. If it isn't feasible to modify the plan, you may still be able to get what's called a "hardship" discharge if:

- you failed to complete your plan due to circumstances "for which you should not justly be held accountable" (like a job loss), and
- your unsecured creditors have received at least what they would have gotten if you had filed for Chapter 7 bankruptcy (that is, at least the value of your nonexempt property less sale costs and the trustee's commission).

If the bankruptcy court won't let you modify your plan or give you a hardship discharge, you can:

- convert your Chapter 13 bankruptcy to a Chapter 7 bankruptcy, unless you received a Chapter 7 discharge in a case filed within the previous eight years (this is explained in Ch. 10), or
- dismiss your Chapter 13 case. This means you'll owe your creditors the balances on your debts from before you filed your Chapter 13 case, less the payments you made, plus the interest that accrued while your Chapter 13 case was open.

As you can imagine, Chapter 13 bankruptcy requires discipline. For the entire length of your case, you will have to live strictly within your means—and even more strictly if your income exceeds the state's median income. The Chapter 13 trustee will not allow you to spend money on anything deemed nonessential. In past years, only about 35% of Chapter 13 plans were successfully completed. Many Chapter 13 filers dropped out early in the process, without ever submitting a feasible repayment plan to

the court. Nevertheless, for the 35% of those who proposed a plan and made it to the end, the rewards often included an earlier and easier path to restoring good credit. Whether this will continue to be the case in these hard times remains to be seen.

How Bankruptcy Stops Collection Efforts

One of the most powerful features of bankruptcy is that it stops most debt collectors dead in their tracks and keeps them at bay for the rest of your case. Once you file, all collection activity (with a few exceptions, explained below) must go through the bankruptcy court—and most creditors cannot take any further action against you directly.

 TIP

You don't need bankruptcy to stop your creditors from harassing you. Many people begin thinking about bankruptcy when their creditors start phoning their homes and/or places of employment. Federal law prohibits this activity by debt collectors once you tell the counselor, in writing, that you don't want to be called. And if you orally tell debt collectors that you refuse to pay, they cannot, by law, contact you except to send one last letter making a final demand for payment before filing a lawsuit. While just telling the counselor to stop usually works, you may have to send a written follow-up letter. (See Ch. 12 for a sample letter.)

Credit Card Debts, Medical Debts, and Attorney Fees

Anyone trying to collect credit card debts, medical debts, attorney fees, debts arising from breach of contract, or legal judgments against you (other than child support and alimony) must cease all collection activities after you file your bankruptcy. They cannot:

- file a lawsuit or proceed with a pending lawsuit against you
- record liens against your property
- report the debt to a credit reporting bureau, or
- seize your property or income, such as money in a bank account or your paycheck.

Public Benefits

Government entities that are seeking to collect overpayments of public benefits such as SSI, Medicaid, or TANF (welfare) benefits cannot do so by reducing or terminating your benefits while your bankruptcy is pending. If, however, you become ineligible for benefits, including Medicare benefits, bankruptcy doesn't prevent denial or termination of the benefits on that ground.

Domestic Relations Proceedings

Almost all proceedings related to a divorce or paternity action continue as before—they are not affected by the automatic stay. These include:

- the setting and collection of current child support and alimony
- the collection of back child support and alimony from property that is not in the bankruptcy estate (see Ch. 4 for more on what's in the bankruptcy estate)
- the determination of child custody and visitation
- a lawsuit to establish paternity
- an action to modify child support and alimony
- proceedings to protect a spouse or child from domestic violence
- withholding of income to collect child support
- reporting of overdue support to credit bureaus
- the interception of tax refunds to pay back child support, and
- withholding, suspension, or restriction of drivers' and professional licenses as leverage to collect child support.

Criminal Proceedings

If a case against you can be broken down into criminal and debt components, only the criminal component will be allowed to continue—the debt component will be stayed while your bankruptcy is pending. For example, if you were convicted of writing a bad check and have been sentenced to community service and ordered to pay a fine, your obligation to do community service will not be stopped by the automatic stay (but your obligation to pay the fine will).

Landlord-Tenant Proceedings

With a few exceptions, the automatic stay does not stop the eviction of a tenant if:

- the landlord obtained a judgment of possession prior to the bankruptcy filing, or

- the tenant is endangering the property or using controlled substances on it.

Ch. 5 explains when evictions on these grounds may occur. It also covers the new requirements imposed on both the tenant and the landlord if there is a dispute about whether an eviction can proceed.

Tax Proceedings

The IRS can continue certain actions, such as a tax audit, issuing a tax deficiency notice, demanding a tax return, issuing a tax assessment, or demanding payment of an assessment. The automatic stay does, however, stop the IRS from issuing a lien or seizing (levying against) any of your property or income.

Pension Loans

The stay doesn't prevent withholding from a debtor's income to repay a loan from an ERISA-qualified pension (this includes most job-related pensions and individual retirement plans). See Ch. 4 for more on how pensions are treated under bankruptcy.

Foreclosures

Foreclosure is the way a mortgage holder obtains title to the property that secures the mortgage. It is the main (and sometimes only) remedy available to a mortgage holder when the home-owner defaults. Foreclosure procedures differ from state to state. In about half the states, foreclosures are carried out in court just like any other civil proceeding (these are called judicial foreclosures). In the other states, foreclosures occur outside of court (called nonjudicial foreclosures) and typically involve complex state rules regarding notices, reinstatement periods, and redemption periods.

When you file bankruptcy, pending foreclosure proceedings are stopped dead in their tracks and won't resume until your bankruptcy is completed or the bankruptcy judge lifts the stay upon request by the mortgage holder. Importantly, one thing that bankruptcy doesn't stop is the passage of time required by a particular foreclosure notice. For instance, in California, a foreclosing party must provide the homeowner with a 90-day notice of default prior to setting a date for the actual foreclosure sale. While a bankruptcy filing would delay the issuance of the 90-day notice in the first place, it won't prevent the passage of time under the 90-day period once the notice is filed. So, a Chapter 7 filing would substantially delay the foreclosure process if it were filed prior to the 90-day notice, but would have little or no effect on the foreclosure if it were filed after the 90-day notice is served. See *The Foreclosure Survival Guide* by Stephen Elias (Nolo) for a more detailed look at how bankruptcy works to delay or prevent foreclosures.

Although foreclosure activities initially are stayed by your bankruptcy filing, the stay won't apply if you filed another bankruptcy within the previous two years and the court, in that proceeding, lifted the stay and allowed the lender to proceed with the foreclosure. In other words, the law doesn't allow you to prevent a foreclosure by filing serial bankruptcies.

Utilities

Companies providing you with utilities (such as gas, heating oil, electricity, telephone, and water) may not discontinue service because you file for bankruptcy. However, they can shut off your service 20 days after you file if you don't provide them with a deposit or other means to assure future payment. They can also cut you off if you don't pay for services you receive after you file for bankruptcy.

Special Rules for Multiple Filers

If you had a bankruptcy case pending during the previous year, then the stay will terminate 30 days after you file unless you, the trustee, the U.S. Trustee, or the creditor asks for the stay to continue as to certain creditors and proves that the current case was filed in good faith.

This rule doesn't apply to any case that was dismissed because you should have filed under Chapter 13 instead of Chapter 7 (see Ch. 2 for more on when a case may be dismissed on that ground).

If a creditor had a motion to lift the stay pending during a previous case that was dismissed, the court will presume that you acted in bad faith in your current case. You will have to overcome this presumption in order to obtain continuing stay relief. If you had more than two cases pending during the previous year, then you will have to seek a court order to obtain any stay relief.

The Bankruptcy Trustee

Until your bankruptcy case ends, your financial assets and problems are in the hands of the bankruptcy trustee, who acts under the supervision of another type of trustee called the U.S. Trustee.

The Bankruptcy Trustee's General Duties

With few exceptions, the bankruptcy trustee assumes legal control of your property and debts as of the date you file. If, without the trustee's consent, you sell or give away property while your case is open, you risk having the transaction undone and your case dismissed.

The bankruptcy trustee's primary duties are:

- to see that your nonexempt property is seized and sold for the benefit of your unsecured creditors
- to make sure that the paperwork submitted in your bankruptcy is accurate and complete
- to schedule and operate the creditors' meeting (the 341 hearing), and
- to administer the case for the court.

The bankruptcy trustee may be a local bankruptcy attorney or a nonlawyer who is very knowledgeable about Chapter 7 or Chapter 13 bankruptcy generally and the local court's rules and procedures in particular.

Just a few days after you file your bankruptcy papers, you'll get a Notice of Filing from the court, giving the name, business address, and business phone number of the bankruptcy trustee. The trustee may follow up with a list of any financial documents the trustee wants to see, such as bank statements, property appraisals, or canceled checks, and the date by which the trustee wants them. In addition, you are supposed to send the trustee a copy of your most recently filed federal tax return at least seven days before the creditors' meeting.

As used in this book, the term "trustee" means the bankruptcy trustee who will actually be handling your case on behalf of the bankruptcy court, unless otherwise stated.

The U.S. Trustee's Office

In addition to the bankruptcy trustee assigned to your case, another type of trustee—a U.S. Trustee—will be involved, usually behind the scenes. The Office of the U.S. Trustee is a part of the United States Department of Justice. Its role is to supervise the bankruptcy trustees who actually handle cases in the bankruptcy court, to make sure that the bankruptcy laws are being followed and that cases of fraud and other crimes are appropriately handled. There are 21 regional U.S. Trustee offices throughout the country.

If a U.S. Trustee decides to take an active part in your case, the parties to the case—including you—will be sent a notice about the proposed action, and you will be given an opportunity to oppose whatever action the U.S. Trustee proposes. Later chapters in this book suggest some ways to respond to various actions the U.S. Trustee might propose.

Happily, most filers never have to deal with the U.S. Trustee. It will likely happen only if they file a Chapter 7 bankruptcy and their bankruptcy papers—or their testimony at the creditors' meeting—indicate that:

- their "current monthly income" is more than the median income for their state (see Ch. 2)
- they earn enough actual income to support a Chapter 13 plan (see Ch. 2)
- they have apparently engaged in illegal actions that warrant investigative follow-up (such as perjury), or
- their case is selected for a random audit (one out of every 250 bankruptcy cases is supposed to be audited under the new bankruptcy rules).

Chapter 7 Bankruptcy Trustee

In a Chapter 7 bankruptcy, the trustee is mostly interested in what you own and what property you claim as exempt. This is because the court pays the trustee a commission on property that is sold for the benefit of the unsecured creditors. The trustee may receive 25% of the first $5,000, 10% of any amount between $5,000 and $50,000, and 5% of any additional money up to $1,000,000.

If your papers indicate that all of your property is exempt (which means you get to keep it), your case initially is considered a "no-asset" case and your creditors are told not to file claims (because you don't have any property that will be sold to pay them). The trustee also won't show much interest in a no-asset case unless your papers suggest that you may be hiding or mischaracterizing assets. After all, if there is no property for the trustee to seize and sell to pay your unsecured creditors, then there is no commission for the trustee.

The first time you will personally encounter the trustee in a Chapter 7 case is when you appear at your creditors' meeting, which you must attend if you don't want your bankruptcy dismissed. Typically, if all of your assets are exempt, you will hear nothing further from the trustee. However, if there are (or it appears that there might be) nonexempt assets in your bankruptcy estate, the trustee may continue your creditors' meeting to another date and ask you to submit appropriate documentation in the meantime. More rarely, the trustee may hire an attorney to pursue nonexempt assets you appear to own, or even refer your case to the U.S. Trustee's office for further action if it looks like you have engaged in dishonest activity.

If there are nonexempt assets for the trustee to seize and sell, you will be expected to cooperate in getting them to the trustee for disposition. You will also be given the opportunity to "buy the assets back" from the trustee at a negotiated price or substitute exempt assets for the nonexempt assets.

If you have nonexempt property that isn't worth very much or would be cumbersome for the trustee to sell, the trustee can—and often will—abandon the property, which means you get to keep it. For example, no matter how much your used furniture may be worth in theory, many trustees won't bother selling it. Arranging to sell used furniture is expensive and rarely produces much if any proceeds for the creditors.

Many people wonder whether a trustee can search their homes to determine whether they are hiding property. While such searches are unusual, part of your duty to cooperate with the trustee could consist of a guided tour of your home upon the trustee's request. And if you don't voluntarily cooperate, the trustee can obtain an order from the court to force the issue.

The McMansion Effect

It's not uncommon these days for people with pricey homes built and bought during the housing bubble to be filing Chapter 7 bankruptcy. Popularly called McMansions, these homes frequently contain pricey furniture as well. If you are a McMansion owner and your personal property disclosure schedules indicate that your furniture is old and not very valuable, your bankruptcy trustee may be more skeptical of your words than they might have been in past years and may send a personal property appraiser up to your house for a look-see.

The trustee is also required, under the supervision of the U.S. Trustee, to assess your bankruptcy papers for accuracy and for signs of possible fraud or abuse of the bankruptcy system.

If You Owe Back Child Support

If you owe back support, the trustee is also required to provide notices to the holder of the support claim and the state child support agency to keep them abreast of your bankruptcy and help them find you after your bankruptcy discharge. Specifically, the trustee is required to provide:

- the payee with information about the state child support enforcement agency and his or her rights under the bankruptcy law
- the state child support enforcement agency with information about the back support and the payee, and
- (when you are granted a discharge), the state child support agency and payee with information about the discharge, your last known address, the last known name and address of your employer, and the name of any creditor who holds a nondischargeable claim or a claim that has been reaffirmed.

Both the payee and the child support enforcement agency can ask these creditors to provide your last known address. The laws specifically authorize these creditors to release such information without any penalty.

Chapter 13 Bankruptcy Trustee

In a Chapter 13 bankruptcy, the trustee's role is to:

- examine your proposed plan and make sure it complies with all legal requirements
- receive the payments you make under the plan and distribute them to your creditors in the manner required by law
- monitor the monthly income and expense reports required in a Chapter 13 case
- monitor your duty to file tax returns with the appropriate federal and state taxing authorities for the four years previous to your filing date and annually while your Chapter 13 case is pending
- monitor your duty to file an annual financial statement charting your income and expenses (see Ch. 2), and
- if you owe back child support, provide the payee and your state's child support enforcement agency with information described in "If You Owe Back Child Support," above.

Chapter 13 trustees pay themselves by keeping 7%–10% of the payments they disburse to creditors.

Many Chapter 13 trustees play a fairly active role in the cases they administer. This is especially true in small suburban or rural judicial districts, or in districts with a lot of Chapter 13 bankruptcy cases. For example, a trustee may:

- give you financial advice, such as helping you create a realistic budget (the trustee cannot, however, give you legal advice)
- actively participate in helping you modify your plan, if necessary
- give you a temporary reprieve or take other steps to help you get back on track if you miss a payment or two, or
- participate at any hearing on the value of an item of property, possibly even hiring an appraiser.

Despite the trustee's great interest in your finances, your financial relationship with the trustee is not as stifling as it may sound. In most situations, you keep complete control over money and property you acquire after filing—as long as you make the payments called for under your repayment plan and you make all regular payments on your secured debts. However, if your income or property increases during the life of your plan (for instance, you receive a substantial promotion or you win the lottery), the trustee can seek to amend your plan to pay your creditors a greater percentage of what you owe them rather than the lesser percentage originally called for in your plan.

Business Bankruptcies

If you own your own business as a sole proprietor or independent contractor, you and your business are considered the same when it comes to filing for bankruptcy. All debts owed and all assets owned by your business are also considered to be yours. While you may have to provide some additional paperwork for your bankruptcy, such as a profit and loss or income and expense statement, the procedures are the same as if you weren't in business—with one important exception. If your business has assets that frequently change, such as inventory, and you file under Chapter 7, the bankruptcy trustee may require you to shut the business down while your bankruptcy is pending, which is usually about three months. If, however, you have a service business, or a manufacturing business that doesn't carry a large or valuable inventory, you will probably be allowed to continue

business operations during the pendency of the bankruptcy.

If you file under Chapter 13, you'll be able to continue business operations, but you'll have to dedicate all profits earned while your bankruptcy is pending to paying your unsecured creditors—which means you may end up paying a greater percentage of your unsecured debt than originally planned for in your Repayment Plan.

If you own a corporation or limited liability company, things are different. You and your corporation (or LLC) are different entities and you must file separate bankruptcies, one for you and one for your company. Worse, if your business does need to go through bankruptcy, you'll need a lawyer do it. Owners of their own corporations and other business entities cannot represent the entity—unless they themselves are lawyers. Because many business owners can't afford the legal fees to file for bankruptcy for the company, owners often let the corporation lapse, debts and all, rather than file for bankruptcy.

If you do decide to take a corporation or limited liability company into bankruptcy, you cannot use Chapter 13—only Chapter 7 and Chapter 11 are available to business entities. In Chapter 11, the business can continue operations but you'll have to pay an attorney in order to represent the business in the bankruptcy, and the fees you will pay will probably be well in excess of $10,000. In Chapter 7, you must liquidate the business.

If you file a personal bankruptcy under Chapter 7 or Chapter 13, corporate-owned assets and liabilities are not part of the bankruptcy, although you can discharge any personal liability you have for corporate debt. In some instances, as part of a personal bankruptcy filed under Chapter 7, the trustee can liquidate the corporation wholly owned by the debtor and treat the assets as the debtor's personal assets— which means they can be sold for the benefit of your creditors unless you protect them under the exemptions available to you for this purpose.

You can read more about business bankruptcies in Ch. 2. Nolo's *Bankruptcy for Small Business Owners: File Chapter 7*, by Stephen Elias and Bethany Laurence, brings you, step by step, through the process of filing a Chapter 7 business bankruptcy.

Nolo Resources on Bankruptcy and Debt

Nolo publishes self-help bankruptcy books that provide readers with all of the information they need to file for Chapter 7 or Chapter 13 bankruptcy, step by step. Look for the latest editions of these books:

- *How to File for Chapter 7 Bankruptcy*, by Stephen R. Elias, Albin Renauer, and Robin Leonard. This do-it-yourself bankruptcy book takes you through the filing process for a liquidation bankruptcy. It gives practical advice and supplies all the official bankruptcy forms you'll need, with complete instructions.
- *Chapter 13 Bankruptcy: Keep Your Property & Repay Debts Over Time*, by Stephen Elias and Robin Leonard. This book takes you through the entire Chapter 13 bankruptcy process, step by step. It provides the official bankruptcy forms, with complete instructions for filling them out. You'll learn how to create a repayment plan, represent yourself in bankruptcy court, and deal with unexpected changes.

In addition to these bankruptcy titles, Nolo publishes books that deal with credit, debt, and other money issues. Here are a few you might find helpful:

- *Solve Your Money Troubles: Debt, Credit & Bankruptcy*, by Robin Leonard and Margaret Reiter. A practical book to help you prioritize debts, negotiate with creditors, stop collector harassment, challenge wage attachments, contend with repossession, respond to creditor lawsuits, and rebuild your credit. Contains sample letters to creditors as well as worksheets and charts to calculate a budget and create a payment plan.
- *Credit Repair*, by Robin Leonard and Margaret Reiter. This book shows how to fix your credit situation quickly, easily, and legally. It teaches you how to read and understand your credit report, fix mistakes, get positive information added to your credit report, avoid credit discrimination, and defend your good credit from fraud and identity theft. Includes sample credit reports and letters to creditors, as well as lists of agencies and organizations to turn to for additional help.
- *Divorce & Money: How to Make the Best Financial Decisions During Divorce*, by Violet Woodhouse, with Dale Fetherling. This book can help you with the overwhelming financial decisions of divorce: selling the house, dividing debts, discovering assets, setting alimony and child support, handling retirement benefits and taxes, and negotiating a fair settlement. Contains worksheets, charts, formulas, and tables.

Who Can File for Bankruptcy

Bankruptcy might be a fine solution to your debt problems—but only if you are eligible to file. For example, you won't be allowed to file for Chapter 7 or Chapter 13 bankruptcy if you don't first seek credit counseling. Before reading the rest of this book to find out what effect bankruptcy will have on your life, you should figure out whether you'll be eligible to file for bankruptcy in the first place.

The Chapter 7 bankruptcy eligibility rules are intended, in large part, to require people to pay back at least a portion of their debts if they are able—in other words, to use Chapter 13 rather than Chapter 7. And if you do file under Chapter 13, your repayment plan will have to treat your unsecured creditors as least as well as they would have been treated in a Chapter 7 bankruptcy. This chapter explains these and other eligibility rules for Chapter 7 and Chapter 13. Ch. 7 provides a hypothetical discussion between a bankruptcy lawyer and a would-be filer regarding which type of bankruptcy would be more appropriate given that person's circumstances.

Credit Counseling

Before you can file for Chapter 7 or Chapter 13 bankruptcy, you must consult a nonprofit credit counseling agency. The purpose of this consultation is to see whether there is a feasible way to handle your debt load outside of bankruptcy, without adding to what you owe.

Counseling Requirements

To qualify for bankruptcy relief, you must show that you received credit counseling from an agency approved by the U.S Trustee's office within the 180-day period before you file your bankruptcy. Once you complete the counseling, the agency will give you a certificate of completion that you must file no later than 15 days after your bankruptcy filing date. It will also give you a copy of any repayment plan you may have worked out with the agency. You can find out which agencies have been approved for your judicial district by visiting the Office of the U.S. Trustee's website at www.usdoj.gov/ust; click "Credit Counseling & Debtor Education" to see the list.

The supposed purpose of credit counseling is to give you an idea of whether you really need to file for bankruptcy or whether an informal repayment plan would get you back on your economic feet. Counseling is required even if it's pretty obvious that a repayment plan isn't feasible (that is, your debts are too high and your income is too low) or you are facing debts that you find unfair and don't want to pay. (Credit card balances inflated by high interest rates and penalties are particularly unpopular with many filers, as are emergency room bills and deficiency judgments based on auctions of repossessed cars.)

Bankruptcy law requires only that you participate in the counseling—not that you go along with whatever the agency proposes. Even if a repayment plan is feasible, you aren't required to agree to it. However, if the agency does come up with a plan, you must file it along with the other bankruptcy documents described in Ch. 10.

CAUTION

The court might agree with the agency's plan. If it's clear from the documents you file that you could complete the repayment plan proposed by the agency, the court may use this as a reason to question your Chapter 7 filing and try to push you into a Chapter 13 repayment plan (see Ch. 10). If that happens, at least you'll have an opportunity to argue about whether you should have to repay all of your debts.

Counseling Costs

Credit counseling agencies may charge a reasonable fee for their services. However, if a debtor cannot afford the fee, the counseling agency must provide services free or at reduced rates.

This means that the service must offer a sliding fee scale and a waiver of fees altogether for people below a certain income level (below 150% of the poverty level for a family of equal size). The Office of the U.S. Trustee, the law enforcement agency that oversees credit counseling agencies, has indicated that a "reasonable" fee might range from free to $50, depending on the circumstances.

Exceptions to the Counseling Requirement

You don't have to get counseling if the U.S. Trustee certifies that there is no appropriate agency available to you in the district where you will be filing. However, counseling can be provided by telephone or (usually) online, so it is

---

Rules Counseling Agencies Must Follow

In addition to providing services without regard to the debtor's ability to pay, counseling agencies have to meet a number of other requirements. They must:

- disclose to you their funding sources, their counselor qualifications, the possible impact of their proposed plan on your credit report, the costs of the program, if any, and how much of the costs will be borne by you
- provide counseling that includes an analysis of your current financial condition, factors that caused the condition, and how you can develop a plan to respond to the problems without adding to your debt

- use trained counselors who don't receive any commissions or bonuses based on the outcome of the counseling services (that is, kickbacks to individual counselors are not allowed, although kickbacks to the agency may be legal), and
- maintain adequate financial resources to provide continuing support services over the life of any repayment plan (that is, if they propose a three-year payment plan, they must have adequate reserves to service your case for three years).

unlikely that approved debt counseling will ever be "unavailable."

You can also avoid this requirement if you certify to the court's satisfaction that:

- You had to file for bankruptcy immediately (perhaps to stop a wage garnishment or foreclosure).
- You were unable to obtain counseling within five days after requesting it.

If you can prove that you didn't receive credit counseling for these reasons, you must certify that to the court and complete the counseling within 30 days after filing (you can ask the court to extend this deadline by 15 days).

You may also escape the credit counseling requirement if, after notice and hearing, the bankruptcy court determines that you couldn't participate because of:

- a physical disability that prevents you from attending counseling (this exception probably won't apply if the counseling is available on the Internet or over the phone)
- mental incapacity (you are unable to understand and benefit from the counseling), or
- your active duty in a military combat zone.

Incentive for Creditors to Settle?

If a credit counseling agency proposes a settlement that would repay at least 60% of your debt to a creditor, and that creditor refuses to go along with the plan, the creditor may be penalized when and if your property is distributed in bankruptcy. The creditor will be allowed to collect a maximum of 80% of the total claim if you can show, by clear and convincing evidence, that the creditor was offered the deal at least 60 days before you filed and the creditor unreasonably refused the offer.

Although this 20% penalty is billed as an incentive for creditors to accept settlement prior to bankruptcy, the creditor stands to lose only 20 cents on the dollar for turning down an offer to lose 40 cents on the dollar. It's not clear why a creditor would agree to take a large hit early to avoid the possibility of a smaller hit down the road. Also, it will generally cost you more to prove that the creditor's refusal was unreasonable than the penalty is worth. And finally, this will be a factor only in Chapter 13 cases; creditors of Chapter 7 debtors rarely recoup 60% of their debt, let alone 80%.

Calculating Your Income Status

In 2005, Congress decided that higher-income people with primarily consumer debts should file Chapter 13 bankruptcy if possible, given their income and expenses. To learn whether you fit within the Chapter 7 or Chapter 13 group, take the following two steps:

- calculate your current monthly income (CMI), and
- compare your CMI to the appropriate median income figure.

Calculate Your Current Monthly Income

The bankruptcy law defines your CMI as your average monthly income received during the six-month period that ends on the last day of the month preceding your filing date—whether or not the income is taxable. When including wages or other sources of income, you must include the gross amount, not the net income you actually receive after deductions from taxes and other withholdings are made.

Your CMI includes income from all sources except:

- payments you receive under the Social Security Act (including Social Security Retirement, SSI, SSDI, TANF)
- payments to victims of war crimes or crimes against humanity based on their status as victims of such crimes, or
- payments to victims of international or domestic terrorism.

Use Worksheet A: Current Monthly Income, below (and in Appendix B), to calculate your CMI by:

- adding up all of the income you received during that six-month period (except for income that falls into the excluded categories), and
- dividing by six to come up with a monthly average.

EXAMPLE: John and Marcia are married and have two young children. They fell quickly into debt after John was forced out of his job because of a work-related injury on April 1, 20xx. Three months later, on July 1, 20xx, John and Marcia decide to file for bankruptcy.

To calculate their CMI, Marcia reviews the family's income for the period between January 1 and June 30, 20xx (the six-month period prior to their bankruptcy filing date). This includes John's *gross* salary for the first three months (he made $8,000 a month as a software engineer), plus $1,800 in workers' compensation benefits for each of the last three months. Marcia made $1,000 a month during the first three months and had no income for the last three months. The total family income for the six-month period is $32,400. Divided by six, the family's CMI is $5,400 (the six month average), even though the monthly amount they actually took in during each of the three months before filing was only $1,800. None of the deductions available for calculating CMI are available to John and Marcia, so their CMI remains at $5,400.

The following types of income should be included in the form:

- wages, salary, tips, bonuses, overtime, and commissions

Worksheet A: Current Monthly Income

Use this worksheet to calculate your current monthly income; use figures for you and your spouse if you plan to file jointly.

Line 1. Calculate your total income over the last six months from wages, salary, tips, bonuses, overtime, and so on.

    A. Month 1 $ _____

    B. Month 2   _____

    C. Month 3   _____

    D. Month 4   _____

    E. Month 5   _____

    F. Month 6   _____

    G. TOTAL WAGES (add Lines 1A–1F) $ _____

Line 2. Add up all other income for the last six months.

    A. Net business, profession, or farm income   _____

    B. Interest, dividends, and royalties   _____

    C. Net income from rents and real property   _____

    D. Pension and retirement income   _____

    E. Alimony or family support   _____

    F. Spousal contributions (if separated and not filing jointly)   _____

    G. Unemployment compensation   _____

    H. Workers' compensation   _____

    I. State disability insurance   _____

    J. Annuity payments   _____

    K. Other   _____

    L. TOTAL OTHER INCOME (add Lines 2A–2K) $ _____

Line 3. Calculate total income over the six months prior to filing.

    A. Enter total wages (Line 1G).   _____

    B. Enter total other income (Line 2L).   _____

    C. TOTAL INCOME OVER THE SIX MONTHS PRIOR TO FILING. Add Lines 3A and 3B together. $ _____

Line 4. Average monthly income over the six months prior to filing. This is called your "current monthly income."

    A. Enter total six-month income (Line 3C).   _____

    B. CURRENT MONTHLY INCOME. Divide Line 4A by six. $ _____

- net income from the operation of a business, profession, or farm (the amount you report as taxable income, after subtracting reasonable and necessary business expenses on IRS Schedule C)
- interest, dividends, and royalties
- net income from rents and other real property income
- pension and retirement income
- regular contributions to the household expenses of the debtor or the debtor's dependents, including child or spousal support
- regular contributions by the debtor's spouse if he or she isn't part of the household either because of a separation or a joint debtor in the bankruptcy
- unemployment compensation
- workers' compensation insurance
- state disability insurance, and
- annuity payments.

Compare Your Household Income to Your State's Family Median Income

The census bureau periodically publishes family median income figures for all 50 states. To compare your current monthly income to the family median income for your state, you'll need to multiply your current monthly income by 12 (or divide the annual household median income figure by 12). Let's do it the first way. In John and Marcia's case, the family's "current monthly income" ($5,400) multiplied by 12 would be $64,800.

Once you've computed your CMI and located the same size household (for your state), compare the two figures to see whether your CMI is more or less than the median income for the

same size household for your state. You can find the state median figures (as of the publication date of this book) in the Median Household Income chart, in Appendix B. You can also find up-to-date figures at the U.S. Trustee's website at www.usdoj.gov/ust (click "Means Testing Information") or at the website of the United States Census Bureau, www.census.gov (click "State Median Income" from the home page).

You can see from the chart in Appendix B that John and Marcia's current monthly income would be more than the family median income in most states.

For Larger Families

Although the U.S. Census Bureau generates median figures for families that have up to seven members, Congress does not want you to use these figures if you have a larger family. The Census figures are to be used for families that have up to four members (these are the numbers you will find in Appendix B). If there are more than four members of your family, you must add $6,900 per additional person to the four-member family median income figure for your state.

If Your Current Monthly Income Is Less Than or Equal to Your State's Family Median Income

If your CMI is less than or equal to your state's family median income, you aren't subject to the means test in a Chapter 7 bankruptcy filing. And, if you decide to file for Chapter 13, you

How to Determine Your Household Size

Determining your household size is very important—the more members you have in your household, the less likely it is that your income will exceed the median for a similarly sized household. For example, assume that your CMI is $6,000, the median income for a household of three is $5,800, and the median income for a household of four is $6,500. It will be to your benefit to have four people in your household instead of three.

Unfortunately, neither Congress nor the courts have given clear guidance on how to calculate your household size. Most courts adopt the census test for a household, which includes all of the people, related and unrelated, who occupy a house, apartment, group of rooms, or single room that is intended for occupancy as separate living quarters. Under this test, you can count your children or stepchildren even if they are not dependents for tax purposes. However, some courts count only dependents as part of the household and require that you list in your bankruptcy papers any money donated to the household by any other person or entity.

Domestic partners count as one household. But mere roommates are not a single household when they have separate rooms within a house but don't act as one economic unit by comingling their incomes and jointly paying expenses. One vexing issue yet to be decided is whether children can be counted as part of a household in situations where they are only living with the parent part time under a custody and visitation agreement.

may propose a plan that is based on your actual expenses and lasts for only three years.

If Your Current Monthly Income Is More Than Your State's Family Median Income

If your current monthly income, as calculated above, exceeds your state's family median income, the consequences depend on whether you are filing for Chapter 7 or Chapter 13 bankruptcy:

Chapter 7: If the majority of your debt is consumer debt (meaning it doesn't come from operating a business, tax debts, or debts for personal injury or property damage you caused to someone else), you'll have to take what's called "the means test." Under this test, which is explained step by step under "Chapter 7 Eligibility Requirements," below, you can't file for Chapter 7 bankruptcy if, after certain expenses are deducted, your remaining income:

- would exceed $10,950 when projected over a five-year period ($182.50 per month), or
- would be equal to at least $6,575 over five years ($110 per month) and would pay at least 25% of your unsecured, nonpriority debts over that same period. Unsecured, nonpriority debts include credit card and department store charge card bills, medical bills, utility bills, and student loans (see "How Debts Are Classified," below, for more on unsecured debts).

If your remaining income would be less than $6,575 when projected over the next five years, you will pass the means test and can file for Chapter 7 if you meet the other eligibility requirements explained in "Chapter 7 Eligibility Requirements," below.

EXAMPLE: Jonas makes $4,500 a month as a section manager in a large general-purpose store. His current monthly income is more than the median income for his state, so he has to pass the means test to file for Chapter 7 bankruptcy. He deducts allowable expenses from his income and comes up with $200 a month extra. Because his excess income comes to $12,000 when projected over the next five years ($200 x 60 months), Jonas fails the means test.

If Jonas had only $125 a month extra ($7,500 over a five-year period), he would have to figure out whether this amount would pay 25% of his unsecured, nonpriority debt in that five-year period. For instance, if Jonas owed $36,000 in credit card debt, he would be barred from Chapter 7 if he could pay $9,000 (25% of the debt) over a five-year period. Because Jonas only has $7,500 extra, however, he would pass the means test and be eligible for Chapter 7, as long as he meets the other eligibility factors.

As noted earlier, no matter how high your income is, you don't have to take the means test if you are a disabled veteran with a disability rating of at least 30%. You can also skip the means test if your debt is not primarily consumer debt—that is, if more than 50% of your debt load comes from business debts, taxes, or debts for personal injury or property damage you caused to someone else (called "tort debts").

Chapter 13: If your current monthly income is more than the median for your state and you file for Chapter 13, you must propose a five-year repayment plan to which you commit all of your disposable income. You will also have to use the

Exceptions to the Higher-Income Rule

There are two exceptions to the higher-income rule:

Veterans. If you are a disabled veteran and the debts you wish to discharge were incurred when you were on active duty or engaged in homeland defense activity, the court must treat you as if you were in the lower income group, regardless of your actual income. The law doesn't clearly indicate what will happen if some of your debts were incurred when you were on active duty and others prior to or after active duty; we'll have to wait and see how courts interpret this provision.

Nonconsumer debts. If the majority of your debts are not consumer debts, you will be treated as if your CMI is below the median income. This would be the case if your debts primarily arose from the operation of a business, or if your debts are primarily taxes or other types of debt that aren't considered to be consumer debt. However, personal mortgages are considered to be consumer debt and they are often high enough to swing your overall debt into the consumer category.

IRS expense standards—and other allowable deductions—to calculate your projected disposable income (the amount of income you'll have to pay into the plan every month for the benefit of your nonpriority, unsecured creditors). These rules are explained in "Chapter 13 Eligibility Requirements," below.

TIP

Choose your filing date to lower your CMI. If your income has been uneven during the six months prior to your projected filing date, you may want delay or speed up your filing if either strategy would move your CMI from the high-income to the low-income category. For instance, if you had a high-paying job during the first three months and a low-paying job during the second three months, each month you wait before filing will reduce your CMI. On the other hand, if you've recently landed a high-paying job after having a low-income job, the sooner you file, the lower your CMI will be.

Chapter 7 Eligibility Requirements

There are several basic eligibility requirements you must meet to file a "consumer" Chapter 7 bankruptcy. In addition, if your current monthly income is more than your state's family median income for a family of your size, and your debts are primarily consumer debts, you will have to pass the means test, explained below. To figure out whether you can meet these requirements, you'll first need to know how various debts are classified.

How Debts Are Classified

The eligibility requirements for Chapter 7 bankruptcy are based primarily on your income, living expenses, and debts. Different types of debts are handled differently in these calculations. This section will help you figure out which numbers to use.

Secured Debts

A debt is "secured" if you stand to lose specific property when you don't make your payments to the creditor. Most secured debts are created when you sign loan papers giving a creditor a security interest in your property—such as a home loan or car loan. But a debt might also be secured if a creditor has filed a lien (a legal claim against your property that must be paid before the property can be sold). Here is a list of common secured debts and liens:

- **Mortgages.** Called deeds of trust in some states, these are loans to buy or refinance a house or other real estate. If you fail to pay, the lender can foreclose on your house.
- **Home equity loans (second mortgages).** If you fail to pay, the lender (typically a bank or finance company) can foreclose on your house.
- **Loans for cars, boats, tractors, motor-cycles, or RVs.** If you fail to pay, the lender can repossess the vehicle.
- **Store charges with a security agreement.** Almost all store purchases on credit cards are unsecured. Some stores, notably Sears and J.C. Penney, however, claim to retain a security interest in all hard goods (durable goods) purchased, or they make customers sign security agreements when they use their store charge card.
- **Personal loans from banks, credit unions, or finance companies.** Often, you must pledge valuable personal property, such as a paid-off motor vehicle, as collateral for these loans. The property can be repossessed if you don't make the payments.

- **Judicial liens.** A judicial lien can be imposed on your property only after somebody sues you and wins a money judgment against you. In most states, the judgment creditor then must record (file) the judgment with the county or state. The recorded judgment creates a lien on your real estate and, in some states, on some of your personal property as well.
- **Statutory liens.** Some liens are automatic, by law. For example, in most states, when you hire someone to work on your house, the worker and the supplier of materials can assert a mechanic's lien (sometimes called a materialman's or contractor's lien) on the house if you don't pay.
- **Tax liens.** If you owe money to the IRS or other taxing authority, the debt is secured if the agency has recorded a lien against your property.

Unsecured Debts

An unsecured debt is any debt for which you haven't pledged collateral and for which the creditor has not filed a lien against you. If the debt is unsecured, the creditor is not entitled to repossess or seize any of your property if you don't pay.

Most debts are unsecured. Some of the common ones are:

- credit and charge card purchases and cash advances
- department store credit card purchases, unless the store retains a security interest in the items you buy or requires you to sign a security agreement
- gasoline company credit card purchases
- back rent

- medical bills
- alimony and child support
- student loans
- utility bills
- loans from friends or relatives, unless you signed a promissory note secured by some property you own
- health club dues
- lawyers' and accountants' bills
- church or synagogue dues, and
- union dues.

Priority Debts

Priority debts are unsecured debts that are considered sufficiently important to jump to the head of the bankruptcy repayment line. This means they are paid first if a Chapter 7 trustee disburses property in the course of the case. This can be very helpful when the priority debt can't be discharged in your bankruptcy (which is usually the case). For example, liability for a recent income tax is both a priority debt and a debt that can't be discharged in bankruptcy. Having your property pay off the tax debt—which you will have to pay anyway—is a lot better than having your property go to pay off debts that would otherwise be discharged in your bankruptcy.

Priority debts that may come up in consumer bankruptcies include:

- wages, salaries, and commissions owed by an employer
- contributions to employee benefit plans
- debts of up to $5,400 (each) owed to certain farmers and fishermen
- up to $2,425 in deposits made for the purchase, lease, or rental of property or

services for personal, family, or household use that were not delivered or provided

- alimony, maintenance, or support, and
- income taxes that became due within the three-year period before the bankruptcy filing date and taxes that were collected or withheld from an employee (trust fund taxes); also, customs, duties, and penalties owing to federal, state, and local governmental units.

The Means Test

By now you know that if your CMI exceeds your state's median income for a similarly sized household, you are required to take what's known as the means test. The means test measures certain expenses and deductions against your CMI to see whether you have any income you can spare to propose a Chapter 13 bankruptcy plan. In the words of the law, the means test determines whether a "presumption of abuse" arises—that is, whether filing a Chapter 7 bankruptcy would be presumed to be an abuse of the bankruptcy laws in the absence of facts proving the contrary.

SKIP AHEAD

If your CMI is below the median income, no need to take the means test. But see the discussion just below regarding "abuse under all the circumstances."

When a presumption of abuse arises, it's up to the filer to rebut the presumption, which means the filer has to convince the court that special circumstances entitle him or her to file under Chapter 7, even though the means test indicates a different result. On the other hand, if no presumption of abuse arises, then the way is clear to file under Chapter 7 (with some exceptions discussed below).

Take the Means Test

The means test itself is contained in Official Form 22A. You'll find a filled-out sample in Appendix C. To complete the test, you must use certain predetermined expenses formulated by the IRS that vary according to state and region. These expenses are available only online, at www.usdoj.gov/ust and are easily obtained for free at www.legalconsumer.com. In fact, all you have to do at www.legalconsumer.com is enter your email address and the calculator will automatically enter the proper predetermined expenses for you. You'll still need to add a bunch of information regarding your actual expenses. The following is a rough and ready guide to help you organize the information you'll need to actually take the test.

Use Worksheet B: Allowable Monthly Expenses, in Appendix B, to help you with the actual figures as you work through the following steps.

RESOURCE

Use a free means test calculator to help you do the math. You can find one at www.legalconsumer.com, a website owned and operated by Albin Renauer, coauthor of *How to File for Chapter 7 Bankruptcy* (Nolo). Start by entering your Zip code, which tailors the information to your state and locality. The site also provides plenty of other bankruptcy information and resources.

You Cannot Use the Car-Ownership Deduction If You Don't Have Car Payments

Until recently, some courts allowed you to deduct the standard predetermined transportation ownership expense for purposes of the means test, even if you weren't making payments on your car. Other courts ruled that you couldn't take this deduction if you weren't making car loan or lease payments.

Recently, in *Ransom v. FIA Card Services, MBNA, America Bank, _ U.S._* (2011), the United States Supreme Court held that in a Chapter 13 bankruptcy, a debtor cannot use the car-ownership deduction if the debtor does not make car loan or lease payments. In a Chapter 13 bankruptcy, the car-ownership deduction is one of the deductions used to determine the amount of debtor's disposable income, and thus the amount that the debtor must repay creditors.

Although the *Ransom* case deals with Chapter 13 bankruptcies, it is extremely likely that courts will apply the same reasoning to the car-ownership deduction in Chapter 7 bankruptcies for means test calculations.

Enter Actual Expenses

In addition to your CMI, which is the starting point for the means test, and the predetermined expenses, you'll also have to provide the following information about your actual expenses computed on a monthly basis:

- all federal, state, and local taxes, such as income taxes, self-employment taxes, Social Security taxes, and Medicare taxes. Do not include property taxes or sales taxes.
- total payroll deductions that are required for your employment, such as retirement contributions, union dues, and uniform costs. Do not include discretionary amounts, such as voluntary 401(k) contributions.
- term life insurance premiums for yourself. Do not include premiums for insurance on your dependents, for whole life, or for any other form of insurance.
- payments you are required to pay under a court or administrative agency order, such as spousal or child support payments. Do not include payments on arrearages.
- payments expended for education that is a condition of employment and for education that is required for a physically or mentally challenged dependent child for whom no public education providing similar services is available
- payments for child care, such as babysitting, day care, nursery, and preschool. Do not include other educational payments.
- payments for health care that is required for the health and welfare of yourself or your dependents, that is not reimbursed by insurance or paid by a health savings account, and that is in excess of the standard health care expense entered on Line 19B. Do not include payments for health insurance or health savings accounts listed in Line 34 of the form.
- payments for telecommunication services other than your basic home telephone and cell phone service—such as pagers, call

waiting, caller ID, special long distance, or Internet service—to the extent necessary for your health and welfare or that of your dependents. Do not include any amount previously deducted.

- payments to care for a member of your household or immediate family because of the member's age, illness, or disability
- payments for security systems and any other method of protecting your family
- actual payments for home energy costs that exceed the IRS expense
- payments for your children's education. The maximum you can deduct is $137.50.
- payments for food and clothing that exceed the predetermined expense, but no more than 5% of the pre-determined expense, and
- charitable contributions (tithing), but only if you have a history of making them.

Enter Monthly Contractual Payments

You are entitled to deduct the contractual monthly payments you owe on your mortgage, car, and other collateral you are making payments on. The deduction will be based on the total payments due over the next five years, divided by 60. If the monthly payments are due to last for five years or more, the deduction will be equal to the monthly payment. However, if your monthly payments are due to end prior to the end of the five-year period, you divide the total due by 60 and use the resulting number as your deduction.

> **EXAMPLE:** You are paying $1,500 a month on a mortgage that has ten years left on it. You also pay $300 a month on a home

---

Mortgage Obligation Payments When Surrendering Your Home

It's not uncommon for people filing bankruptcy to be in some stage of foreclosure and months behind on their payments. Some courts refuse to allow a deduction for mortgage payments when it's clear that the filer doesn't intend to keep the house. Other courts let you deduct them as long as you are still liable for them, regardless of what your intent might be for the future. The best approach is to first run the means test without counting the mortgage. If you pass without this deduction, then don't make it. If you need the deduction, however, then you'll need to be prepared to argue in a hearing that your court should follow the courts that allow it. This issue will likely be decided by the U.S. Supreme Court in 2011.

---

equity loan that has three years left on it. And you have a car note for $200 a month that has two years left. The monthly deduction for the mortgage will be $1,500, since the mortgage is due to last beyond the next five years. To calculate the deduction for the home equity loan, you first multiply $300 by 36 (the number of months left on the loan) and then divide that amount by 60 (the amount left amortized over a five-year period). The resulting deduction will be $180 a month. Finally, multiply $200 by 24 to obtain the amount you have left to pay on the car note ($4,800) and divide by 60, for a monthly deduction of $80. In this example, the total deduction for the mortgage, home equity loan, and car note is $1,760 a month.

Use Worksheet C in Appendix B to help you
calculate the actual figures.

Enter One-Sixtieth of Arrearages

You are entitled to deduct a monthly amount
equal to one-sixtieth of the arrearage you owe on
a secured debt, such as a mortgage or car note.
Incidentally, the one-sixtieth fraction represents
a monthly payment over a five-year period. For
example, if you owe three missed payments on
your mortgage totaling $4,500, the deduction
would be $75 a month (one-sixtieth of $4,500).
Before using this deduction, however, see "Mortgage Obligation Payments When Surrendering
Your Home," above.

Enter One-Sixtieth of Your Priority Debts

You are entitled to deduct a monthly amount
equal to one-sixtieth of your priority debts. The
reason for this is that priority debts must be paid
in full over the life of a Chapter 13 plan, and this
deduction represents the amount you'll have to
pay. For instance, recent taxes (taxes that first
became due within the three years immediately
preceding your bankruptcy filing date) are
priority debts. If you owe $5,000 in recent taxes,
you'll deduct one-sixtieth of that amount, or
about $83 a month.

The Trustee Fee

You are entitled to deduct the commission the
trustee would earn in a Chapter 13 case if you
filed one, which is roughly 10% of all payments
that would be made under the plan. This is a
difficult figure to come up with without more
information about which payments you must
make under the plan and which payments you

can make directly, so you should wrestle with
it only if you can't pass the means test by other
way.

A sample completed means test (Form 22A)
is included in Appendix C. By providing all this
requested information and using the sample as a
guide, you should be able to produce a result on
the www.legalconsumer.com calculator that will
tell you whether you pass the means test.

Special Circumstances

If abuse is presumed despite all the expenses and
deductions, you still may wriggle out of Chapter
13 and into Chapter 7 if you can prove that
special circumstances override the presumption.
See "Proving Special Circumstances," below.

When Your Leftover Income Fits Within the $110 to $187.50 Range

If you have some income left over after all the
deductions, and the income is less than $110,
you are home free. On the other hand, if the
income is over $187.50, abuse is presumed
(unless you can show special circumstances).
What happens if your income is right in the
middle? You'll need to compute your unsecured
debt (see the discussion of unsecured debt,
above) and enter that amount. The program at
www.legalconsumer.com will do the rest and
tell you whether or not abuse is presumed. The
test is whether the amount of leftover income
will pay at least 25% of your unsecured, nonpriority debt.

Abuse Under All the Circumstances

Even if you pass the means test, you aren't out of the woods. As you know, the means test is based on your CMI, a figure that may have no relationship to your actual income at the time you file bankruptcy. For instance, you may have been unemployed during that six-month look-back period, but when you file your bankruptcy you've just landed a plum job. Even though you pass the means test with flying colors, your actual income, when compared to your actual expenses leaves you a few hundred extra dollars every month. Bankruptcy law allows the trustee to challenge your Chapter 7 bankruptcy on the basis that this extra actual income would fund a Chapter 13 program. They advance this argument under a law that allows the court to dismiss or convert a case upon a finding of "abuse under all the circumstances." Most courts sign off on this approach (using your actual income and expenses to determine abuse rather than your CMI).

Cases are sometimes ordered dismissed or converted to Chapter 13 under the "abuse under all the circumstances" test when the filer's mortgage and car payments are unreasonably high for someone filing bankruptcy and the judge decides that lesser obligations would free up some money for a Chapter 13 plan. For

Proving Special Circumstances

If the U.S. Trustee seeks to dismiss or convert your Chapter 7 bankruptcy on the ground of presumed abuse, you can defend against that motion by showing that special circumstances apply in your case. These special circumstances must increase your expenses or decrease your income to bring your net monthly income down to a level that passes the means test. While the new bankruptcy law does not define the term "special circumstances," Congress cited as examples "a serious medical condition" or "a call or order to active duty in the Armed Forces."

And recently the U.S. Trustee's office noted that common special circumstances it may consider include:

- job loss or reduction in income for which there is no reasonable alternative
- a one-time "bump" in prepetition income that is not likely to happen again
- the debtors have separate households due to pending divorce or job relocation, and have filed a joint bankruptcy petition, and
- a postpetition household size increase due to pregnancy or a reasonable need to support an additional person.

For instance, assume you were activated from the reserves and faced a sharp drop in income as well as the costs of moving your family. If the judge agrees that these are special circumstances, and your changed economic picture gives you a net monthly income that passes the means test, you will be able to file a Chapter 7 bankruptcy. See Ch. 10 for more on using special circumstances to get you past the means test.

example, if Andy's monthly mortgage payments are $5,000 on a $750,000 note in an area where the median home price is $400,000, or Brianna is paying $900 a month on a note secured by a new-model Mercedes, the court may disallow a portion of these expenses and rule that Andy and Brianna could now afford a Chapter 13 plan. Of course this means that Andy would have to give up his house and Brianna her car, if they wanted to proceed in the bankruptcy court, rather than having their cases dismissed.

Bad Faith

Another doctrine that may affect your eligibility for bankruptcy is what's commonly called "bad faith." Under this doctrine, a judge can dismiss your bankruptcy if he or she believes you filed for reasons other than to get a fresh start, or you engaged in prebankruptcy behavior that is inconsistent with the need for a bankruptcy discharge. For example, in one recent case the court dismissed a case because the debtor purchased an expensive motorcycle shortly before filing and could have easily paid off his debts in a Chapter 13 bankruptcy had he not had to make the high monthly payments on his motorcycle.

Individuals and Businesses Can File for Chapter 7 Bankruptcy

Individuals and businesses can file for Chapter 7 bankruptcy. When individuals file, they get rid of their debts and go on with their lives. When business entities file, the business is liquidated, the assets are sold, and the proceeds go to the unsecured creditors. In between these extremes

are individuals who are also in business as sole proprietors or independent contractors.

Sole Proprietors

If you run your business as a sole proprietor, you and your business are considered to be one and the same. If there are business assets, they are subject to being sold for the benefit of your creditors—unless they qualify for an exemption (see Ch. 4). If, on the other hand, your business is service or profession oriented—such as contractors, lawyers, accountants, electricians, real estate agents, and the like—there are usually no assets worth selling and your business can continue without interruption. Retail businesses that have inventories or other assets that might generate income for the creditors typically must cease operations upon filing bankruptcy. This gives the trustee time to inventory and value the assets as of the date of the bankruptcy filing and decide whether they are covered by any exemption you claim or whether they can be seized and sold for the benefit of your creditors. Also, in some circumstances a trustee may close a business in order to avoid potential liability in the event that a customer is injured.

Owners of Small Business Entities

Owners of a small business that has incorporated or formed as a limited liability company (LLC) often have a choice to make, because there are two potential bankruptcy debtors: the owners personally and the business entity. You can:

- file as an individual and leave the business intact

- file as an individual and also have the business entity file separately, or
- have the business entity file and not file as an individual.

These decisions will depend on the following factors:

- the degree to which you have followed the necessary formalities in maintaining the business as a separate entity. For instance, did you maintain corporate minutes, issue stock or memberships, hold corporate meetings and pass resolutions as appropriate? Did you title business assets in the name of the business and keep your individual and business financial transactions separate (by using separate checkbooks, maintaining separate books, and observing basic rules of accounting regarding use of the business assets, income, and expenses)?
- the degree to which the business entity has its own debts and property separate and apart from the owner's, and
- the degree to which the owner has personally signed off on loans and other debt.

One large downside to taking a business entity through Chapter 7 is that you have to use a lawyer. Even if you are the sole owner of the entity, you can't represent it in the bankruptcy court. Lawyers don't come cheap, and this fact alone may drive your decision as to whether to have the entity file or just let it lapse and deal with your personal liability for any corporate debt in a personal bankruptcy.

 TIP

If you are filing a business-related bankruptcy, make sure you have good records. Although all bankruptcy debtors may be required to produce records of certain financial transactions as part of the bankruptcy case, this requirement is especially common when the debtor is in business (or has recently been in business). If the bankruptcy trustee moves to dismiss the case on the ground that the absence of financial records makes the case impossible to administer, the court might not accept the excuse that you're a sloppy bookkeeper, especially if you are a professional or in a type of business that requires some degree of sophistication.

Partnerships

Similarly, if you are a member of a business partnership with people other than your spouse, you can file for Chapter 7 bankruptcy as a consumer and include all business debts on which you are personally liable. Your partners will remain fully liable for the debts you wipe out, however.

 **SEE AN EXPERT**

If you are a member of a business partnership, consider consulting a small business lawyer before you file for bankruptcy. Your obligation to your partners may be governed by a buy-sell agreement that requires you to terminate your partnership interest before filing for bankruptcy. If you don't follow that agreement or any other understanding you and your partners have, you probably will be putting the partnership's property at risk.

And your partners (or ex-partners) may ask the bankruptcy court to lift the automatic stay so they can file a lawsuit against you. A lawyer can help you assess your obligations and options.

You Haven't Had a Previous Bankruptcy Discharge

You can't file for Chapter 7 bankruptcy if you previously had your debts discharged in:

- a Chapter 7 bankruptcy *filed* within the previous *eight* years, or
- a Chapter 13 bankruptcy *filed* within the previous *six* years.

EXAMPLE: On June 14, 2004, you filed for Chapter 7 bankruptcy. You received your discharge on November 2, 2004. You've fallen on hard times again and are considering filing another Chapter 7 case. You cannot file before June 15, 2012.

You Aren't Barred by a Previous Bankruptcy Dismissal

You can't file for Chapter 7 bankruptcy if your previous bankruptcy case was dismissed within the past 180 days for any of the following reasons:

- You violated a court order.
- The court ruled that your filing was fraudulent or an abuse of the bankruptcy system.
- You requested the dismissal after a creditor asked the court to lift the automatic stay.

EXAMPLE: You filed for Chapter 7 bankruptcy on February 12, 2011, after your

landlord started eviction proceedings. A week after you filed, your landlord filed a motion with the bankruptcy court to have the automatic stay lifted to continue the eviction proceedings. You dismissed your case. You've found a new place to live, but your debt problems haven't gone away and you want to refile. You must wait at least 180 days before filing again—that is, until August 12, 2011.

Prefiling Transfers of Real and Personal Property

Certain types of prefiling activities have such serious consequences that, as a practical matter, they render you ineligible to file bankruptcy for a period of time. Transactions involving the gift or sale of any type of personal property or real estate during the two-year period immediately preceding your filing date are heavily scrutinized in bankruptcy.

The basic problem here is that some filers are tempted to unload various assets so that the bankruptcy trustee won't find and seize the property and sell it for the benefit of the creditors. These transactions often take the form of selling the property to a friend or relative for a nominal amount, such as $1.00 with the understanding that the friend will cough up the property after the bankruptcy is completed. Other common examples are taking one's name off of a joint account, deed, or vehicle title (which is really a gift of half of the property to the other owner).

EXAMPLE: You want to file for Chapter 7 bankruptcy but you realize that you are listed on a deed as the co-owner of property where a friend is living—which was necessary to buy the property because your friend had bad credit. After learning that the trustee could take that property and sell it for the benefit of your unsecured creditors, you have yourself taken off the deed before filing. Assuming you wouldn't want to commit perjury in your bankruptcy papers, you would have to list that transaction, and your entire bankruptcy might go down the tubes.

Whatever form they take, prebankruptcy gifts and sales for substantially less than the property is worth are frequently judged to be fraudulent transfers, which can result in the transferred property being seized and sold for the benefit of the creditors, and the bankruptcy being dismissed. And even if you convince the bankruptcy trustee that you had an honest intent, the trustee can still demand that the person to whom you transferred the property give it back to be sold for the benefit of the creditors. And in these situations, it usually is not possible to claim the transferred property as exempt, which means you won't get any of the sale proceeds.

If you learn that you did a no-no, you may be tempted to try to undo it (in other words, get the property back, put your name back on the deed, etc.). This is even worse, since it indicates you are trying to deceive the court. About the best way to handle prebankruptcy transfers is to wait out the two-year period. For example, if you transferred your car to a relative for a nominal sum, you would wait for two years after the transfer to file. The bankruptcy papers you file ask you to list all transfers you made during the

Avoidable Transfers Don't Require a Guilty Mind

The concept of avoidable transfers is actually a simple one. When you file bankruptcy, all your property is part of your bankruptcy estate. This property consists of the property you own on the date you file, and in some circumstances the property you had before you filed. Whether you sold the property for less than its market value—for instance, a $3,000 car to a friend for $1,000—or just gave it away, it doesn't matter. It also doesn't matter whether your method of sale was direct—cash in exchange for the property—or a retitling that resulted in your interest being transferred to the other party. The property belongs to your bankruptcy estate and it's the trustee's job to avoid the transfer (collect it for the benefit of your creditors).

If your mindset was innocent—you had no idea you were going to file for bankruptcy when you transferred the property—the trustee will simply collect it from the transferee and distribute it to your creditors according to bankruptcy priority rules. Your bankruptcy won't be affected. However, if it appears that you deliberately got rid of it because you were planning your bankruptcy, the trustee can take your case to the bankruptcy judge and ask that your bankruptcy discharge be denied. Whether the judge denies your discharge will depend on the individual facts of your case.

coverage period, and if you can honestly answer no, you're in business.

I'm often asked, how will the trustee find out about a particular transfer? If title is involved (as with cars, boats, and real estate), the transfer will show up in the trustee's routine search of the various state and local databases (such as the DMV) that would document the transfer. Also, when you go to your creditors' meeting, you must affirm under oath that you've truthfully answered the questions in your Statement of Financial Affairs, the form where you are asked about prebankruptcy transfers. Trustees are skilled in picking up any hesitancy you have on this point. If they suspect something is wrong, they can follow up the meeting by questioning you under oath in a deposition-like proceeding. Most importantly, it's a bad idea to commit perjury. Period.

In my experience, a lot of property that is transferred prior to bankruptcy could easily have been retained and claimed as exempt. In other words, the transfer has occurred out of ignorance of the bankruptcy laws, which isn't surprising given the price that bankruptcy lawyers charge for their information. Still it makes me sad that people get themselves into this situation for no good reason.

Preference Payments

A basic principle of bankruptcy law is that all creditors deserve to be treated fairly in comparison to each other. In many cases, fair treatment means that no one gets anything. In some cases, it means that your unsecured creditors share equally in the proceeds if the trustee takes your nonexempt property and sells it.

This principle is undermined if you make a payment to some creditors and not others before you file for bankruptcy. Payments like these may be considered "preferences" because you are favoring some creditors over others. When payments qualify as preferences, the trustee can demand that the creditor return the money to your bankruptcy estate, where it will be divided equally among all of your creditors (subject to any exemptions you can claim).

For consumer debtors (those whose debts are primarily for personal debt rather than business debt), any payment of more than $600 might be considered a preference if it was made within a year to insider creditors (business associates, friends, or relatives), or within three months to others (see below). If, however, you are a business debtor—that is, a majority of your debt arises from your business activities—the court will look only at transactions that exceed $5,475. (Above I explain how to determine whether you are a business debtor for purposes of this rule.)

Payments to Insiders

The time period during which payments will be considered a preference depends on whether the creditor is an insider (a business associate, friend, or relative). If you pay more than $600 (or $5,475 if you are primarily a business debtor) to any creditor who's an insider during the year before you file for bankruptcy, that payment is a preference. For example, if you use your tax refund to pay back an emergency loan from your sister, brother, or mother, you have preferred that creditor over your other unsecured creditors. Bluntly put, when in bankruptcy, you are required to treat your mother and Visa equally.

EXAMPLE: In October, Robin borrows $2,000 from her mother to pay off a supplier. In March of the following year, Robin receives a tax refund of $3,000. She pays her mother back and uses the remaining $1,000 to catch up on other bills. Even though no one could blame Robin for paying back her mom, this would likely be considered a preference payment if she files for bankruptcy within the year. She'll have to disclose it in her bankruptcy paperwork, and her mom may have to cough up the money.

There is one important exception to this rule: A payment to an insider won't be considered a preference if you made the payment more than 90 days prior to filing for bankruptcy and you weren't insolvent at the time. For example, if you repaid a $3,000 loan from your mother more than three months before you file, and you can show that the value of your assets was greater than your liabilities at the time you repaid her, the payment won't be considered a preference. This insolvency rule also applies to preferences to noninsiders.

Insolvency is presumed during the 90-day period before you file for bankruptcy, so if you made a preference payment within the past 90 days, you should expect it to be undone if you file for bankruptcy.

Payments to Others

If the creditor is not an insider, but instead is a regular "arms-length" creditor like most of your business creditors, such as a vendor or credit card company, the rules are different. The court will look at your transactions with that creditor for only three months before you file for bankruptcy. During this time period, any payment of more than $600, or $5,475 if you are primarily a business debtor, will be considered a preference.

Payment of criminal restitution, like other debts, can be considered a preference if made within the three-month period prior to your bankruptcy filing and is over the $600 threshold.

Antecedent Debt Rule

To qualify as a preference, the payments must be made on an "antecedent" debt. In other words, the debt must already be past-due and owing. Even if you are current on an account, it might still qualify as an antecedent debt. For example, you may be current on a large credit card debt because you have been making the minimum monthly payments. As long as interest is being charged on the underlying debt, however, it will be considered an antecedent debt, and paying off the debt would be considered a preference.

Payments Made in the Ordinary Course of Business or Financial Affairs

A payment is not a preference if it is made in the ordinary course of business or the debtor's financial affairs.

EXAMPLE: Tim, a masonry contractor, owes Tom's Tile $3,500 from a past job. Although it's always been Tim's practice to immediately pay for his supplies as soon as he's paid for the job, he hasn't paid Tom's Tile because of a dispute over the quality of materials provided. Tim lands another job, for which he secures $10,000 worth of tile on credit from ABC Masonry Supplies. Two months later, when he is paid for the job, he pays ABC $10,000, which brings his ABC account current. This transaction would most likely qualify as one made in the ordinary course of Tim's business, because it meets his normal practice of immediately paying his suppliers.

Regular payments for personal expenses—such as utilities or services—typically also qualify as payments made in the ordinary course of business or financial affairs, rather than preferences. And regular monthly payments on long-term debt (for example, making a usual monthly payment on a mortgage, credit card bill, or student loan) also fall within this exception.

Even if a payment to a creditor was not made in the ordinary course of business or financial affairs, it still may escape the trustee's clutches if the debtor receives "new value" as a result of making the payment. This means the debtor is receiving some current benefit for making the payment, not just paying off an old debt. For instance, let's say Tim, from the example above, paid off Tom's Tile so he could order more materials on credit from that company. This extension of credit might be considered new value received for paying off the old debt, which means the payment wouldn't be a preference.

TIP

Transferring balances may be a preference. At least one court has found that transferring your balance from one credit card to another might be considered a preference. In that case, the debtor used her credit on one credit card to pay off her debt on another credit card. Because she made the transfer within three months of filing for bankruptcy, and she could have used the money for any purpose (in other words, she didn't have to use it to pay off her

other card), the court ruled that the transfer was a preference. (*In re Dilworth*, 560 F.3d 562 (8th Cir. 2009).)

If You've Made Preference Payments

The consequences of violating the preference rules can be harsh. The bankruptcy trustee is authorized to take back the money and distribute it among your creditors. If you paid back a family member, this may cause some tension. Even if you paid back a creditor that isn't an insider, it could cause problems. For example, if you paid back a credit card issuer so you could keep your card, the issuer will probably revoke your credit card if it has to cough up the money to the trustee. The same problem could come up if you paid a debt to a core vendor or a commercial landlord or equipment leasing company.

The trustee may not go after every preference payment. For example, the trustee might decide not to go after a preference if the cost of suing to collect it would outweigh the amount to be gained. If you can claim an exemption that covers the preference, the trustee has even less incentive to pursue it. For example, assume your state has a wildcard exemption (discussed in Ch. 6) for up to $5,000 of any property. If the trustee discovers a preference payment of up to $5,000, and you haven't used any of the wildcard exemption, the trustee has no reason to undo the preference. Even if the trustee went to the trouble to get the preference back, you would get to keep the money when it is returned to the bankruptcy estate; forcing your creditor to pay the money back wouldn't raise any money for your other creditors.

Even though you can't pay a favorite creditor before you file, nothing prevents you from doing so after you file, as long as you do it with income earned after you file for bankruptcy or with property that isn't in your bankruptcy estate.

Presumptions of Fraud

If you charge a credit card for an amount exceeding $550 for luxuries within three months of filing, or take out a cash advance from any one creditor exceeding $825 within 70 days before filing, the charge or advance will be presumed to be fraudulent if the creditor challenges them in court. As a general rule, few if any creditors will actually challenge such small amounts, because it will cost them more in lawyer fees. But to be safe it's advisable to wait out the three month, or 70-day period before filing.

You can also get into trouble if you:

- run up large debts for luxury items when you clearly are broke and have no way to pay the debts, or
- conceal property or money from your spouse during a divorce proceeding.

These activities cast a suspicion of fraud over your entire bankruptcy case.

You Can Produce a Tax Return, Wage Stubs, and a Credit Counseling Certificate

To file a Chapter 7 case, you must produce your most recent filed tax return. You'll also need a certificate showing that you completed a credit counseling course and wage stubs for the previous 60 days. (See Ch. 10 for more on these requirements.)

You Have Taken an Approved Personal Financial Management Course

You are required to take an approved personal finance course before the court will discharge your debts in a Chapter 7 bankruptcy. The agencies providing this service must be approved by the Office of the U.S. Trustee and must offer approximately two hours of required curriculum. Unlike the credit counseling agencies, personal financial management agencies don't have to be nonprofits, but they must offer in-person services on a sliding fee scale. For more information about the requirements for these agencies and how to find one in your area, visit the U.S. Trustee's website at www.usdoj.gov/ust; click "Credit Counseling & Debtor Education."

Before you can receive your Chapter 7 discharge, you must file an official form (Form 23) with the bankruptcy court, showing that you have completed this counseling. This must be accompanied by a certificate of completion from the counseling agency. You must file these forms no later than 45 days after the date on which your creditors' meeting was first scheduled. If you miss this deadline, the court may close your case without discharging your debts. This means you'll have to pay to reopen your case so you can file the form and request a discharge.

Chapter 13 Eligibility Requirements

Like Chapter 7 bankruptcy, Chapter 13 bankruptcy has several important eligibility requirements.

Prior Bankruptcy Discharges

You can't get a Chapter 13 discharge if you received a discharge in a previous Chapter 13 case in the last two years, or a discharge in a Chapter 7 case filed within the last four years. You aren't barred from filing a Chapter 13 in these circumstances, but you can't get a discharge. For instance, you can file a Chapter 13 bankruptcy the instant you receive a Chapter 7 discharge (to handle liens that survived your Chapter 7 case or manage repayment of debts that weren't discharged in that case), and you can operate under a plan confirmed by the court for a three- to five-year period. But you can't get the Chapter 13 discharge, which means you'll still owe any debt that you don't pay off in the course of your Chapter 13 case. (Filing for Chapter 13 after receiving a Chapter 7 discharge is colloquially known as a "Chapter 20 bankruptcy.") You may be wondering what good it would do you to file a Chapter 13 case when you don't qualify for the discharge. Simply, it provides a structured way for you to handle your debt load that might not be available outside of bankruptcy.

Businesses Can't File for Chapter 13 Bankruptcy

To file a Chapter 13 bankruptcy case, you must be an individual (or a husband and wife filing jointly). If you own your own business as a sole proprietor or partner, you can include all business debts on which you have personal liability. You have to file your case in your name, however, and not in the name of your business, because a business cannot file for Chapter 13 bankruptcy. On your bankruptcy papers, you will need to list all fictitious business names or DBAs ("doing business as" names) that you've used as a sole proprietor or partnership.

> **EXAMPLE:** Shelby Ferra operates a graphic design business under the name "Shelby Designs," and also has a seasonal tax preparation business called "AAA Tax Preparation Services." Shelby's bankruptcy petition would read as follows: Shelby Ferra AKA Shelby Designs AKA AAA Tax Preparation Services. There is no limit to the number of "akas" in a bankruptcy petition, provided that they aren't separate business entities requiring their own bankruptcy filings.

As with Chapter 7 bankruptcy, if you operate your business as a sole proprietorship or in a partnership with your spouse or another party, you or you and your partner are personally liable for the debts of the business. For bankruptcy purposes, you and your business (or your share of a partnership) are one and the same. There is one exception: stockbrokers and commodity brokers cannot file a Chapter 13 bankruptcy case, even for personal (not business) debts.

You cannot file a Chapter 13 bankruptcy on behalf of a corporation, limited liability company (LLC), or partnership as such. If you want to file a reorganization bankruptcy in that situation, you must file a business Chapter 11 bankruptcy, which is beyond the scope of this book.

> ### Chapter 11 Alternative for Business Entities
>
> Although business entities don't qualify to file Chapter 13 bankruptcy, they certainly can file under Chapter 11. Unfortunately, Chapter 11 bankruptcy is hideously expensive because of attorney fees and the need for both intensive and endless negotiations with secured creditors and creditor committees. Still, if you have a going business and the ability to raise cash in the range of $100,000 or more, Chapter 11 may be a way to save it. For a general overview of Chapter 11 bankruptcy, see *Business Reorganizations* by Myles H. Alderman, Jr., Esq. (Outskirts Press, Inc.).

Your Debts Must Not Be Too High

You do not qualify for Chapter 13 bankruptcy if your secured debts exceed $1,010,650 or your unsecured debts are more than $336,900. If you need help figuring out which of your debts are secured and which are unsecured, see "How Debts Are Classified," above.

You Must Be Current on Your Income Tax Filings

You will have to offer evidence that you have filed your federal and state income tax returns for the four tax years prior to your bankruptcy filing date. This evidence can be provided by the returns themselves or by transcripts of the returns obtained from the IRS. You have to provide this evidence no later than the date set for your first meeting of creditors (about a month after you file). The trustee can keep the creditors' meeting open for up to 120 days to give you time to file the returns, and the court can give you an additional 120 days. Ultimately, if you don't produce your returns or transcripts of the returns or transcripts for those four preceding years, your Chapter 13 will be dismissed.

Your Proposed Repayment Plan Must Satisfy Legal Requirements

Your eligibility for Chapter 13 bankruptcy depends on your ability to propose a plan that the court will approve of (confirm).

To determine whether a judge will confirm your plan, follow these steps:

Step 1: Compute your current monthly income (CMI) and compare it to the median income figure for your state (see Appendix B).

Step 2A: If your CMI exceeds the median income figure, use Worksheet C in Appendix B to compute your disposable income (income available to pay your unsecured nonpriority debt after all required payments will be taken care of under your plan). A copy of Worksheet C is in Appendix B.

If you are married but living separately, and filing a joint Chapter 13, you must count the income of both spouses when computing your disposable income on Form 22C. However, you do not have to include Social Security benefits received by either spouse when making that computation. But if only one spouse is filing the Chapter 13, the filing spouse may have to include Social Security received by the other spouse (or by anyone else) if it is contributed to the filer's household on a regular basis.

Step 3D: If your CMI is less than the median income for your state, compute your disposable income by subtracting your actual living expenses from your net income (See sample Forms I and J in Appendix C).

Step 3A: If you have enough disposable income to pay the percentage of your unsecured nonpriority debt that is required by your court (after paying all required debt under the plan), you qualify for Chapter 13.

Step 3B: If you have negative disposable income, forget about Chapter 13, unless you can reduce your living expenses or sell some property to create a positive disposable income.

CAUTION

Your plan might not be confirmed if your actual expenses look too low. If your current monthly income is less than your state's family median income, you can use your actual expenses to calculate how much you could devote to a Chapter 13 plan, provided those expenses are reasonable. Some people are tempted to decrease their stated expenses in order to increase their disposable income so they can qualify for Chapter 13. If it appears that your expenses are unreasonably low, however, the court may reject your plan as unreasonable.

Child Support and Alimony Owed to the Government

The general rule is that a Chapter 13 plan may be confirmed only if it provides for all priority debts to be paid in full over the life of the plan. However, if all of your disposable income is dedicated to repayment of debts over a five-year period, the plan may be confirmed even if you won't be able to fully repay back child support and alimony you owe to a governmental unit (such as a child support enforcement agency) during the five-year period. But, you will still be liable for the remaining back support after your Chapter 13 discharge.

RESOURCE

Get help calculating expenses in Chapter 13. If your disposable income falls short, it may be because you've deducted too many expenses or misinterpreted the meaning of a particular expense. There are many twists and turns to accurately computing the appropriate expenses in a Chapter 13 case, whether you are using the IRS expenses or actual expenses. A bankruptcy lawyer versed in the new law can be very helpful in this situation. You'll find additional guidance in *Chapter 13 Bankruptcy: Keep Your Property & Repay Debts Over Time*, by Stephen Elias and Robin Leonard (Nolo).

When Your CMI Is Different From Your Actual Monthly Income

Under the old law, a court would not confirm a Chapter 13 plan unless it was clear that the debtor's actual income could support a confirmable plan over three to five years. Under the new law, the court is supposed to decide whether to confirm a plan based on a figure—your current monthly income (CMI)—that does not necessarily reflect your actual income. Because your CMI is based on the six-month average prior to your filing date, your actual income may be much less or much more.

Since the bankruptcy laws changed in 2005, courts have differed on what to do when a debtor's "current monthly income" figure is different from the debtor's actual monthly income. Some judges based Chapter 13 plan payments on a projected disposable income that was calculated using the CMI, even if the CMI was different from the debtor's actual monthly income. Other judges were more flexible and permitted plans based on the debtor's actual income going forward. Similarly, in some cases judges considered phantom expenses (such as mortgage payments even though the debtor's intention was to walk away) while others did not.

Fortunately the U.S. Supreme Court recently provided some guidance on this issue in *Hamilton v. Lanning*, 560 U.S. __ (2010).

The Court ruled that, when deciding whether to confirm a Chapter 13 plan, bankruptcy courts can take into consideration changes in income or expenses that have occurred, or are known or virtually certain to occur, at the time of confirmation (confirmation usually occurs about two to three months after the petition is filed). In other words, when called on to confirm a Chapter 13 plan, courts can base their decision on the reality of the debtor's income going forward rather than on the formula created by Congress, which looks backward six months. However, the key word here is *change*. If there has been no significant change from the time the current monthly income and allowable expenses were computed, those figures will determine the amount to be repaid to unsecured creditors under the plan.

Importantly, the *Lanning* decision only addresses the test for computing disposable income in a Chapter 13 case. It remains to be seen whether the court's general approach—reality over formula—will govern in cases dealing with determining Chapter 7 eligibility under the means test (the means test formula is virtually identical to the disposable income test, although the purposes of two tests are different.)

In Step 2A, you calculated your mandatory debts and deducted them from the income you had left after deducting your IRS or actual expenses. If you have any remaining income after paying your mandatory debts, you will have to commit that income to paying your unsecured, nonpriority debts.

If your current monthly income is more than your state's median, you have to commit all of your projected disposable income to your plan for a five-year period. If your current monthly income is less than your state's median, you have to commit all of your disposable income to your plan for at least three years. Depending on which category you fit into, your plan will have to show what your projected disposable income can accomplish during the period in question.

For instance, if you are in the five-year category, will your projected disposable income cover all mandatory debts and necessary payments when spread out over 60 monthly payments? If there is anything left, does your plan apply that money to your unsecured, nonpriority debts? If so, then your plan should be confirmed by the court.

Similarly, if your current monthly income is less than the state's median, you need only commit to a three-year plan. So if you can make all required payments within 36 monthly payments, your plan will be confirmed provided that anything left over goes to your unsecured, nonpriority creditors. If you'll need a longer repayment period to pay all required debts, you can ask the court's permission at your confirmation hearing.

By now, you should understand that it's possible to propose a confirmable Chapter 13 plan without paying anything to your unsecured, nonpriority creditors—including credit card companies and hospital bills—assuming you have no nonexempt property (see below).

Your Proposed Payments Must Equal the Value of Your Nonexempt Assets

The total amount of payments to your unsecured creditors under your proposed plan must equal at least what those creditors would have received had you filed for Chapter 7 bankruptcy—that is, the value of your nonexempt property less what it would cost to sell the property and the amount of the trustee's commission. (Exempt property is the property you are allowed to keep if you file a Chapter 7 case. The important topic of exempt property is discussed in Ch. 1 and explained in more detail in Chs. 4 and 5.)

As emphasized throughout this book, many bankruptcy filers have little or no nonexempt property and thus probably need not be concerned with this particular eligibility requirement.

However, if you do have nonexempt property, you will have to perform what's called a "liquidation analysis" to determine how much your unsecured creditors would actually receive if you used Chapter 7 (and therefore, how much they are entitled to receive under your Chapter 13 plan).

Start with the value of your equity in the property. If a portion of the property is exempt, subtract the exempt amount. For example, many states exempt up to a certain amount of equity in a car. If you own a car outright that's worth $10,000, and the exemptions you are using allow you to exempt $4,000 of equity in a car, your total nonexempt amount is $6,000.

Next, subtract the trustee's commission. This amount represents what the trustee would get to keep if your property were taken and sold in a Chapter 7 case. Because this amount would not be distributed to your creditors, you can subtract it from the amount you have to pay them in a Chapter 13 case.

For each item of property sold, the trustee gets 25% of the first $5,000, 10% of the next $50,000, and 5% of the rest up to one million dollars. So, if you have a nonexempt bank account containing $25,000, the trustee gets to keep $1,250 (25% of $5,000) plus $2,000 (10% of the remaining $20,000) for a total of $3,250. Put another way, your creditors would receive $21,750 instead of $25,000.

In addition to the trustee's commission, you can also subtract the costs of taking the property and selling it. For certain types of property, there are few (if any) costs of sale. Cash on hand, bank accounts, and investments that can easily be converted to cash fit within this category of property. However, other types of property—such as a home, a car, or furniture—have significant resale costs. Because your unsecured creditors wouldn't get any of this money in a Chapter 7 case, they also aren't entitled to it in your Chapter 13 case. And, because personal property (a piano or furnishings, for example) often sells at auction for significantly less than its replacement value, you might be able to argue for an even lower total.

You Have Taken an Approved Personal Financial Management Course

As in Chapter 7, you (and your spouse, if you're filing jointly) are required to take a course on personal financial management before you can obtain a Chapter 13 discharge. This course is known by several names, including predischarge counseling and budget counseling. It's important to distinguish this mandatory counseling from the credit counseling you were required to take before you filed your bankruptcy. This course takes about two hours and can be taken online or through the mail, the same as with credit counseling. As with the credit counseling, you are entitled to pay on a sliding scale if you can't afford the full price. As a general rule, you can save some money if you sign up with the same company for both counseling sessions—the one before you file and the one after you file.

You can take this course at any time during your Chapter 13 case, but you will have to provide evidence that you've completed the counseling before the court will issue a Chapter 13 discharge. For more information about these counseling agencies, visit the U.S. Trustee website at www.usdoj.gov/ust. Click "Credit Counseling & Debtor Education." ●

How Bankruptcy Affects Your Debts

Most people consider bankruptcy because they want to get rid of debts—either immediately (in a Chapter 7 bankruptcy) or over time (in a Chapter 13 repayment plan bankruptcy). Most of your debts will, in fact, be wiped out in a bankruptcy of either type. Some, however, will not—which means you will still be responsible for paying them.

If you successfully complete your bankruptcy, whether Chapter 7 or Chapter 13, you will receive a notice from the court discharging all debts that are legally dischargeable. Although the notice lists the types of debts that are dischargeable, it doesn't tell you which of your particular debts are discharged and which are not. This chapter explains what types of debts are discharged in Chapter 7 and Chapter 13 bankruptcies, and which debts you might still owe after your bankruptcy case is over.

Debts That Will Be Discharged in Bankruptcy

Whether you file for Chapter 7 or Chapter 13 bankruptcy, certain types of debts will be discharged—that is, you will no longer be responsible for repaying them—at the end. In a Chapter 7 bankruptcy, you won't have to repay any portion of these debts directly: The bankruptcy trustee will divide your nonexempt assets (if you have any) among your creditors, then the court will discharge any amount that remains unpaid. In a Chapter 13 bankruptcy, your repayment plan will most likely provide for some portion of these debts to be paid back. If you complete your plan successfully, the remaining unpaid amount will be discharged.

Credit Card Debts

Without a doubt, the vast majority of those who file for bankruptcy are trying to get rid of credit card debts. Happily for these filers, the vast majority of bankruptcies succeed in this mission. With a few rare exceptions for cases involving fraud or luxury purchases immediately prior to your bankruptcy (outlined in "Debts That Survive Chapter 7 Bankruptcy," below), you can expect to get rid of your credit card debt in a Chapter 7 or Chapter 13 bankruptcy.

Medical Bills

Many people who file for bankruptcy got into financial trouble because of medical bills. More than 50 million Americans have no medical insurance. Many more millions of working Americans either have inadequate insurance from their employer or can't afford to use the plans that are available to them because of high deductibles.

Luckily, bankruptcy provides an out: Your medical bills will be discharged at the end of your bankruptcy case. In fact, billions of dollars in medical bills are discharged in bankruptcy every year.

Lawsuit Judgments

Most civil court cases are about money. If someone wins one of these lawsuits against you, the court issues a judgment ordering you to pay. If you don't come up with the money voluntarily, the judgment holder is entitled to collect on it by, for example, grabbing your bank account, levying your wages, or placing a lien on your home.

Money judgments and the debts that underlie them are almost always dischargeable in bankruptcy, regardless of the facts that led to the lawsuit in the first place. There are a couple of exceptions (discussed in "Debts That Survive Chapter 7 Bankruptcy," below), but in the vast majority of cases, money judgments are discharged. Even liens on your home arising from a court judgment can be cancelled if they interfere with your homestead exemption. (See "Secured Debts Are Dischargeable, But the Lien Remains the Same," below.)

Obligations Under Leases and Contracts

Increasingly in our society, things are leased rather than owned, be it a lease of real property (such as an apartment) or personal property (such as a car). If you enter into a lease contract and then become unable to make the monthly payment or otherwise perform your obligations under the lease, there will be consequences. The other party may want to hold you to the deal, and failing that, expect you to pay damages as a result of your breach (the damages are typically a reasonable, predetermined amount, or the actual financial hit the other party takes when you don't come through). If you don't pay damages voluntarily, the other party can go after you in a lawsuit.

Some debtors also have ongoing contractual obligations, such as a contract to sell or buy real estate, buy a business, deliver merchandise, or perform in a play. The other party may want to force you to hold up your end of the deal and may sue you for breach of contract damages if you fail to perform.

Obligations and liabilities under these types of agreements can also be cancelled in bankruptcy. Almost always, filing for bankruptcy will convert your lease or contractual obligation into a dischargeable debt, unless:

- The trustee believes that the lease or contract can be sold to a third party to raise money to pay your unsecured creditors.
- The court finds that you filed for bankruptcy for the specific purpose of getting out of a personal services contract (such as a recording contract).

If you wish, you can choose to keep the contract or lease in effect by "assuming" it. For example, you may have a time-share contract that you have been paying on for years and are close to paying off. Rather than canceling the contract, you may wish to keep it in effect. Or, you may be leasing essential equipment for your business and want to "assume" the lease. You indicate your choice—whether to assume or reject a lease or contract—in a document called a Statement of Intention.

Personal Loans and Promissory Notes

Money you borrow in exchange for a promissory note (or even a handshake and an oral promise to pay the money back) is almost always dischargeable in bankruptcy. As with any debt, however, the court may refuse to discharge a loan debt if the creditor can prove that you obtained the loan fraudulently. But that almost never happens.

Debts Owed to Coborrowers Who Paid the Original Debt

If you have jointly incurred a debt with another person, and that person pays off the debt in full, the debt you owe to the cosigner for your share of the debt (that was paid off) is dischargeable in Chapter 7 bankruptcy. However, this rule doesn't necessarily apply if the coborrower is your spouse and you have taken responsibility for payment of the debt in a divorce or separation agreement.

Other Obligations

The sections above outline the most common debts that are discharged in bankruptcy, but this isn't an exhaustive list. Actually, you can pretty much count on discharging any obligation or debt unless it fits within one of the exceptions discussed below.

Debts That Survive Chapter 7 Bankruptcy

Under bankruptcy law, there are several categories of debt that are "not dischargeable" in Chapter 7 (that is, you will still owe them after your bankruptcy is final):

- Some of these debts can't be discharged under any circumstances.
- Some will not be discharged unless you convince the court that the debt fits within a narrow exception to the rule.
- Some may survive your bankruptcy, but only if the creditor files a formal objection and convinces the court that they should.

Secured Debts Are Dischargeable, But the Lien Remains the Same

Secured debts are typically contractually linked to specific items of property, called collateral. If you don't pay the debt, the creditor can take the collateral. The most common secured debts include loans for cars and homes.

If you have a debt secured by collateral, bankruptcy eliminates your personal liability for the underlying debt—that is, the creditor can't sue you to collect the debt itself. But bankruptcy doesn't eliminate the creditor's hold, or "lien," on the property that served as collateral under the contract.

Other types of secured debts arise involuntarily, often as a result of a lawsuit judgment or an enforcement action by the IRS on taxes that

are old enough to be discharged. In these cases too, bankruptcy gets rid of the underlying debt, but may not eliminate a lien placed on your property by the IRS or a judgment creditor.

Chapter 7 bankruptcy offers several options for dealing with secured debts, ranging from buying the property from the creditor for its replacement value, reaffirming the debt, surrendering the property, or (in some cases) getting rid of the debt while keeping the property and continuing to make payments as before. Secured debts and options for dealing with them in Chapter 7 bankruptcy are discussed in Ch. 6.

Debts Not Dischargeable Under Any Circumstances

There are certain debts that bankruptcy doesn't affect at all: You will continue to owe them just as if you had never filed.

Domestic Support Obligations

Obligations defined as "domestic support obligations" are not dischargeable. Domestic support obligations are child support, alimony, and any other debt that is *in the nature of* alimony, maintenance, or support. For example, one spouse may have agreed to pay some of the other spouse's or the children's future living expenses (shelter, clothing, health insurance, and transportation) in exchange for a lower support obligation. The obligation to pay future living expenses may be treated as support owed to the other spouse (and considered nondischargeable), even though no court ordered it.

To be nondischargeable under this section, a domestic support obligation must have been established—or must be capable of becoming established—in:

- a separation agreement, divorce decree, or property settlement agreement
- an order of a court that the law authorizes to impose support obligations, or
- a determination by a child support enforcement agency (or other government unit) that is legally authorized to impose support obligations.

A support obligation that has been assigned to a private entity for reasons other than collection (for example, as collateral for a loan) is dischargeable. This exception rarely applies, however: Almost all assignments of support to government or private entities are made for the purpose of collecting the support.

Other Debts Owed to a Spouse, Former Spouse, or Child

You can't discharge any debt you owe to a spouse, former spouse, or child that was incurred:

- in the course of a divorce or separation, or
- in connection with a separation agreement, divorce decree, or other court order.

Simply put, debts you owe to a child or former spouse because of a divorce are not dischargeable in Chapter 7. (However, they can be discharged in Chapter 13—see "Debts Discharged in Chapter 13 (But Not in Chapter 7)," below.)

Importantly, while your bankruptcy will get rid of your obligation to pay the creditor, you are still liable to your ex-spouse for your share if the creditor goes after him or her for payment. Assume, for example, that Linda and Paul agree in their marital settlement agreement that Paul will be responsible for the couple's credit card debt (roughly $50,000), while Linda will assume responsibility for the family car, a 2009 BMW on which they owe $50,000. If Paul files for bankruptcy, he will no longer owe anything to the credit card creditors, but if the creditors try to collect from Linda as a joint debtor, Linda can hold Paul responsible. Similarly, if Linda defaults on the BMW and files bankruptcy after a deficiency judgment of $20,000 is obtained, Paul can sue Linda for the $20,000 if he is forced to pay it. Of course if both Linda and Paul file bankruptcy, then they are both freed of obligations to the creditors and each other.

Fines, Penalties, and Restitution

You can't discharge fines, penalties, or restitution that a federal, state, or local government has imposed to punish you for violating a law. Examples include:

- fines or penalties imposed under federal election law
- fines for infractions, misdemeanors, or felonies
- fines imposed by a judge for contempt of court
- fines imposed by a government agency for violating agency regulations
- surcharges imposed by a court or agency for enforcement of a law, and
- restitution you are ordered to pay to victims in federal criminal cases.

Certain Tax Debts

Regular income tax debts are dischargeable if they are old enough and meet the other requirements (discussed below). Other types of taxes may not be dischargeable at all. The specific rules depend on the type of tax.

Fraudulent income taxes. You cannot discharge debts for income taxes if you didn't file a return or you were intentionally avoiding your tax obligations.

Property taxes. Property taxes aren't dischargeable unless they became due more than a year before you file for bankruptcy. Even if your personal liability to pay the property tax is discharged, however, the tax lien on your property will remain. From a practical standpoint, this discharge is not meaningful, because you'll have to pay off the lien before you can transfer the property with clear title. In fact, you may even face a foreclosure action by the property tax creditor if you take too long to come up with the money.

Other taxes. Other types of taxes that aren't dischargeable are business related: payroll taxes, excise taxes, and customs duties. Sales, use, and poll taxes are also probably not dischargeable.

Debt Incurred to Pay Nondischargeable Taxes

In a Chapter 7 bankruptcy, you can't discharge debts that you incurred to pay taxes owed to a government entity. For example, if Jose uses his Visa card to pay his income taxes of $2,000, Visa can bill Jose for the $2,000 after the bankruptcy is over. Similarly, if Valerie borrows $5,000 from her credit union to pay her property tax, the debt will survive her bankruptcy. However, even though this type of debt is not legally discharged, it may be that the creditor doesn't screen bankruptcies to contest this type of debt and may not attempt to collect it after your bankruptcy.

This type of debt is dischargeable in a Chapter 13 bankruptcy, however. For instance, if Jona owes $25,000 in back taxes after an audit, and uses a credit card to pay it off, Jona would be on the hook for $25,000 after a Chapter 7 bankruptcy. However, if she files for Chapter 13, she can get rid of the balance of the debt when her plan ends after three or five years (the length of her plan will depend on her income), even though her plan had been paying pennies on the dollar toward the debt.

SEE AN EXPERT

Get help for business tax debts. If you owe any of these nondischargeable tax debts, see a bankruptcy attorney before you file.

Court Fees

If you are a prisoner, you can't discharge a fee imposed by a court for filing a case, motion, complaint, or appeal, or for other costs and expenses assessed for that court filing, even if you claimed that you were unable to afford the fees. (You can discharge these types of fees in Chapter 13—see "Debts Discharged in Chapter 13 (But Not in Chapter 7)," below.)

Intoxicated Driving Debts

If you kill or injure someone while you are driving and are illegally intoxicated by alcohol or drugs, any debts resulting from the incident aren't dischargeable. Even if a judge or jury finds you liable but doesn't specifically find that you were intoxicated, the debt may still be nondischargeable. The judgment against you won't be discharged if the bankruptcy court (or a state court in a judgment collection action) makes an independent determination that you were, in fact, intoxicated.

Note that this rule applies only to personal injuries: Debts for property damage resulting from your intoxicated driving are dischargeable.

Condominium, Cooperative, and Homeowners' Association Fees

You cannot discharge fees assessed after your bankruptcy filing date by a membership association for a condominium, housing cooperative, or lot in a homeownership association if you or the trustee have an ownership interest in the condominium, cooperative, or lot. As a practical matter, this means that any fees that become due after you file for Chapter 7 bankruptcy will survive the bankruptcy, but fees you owed prior to filing will be discharged. (You can discharge postfiling fees in Chapter 13—see "Debts Discharged in Chapter 13 (But Not in Chapter 7)," below.)

Debts for Loans From a Retirement Plan

If you've borrowed from your 401(k) or other retirement plan that is qualified under IRS rules for tax-deferred status, you'll be stuck with that debt. (You can, however, discharge a loan from a retirement plan in Chapter 13—see "Debts Discharged in Chapter 13 (But Not in Chapter 7)," below.)

Debts You Couldn't Discharge in a Previous Bankruptcy

If a bankruptcy court dismissed a previous bankruptcy case because of your fraud or other bad acts (misfeasance), you cannot discharge any debts that you tried to discharge in that earlier bankruptcy. (This rule doesn't affect debts incurred since the date you filed the earlier bankruptcy case.)

EXAMPLE: You filed for Chapter 7 bankruptcy in January 2005 and received a discharge in May 2005. You need to file for bankruptcy again in 2012, but eight years haven't elapsed since your previous filing. In desperation, you use a fake Social Security number on your 2012 filing. Your ploy is discovered and your bankruptcy is dismissed because of your fraud. You file again in 2013. Even though eight years have passed since your 2005 filing, none of the debts you incurred prior to your fraudulent 2012 filing will qualify for discharge.

Debts Not Dischargeable Unless You Can Prove That an Exception Applies

Some debts cannot be discharged in Chapter 7 unless you show the bankruptcy court that the debt really is dischargeable because it falls within an exception. The two most common examples of this type of debt are student loans and certain taxes.

Student Loans

Student loans are very difficult to discharge. The law excludes student loans from the discharge, whether they are issued or insured by the government or a nonprofit institution, or by a private commercial lender (provided that the loan is a qualified education loan incurred by an individual). To qualify as an education loan, the loan must contain certain payback provisions that give the borrower some slack in times of economic difficulty or when attending an educational institution. The only way out of an educational loan in bankruptcy is to establish undue hardship, which is harder to do than you might think.

To discharge your student loan on the basis of "undue hardship," you must file a separate action in the bankruptcy court and obtain a court ruling in your favor on this issue. To succeed, an action to discharge a student loan debt typically requires the services of an attorney, although it's possible to do it yourself if you're willing to put in the time. (See Ch. 10 for general information about going to bankruptcy court.)

In determining undue hardship, most bankruptcy courts look at three factors (listed below). If you can show that all three factors are present, the court is likely to grant you an undue hardship discharge of your student loan. These factors are:

- **Poverty.** Based on your current income and expenses, you cannot maintain a minimal living standard and repay the loan.
- **Persistence of hardship.** Your current financial condition is likely to continue indefinitely—that is, your situation is hopeless or virtually hopeless. This factor is most likely to be present if you are elderly or you or a spouse has a disability that restricts your opportunities to earn a decent living.
- **Good faith.** You've made a good-faith effort to repay your debt. (You're not likely to be granted a hardship discharge if you file for bankruptcy immediately after getting out of school or if you haven't looked extensively for employment and made efforts to maximize your income.)

Special Rules for HEAL and PLUS Loans

The federal Health Education Assistance Loans (HEAL) Act, not bankruptcy law, governs HEAL loans. Under the HEAL Act, to discharge a loan, you must show that the loan became due more than seven years ago and that repaying it would not merely be a hardship, but would impose an "unconscionable burden" on your life.

Parents can get Parental Loans for Students (PLUS Loans) to finance a child's education. Even though the parent does not receive the education, the loan is treated like any other student loan if the parent files for bankruptcy. The parents must meet the undue hardship test to discharge the loan.

Courts rarely allow student loans to be discharged. They take the position that Congress wants student loans to be repaid, absent exceptional circumstances. They also recognize that federal student loan regulations require a lot of flexibility on the creditor's part, including moratoriums on payments, temporary reductions in payments, and extensions of the repayment period that lower the monthly payments to an affordable amount. These options give debtors other ways (short of filing for bankruptcy) to seek relief from student loan debt.

In some cases, however, courts have found that it would be an undue hardship to repay the entire loan and relieved the debtor of a portion of the debt. Other courts take the position that it's an all-or-nothing proposition—either the entire loan is discharged or none of it is discharged. Ask a local bankruptcy attorney how courts in your area handle student loans.

Regular Income Taxes

People who are considering bankruptcy because of tax problems are almost always concerned about income taxes they owe to the IRS or the state equivalent. There is a myth afoot that income tax debts are not discharged in bankruptcy. This is not true if you are able to meet certain conditions. Here are the specifics.

You can discharge federal or state income tax debt in Chapter 7 bankruptcy if all of the following are true:

- You filed a tax return for the tax year or years in question.
- The return was filed at least two years before your bankruptcy filing date.
- The tax return was due at least three years before you file for bankruptcy (either April 15th of the following year or October 15th if you requested an extension).
- The taxing authority has not assessed your liability for the taxes within the 240 days before your bankruptcy filing date (this time period can be extended if the IRS has suspended collection activities because of an offer in compromise or a previous bankruptcy filing).
- You did not willfully attempt to evade the tax.

EXAMPLE: Fred filed a tax return in August 2008 for the 2007 tax year. In March 2010, the IRS audited Fred's 2007 return and assessed a tax due of $8,000. In May 2011, Fred files for bankruptcy. The taxes that Fred wishes to discharge were for tax year

---

Pending Legislation Would Allow Discharge of Private Student Loans

Private student loans are loans not offered or guaranteed by the federal government. Prior to the 2005 changes to bankruptcy law, private student loans were dischargeable in bankruptcy. The 2005 changes reversed that, making private student loans the same as federal or federally backed student loans— that is, not dischargeable unless you can meet the stringent guidelines of undue hardship. However, Senate Bill 3219, introduced by Senator Dick Durbin, would once again allow private student loans to be discharged in bankruptcy, just like other unsecured debt. To check on the status of this legislation, visit the Library of Congress's website at http://thomas.loc.gov.

2007. The return for those taxes was due on April 15, 2008, more than three years prior to Fred's filing date in May 2011. The tax return filed in August 2008 was at least two years prior to Fred's bankruptcy filing date. Finally, the assessment date of March 2010 was well prior to 240 days of the filing date. There is no evidence that Fred schemed to not pay his tax (in other words, that he illegally tried to avoid paying). Because Fred met all five conditions for discharging an income tax liability, Fred can discharge those taxes.

Even if you meet each of the five requirements for discharging tax liability, any lien placed on your property by the taxing authority will remain after your bankruptcy. The result is that the taxing authority can't go after your bank account or wages, but you'll have to pay off the lien before you can sell your real estate with a clear title.

Taxes Due Under Late-Filed Returns

For some time the IRS considered prior income tax obligations to be nondischargeable if the debtor failed to file the return on time, even though the return was filed at least two years prior to the bankruptcy filing date. Recently, the IRS has admitted to the error of its ways and, as provided in Section 523(a)(1)(B) of the bankruptcy code, will only apply the late-filed rule if the returns were filed within the two-year period.

CAUTION

Debts incurred to pay nondischargeable taxes will also be nondischargeable in Chapter 7 bankruptcy. If you borrowed money or used your credit card to pay taxes that would otherwise not be discharged, you can't eliminate that loan or credit card debt in Chapter 7 bankruptcy. In other words, you can't turn a nondischargeable tax debt into a dischargeable tax debt by paying it on your credit card. (Note: These debts can be discharged in Chapter 13 bankruptcy, however, as explained below.)

Debts Not Dischargeable in Bankruptcy If the Creditor Successfully Objects

Four types of debts may survive Chapter 7 bankruptcy, but only if:

- The creditor files a formal objection—called a complaint to determine dischargeability—during the bankruptcy proceedings.
- The creditor proves that the debt fits into one of the categories discussed below.

Debts From Fraud

In order for a creditor to prove that one of your debts should survive bankruptcy because you incurred it through fraud, the debt must fit one of the categories below.

Debts from intentionally fraudulent behavior. If a creditor can show that a debt arose because of your dishonesty, the court probably will not let you discharge the debt. Here are some common examples:

If Your Debts Will Be Discharged Unless a Creditor Objects

Even though creditors have the right to object to the discharge of certain debts, many creditors—and their attorneys—don't fully understand this right. Even a creditor who knows the score might sensibly decide to write off the debt rather than contesting it. It can cost a lot to bring a "dischargeability action" (as this type of case is called). If your debt isn't huge, a creditor might decide that it will be cheaper to forgo collecting the debt than to fight about it in court.

For these reasons, the fact that a particular debt may not be discharged if a creditor objects shouldn't necessarily prevent you from filing for bankruptcy. It all depends on your total debt burden: If you are filing primarily to get rid of a debt that won't be discharged if a creditor objects, you might end up with a bankruptcy on your record for nothing. If, on the other hand, you have other debts that will certainly be discharged (such as credit card debts), those debts will be gone after you file for bankruptcy, even if a creditor successfully objects to the discharge of one debt.

- You wrote a check for something and stopped payment on it, even though you kept the item.
- You wrote a check against insufficient funds but assured the merchant that the check was good.
- You rented or borrowed an expensive item and claimed it was yours in order to use it as collateral to get a loan.

- You got a loan by telling the lender you'd pay it back, when you had no intention of doing so.
- You received payments from unemployment insurance or other benefit programs because of your fraud or misrepresentation.

For this type of debt to be nondischargeable, your deceit must be intentional, and the creditor must have relied on your deceit in extending credit or awarding benefits. Again, these are facts that the creditor has to prove before the debt will be ruled nondischargeable by the court.

Debts from a false written statement about your financial condition. If a creditor proves that you incurred a debt by making a false written statement, the debt isn't dischargeable. Here are the rules:

- The false statement must be written —for instance, made in a credit application, rental application, or resume.
- The false statement must have been "material"—that is, it was a potentially significant factor in the creditor's decision to extend you credit. The two most common materially false statements are omitting debts and overstating income.
- The false statement must relate to your financial condition or the financial condition of an "insider"—a person close to you or a business entity with which you're associated.
- The creditor must have relied on the false statement, and the reliance must have been reasonable.
- You must have intended to deceive the creditor. This is extremely hard for the creditor to prove based simply on your behavior. The creditor would have to show outrageous behavior on your part, such as

adding a "0" to your income (claiming you make $180,000 rather than $18,000) on a credit application.

Recent debts for luxuries presumed fraudulent. If you run up more than $550 in debt to any one creditor for luxury goods or services within the 90 days before you file for bankruptcy, the law presumes that your intent was fraudulent regarding those charges. The charges will survive your bankruptcy unless you prove that your intent wasn't fraudulent. The term "luxury goods and services" does not include things that are reasonably necessary for the support and maintenance of you and your dependents (what that means will be decided on a case-by-case basis).

Recent cash advances. If you get cash advances from any one creditor totaling more than $825 under an open-ended consumer credit plan within the 70 days before you file for bankruptcy, the debt is presumed to be nondischargeable. "Open-ended" means there's no date when the debt must be repaid, but rather, as with most credit cards, you may take forever to repay the debt as long as you pay a minimum amount each month.

RELATED TOPIC

Additional information on credit card issuers' attempts to have credit card debt declared nondischargeable because of fraud is provided in Ch. 9.

Debts Arising From Debtor's Willful and Malicious Acts

If the act that caused the debt was both willful *and* malicious (that is, you intended to inflict an injury to person or property), the debt isn't dischargeable if the creditor successfully mounts an objection in the bankruptcy court.

Generally, crimes involving the intentional injury to people or damage to property are considered willful and malicious acts. Examples are assaults, rape, arson, or vandalism.

Other acts that would typically be considered to be willful and malicious include:

- kidnapping
- deliberately causing extreme anxiety, fear, or shock
- libel or slander, and
- illegal acts by a landlord to evict a tenant, such as removing a door or changing the locks.

If you were simply careless (you should have taken more care, as is true in most automobile accidents), or even reckless (for example, you caused an injury by driving far too fast), the debt will still be discharged. Because creditors have a hard time proving that a debt arises from both a willful and malicious act, these debts are often ordered discharged by the court when contested on this ground.

Willful and Malicious Acts Are Different in Chapter 13

In Chapter 7 bankruptcy, these debts are nondischargeable only if the underlying act is found by the court to be both willful *and* malicious. Under Chapter 13 bankruptcy, however, the underlying act need only be willful *or* malicious. On the other hand, debts for property damage, which can survive Chapter 7 under the willful and malicious rule, can be discharged in a Chapter 13 bankruptcy.

Debts From Embezzlement, Larceny, or Breach of Fiduciary Duty

A debt incurred as a result of embezzlement, larceny, or breach of fiduciary duty is not dischargeable if the creditor successfully objects to its discharge.

"Embezzlement" means taking property entrusted to you for another and using it for yourself. "Larceny" is another word for theft. "Breach of fiduciary duty" is the failure to live up to a duty of trust you owe someone, based on a relationship where you're required to manage property or money for another, or where your relationship is a close and confidential one. Common fiduciary relationships include those between:

- business partners
- attorney and client
- estate executor and beneficiary
- guardian and ward, and
- husband and wife.

Debts or Creditors You Don't List

Bankruptcy requires you to list all of your known creditors on your bankruptcy papers and provide their most current addresses. This gives the court some assurance that everyone who needs to know about your bankruptcy will receive notice. As long as you do your part, the debt will be discharged (as long as it's otherwise dischargeable under the rules), even if the official notice fails to reach the creditor for some reason beyond your control—for example, because the post office errs or the creditor moves without leaving a forwarding address.

Suppose, however, that you forget to list a creditor on your bankruptcy papers or carelessly misstated a creditor's identity or address. In that situation, the court's notice may not reach the creditor and the debt may survive your bankruptcy. Here are the rules:

- If the creditor knew or should have known of your bankruptcy through other means, such as a letter or phone call from you, the debt will be discharged even though the creditor wasn't listed. In this situation, the creditor should have taken steps to protect its interests, even though it didn't receive formal notice from the court.
- If all of your assets are exempt—that is, you have a "no-asset" case—the debt will be discharged (unless the debt is otherwise nondischargeable). In this situation, the creditor wouldn't have benefited from receiving notice anyway, because there is no property to distribute. However, if the lack of notice deprives a creditor of

If an Unknown Creditor Pops Up After Bankruptcy

If a creditor comes out of the woodwork after your bankruptcy case is closed, you can always reopen your case, name the creditor, and then seek an amended discharge. If it's the kind of debt that will be discharged anyway, many courts won't let you reopen because there is no need to. The debt is discharged by law and most creditors know this. However, if the creditor continues to try to collect the debt, you can haul the creditor into the bankruptcy court on a contempt charge (for violating the court's discharge order).

the opportunity to successfully object to the discharge by filing a complaint in the bankruptcy court (such as for a fraudulent debt), the debt may survive your bankruptcy.

Debts That Survive Chapter 13 Bankruptcy

In a Chapter 13 bankruptcy, you are supposed to pay off your debts over time, but few debtors pay back 100% of their debts. The typical Chapter 13 plan pays 100% of back child support (except support owed to a government agency), back taxes, and other debts classified as priority debts, and some percentage of other unsecured debts, depending on the debtor's disposable income and the value of the debtor's nonexempt property. (See Ch. 2 for more on Chapter 13 plans.) This section explains what happens to any remaining nonpriority, unsecured debt when your Chapter 13 plan is complete.

As in Chapter 7, several categories of debt may not be discharged in Chapter 13 bankruptcy:

- Some debts can't be discharged under any circumstances and you'll be stuck with them after your case is over.
- Student loans won't be discharged unless you convince the court that it would be an undue hardship to pay off the loan.
- Fraudulent debts won't be discharged, but only if the creditor convinces the court that they shouldn't be.

Debts Not Dischargeable Under Any Circumstances

Certain types of debts survive Chapter 13 bankruptcy, regardless of your income or circumstances.

Domestic Support Obligations

In both Chapter 7 and Chapter 13 bankruptcies, child support and alimony you owe directly to an ex-spouse or child are nondischargeable. (See "Debts That Survive Chapter 7 Bankruptcy," above, for more on these obligations.) Your Chapter 13 repayment plan must provide for 100% repayment of these debts. Although you don't have to completely pay back support you owe to a governmental child support collection agency during the life of your plan, any amount that is left over after you complete your plan is not dischargeable.

> **EXAMPLE:** In the final decree issued in his divorce, Fred was ordered to pay his ex-wife $500 a month for child support. Shortly after the divorce, Fred's ex-wife applied for welfare and assigned her child support rights to the county providing the welfare. Over time, Fred fell behind on his child support to the tune of $25,000 principal and interest. When Fred files for bankruptcy under Chapter 13, his plan—later confirmed by the court—requires him to pay $15,000 of the $25,000 arrearage. When Fred receives his Chapter 13 discharge, he will still owe the $10,000 that won't be paid through his plan.

Criminal Penalties

Debts you owe on fines or restitution orders contained in the sentence for conviction of any crime (yes, even traffic tickets) may not be discharged in Chapter 13.

Fines or Penalties Owed to a Government Agency

If you have been fined by a government agency for some reason, or subjected to a penalty or a forfeiture of property, this debt will not be discharged. However, if the government agency assesses the fine because you were overpaid benefits due to your failure to report income or for some other faulty behavior, only the fine itself is not dischargeable. The amount you were overpaid is dischargeable like any other unsecured debt. However, if the agency files an action in court alleging that you obtained the overpayment through fraud, the court can rule that the overpayment is not dischargeable.

> **EXAMPLE:** Mary was receiving unemployment insurance benefits, and then found a job. While she originally intended to report the job to the unemployment insurance agency—which would result in a termination of the benefits—she found that her wages were insufficient for her needs and decided to continue receiving the unemployment benefits. When she was caught about six months later, she had received over $10,000 in overpayments. She signed an agreement to repay the $10,000 overpayment as well as a $5,000 fine because of her intentionally fraudulent behavior. In bankruptcy, the $5000 fine is not dischargeable as matter of law. However, the $10,000 would be discharged unless the government agency filed an affirmative action in bankruptcy court, asking the judge to except the overpayment from discharge because of fraud.

Certain Taxes

Recent income tax debts—those that first became due within the three-year period prior to your filing date—are priority debts and have to be paid in full in any Chapter 13 plan. If your Chapter 13 ends prematurely for any reason, the tax debts you have not yet repaid will remain; you will either have to pay them outside of bankruptcy or convert your Chapter 13 to a Chapter 7 bankruptcy. (See "Debts That Survive Chapter 7 Bankruptcy," above, for information on which taxes are dischargeable.) If there is evidence in the tax records that you tried to avoid your duty to file an honest return or pay your taxes, the taxes will survive bankruptcy without exception. If you operated a business, you can't discharge taxes that you failed to withhold from an employee. And, in a departure from pre-2005 bankruptcy rules, tax debts for which you did not file returns are not dischargeable under any circumstances.

Intoxicated Driving Debts

If you operate a vehicle while illegally intoxicated by alcohol or drugs, and you kill or injure someone, any debt arising out of the injury is not dischargeable. But what if you are sued and the judge or jury finds you liable but doesn't specifically find that you were intoxicated? This may not help you: The judgment against you won't be discharged if the bankruptcy court (or a state court in a judgment collection action) determines that you were, in fact, intoxicated.

Note that this rule applies only to personal injuries: Debts for property damage resulting from your intoxicated driving are dischargeable.

Debts Arising From Your Willful or Malicious Actions

If a creditor obtains a judgment against you in civil court for personal injury or death caused by your willful or malicious act, the judgment will be nondischargeable. For example, O.J. Simpson was acquitted of criminal charges but found liable, in a civil suit, for wrongful death—which fits the definition of a "willful or malicious act." Under this rule, O.J. could not discharge the debt in Chapter 13 bankruptcy.

Unlike the "willful and malicious" category of debts that may be nondischargeable in Chapter 7, a creditor in a Chapter 13 case need not go to court to prove that the debt should not be wiped out. Instead, these debts are automatically nondischargeable. Note that the act which gives rise to the debt need only be willful *or* malicious to be nondischargeable in Chapter 13, which greatly expands the types of debt that will survive discharge. For instance, a judgment for injury caused by your reckless driving would most likely survive Chapter 13 bankruptcy on the ground of "maliciousness," whereas it might be discharged in Chapter 7 because reckless driving, through malicious, is seldom considered willful.

Finally, unlike Chapter 7, which includes damage to property, this exception to a Chapter 13 discharge applies only to debts arising from personal injury or death.

Debts or Creditors You Don't List

Bankruptcy requires you to list all your creditors on your bankruptcy papers and provide their most current addresses. That way, the court can mail out notice of your bankruptcy with the best chance of reaching them. If you do your part and the official notice fails to reach the creditor for some reason beyond your control—for example, because the post office errs, or the creditor moves without leaving a forwarding address—the debt will still be discharged (as long as it is otherwise dischargeable). Also, if the creditor knew or should have known of your bankruptcy through other means, such as a letter or phone call from you, the debt will be discharged.

Suppose, however, that you forget to list a creditor on your bankruptcy papers or carelessly misstate a creditor's identity or address. In that situation, the court won't notify the creditor and the debt almost always will survive your bankruptcy (unless the creditor wouldn't have received any payments under your plan, a very rare occurrence). The general rule is that debts not listed in a Chapter 13 case survive the bankruptcy. This means, of course, that you should be extra careful to list all of your creditors in a Chapter 13 case. Also, if a creditor fails to file a proof of claim, you would be well advised to file one for it, especially if the claim is for a secured debt.

Student Loans

As in Chapter 7, a student loan cannot be discharged in Chapter 13 unless you show the bankruptcy court that paying the loan back would be a substantial hardship. See "Debts That

Survive Chapter 7 Bankruptcy," above, for more on the rules for discharging student loans.

Student Loan Interest May Be Discharged in a Chapter 13 Plan

In *United Student Aid Funds, Inc. v. Espinosa*, No. 08–1134 (U.S., March 23, 2010), the Chapter 13 debtor submitted a plan, which the bankruptcy court confirmed, that provided for payment of the student loan principal but discharge of the accrued interest. The lender did not object and the interest was discharged upon completion of the plan. The lender then attempted to collect the interest it considered due, arguing that discharge of a student loan, and accompanying interest, may only be accomplished if the debtor sues the lender in an adversary action to determine the loan's dischargeability, and the court finds repayment of the loan would constitute an undue hardship. The U.S Supreme Court refused to set aside the discharge order, ruling that the lender had actual notice of the bankruptcy (and the plan that provided for the discharge of the interest), and could have appeared in the bankruptcy to protect its rights. However, the Supreme Court made clear that discharging student loans (rather than interest) through plan confirmation violates the bankruptcy code and it's uncertain how courts will treat this situation in the future.

Fraudulent Debts

Debts based on fraud, theft, or breach of fiduciary duty are not dischargeable in Chapter 13. (See "Debts That Survive Chapter 7 Bankruptcy," above, for a description of these types of debts.) Bankruptcy courts in Chapter 13 cases use the same procedure for determining the dischargeability of these debts as they use in Chapter 7 cases—that is, the debt will be discharged if the creditor fails to come forward and establish fraud in the bankruptcy court.

Debts Discharged in Chapter 13 (But Not in Chapter 7)

Certain debts that cannot be discharged in Chapter 7 (see "Debts That Survive Chapter 7 Bankruptcy," above) can be discharged in Chapter 13. They are:

- marital debts created in a divorce or settlement agreement
- debts incurred to pay a nondischargeable tax debt
- court fees
- condominium, cooperative, and home-owners' association fees incurred after the bankruptcy filing date
- debts for loans from a retirement plan, and
- debts that couldn't be discharged in a previous bankruptcy.

In most cases, bankruptcy filers may convert their cases from one chapter to another. If, for example, a court finds that a Chapter 7 filing is an abuse of the bankruptcy system under the means test, the filer can convert to Chapter 13 rather than dismissing the case altogether. Or, you may decide to convert—because a particular debt will only be discharged in Chapter 13, for example, or because you won't be able to complete a Chapter 13 repayment plan. Once you make the switch, you are subject to the dischargeability rules of the chapter to which you converted, not the chapter you started out using.

EXAMPLE: Connie files for Chapter 13 bankruptcy because she owes a lot of debt from a divorce and has been told that those debts can be discharged in Chapter 13 but not in Chapter 7. Connie proposes a feasible Chapter 13 plan that pays only 25% of her divorce-related debt. Halfway through the plan, Connie loses her job and can't continue her payments. She converts to Chapter 7. Her Chapter 7 discharge won't include the divorce-related debts. However, Connie will receive a credit for the amounts she paid on those debts during her Chapter 13 case.

How Joint Debts Are Handled

Debts for which you have a joint debtor—another person who owes the debt along with you—raise some tricky issues. Let's look at the different kinds of joint debtors and how your bankruptcy filing might affect them.

Cosigners and Guarantors

A cosigner or guarantor is someone who signs onto your debt in order to back up or guarantee your payment. If you don't pay, the cosigner or guarantor is legally responsible for payment. If you discharge a debt for which you have a cosigner or guarantor, your joint debtor will still owe the entire thing, even though you are no longer on the hook to repay it.

If you want to file for Chapter 7 bankruptcy but don't want to stick your cosigner or guarantor with the debt, you can make an agreement with the creditor to reaffirm the debt—that is, to continue to owe it after your bankruptcy ends.

 TIP

It's usually better to reimburse the cosigner than to reaffirm the debt. For a variety of reasons, it's almost always a good idea to discharge the debt and agree to owe your cosigner for any potential liability, rather than to reaffirm it and continue to owe your original creditor. This approach gives you more flexibility regarding repayment than you'd have if you defaulted on your payments to the regular creditor under a reaffirmation agreement. Also, the creditor may decide not to try to collect from the cosigner,

Bankruptcy and Preferences

If you file for Chapter 7 bankruptcy and have a joint debtor who is a relative, close friend, or business associate, the joint debtor may have to pay the bankruptcy trustee any amount that you pay the creditor on the loan. Here's how this works.

As mentioned in Chapter 2, when you file for bankruptcy, the bankruptcy trustee will look to see whether you made any payments to creditors within the 90 days before you filed—or within one year of filing, if those payments were made to, or for the benefit of, a relative or close business associate. These payments are called "preferences" and they're not permitted if they exceed certain limits. The idea is that you shouldn't be allowed to single out certain creditors for special treatment just before you file for bankruptcy.

If you make a preferential payment to a creditor, the bankruptcy trustee can demand that the creditor turn over the amount of payment to the trustee, so that it can be divided equally among your unsecured creditors. If the creditor pays up and the debt is then discharged in bankruptcy, you won't owe anything, but your joint debtor will be on the hook for whatever remains of the original debt.

If the creditor can't or won't cough up the preference money you paid, the trustee could sue the creditor. But an easier route for the trustee may be to go after your joint debtor— who benefited from the preference because your payment wiped out or reduced his or her liability for the debt. In this scenario, believe it or not, the joint debtor would have to pay the trustee the amount of the preference. The joint debtor then continues to be liable for the debt, less the amount of the preference kept by the creditor.

Fraudulent transfers are closely related to preferences. If, in the two years before filing for bankruptcy, you transfer property to a friend, relative, or other insider without an exchange of equal value, the transfer may be considered fraudulent. Fraudulent transfers give the trustee the right to seize the transferred property for the benefit of your creditors. They may also result in the dismissal of your bankruptcy case.

which means neither one of you would have to repay the debt. And finally, it's possible that the cosigner will also decide to file bankruptcy.

If you file for Chapter 13 bankruptcy, you can include the cosigned or guaranteed debt as part of your repayment plan, and your joint debtor will not be pursued during your bankruptcy case—typically, at least three years. If you can, you should pay the debt in full during your case. If you don't, you will be entitled to discharge whatever balance remains when your case is over (assuming the debt is otherwise dischargeable in a Chapter 13 bankruptcy). But in that situation, the creditor can still go after the joint debtor for the balance.

Spousal Responsibility for Debts

Married people can file for bankruptcy jointly or separately. If they file jointly, all of their debt is subject to the rules explained above. If only one spouse files, state marital property rules determine which debts qualify for discharge.

Community Property Rules

Some states use what's called a "community property" system to determine who owns marital property, including debts. These states are Arizona, California, Idaho, Louisiana, Nevada, New Mexico, Texas, Washington, and Wisconsin. (Spouses in Alaska can elect to have their property treated as community property, if they make a written agreement to that effect.)

In community property states, both spouses owe debts incurred by either spouse during the marriage even if one spouse incurs a debt without the other spouse's knowledge. These are termed "community" debts. Debts incurred by a spouse prior to the marriage are considered separate debts, as are debts incurred after separation and divorce.

For example, when Justine and Paul marry in California, each has about $10,000 in credit card debt. In addition, Paul owes taxes to the IRS and Justine owes her uncle $3,000 on a loan she used to buy a car. After they marry, Justine and Paul buy a home and take out a second mortgage a few years later. They also obtain an unsecured loan of $15,000 from a bank to buy a car. When hard times hit in 2008, they separate. Shortly after the separation, Justine hits the credit cards hard and adds an additional $20,000 to her personal debt. Under these facts, all the credit card debt is separate debt because Paul

---

Creditors Seldom Sue Nonfiling Spouses for Marital Debts

When a debt is jointly owed because of state marital property rules, and is not discharged as to the nonfiling spouse in a bankruptcy filed by just one spouse, creditors seldom if ever sue the nonfiling spouse for the debt unless his or her name is on the contract underlying the debt. This is primarily because there is a huge aftermarket for buying judgments and then trying to collect on them—to have any value in this market a judgment must be noncontroversial. Also, it takes time and money to impose liability on a nonsigning spouse, since state marital property laws are seldom absolute and require a showing that the debt was not a necessity or in some other category that would allow the nonfiling spouse to escape liability. In short, most creditors determine that it just isn't practical to try to collect the debt from a nonfiling spouse who never signed onto the debt. Similarly, a spouse who is added to an existing credit card owned by the other spouse is not liable for the debt unless he or she signs the request.

---

and Justine incurred it before marriage and after separation. So, too, is Justine's debt to her uncle and Paul's debt to the IRS. However, the home mortgages and the bank loan are community debts.

In bankruptcies filed in community property states, community debts are discharged even if only one spouse files—which means that the nonfiling spouse will benefit from the filing spouse's discharge. However, the nonfiling spouse's separate debts are not discharged and will survive the bankruptcy.

Using the facts in the previous example, if Justine files for bankruptcy in a community property state, she will discharge her credit card debt and her debt to her uncle. The debt owed on the house, although a community debt, will be handled differently because it is secured debt. (See Ch. 7 for more on how secured debts are treated in bankruptcy). The bank loan is also community debt and will likely be discharged, even though Paul doesn't file. Justine's bankruptcy will not affect Paul's separate credit card debt or his separate debt to the IRS.

Common Law Property Rules

All states that don't use the community property system for dealing with marital debts are termed common law states. The rules for those states are a bit simpler. All debts either spouse incurs before the marriage are that spouse's separate debts. Debts incurred during the marriage might be either separate or joint: If the debt is jointly undertaken (for example, it was incurred from a joint account or the creditor considered the credit information of both spouses in deciding to extend the loan) or the debt benefits the marriage (for example, the debt was for necessary items, such as food, clothing, or child care), it is jointly owed by both spouses. Otherwise, a debt that one spouse incurs separately remains that spouse's separate debt.

When one spouse files for bankruptcy in a common law state, the only debts that come into play are that spouse's separate debts and any debts that can be classified as joint. The other spouse's separate debts continue unaffected by the bankruptcy filing.

Business Partners

As a general rule, all partners are responsible for partnership debts unless the partnership has special provisions limiting the liability of certain classes of partners (as in a limited partnership). If you are in a partnership and file for bankruptcy, you can get rid of your personal liability for partnership debts. However, the remaining partnership and individual partners (if there are any—often partnerships are dissolved if one partner leaves or declares bankruptcy) will still be on the hook. ●

Your Property and Bankruptcy

This chapter explains what happens to the property you own when you file for bankruptcy. It also covers exemptions—the rules that determine which property you can keep, which property you'll have to give up in Chapter 7 bankruptcy, and in some cases how much you have to pay out in Chapter 13 bankruptcy.

In Chapter 7, if property is "exempt," you will probably be able to keep it; you may have to forfeit nonexempt property or property that is worth more than the applicable exemption, to the bankruptcy trustee to pay off your creditors.

In Chapter 13, if property is not exempt, your plan will have to provide that your unsecured creditors will be paid at least as much as they would receive in a Chapter 7 bankruptcy. In essence, this would amount to the value of the property, less any exemption you would be entitled to, less costs of sale, and less the trustee's commission.

For the purpose of this book, there are three types of property: real estate, personal property you own outright, and personal property that is collateral for a debt (typically a car). In this chapter, we focus only on what happens to personal property you own outright. Ch. 5 discusses what happens to real estate, including how bankruptcy can be used to deal with foreclosures. Ch. 6 explains what happens to personal property that is collateral for a debt you are making payments on.

CAUTION

Exempt property can be taken to pay child support and alimony. This chapter explains the rules that protect certain types of property from being seized by creditors or the bankruptcy trustee to pay your debts. However, your exempt property is not protected if you owe money to a former spouse for child support or alimony: These obligations must be met, even if it means that you lose property that would otherwise be exempt.

Most Chapter 7 filers emerge from bankruptcy with their property intact because most of what they own is exempt and the benefit to the creditors of seizing and selling what is not exempt is often not worth the cost. But that is not always the case. Also, in Chapter 13, you are entitled to keep your property regardless of its value, but your plan must pay your unsecured creditors at least as much as they would have received had you filed a Chapter 7 bankruptcy. (See Ch. 2 for more on this.)

Your Bankruptcy Estate

The property you own on the day you file for bankruptcy is called your "bankruptcy estate." With a few important exceptions (discussed below), property and income you acquire after you file for Chapter 7 bankruptcy aren't included in your bankruptcy estate. When you file for bankruptcy, the forms you have to fill out require you to list all of the property in your bankruptcy estate.

What's in Your Bankruptcy Estate

Several broad categories of property make up your bankruptcy estate:

Property you own and possess when you file. Everything in your possession that you own, whether or not you owe money on it—for example, a car, real estate, clothing, books, television, stereo system, furniture, tools, boat, artworks, or stock certificates—is included in your bankruptcy estate. Property that you have in your possession but belongs to someone else (such as the car your friend stores in your garage or the television you borrowed from your sister) is not part of your bankruptcy estate, because you don't have the right to sell it or give it away.

Property you own but don't possess when you file. You can own something even if you don't have physical possession of it. For instance, you may own a car that someone else is using. Other examples include a deposit held by a stockbroker, a security deposit held by your landlord or a utility company, or a business in which you've invested money.

Property you are entitled to receive. Property that you have a legal right to receive but haven't gotten yet when you file for bankruptcy is included in your bankruptcy estate. Common examples include:

- wages, royalties, or commissions you have earned but have not yet been paid
- a tax refund legally due you
- vacation or termination pay you've earned
- property you've inherited but not yet received from someone who has died
- proceeds of an insurance policy, if the death, injury, or other event that gives rise to payment has already occurred, and
- money owed you for goods or services you've provided (often called "accounts receivable").

Community property. If you live in a community property state, all property either spouse acquires during the marriage (but not during separation) is ordinarily considered "community property," owned jointly by both spouses. (The community property states are

Arizona, California, Idaho, Louisiana, Nevada, New Mexico, Texas, Washington, and Wisconsin, and—if you have a written community property agreement or trust—Alaska.) Gifts and inheritances to only one spouse are the most common exceptions—these are the separate property of the spouse who receives them. If you're married and file jointly for bankruptcy, all the community property you and your spouse own, as well as all of both of your separate property, is considered part of your bankruptcy estate. If your spouse doesn't file, then your bankruptcy estate consists of all of the community property and all of your separate property—your spouse's separate property isn't included.

Marital property in common law property states (all states that aren't community property states). If you are married and filing jointly in a common law state, your bankruptcy estate includes all the property you and your spouse own, together and separately. If you are filing alone for bankruptcy in a common law property state (all states other than the community property states listed above), your bankruptcy estate includes:

- your separate property (property that has only your name on a title certificate or that was purchased, received as a gift, or inherited by you alone), and
- half of the property that is jointly owned by you and your spouse, unless you own the property as tenants by the entirety.

CAUTION

"Tenancy by the entirety" property often is handled differently in bankruptcy. Property you and your spouse jointly own as "tenants by the entirety" usually receives special protection in bankruptcy if (1) it is located in Delaware, the District of Columbia, Florida, Hawaii, Illinois, Indiana, Maryland, Massachusetts, Michigan, Missouri, North Carolina, Pennsylvania, Tennessee, Vermont, Virginia, or Wyoming and (2) only one spouse files for bankruptcy. In that event, the filing spouse's creditors (and therefore the bankruptcy court) typically cannot take property that both spouses own as tenants by the entirety. If both spouses file, however, this protection doesn't apply. If you and your spouse own "tenancy by the entirety" property, consult a local bankruptcy lawyer before you file.

Certain property you acquire within 180 days after filing for bankruptcy. Most property you acquire or become entitled to after you file for bankruptcy isn't included in your bankruptcy estate. But there are a few exceptions. If you acquire or become entitled to the following items within 180 days after you file, you must notify the trustee:

- an inheritance through a will or by operation of law (property you receive through a living trust, a beneficiary designation, or through any other transfer device that occurs upon a person's death, other than a will, is not included in this exception)
- property you receive or have a right to receive from a marital settlement agreement or divorce decree, and
- death benefits or life insurance policy proceeds.

Unless an exemption applies, the trustee can take this property and distribute it to your creditors.

Property (revenue) generated by estate property. This type of property typically consists of the proceeds of contracts—such as those providing for rent, royalties, and commissions—that were in effect at the time of the bankruptcy filing, but which produced earnings after that date. For example, if you are a composer or author and receive royalties each year for a book that was written before you filed for bankruptcy, the trustee may collect those royalties as property of your estate. Proceeds from work you do after your filing date belong to you.

Property that appreciates in value after you file. If you own property that has appreciated in value after you file for bankruptcy, the amount of the appreciation is also part of your bankruptcy estate and, absent an available exemption, can be taken by the trustee right up until the time your bankruptcy case is closed. For example, assume your home has equity worth $100,000 when you file and you live in a market where the real estate prices are appreciating. The trustee decides to keep your case open. A few years later, while your case is still open, the equity in your home appreciates to $150,000 and your exemption protects only $100,000. At this point the trustee can decide to sell your home, give you the $100,000 exemption, and use the $50,000 to pay your unsecured creditors.

Property you transferred prior to your bankruptcy. The rules discussed in Ch. 2 regarding preferences and fraudulent transfers create a type of property—property illegally transferred or paid out in a preference—that is considered part of your bankruptcy estate. However, since by definition you no longer own or have possession of the property, the bankruptcy trustee is authorized to "avoid" the transfer or preference—this means the trustee can sue the party who has received the property to have it returned to the bankruptcy estate, and then sell the property for the benefit of your creditors.

Consigned property. Under the bankruptcy code, property your business stocks on a consignment basis (for example folk art in a crafts shop) is considered to be an asset of your business and can be liquidated without payment to the people who have placed the property with you on consignment.

Property That's Not Part of Your Bankruptcy Estate

Property that is not in your bankruptcy estate is not subject to the bankruptcy court's jurisdiction, which means that the bankruptcy trustee can't take it to pay your creditors under any circumstances.

The most common examples of property that doesn't fall within your bankruptcy estate are:

- Social Security payments, whether they be past, present, or future (Section 407 of the Social Security Act)
- property you buy or receive after your filing date (with the few exceptions described above)
- pensions subject to the federal law known as ERISA (commonly, defined benefit pensions)
- property pledged as collateral for a loan where a licensed lender (pawnbroker) retains possession of the collateral
- property in your possession that belongs to someone else (for instance, property you are storing for someone), and

- wages that are withheld, and employer contributions that are made, for employee benefit and health insurance plans.

 CAUTION

Even if they are technically part of your bankruptcy estate, most retirement plans are exempt, which means you'll get to keep them anyway. For example, IRAs and 401(k) plans are exempt in all states (although the exemption for IRAs is limited to $1,095,000 per person). For more information, see Appendix A.

Funds placed in a qualified state tuition program or Coverdell education savings account are also not part of your bankruptcy estate, as long as:

- You deposit the funds into the account at least one year before filing for bankruptcy.
- The beneficiary of the account is your child, stepchild, grandchild, step-grandchild, or in some cases, foster child.

This exclusion applies to all funds placed in the account at least two years previous to your filing date. It is limited to funds of $5,175 or less placed in the account within a one-year period beginning two years before you file for bankruptcy.

Inventory Your Property

If you decide to file for bankruptcy, you'll be required to list all property that belongs in your bankruptcy estate. Whether you can hold on to that property, or at least some of the property's value in dollar terms, depends on what the property is worth, which exemptions are available to you, and what type of bankruptcy you file. The best way to start finding out what you'll be able to keep in Chapter 7 or pay out in Chapter 13 is to create an inventory (list) of your property and match it with the available exemptions.

The simplest strategy is to start with the property items that you are most interested in keeping—and worry about the rest of your property only if and when you actually file for bankruptcy. Or, you can be more systematic and make a list of every single thing in your bankruptcy estate. If you're married and would be filing jointly, enter all property owned by you and your spouse (or the property that you both care about). Use Worksheet E: Personal Property Checklist in Appendix B to identify the property in your bankruptcy estate.

Value Your Property

Use Worksheet F: Property Value Schedule, below (and in Appendix B), to figure out what each item is worth. It's easy to enter a dollar amount for cash and most investments. If you own a car, start with the middle *Kelley Blue Book* price or, alternatively, the middle price calculated by the National Automobile Dealers Association (at www.nada.org). If the car needs repair, reduce the value by what it would cost you to fix the car. You can find the *Kelley Blue Book* at a public library or online at www.kbb.com. Alternatively, you can use the valuations provided at www.nada.org.

For bankruptcy purposes, you are supposed to compute the property's replacement value: what it would cost to buy that specific property—considering its age and condition—from a retail merchant. If you use the Internet, visit eBay (www.eBay.com) to get a fix on the going price for just about anything. Or briefly describe the item in Google (or your search engine of choice) and see what turns up. As long as your valuations are based on the going retail price for the item in question, you should use the lowest value you can find, which means you are more likely to be able to keep the property under your state's exemption laws.

If you are filing separately and own something jointly with someone (other than a spouse with whom you would file for bankruptcy), reduce the value of the item to reflect only the portion you own. For example, you and your brother jointly bought a music synthesizer worth $10,000. Your ownership share is 40% and your brother's is 60%. You should list the value of the property you own as $4,000, not $10,000.

Even if you are married and filing separately in a community property state, include the total value of all the community property as well as the value of your separate property.

If you are married, you own the property with your spouse as tenants by the entirety, and you are filing separately, your ownership interest may not be 50% for purposes of computing your exemption. (Talk to a lawyer to find out what percentage of your tenancy by the entirety property you can claim as exempt.)

Worksheet F: Property Value Schedule

List the total replacement value of each item in your Personal Property Checklist.

Item	Replacement Value
1. Cash	$ _____
2. Bank accounts	_____
3. Security deposits	_____
4. Household goods and furniture	_____
5. Books, pictures, etc.	_____
6. Clothing	_____
7. Furs and jewelry	_____
8. Sports and hobby equipment	_____
9. Interest in insurance	_____
10. Annuities	_____
11. Pensions and profit-sharing plans	_____
12. Stock and interest in business	_____
13. Interest in partnership and ventures	_____
14. Bonds	_____
15. Accounts receivable	_____
16. Alimony and family support	_____
17. Other liquidated debts, tax refund	_____
18. Future interests & life estates	_____
19. Interests due to another's death	_____
20. Other contingent claims	_____
21. Intellectual property rights	_____
22. Licenses and franchises	_____
23. Vehicles	_____
24. Boats, motors, and accessories	_____
25. Aircraft and accessories	_____
26. Office equipment, furniture, and supplies	_____
27. Machinery, fixtures, etc.	_____
28. Inventory	_____
29. Animals	_____
30. Crops—growing or harvested	_____
31. Farm equipment	_____
32. Farm supplies, chemicals, and feed	_____
33. Anything not listed above	_____
TOTAL	$ _____

Be Careful of Joint Ownership Accounts

Joint accounts are often created for purposes other than ownership of the funds in the account. For example, parents commonly put a child on their account to provide an easy means of inheritance. Should the parent die, the account automatically goes to the child. Or, the child may be added to the account to handle economic transactions for the parent. In these situations, it's clear to the parent and child that the funds belong to the parent, but absent a formal statement of this fact when setting up the account, a Chapter 7 bankruptcy trustee (in a bankruptcy filed by the child) might reasonably view the account as also belonging to the child. If so, the account (or at least half the account) might be considered property of the child's bankruptcy estate to be seized and sold unless the child claims it as exempt.

Fortunately, a legal doctrine known as "bare legal title" is sometimes used to exclude this type of property from the bankruptcy estate. In essence, the bankruptcy court rules that the parent has an equitable claim to the funds, which leaves the child with bare legal title to the account but with no right to the funds themselves.

Understanding Exemptions

Bankruptcy is intended to give debtors a fresh start—not to leave them utterly destitute. You are entitled to keep certain property that the laws applicable to your bankruptcy categorize as exempt. Creditors cannot take exempt property as part of their collection efforts, and the bankruptcy trustee can't take it, either. Exempt property can literally range from "the shirt on your back" to a million-dollar estate, depending on which exemptions you are entitled to use.

State Exemption Systems

Every state has its own fairly lengthy list of exempt property. (You can find these lists in Appendix A.) In addition, some states offer bankruptcy filers an alternative choice of exemptions—a list of exempt property found in the federal Bankruptcy Code. States that offer this choice are: Arkansas, Connecticut, Hawaii, Massachusetts, Michigan, Minnesota, New Hampshire, New Jersey, New Mexico, Pennsylvania, Rhode Island, Texas, Vermont, Washington, and Wisconsin. In these states, you must choose between the state exemption system and the federal exemption system (no mixing or matching allowed).

Although California doesn't make the federal Bankruptcy Code exemptions available, it also has two separate exemption systems—but both are created by state law. Debtors who use the California exemptions must choose between System 1 (the regular state exemptions available to debtors in and out of bankruptcy) and System 2 (state exemptions available only in bankruptcy and very similar to the federal exemptions). Here, too, no mixing and matching.

How Exemptions Work

Under both the federal and state exemption systems, some types of property are exempt regardless of value. For example, in some states, home furnishings, wedding rings, or clothing are exempt without regard to value. In Washington, DC, homes are exempt regardless of their value or the value of the bankruptcy filer's ownership (equity) in the home.

Other kinds of property are exempt up to a limited value. For instance, cars are often exempt up to a certain amount—typically $2,500 to $3,000. The home equity exemption ranges from nothing in New Jersey to $5,000 in South Carolina to $500,000 in Massachusetts, to no limit other than acreage in Florida, Texas, and a few Midwestern states.

When there is a dollar limit on an exemption, any equity above the limit is considered nonexempt. (Your equity is the amount you would get to keep if you sold the property.) Even though a portion of your ownership in these items is exempt, the trustee can seize and sell property in which your equity exceeds the exemption limit,

---

Exemption Doesn't Protect a Later Sale of Property If Its Value Appreciates Above the Exemption Amount

Sometimes, the value of an item of property is lower than the exemption amount when you file for bankruptcy, but later appreciates above the exemption amount. If the trustee doesn't object to the exemption within the appropriate time period, can it later sell the property?

This issue was considered by the U.S. Supreme Court in *Schwab v. Reilly*, 560 U.S. — (2010). In this case the property value was lower than the exemption amount when the debtor filed for bankrupty. However, when the property appreciated in value, the trustee wanted to sell the property, pay the debtor his claimed exemption, and distribute the rest to the unsecured creditors. The debtor argued that since the trustee did not object to the exemption within the statutory time limit (30 days), he couldn't take the property. The Supreme Court ruled that the trustee was entitled to sell the property as long as he would receive enough from the sale to pay the debtor the amount of his claimed exemption. In other words, the exemption does not prevent property from being sold as long as the debtor is paid what he is entitled to under the exemption statutes.

This Supreme Court case has subsequently been used in a 9th Circuit Court of Appeals case to support the sale of a debtor's home several years after the bankruptcy discharge was granted—because the value of the home appreciated past the amount of the homestead exemption that was in force when the bankruptcy was filed. As long as the trustee keeps the case open, the debtor's property remains property of the bankruptcy estate and can be sold for the benefit of the creditors. Once again, the exemption claim only protects equity as provided for by statute, but doesn't prevent a later sale of the property if its value exceeds the exemption.

give you your exemption amount, and distribute the remainder to your unsecured creditors.

Many states offer a "wildcard" exemption —a dollar amount that you can apply to any property, in order to make it (or more of it) exempt. This type of exemption typically runs from a few hundred to several thousand dollars (but close to $23,000 in California's System 2 exemptions). If you use the federal exemptions, the wildcard is roughly $11,000 for individuals and $22,000 for couples.

> **EXAMPLE:** Lucinda and Freddie file a joint bankruptcy petition in Vermont, which allows a choice between the Vermont state exemptions and the federal exemptions. Lucinda and Freddie rent their home but own a travel trailer with a value of roughly $20,000, which they want to keep. The Vermont state exemptions provide a wildcard allowance up to a maximum of $7,400, not nearly enough to protect the travel trailer. However, the federal exemptions provide a wildcard exemption for couples of $22,400 on any type of property. Lucinda and Freddie choose the federal exemptions, which also protect their other property, such as their furniture, animals, and tools of the trade.

When the Trustee Takes Property

As mentioned earlier, the trustee will seize and sell property only in a Chapter 7 bankruptcy. As a practical matter, the trustee won't seize and sell property unless the value of the nonexempt portion, after the costs of storage and sale are deducted, is high enough to make it worth the trustee's while. For example, even if your used furniture exceeds the exemption limit in your state (assuming there is one), the trustee is unlikely to seize and sell the furniture unless it is quite valuable and could obviously be resold for an amount that will cover your exemption (whatever it is) and still leave enough for your unsecured creditors to generate a decent commission for the trustee. (See "The Bankruptcy Trustee" in Ch. 1 for more on how trustees get paid.)

The kinds of property listed below are typically not exempt unless by application of a wildcard. If you are concerned about keeping any of these items, you should pay close attention to the exemptions that are available to you:

- interests in real estate other than your home (see Ch. 5 for more on residential property exemptions)
- substantial equity in a newer-model motor vehicle
- expensive musical instruments unrelated to your job or business
- stamp, coin, and other valuable collections
- cash, deposit accounts, stocks, bonds, and other investments
- business assets (other than tools of the trade, which are typically exempt)
- valuable artwork
- expensive clothing and jewelry
- antiques, or
- IRAs that have been inherited and that no longer have any restrictions on withdrawal (most courts take this position; a few, however, have afforded inherited IRAs the same protection as they would any other IRA).

Residency Requirements for Exemption Claims

Prior to 2005, filers used the exemptions available in the state where they filed for bankruptcy. Now, however, some filers may have to use the exemptions available in the state where they used to live. Congress became concerned about people gaming the system by moving to states with liberal exemptions just to file for bankruptcy. As a result, it passed residency requirements filers have to meet before claiming a state's exemptions. Here are the new rules:

- If you have made your current state your home for at least two years, you will file in that state and use that state's exemptions (subject to the homestead cap explained in Ch. 5).
- If you have made your current state your home for more than 91 days but less than two years, you will file in that state and use the exemptions of the state where you lived for the better part of the 180-day period immediately prior to the two-year period preceding your filing.
- If you have lived in your current state for fewer than 91 days, you must wait until you have lived there for 91 days to file in that state (then use whatever exemptions are available to you according to the rules above).
- If the state you are filing in offers the federal homestead exemption, you can use that exemption list regardless of how long you've been living in the state.
- If this system deprives you of the right to use any state's exemptions, you can use the federal exemptions, even if the state where you file doesn't offer this choice.

Where You Make Your Home

When we refer to the state "where you make your home," we mean the place where you are living and intend to remain living for the indefinite future, the place where you work, vote, receive your mail, pay taxes, bank, own property, participate in public affairs, register your car, apply for your driver's license, and send your children to school. Congress refers to this state as your "domicile." Your domicile might be different from where you are actually living if you spend time in one state but consider another state to be your true home. For example, members of the military, professional athletes, and corporate officials all might spend significant amounts of time working in another state or country; their domicile is the state where they make their permanent home.

Domicile has been defined as "the place where a man has his true fixed and permanent home and principal establishment and to which whenever he is absent he has the intention of returning." This means something more than your residence, which generally means wherever you are living at any given time. Even if you reside in one state, your domicile may be elsewhere—and your domicile determines which exemptions you can use.

For example, some states allow their exemptions to be used only by current state residents, which might leave former residents who haven't lived in their new home for at least two years without any available state exemptions.

A longer residency requirement applies to homestead exemptions: If you acquired a home in your current state less than 40 months before your filing date, your homestead exemption may be subject to a $136,875 cap regardless of which state's exemption system you use. (Ch. 5 covers homestead exemptions in detail.)

RESOURCE

Find your exemptions online. You can search the exemptions for your state at www. legalconsumer.com, which also has plenty of other resources for bankruptcy filers.

EXAMPLE 1: Sammie Jo lives in South Carolina from July 2010 until January 2011, when she gets lucky at a casino, moves to Texas, and buys a car for $15,000. In March 2012, Sammie Jo files for bankruptcy in Texas. Because Sammie Jo has been living in Texas for only 14 months—not two years— before she files for bankruptcy, she can't use the Texas exemption for cars, which can be up to $30,000 depending on the value of other personal property claimed as exempt. Because Sammie Jo filed in March 2012, the two-year period begins in March 2010. And because Sammie Jo lived in South Carolina for the better part of the two-year period preceding the bankruptcy filing date, the South Carolina state exemptions are the only state exemptions available to her. As it turns out, the South Carolina exemption for cars is only $1,200, which means Sammie Jo will probably lose her car if she uses the South Carolina state exemptions.

As it turns out, however, Texas offers the federal exemptions as an alternative to its state exemptions. Under the new bankruptcy law, the state where a person files determines whether the federal exemptions are available, regardless of how long the person has lived in that state. This means that Sammie Jo can use the federal exemptions instead of the South Carolina state exemptions. Under the federal exemptions, Sammie Jo is entitled to exempt a motor vehicle up to $3,225—still not enough to cover her car, which is now worth $14,000. But wait. The federal exemptions also provide a wildcard of $1,075 plus $10,125 of unused homestead exemption. Sammie Jo rents rather than owns her home (and doesn't need a homestead exemption), so she can add the entire wildcard of $11,200 to her $3,225 vehicle exemption, for a total exemption applicable to her car of $14,425.

EXAMPLE 2: Julia lives in North Dakota for many years until she moves to Florida on January 15, 2011. She files for bankruptcy in Florida on November 30, 2012. Because she hasn't lived in Florida for two years (her two-year anniversary is January 14, 2013), Julia must use the exemptions from the state where she lived for the better part of the 180-day period preceding the two-year period—which is North Dakota. As it turns out, Julia's largest property item is a prepaid medical savings account deposit of $20,000. While this would be exempt under Florida law, North Dakota has no exemption for this item. Nor are the federal exemptions available in Florida. So the trustee will most likely seize the medical savings account and use it to pay Julia's creditors. Had Julia waited another month and a half to file, she would have been able to use Florida's exemptions and keep her medical savings account.

Using the Exemptions Appendix

You can find the exemptions for all 50 states in Appendix A. If you are considering filing for bankruptcy in one of the states listed below, you'll also want to look at the federal exemptions, which are listed right after Wyoming.

States That Offer the Federal Exemptions	
Arkansas	New Mexico
Connecticut	Pennsylvania
Hawaii	Rhode Island
Massachusetts	Texas
Michigan	Vermont
Minnesota	Washington
New Hampshire	Wisconsin
New Jersey	

Use Appendix A to find the applicable exemptions for your property, using the rules set out above to determine which exemptions to use. Do this by comparing the type and value of your property, and the amount of equity you have in the property, with the exemptions. (You can find definitions of many of the terms in Appendix A in the Glossary at the back of this book.)

Remember, if you are filing in a state that offers the federal bankruptcy exemptions, you should also check the federal exemption chart (it comes right after Wyoming). Items that aren't exempt under the state exemptions available to you may be exempt under the federal system, and vice versa. However, you must pick one system or the other to use in your bankruptcy—you can't mix and match.

If you are married and filing jointly, you can double the federal exemptions and any state exemptions unless the chart says that you can't. This will be indicated either at the top of the chart for the particular state or next to a particular exemption.

Assuming you live in California, and meet the residency requirements for claiming that state's exemptions, you may choose System 1 (the regular state exemptions) or System 2, a state list that is derived from the federal exemptions but differs in important particulars. If you file in California but don't meet the residency requirements, you can't use either California system—you'll have to use the rules set out above to figure out which exemptions you can use.

Federal Nonbankruptcy Exemptions

If you are using the exemptions of a particular state rather than the federal exemptions, you may also exempt property listed in Appendix A under Federal Nonbankruptcy Exemptions. Don't confuse those with the federal bankruptcy exemptions, which may be used only if a state allows, and only as an alternative to the state exemptions.

Your Home

One of the biggest worries you may face in deciding whether to file for bankruptcy is the possibility of losing your home, whether you own or rent. If so, you'll be relieved to know that the bankruptcy system is not designed to put you out on the street.

If you can get and stay current on your mortgage payments, and your equity in your home is fully protected by an available exemption, your chances of keeping your home look good. If, however, your equity in the home is significantly more than the amount you are entitled to keep (called the "homestead exemption"), you might lose your home if your file under Chapter 7. In this situation, Chapter 13 bankruptcy will likely be a better option, assuming you qualify.

If you are behind on your mortgage payments when you file bankruptcy, the story is different. Your lender will probably be able to get permission from the bankruptcy court to initiate foreclosure proceedings.

If you are a renter facing eviction based on a court order, filing for bankruptcy is unlikely to improve your situation in most cases. If, however, you owe back rent but your landlord has not yet obtained a judgment of eviction, you can use bankruptcy to temporarily postpone the eviction in addition to discharging any liabilities arising from your tenancy.

This chapter covers:

- issues facing homeowners who file under Chapter 7
- issues facing homeowners who file under Chapter 13, and
- issues facing renters who file for bankruptcy under either chapter.

Homeowners Filing for Bankruptcy Under Chapter 7

If you are current on your house payments, you can figure out how bankruptcy will affect your home ownership by doing some simple math:

- Compute your equity in your home.
- Choose the appropriate homestead exemption.
- Compare your equity to the homestead exemption.

If your equity is less than the homestead exemption, your home is protected. If your equity is more than the homestead exemption, your home is at risk. (See "If You Are Behind on Your Mortgage Payments," below, if you aren't current on your payments.)

Compute Your Equity

Your equity in your home is how much money you would end up with if you sold it. This is typically what it would cost you to sell the same property *less* what you will have to pay to others out of the sales price because of legal claims (liens) they have against the property (such as claims by your mortgage lender or the county tax collector). Don't include the costs of selling the house—such as closing costs or broker's fees—in your calculations. These costs will, however, be important in deciding later whether your home is safe from being sold by the trustee for the benefit of your creditors.

> **EXAMPLE:** Your house will sell for $300,000. You have a mortgage for $200,000. There are no other debts that have to be paid out of the sales proceeds.

Your equity is $100,000. If there is a lien on your home, you must subtract that as well. For example, if you didn't pay the contractor who remodeled your kitchen and the contractor put a $20,000 lien on your home, your equity would be reduced by that lien amount, to $80,000.

If there's a money judgment lien on your home that would deprive you of your full homestead exemption if the property were sold, you can ask the bankruptcy judge to remove the lien. But even if you plan to petition to have the lien removed, don't include the amount of the lien when calculating your equity in the home. You can find out more about lien avoidance procedures in Ch. 10.

Assess the Fair Market Value of Your Property

When computing your equity, you must first assess your home's fair market value. When home values deteriorate, it's often difficult to know what a home is worth without actually selling it. Home values have traditionally been determined by comparables—what similar homes in the neighborhood have sold for. However, comparables are hard to come by when homes aren't being sold. And even when they are being sold, they aren't necessarily sold under normal market conditions. For example, homes that have sat empty for months as a result of a foreclosure sale may ultimately be sold—for half or less of their previous value—to investors who are looking for rock bottom prices. If you use sales under those conditions to judge your home's value, you may not get what you think your home is worth. Still, in the final analysis, its

value can only be determined by what it would sell for, and it may not sell for much more than was paid for the distressed home down the street. Probably the best way to pin a value on your home is to find a real estate agent who can give you an estimate. You may be shocked at what you hear, but the amount will be the agent's best guess at what they could get for it if you put it up for sale. Alternatively, you can use the information databases available on the Internet (see below).

Fortunately, not every area in the country is experiencing a downturn in real estate values. If you happen to live in one such blessed area, you may run into the problem of having too much equity. If your home likely would sell for significantly more than the value placed on it by real estate professionals or Internet resources, you have to determine whether that equity is protected by your state's exemption laws. If the real estate market in your neck of the woods heats up and values start appreciating, you must make sure that your appraisal occurs just before your filing date, so you can be sure your homestead exemption covers your equity.

Realtors in your area will know what similar homes have sold for and can give you a pretty accurate estimate of what they could get for your home. Although prices might rise by a few percentage points a year (at least in your neck of the woods), you shouldn't have too much trouble valuing your home.

 **RESOURCE**

Using the Internet to find sales prices for comparable homes in your area. For a modest fee, you can get details on comparable houses—including neighborhood information, sales history, address, number of bedrooms and baths, square footage, and property tax information—from SmartHomeBuy at www. smarthomebuy.com. Less-detailed information (purchase price, sales date, and address) is available free from sites including www.homevalues. com, www.zillow.com, www.domania.com, www.homeradar.com, and http://list.realestate. yahoo.com/re/homevalues. Simply enter your home's address or Zip code.

Rapid appreciation in your home's value is obviously good news, but can be a real problem if you're filing for bankruptcy. The more equity you have in your home, the more likely you will have to forfeit it to pay your creditors in a Chapter 7 bankruptcy (unless the available homestead exemption is large enough to cover the increase). And the harder it is to accurately predict your home value on the date you file for bankruptcy, the harder it will be to figure out whether your house will be safe in Chapter 7 or whether you should file for Chapter 13 instead. In hot real estate markets, you must make sure your appraisal occurs just before your filing date, so you can be sure your homestead exemption covers your equity.

TIP

The trustee may keep your bankruptcy case open in an appreciating housing market. In Chapter 7 bankruptcy you typically get a discharge about three months after you file. However, your case closes only when the bankruptcy trustee closes it. While closure and discharge often happen at around the same time, in some situations the trustee will keep the case open for an indefinite period of time. This usually happens when the trustee expects that property of the estate will increase in value and that this increase can be used to benefit the unsecured creditors. For example, as discussed in Ch. 4, if real estate values are appreciating in your area, the trustee may keep the case open until your home appreciates enough so that the trustee can sell it, pay you the amount of your exemption, and pay your creditors a portion of the proceeds. Only if your bankruptcy case is closed can you be sure that your home won't be sold to take advantage of an appreciating market.

Identify Liens on Your Property

When computing your equity, you must subtract any liens on the property. A lien is a legal claim on property that can only be removed voluntarily by the lienholder or by a court order. A mortgage, for example, is a debt that is secured by the property in the form of a lien.

Because a lien claims a right to some portion of the property's value, it "clouds" the owner's title to the property. Buyers don't want to buy property that is encumbered by liens—and insurance companies don't want to issue title insurance in this situation, either. As a practical matter, this means you will have to pay off liens in order to sell your house (unless you can get rid of the liens in your bankruptcy—which may be the case with liens arising from money judgments).

In addition to a mortgage, other typical liens arise from:

- second deeds of trust
- home equity loans and lines of credit
- money judgments issued by a court
- child support arrearages
- delinquent income or property taxes, and

Liens Exist Only If They're Recorded

A lien on real estate exists only if it has been recorded in the local land records office. For this reason, you can tell whether you have any liens against your property by paying that office a visit and searching its database. It's not uncommon for people to assert liens based merely on language in written agreements. For example, an agreement stating that Johnny owes Florence $2,000 and that Florence will have a lien on Johnny's home to secure repayment of the loan, does not by itself create the lien. The contract must be properly recorded.

- debts owed to people who improved the property but who weren't paid for some reason (these are called mechanic's and materialman's liens).

To compute your equity, deduct all liens on your home from its fair market value (what you could sell it for). If a debt is not secured by a lien on your home, you don't have to count it when computing your equity.

As explained above, you shouldn't count liens that can be removed in bankruptcy when calculating your equity. See "Eliminating Liens in Chapter 7 Bankruptcy" in Ch. 6 and "Lien Avoidance Motions" in Ch. 10 for more information on lien avoidance.

Choose Your Homestead Exemption

Your homestead exemption is the amount of equity in your home you are entitled to keep if you file for Chapter 7 bankruptcy. Every state has its own homestead exemption rules—and the exemption available to you will help determine whether you keep or lose your home. Because bankruptcy law imposes strict residency requirements for the use of a state's exemptions, however, you may not qualify for the exemption you want to use. This section explains the various types of homestead exemptions available, and how to figure out which one to use.

Types of Homestead Exemptions

Homestead exemptions vary tremendously from state to state. In fact, in a few states, the homestead exemption isn't a monetary amount at all—it's based on your lot size. On the other hand, in a handful of states there is no homestead exemption at all. Some states are at the other extreme, and allow you to protect a very large amount of equity (for example, $500,000 in Massachusetts). In a few states, the homestead exemption is based on a combination of lot size and a monetary amount.

How Does Your State Calculate Its Homestead Exemption?	
Unlimited homestead exemption	District of Columbia
Homestead exemption based on lot size only	Arkansas, Florida, Iowa, Kansas, Oklahoma, South Dakota, Texas
Homestead exemption based on lot size and equity	Alabama, Hawaii, Louisiana, Michigan, Minnesota, Mississippi, Nebraska, Oregon
Homestead exemption based on equity only	Federal bankruptcy exemptions and: Alaska, Arizona, California, Colorado, Connecticut, Delaware, Georgia, Idaho, Illinois, Indiana, Kentucky, Maine, Massachusetts, Missouri, Montana, Nevada, New Hampshire, New Mexico, New York, North Carolina, North Dakota, Ohio, Rhode Island, South Carolina, Tennessee, Utah, Vermont, Virginia, Washington, West Virginia, Wisconsin, Wyoming
No homestead exemption	Maryland, New Jersey, Pennsylvania

Homestead Exemptions Protect Only Residences

With very few exceptions, you must reside in the home as your primary residence when you file for bankruptcy in order to claim a homestead exemption. Homestead exemption laws do not protect second homes, vacation homes, or other real estate in which you aren't living when you file. They do, however, typically apply to mobile homes, R.V.s, and boats that you use as your primary residence.

Declared Homesteads

In California and many other states, the homestead exemption automatically kicks in when you file for bankruptcy. However, some states (listed below) require you to file a "Declaration of Homestead" with the county recorder in order to use the state's homestead exemption in bankruptcy. In rare cases, some states will allow you to claim an exemption for a declared homestead even if you aren't living in the home when you file.

States That Require a Declaration of Homestead	
Alabama	Texas
Idaho	Utah
Massachusetts	Virginia
Montana	Washington
Nevada	

States With Two Exemption Systems

In 15 states and the District of Columbia, you must choose between two different homestead amounts—one offered by the state and one offered under the federal Bankruptcy Code. California also offers a choice between two different amounts, but both amounts are offered under California state law. (See Ch. 4 for more on these dual systems.)

Wildcard Exemptions

In some states, you can increase the amount of your homestead exemption with a state "wildcard" exemption—that is, a dollar amount that your state allows you to apply to any property, in order to make it (or more of it) exempt. The chart below lists the state wildcard exemptions that you can apply to real estate; although other states have wildcard exemptions, they can be applied only to personal property.

> **EXAMPLE:** In Connecticut, the base homestead exemption is $75,000. In addition, Connecticut has a wildcard exemption of $1,000 applicable to any property. This means that if you don't use the wildcard exemption for other types of property, you can use it for your homestead, which would increase the exemption from $75,000 to $76,000.

State Wildcard Exemptions Applicable to Real Estate	
Connecticut	$1,000
Georgia	$600
Indiana	$4,000
Kentucky	$1,000
Maine	$400
Maryland (because Maryland has no homestead exemption, this is the only exemption you can use on your home)	$5,500
Missouri	$1,250
New Hampshire	$8,000
Ohio	$400
Pennsylvania	$300
Vermont	$400
Virginia (available only if you are a disabled veteran)	$2,000
West Virginia	$800

Choosing Between Exemption Systems Can Be Painful

As mentioned, California has two exemption systems and about 17 states give you a choice between the state exemptions and the federal exemptions. Sometimes it is an agonizing choice as to which system to use. For instance California System 1 allows up to $175,000 in home equity protection (depending on age, disability, and other factors) whereas System 2 only allows about $23,000. On the other hand, System 2 lets you use the $23,000 (called the wildcard exemption) for any kind of property—personal or real estate. System 1 only lets you use the homestead exemption for home equity and doesn't provide a general purpose exemption for personal property.

To see how this plays out, assume you have $50,000 worth of equity in your home and a car worth $15,000. If you use System 1 you can keep your home but you may have to give up your car, since that system only allows you to keep $2,550 worth of vehicle equity. In System 2, you could keep the car (by applying the $23,000 wildcard exemption to the $15,000 equity in your car), but would likely lose your home. Since you can't mix or match, you'll ultimately have to choose one system or the other, and it can be a painful decision indeed.

Tenancy by the Entirety

In 18 states, spouses are allowed to own property together in a form known as "tenancy by the entirety." If only one spouse files for bankruptcy, property the couple owns as tenants by the entirety is, generally, not part of the bankruptcy estate. In other words, the property is exempt in its entirety, regardless of its value. If, however, both spouses file, the property will be part of their bankruptcy estate and will be subject to the appropriate homestead exemption available to the couple under the rules discussed below.

States That Allow Spouses to Own Property in Tenancy by the Entirety

Delaware	Missouri
District of Columbia	North Carolina
Florida	Ohio
Hawaii	Pennsylvania
Illinois	Rhode Island
Indiana	Tennessee
Maryland	Vermont
Massachusetts	Virginia
Michigan	Wyoming

Choose the Appropriate Homestead Exemption

As explained in Ch. 4, residency requirements determine which exemptions filers can use. In addition to these general rules, Congress passed even stricter residency requirements for claiming a state's homestead exemption, to discourage people from moving to states with more generous homestead exemptions just to file for bankruptcy.

If You Have Been Domiciled in Your State for at Least Two Years and You Acquired Your Current Home at Least 40 Months Before Filing

You can use your current state's homestead exemption without restriction.

> **EXAMPLE:** Mary and Peter are domiciled in Vermont. They have owned their home for five years. They file for bankruptcy in Vermont and can use Vermont's homestead exemption without limitation (because they lived in Vermont for at least two years and acquired their home at least 40 months prior to filing their bankruptcy). Because Vermont offers the federal exemption option, Mary and Peter can choose either the Vermont state homestead exemption or the federal homestead exemption. As it turns out, the Vermont state homestead exemption is $75,000 compared to a maximum federal homestead exemption of roughly $42,000 (for a couple filing together).

If You Have Been Domiciled in Your State for at Least Two Years and You Bought Your Home Within 40 Months of Filing, Using the Proceeds From the Sale of Another Home in the Same State

If you acquired your current home within 40 months of filing, but purchased it with the proceeds from the sale of another home in the same state that occurred at least 40 months earlier, you can use your current state's homestead exemption without restriction.

> **EXAMPLE:** Violet and Robin have lived in Nevada for six years. When they first moved there, they bought a home for $175,000. Three years later, they sold that home

and bought another home for $250,000. Although they have owned their current home for less than 40 months, they bought it with the proceeds of another Nevada home that they purchased more than 40 months before filing. Violet and Robin can claim Nevada's homestead exemption without restriction.

If You Acquired Your Home Within 40 Months of Filing and Have Been Domiciled in Your State Two Years or More

If you acquired your current home within the previous 40 months and have made your home in your state for at least two years, you can use that state's homestead exemption, subject to a $136,875 cap.

> **EXAMPLE 1:** Three years ago, John and Susie moved from Massachusetts to Maine, where they bought a home. If they file for bankruptcy in Maine, they can claim the Maine homestead exemption because they have lived there longer than two years. However, because they bought the Maine home within the 40-month period prior to their bankruptcy filing, they will be limited to a homestead cap of $136,875. Maine's homestead allowance for joint filers who are over the age 60 is $140,000, so John and Susie (who are both 65 years old) will lose about $3,000 worth of homestead exemption because of the residency cap.

> **EXAMPLE 2:** Massachusetts provides a homestead exemption of $500,000. After moving from Vermont to Boston in 2010, Julius and his family buy a fine old Boston home in 2011 for $700,000.

After borrowing heavily against the home because of financial reversals, Julius files for bankruptcy in early 2012. At the time Julius owns $250,000 equity in the house. Although the Massachusetts homestead exemption of $500,000 would easily cover Julius's equity, Julius may claim an exemption of only $136,875 because he acquired the Massachusetts house from another state within the previous 40 months.

If You Have Lived in Your State for Less Than Two Years

If you moved to your current state within two years before filing bankruptcy, you must use the homestead exemption available in the state where you made your home for the better part of the 180-day period prior to the two-year period, subject to the $136,875 cap. However if the state where you are filing offers the federal homestead exemption, you can use that exemption regardless of how long you've been living in that state or when you bought your home.

> **EXAMPLE 1:** Eighteen months ago, Fred moved from Florida to Nevada, where he purchased his current home with $400,000 he received from a recent inheritance. Fred files for bankruptcy in Nevada, his current state. Because Fred has not lived in Nevada for two years, and because he lived in Florida for the 180-day period prior to the two-year period preceding his bankruptcy filing, he must use Florida's homestead exemption, subject to the $136,875 cap. The cap imposes an extreme penalty on Fred. Florida's homestead exemption is unlimited while Nevada's is $300,000. However, because Fred can protect only

$136,875, most of his equity in his home is nonexempt, which means that the trustee will undoubtedly sell the home, give Fred his $136,875, and distribute the balance to Fred's unsecured creditors.

> **EXAMPLE 2:** Joan moves from New Jersey to Vermont, where she buys a home. Less than two years after moving to Vermont, Joan files for bankruptcy in that state. Because Joan was living in New Jersey for the better part of the 180-day period preceding the beginning of the two-year prebankruptcy filing period, she must either use New Jersey's state homestead allowance or the federal homestead allowance if Vermont allows it—which it does. New Jersey provides no homestead exemption at all, but the federal homestead exemption is approximately $21,000 (a combination of the homestead allowance for one filer and the $1,075 wildcard exemption). Joan chooses to use the federal homestead allowance—a no-brainer.

If You Have Committed Certain Crimes, Torts, or Deception Against Creditors

Even if you qualify for an "uncapped" homestead exemption under the rules explained above, your exemption might be limited if you have engaged in particular types of misconduct. If you have committed a felony, a securities act violation, or certain crimes or intentional torts that have led to death or serious bodily injury, your homestead exemption may be capped at $136,875, depending on how the court sees your circumstances. For instance, the court might decide to lift the cap if it finds that the homestead in question is reasonably necessary for you to support yourself and your dependents.

Even if you haven't committed a crime or tort, your homestead exemption might be limited if you have tried to cheat your creditors. If you have disposed of nonexempt property with the intent to hinder, delay, or defraud a creditor at any time within the ten years before you file for bankruptcy, the value of your interest in your current home will be reduced by the value of the property you unloaded, which means you may be left with little or no homestead protection.

Find Your Homestead Exemption

Once you have decided which state's homestead exemption you can use, turn to Appendix A at the back of this book and look in the top box for that state.

If you are married and filing jointly with your spouse, check to see whether you can double your state's homestead amount.

If the chart for your state indicates that the federal exemptions are available, compare your state's exemption with the federal homestead exemption, which currently is $20,200 for a single filer and double that for a married couple filing jointly, plus a general-purpose (wildcard) exemption of $1,075 for a single filer and double that for joint filers. So, under the federal exemptions, a married couple may exempt up to $40,400 plus $2,150, for a combined total homestead exemption of $42,550.

In California, the alternate exemption system designed for use in bankruptcy (System 2) allows only $22,075 for a homestead, whether you file alone or jointly with a spouse. However, California's primary state exemption system (System 1) allows $75,000 for single filers, $100,000 for heads of households, and $175,000 for elderly, disabled, and poor filers, so people in

California who have significant equity in their homes tend to choose System 1.

 CAUTION

Special considerations in Michigan when choosing homestead exemptions. Michigan has two homestead exemptions, one of which can only be used when filing bankruptcy. (Mich. Comp. Laws § 600.5451(1)(n)). Several bankruptcy courts in Michigan have ruled that state-originated bankruptcy-only exemptions are unconstitutional and have refused to honor this particular homestead exemption. Courts in other states have considered this issue, and most have ruled that such statutes are constitutional. (For a list of other states that have bankruptcy-only exemptions, see Appendix A.) However, if you are filing for bankruptcy in Michigan, make sure you use the right homestead exemption or find out how your local bankruptcy court treats the bankruptcy-only homestead exemption.

Compare Your Equity to the Homestead Exemption

Now that you've computed your equity and located the appropriate homestead exemption, it's time to put the two together. This comparison will tell you whether you can safely file for Chapter 7 bankruptcy and keep your home, or whether you should consider other options—such as filing under Chapter 13.

If You Have No Equity in Your Home or You Are Under Water (Upside Down)

If the total amount of debt against your home is equal to or more than its market value, you have no equity and aren't at risk of losing the home in bankruptcy as long as you keep current on your payments. This is true no matter how large or small the homestead exemption that's available to you and no matter how upside down you are. The trustee wouldn't get any money out of selling your home—all of the proceeds would go to the mortgage company and other creditors who have liens on the property.

EXAMPLE: Your home is worth $325,000. You still owe $425,000 and the IRS has placed a $50,000 lien on the home for back taxes. If the trustee sells the home, the mortgage owner and IRS will have to be paid first, which would leave no money at all for your creditors. In other words, even if you live in a state that offers little or no homestead protection, you will still keep your home because the trustee can't profit from selling it. If you want to avoid a foreclosure, you can sell the home for less than you owe for it (a short sale) or offer up a "deed in lieu of foreclosure."

If You Have Some Equity in Your Home

If the total amount of debt against your home is less than its market value, you will want to compare the difference—your equity—with the homestead exemption available to you. As long as the homestead exemption covers your equity, the trustee won't have any interest in selling your home; there wouldn't be any equity left over to pay your unsecured creditors, and the trustee wouldn't get any commission for the sale. Even if your equity exceeds the homestead limit, the trustee will have to figure in the costs of sale

(about 6% of its selling price) before deciding whether it makes sense to sell the home.

EXAMPLE: The real estate broker you used when you bought your home told you that it is currently worth $300,000. You owe your mortgage lender $200,000 and the IRS (which has issued a Notice of Federal Tax Lien) $35,000. The equity in your home is $65,000 ($300,000 minus $200,000 minus $35,000). If the trustee sells your $300,000 home, he or she will net approximately $275,000 because of the costs of sale and the trustee's commission. After paying the tax lien and the mortgage, the trustee would clear $40,000. If your homestead exemption is equal to or greater than $40,000, the trustee will gain nothing by selling the home. If a significant chunk of the $40,000 is unprotected by a homestead exemption, however, your home is in danger of being sold for the benefit of your unsecured creditors.

If Your Equity Is Significantly More Than Your Homestead Exemption

The homestead exemptions in many states are adequate to cover all or most of a person's equity, primarily because a combination of sinking prices and massive borrowing during the bubble years has drained whatever equity might have once existed.

In a few parts of the country, however, this is not necessarily the case. In the great housing bubble of 2004–2006, housing prices shot up so rapidly that people suddenly found themselves with lots of equity and, therefore, at significant risk of losing their homes if they filed for Chapter 7. Even though the bubble has burst in many parts of the country, prices have held relatively steady in other areas (for instance, in San Francisco, Vermont, and parts of New York City). Homeowners whose homes have maintained their increased value have equity levels in them that greatly exceed their states' homestead exemptions, putting these homes at risk in a Chapter 7 bankruptcy filing.

If you have nonexempt equity in your home (equity that isn't protected by your homestead exemption) and would lose it if you filed for Chapter 7 bankruptcy, you'll probably want to explore other options. For instance, if your home would sell for $300,000, the total liens are $100,000, and your state's homestead exemption is $100,000, you would have $100,000 of unprotected equity. The trustee would probably sell your home, pay off the $100,000 mortgage, pay you your $100,000 homestead exemption, and use the extra $100,000 (less costs of sale) to pay your unsecured creditors. If some of this money were left after your unsecured creditors were paid in full and the trustee took his or her cut, you would get that balance in addition to your homestead exemption.

If you have too much equity in your home, you may be able to use some of it to pay off your other debts and avoid bankruptcy altogether. If you still need to file for bankruptcy after paying down your equity, you may be able to save your house, although you will have to be extremely careful about when you file your bankruptcy. (See "Reducing Your Equity: Timing Is Key," below.)

There are several ways to reduce your equity:

1. **Refinance your mortgage for more than you currently owe.** This has become more difficult to do since banks have tightened up on their lending standards, often due to their inability to know what a home is worth but also because of their desire to avoid making loans that look like the bad loans of old. Still, if you have good credit and home prices have stabilized to some extent when you read this book, this may be a viable approach to reducing your equity.

2. **Offer to substitute cash for the amount of nonexempt equity.** If you want to file for Chapter 7 bankruptcy but you're afraid you will lose your house because your equity exceeds the homestead amount, you might be able to save your house if you can pay the difference to the trustee. You may be able to raise the cash by selling exempt property or using income you earn after you file.

3. **File for Chapter 13 bankruptcy.** Chapter 13 bankruptcy lets you pay your debts out of your income, rather than by selling your property. Thus, if you file for Chapter 13 bankruptcy, you won't have to give up your home, even if you have significant nonexempt equity. However, that nonexempt equity will determine how much you have to pay unsecured creditors over the life of your plan (as explained in Ch.2, "Chapter 13 Eligibility Requirements").

EXAMPLE: Dallas has $85,000 equity in her home. She wants to file bankruptcy but lives in a state with a $50,000 homestead limit and might lose her house in a Chapter 7 bankruptcy. She files a Chapter 13 bankruptcy and proposes a viable five-year plan. Over the life of the plan, she will have to pay her unsecured creditors at least $553 a month or 100% of the unsecured nonpriority debt, whichever is less. This is because Dallas would have to pay her unsecured creditors at least as much as they would have received had the house been sold in a Chapter 7 bankruptcy. See Ch. 2 for more on how this determination is made.

Reducing Your Equity: Timing Is Key

If you decide to take steps to reduce the equity in your house, keep an eye on the calendar. Most likely, you will have to wait at least 90 days after refinancing or making payments on an equity line of credit before you file for bankruptcy. If you pay $600 or more to a regular creditor in the 90 days before you file, the payment can be set aside as a forbidden "preferential payment to a creditor." There's an exception for payments made in the normal course of business (for example, payments by small business owners going into bankruptcy) or for necessities of life, such as housing, utilities, food, and the like.

If you pay $600 or more to a relative or close business associate during the year before you file for bankruptcy, these payments can also be set aside, unless they were made in the normal course of business. And any transfer you make for the purpose of putting your property beyond the reach of creditors during the *ten years* preceding your bankruptcy filing can deprive you of your homestead exemption altogether. See a bankruptcy lawyer if you wish to engage in this sort of planning.

If You Are on a Fixed Income

If you have excess equity in your home, you may be tempted to take out a loan and use it to pay your debts. However, if you are on fixed income because of retirement or disability, you may not be able to make the payments on a loan. In other words, by borrowing to pay your debts, you may end up defaulting on the loan and losing your home to the lender.

> **EXAMPLE:** Trudy bought her home in 1956 for $56,000. Over the years, the value of the house has increased to $400,000. Trudy owes $175,000 in credit card debt and is considering filing for bankruptcy. Trudy wants to borrow against her home and pay off the debt, but her sole income is $800 a month from Social Security. She won't be able to make the payments on the loan.

Although this is a difficult situation, Chapter 7 bankruptcy is not the answer—you would lose your home to the trustee. You might be able to buy a new home with the proceeds from your homestead exemption (the trustee would pay you that in cash), but for many, the loss of a home would be traumatic.

In Trudy's case, depending on her age, the best option may be a reverse mortgage she can use to pay off the debt and augment her fixed income while remaining in her home for the rest of her life. The downside to this is that she won't be able to pass the home down to her kids or other heirs—when she dies.

If You Are Behind on Your Mortgage Payments

If you are behind on your mortgage payments when you file for Chapter 7 bankruptcy, you will almost certainly lose your home to foreclosure unless you can get current in a hurry. As a general rule, your mortgage lender will ask the bankruptcy court to lift the automatic stay (the court order that bars creditors from trying to collect their debts, discussed in Ch. 1), and the court will probably grant the request, allowing the mortgage lender to begin or resume foreclosure proceedings.

The only way Chapter 7 bankruptcy can help you is if you can stave off foreclosure for the length of your bankruptcy case. When the case is over, and your other debts are wiped out or reduced, you may have an easier time getting and remaining current on your mortgage payments, assuming the lender hasn't yet accelerated (called in) the loan.

Negotiating With the Lender

If you've missed only a few mortgage payments, your lender may be willing to negotiate. What the lender agrees to will depend on your credit history, the reason for your missed payments, and your financial prospects.

Here are the possible options your lender might agree to:

- spread out the missed payments over a few months
- reduce or suspend your regular payments for a specified time and then add a portion of your overdue amount to your regular payments later on

---

Get Some Help Negotiating Your Modification

If you are trying to make your mortgage more affordable, either temporarily or in the long term, consider using a free HUD-certified housing counselor. These nonprofit counselors typically are employed by local community action agencies, but also can be located through a couple of national networks. To become certified, these counselors must attend an intensive week-long training sponsored by HUD, which schools them in every aspect of the mortgage business and the various modification procedures used for mortgages insured or owned by the various federal housing entities (Freddie Mac, Fannie Mae, FHA). These counselors may have contacts within the various banks and companies involved in servicing mortgages and can assist you in working out a deal to make your mortgage more affordable. You can find a HUD-certified counselor at:

- HUD. Go to www.hud.gov/foreclosure/index.cfm, or call 800 569-4287.
- The Homeownership Preservation Foundation. Go to www.995hope.org or call 888-995-HOPE.
- The National Foundation for Credit Counseling. They can be reached at 866-557-2227.
- Making Home Affordable at www.makinghomeaffordable.gov (click the counselor tab).

- extend the length of your loan and add the missed payments at the end
- suspend the principal portion of your monthly payment for a while and have you pay only interest, taxes, and insurance, or
- refinance your loan to reduce future monthly payments.

If the Lender Starts to Foreclose

If your debt problems look severe or long-lasting, the lender may take steps toward foreclosure. In most cases, the lender will accelerate the loan before foreclosure actually occurs. This means you must pay the entire balance immediately. If you don't, the lender is entitled to foreclose.

There are two different kinds of foreclosure. One is called a "judicial" foreclosure, so named because the lender must file papers in court and obtain the court's approval before foreclosing. In many judicial foreclosure states, this kind of foreclosure can take well over a year before you would lose your house. If you file Chapter 7 bankruptcy, you will add two or three extra months to that period (depending on whether your lender gets permission from the judge to proceed with the foreclosure before your bankruptcy runs its course). And, if you are salting away at least a portion of your mortgage payment each month, even a three-month delay can result in a substantial increase in your savings.

The other kind of foreclosure is called a "nonjudicial" foreclosure, so named because the lender does not have to go to court in order to foreclose. Instead, a third-party trustee (not the bankruptcy trustee) sells your property after sending you a series of notices. This trustee is the person or business named in the deed of trust that you signed (or their successors in interest) instead of, or in addition to, the traditional mortgage when you purchased or refinanced your property. In some states (especially in the South), nonjudicial foreclosures can happen within a month or two, while in other states nonjudicial foreclosures take as long as or longer than judicial foreclosures—a year or more in some cases.

States Where Judicial Foreclosure Is Customary	
Arizona (sometimes)	New Mexico (sometimes)
Connecticut	New York
Delaware	
Florida	North Dakota
Hawaii	Ohio
Illinois	Oklahoma (if the homeowner requests it)
Indiana	Pennsylvania
Iowa	South Carolina
Kansas	South Dakota (if the homeowner requests it)
Kentucky	
Louisiana	Vermont (sometimes)
Maine	West Virginia (sometimes)
Nebraska	Wisconsin
New Jersey	Wyoming

States Where Nonjudicial Foreclosure Is Customary

Alabama	New Mexico (sometimes)
Alaska	North Carolina
Arizona (sometimes)	
Arkansas	Oklahoma (unless homeowner requests judicial)
California	
Colorado	Oregon
District of Columbia	Rhode Island
Georgia	South Dakota (unless homeowner requests judicial)
Idaho	
Maryland	Tennessee
Massachusetts	Texas
Michigan	Utah
Minnesota	Vermont (sometimes)
Mississippi	Virginia
Missouri	Washington
Montana	West Virginia (sometimes)
Nevada	
New Hampshire	Wyoming

When the Automatic Stay Will Be Lifted to Permit Foreclosure

If you file for bankruptcy and are behind on your payments, expect the mortgage lender to come to court and ask the judge to lift the automatic stay. (See Ch. 1 for more on the automatic stay.) If you have nonexempt equity in your home, the bankruptcy trustee is likely to successfully oppose the motion and sell the property for the benefit of your unsecured creditors (after the lender is paid off and you are paid the amount protected by the applicable exemption). If you have no equity, however, the trustee will probably not oppose the motion to lift the stay and will let the foreclosure go through.

During a foreclosure, you have several options (although if the creditor begins a nonjudicial foreclosure, some of them may not be available to you simply because of time constraints):

- Sell your house. If you don't get any offers that will cover what you owe your lender, the lender may agree to take less. This is called a "short sale."
- Get a new loan that pays off all or part of the first loan and puts you on a new schedule of monthly payments. If the original lender has accelerated the loan, you'll need to refinance the entire balance of the loan to prevent foreclosure.
- Reinstate the loan. If the lender hasn't accelerated the loan, you can prevent foreclosure simply by paying the missed payments, taxes, and insurance, plus interest.
- File for Chapter 13 bankruptcy. The section below explains how Chapter 13 bankruptcy can save your home if you are behind on your mortgage.
- Plan to lose your home. Take advantage of the foreclosure procedures—and delays inherent in bankruptcy—to stay in your home for as long as possible. See "If Foreclosure Is Unavoidable," below.
- Use faulty mortgage documents and lenders' use of robosigners in the foreclosure process as a negotiating tool to

get the lender to agree to new mortgage terms. See "Using Foreclosure Document Deficiencies to Negotiate New Mortgage Terms," just below.

Using Foreclosure Document Deficiencies to Negotiate New Mortgage Terms

In order to foreclose on real estate, the party bringing the action has to be able to prove that it owns the mortgage. To do this, it must be able to produce the original promissory note or other proof showing that it is the current legal owner of the note. Because of the way mortgages were merchandized in the last few decades, many foreclosing parties have difficulty showing they own the mortgage. Much more recently, it has come to light that many foreclosures have been initiated on the basis of affidavits (statements under oath) falsely stating that the affiant had personal knowledge of the facts contained within the documents being sworn to. In fact, common practice has been for individuals to swear to thousands of affidavits a month without any knowledge whatsoever of what was in the paperwork.

Homeowners can use possible defects in the mortgage ownership paper trail and the faulty ways in which foreclosure documents have been prepared to negotiate with the lender. Homeowners may be able to get lenders to agree to a significant reduction of the mortgage principal as well as lower payment amounts and interest rates.

Homeowners Filing for Bankruptcy Under Chapter 13

If you own your home and file for bankruptcy under Chapter 13, you won't face the same issues as you would under Chapter 7. Chapter 13 repayment plans are funded out of your projected disposable income, not your nonexempt property. As long as you can propose a legal plan out of your projected disposable income, you can keep your home no matter how much equity you have—or how large the homestead exemption available to you. As always, however, the devil is in the details.

Under the law governing Chapter 13, you must propose a repayment plan that pays your unsecured creditors at least as much as they would receive if you had filed for Chapter 7 bankruptcy. For example, if you have $100,000 worth of unprotected (nonexempt) equity in your home, you will have to pay your unsecured creditors at least $100,000 over the life of your plan less what it would cost to sell the property and pay the trustee's commission. If you don't have adequate projected disposable income to pay that amount, the court will not confirm your plan and you'll find yourself in Chapter 7, or outside of bankruptcy if you choose to dismiss your Chapter 13 case. (See "Chapter 13 Eligibility Requirements," in Ch. 2, for more on how projected disposable income is computed. You may be in for a surprise.)

Determining Which State's Exemptions Apply

The starting point is to figure out which exemptions are available to you. "Choose Your Homestead Exemption," above, helps you make that determination for homestead exemptions in a Chapter 7 case. The same rules apply in a Chapter 13 case for the purpose of deciding the minimum amount your unsecured creditors must be paid. These rules are:

- If you acquired your home at least 40 months before filing, and have been domiciled in your state for at least two years, you can use your state's homestead exemption without restriction.

- If you acquired your home less than 40 months ago but you have made your home in your current state for at least 40 months and you purchased your current home with the proceeds from the sale of a former home in your current state, you can use your current state's homestead exemption without restriction.

- If you have made your home in your current state for at least two years but you acquired your home less than 40 months previous, you must use your current state's homestead exemption subject to a $136,875 cap.

- If you have made your home in your current state for less than two years, you must use the homestead exemption of the state where you were living for the better part of the 180-day period prior to the two-year period, subject to the $136,875 cap.

- If the state you are filing in offers the federal homestead exemption, you can use that exemption regardless of how long you've been living in the state or when you bought your home.

- If you don't qualify for any state's homestead exemption, you can use the federal homestead exemption.

For a discussion and examples of these rules, review "Choose Your Homestead Exemption," above.

 CAUTION

You must count all of your nonexempt property. In most cases, the equity you own in your home will be the big-ticket item that determines how much you must pay your unsecured creditors in a Chapter 13 bankruptcy. However, if you own other valuable property that is nonexempt, you must add in the value of that property to determine how much your unsecured creditors must get under your repayment plan. Chs. 4 and 6 discuss exemptions for other kinds of property; residency requirements apply to those exemptions as well.

Selling or Refinancing Your Home to Increase Your Disposable Income

As discussed in Ch. 2, you qualify for Chapter 13 only if you have enough projected disposable income to remain current on certain obligations and pay 100% of any arrearages owed on them. For instance, your repayment plan must propose to pay:

- 100% of all support arrearages owed to a child or ex-spouse, as well as your current required payments on those obligations

- 100% of all arrearages on a mortgage as well as the current monthly payments (assuming you plan to keep your home), and

- an amount to your unsecured creditors equal to the value of your nonexempt property.

These and other requirements often make it difficult, if not impossible, to propose a viable Chapter 13 plan. In this situation, you may wish to use some or all of the equity in your home to help fund your Chapter 13 plan—particularly if your equity, when added to your projected disposable income, is sufficient to make your plan confirmable, but isn't enough to make a serious dent in your debt load.

> **EXAMPLE:** Ethan owes $125,000 in credit card debt and is contemplating bankruptcy. However, his income is insufficient to propose a confirmable Chapter 13 plan (because he owes back child support and taxes that he must pay in full). Chapter 7 also isn't an attractive option for Ethan because he would lose nonexempt property that he really wants to keep: stock options and shares in a family corporation. Fortunately, Ethan owns a home that would produce $50,000 after costs of sale. If Ethan sells his home and devotes the proceeds to his plan, the plan will then become confirmable.

In order to use property to fund a Chapter 13 plan, you either must have:

- the sale proceeds in hand when you file your bankruptcy petition or shortly afterwards, or
- a feasible plan of sale that will convince the judge that you really will be able to sell the property and devote the proceeds to the plan.

Of course, if refinancing or borrowing against your home would pay off your debts outside of bankruptcy and still leave you with a manageable loan payment, this might be your best option.

If Your Mortgage Is in Arrears but Foreclosure Hasn't Started

If you are behind on your mortgage and want to keep your home, Chapter 13 will likely be your bankruptcy chapter of choice. As discussed above, filing for Chapter 7 bankruptcy usually won't prevent a lender from ultimately foreclosing on a mortgage default. But Chapter 13 is different. If you have enough disposable income to propose a plan that (a) makes your regular payments on your mortgage and (b) pays off your arrearage in a reasonable period of time, you will be allowed to keep your home as part of your Chapter 13 case.

> **EXAMPLE:** Kenny and Zoe, a married couple, pay $2,000 a month on their mortgage. They have fallen five payments behind and owe an arrearage of $10,000. If they file for Chapter 7 bankruptcy, the lender will get the bankruptcy stay lifted and proceed to foreclose on the loan. Because they want to keep their home, Kenny and Zoe file a Chapter 13 bankruptcy and propose a repayment plan that will, among other things:
> - pay their monthly mortgage of $2,000, and
> - pay roughly $300 a month toward the arrearage.

Mortgage Modifications Under Chapter 13

In Chapter 13, the bankruptcy court is authorized, in some situations, to modify the principal owed on a mortgage to conform to the actual value of the property at the time the bankruptcy is filed. This is colloquially known as a cramdown. Unfortunately, the court is prohibited from cramming down mortgages owed on a primary residence. For example, suppose John and Carrie, a married couple, own their residence and a rental unit. Both their residence and rental unit have decreased in value so that they are worth only 75% of the mortgage principal. If John and Carrie file a Chapter 13 bankruptcy, the court may confirm a plan under which the mortgage on the rental unit will be crammed down 25% to match the unit's current market value. However, the court would not approve the reduction of the mortgage on John and Carrie's residence.

If Your Mortgage Is in Arrears and the Lender Has Started to Foreclose

If your lender has started to foreclose, you can file for Chapter 13 bankruptcy and make up your missed payments, reinstate the loan, and keep making the payments under the original contract. This is called "curing the default." Your right to cure the default depends on how far along the foreclosure proceeding is. If the lender has accelerated the loan or obtained a foreclosure judgment, you usually can still cure the default. If the foreclosure sale has already occurred, however, Chapter 13 usually won't help. Cases have held that the bankruptcy court

has no jurisdiction to undo a sale, even if state law might otherwise allow.

TIP

Use Chapter 13 bankruptcy to buy time. If your lender has begun foreclosure proceedings, you can file for Chapter 13 bankruptcy to put the automatic stay in place to stop further foreclosure activity. During the time it takes for the lender to file a motion to have the stay lifted, for the court to schedule it, and for you to appear to argue it, you may be able to sell the house. You can then dismiss your case (unless, of course, you have other debts you want to take care of through Chapter 13). If you do use Chapter 13 for this limited purpose, you can do it only once over a one-year period.

TIP

Use Chapter 13 bankruptcy to challenge the validity of the mortgage documents and the foreclosure process. Chapter 13 bankruptcy provides a good forum for challenging the legality of the mortgage. In Chapter 13, the mortgage creditor's claim can be opposed on the ground that the creditor can't prove ownership of the promissory note and therefore can't establish its right to receive payments under the mortgage during the life of the Chapter 13 plan. Further, if a foreclosure has been initiated prior to filing the Chapter 13, or the creditor seeks permission from the bankruptcy judge to proceed with a foreclosure, the filer (debtor) can challenge the legitimacy of the foreclosure documents and accompanying affidavit, and defeat the foreclosure as part of the Chapter

13 procedure. See "Using Foreclosure Document Deficiencies to Negotiate New Mortgage Terms," above, to learn more about possible challenges to affidavits and mortgage ownership.

If Foreclosure Is Unavoidable

If you owe significantly more on your mortgage than your home is worth, or you can't afford your mortgage (perhaps because of a reset in interest rates or a loss of income), consider using your state's foreclosure procedures to your best advantage. Depending on your state and your mortgage lender's policies, you can easily remain in your home for many months without paying a dime to anyone. By paying yourself all or a part of your mortgage instead of sending it to your lender, you can easily amass a savings of many thousands of dollars that will be available to you when you seek out new shelter. For example, assume that Kenny's mortgage payment increases from $1,200 to $1,500 because of a mortgage interest reset. Kenny has been able to afford the $1,200, but he can't meet the $300 monthly increase. As it turns out, Kenny owes $175,000 on his mortgage but his house is now only worth $110,000. Kenny decides to walk away from the mortgage. He stops making his mortgage payments and instead puts $1,200 a month into his own bank account. In the state where the house is located—Iowa—Kenny will probably have at least 18 months of payment-free shelter before he has to move, meaning he will be able to save over $21,000 just by living in his house payment free.

Importantly, if you react to foreclosure by selling your home (typically in a short sale) or offering the lender the deed back "in lieu of

foreclosure," you will have to move out of the house much earlier than if you just wait out the foreclosure procedures in your home, and you will thus forgo this unique opportunity to amass a considerable savings. For more information on your state's foreclosure laws and strategies for remaining in your home payment-free for the maximum period of time, see *The Foreclosure Survival Guide,* by Steven Elias (Nolo).

SEE AN EXPERT

If your lender has sent you a fore-closure notice, it may be time to consult with a bankruptcy or real estate attorney—quickly. You may have special legal options—and risks—in your state that are not discussed above. See "The Risk of Deficiency Judgments," below. If you think you can't afford an attorney, remember that you won't be paying your mortgage. For most people, just one month's mortgage payment is enough to buy an attorney's advice, if not outright repre-sentation. And if the attorney can help you stay in your home, payment free, for longer than you could stay there without the attorney's help, which is frequently the case, the attorneys' fees would be well worth it.

The Risk of Deficiency Judgments

In most states and with certain property and types of loans, the lender can get a deficiency judgment following a foreclosure. A "deficiency judgment" is a judgment for the difference between what you owe and what the lender gets for the property at auction. The creditor can use this deficiency judgment to collect the rest of the debt by seizing your other available property.

The possibility of a deficiency judgment could affect your strategy when facing a foreclosure. For instance, if you are at risk of a deficiency judgment, you might try to deed the property back to the lender, in exchange for a release from liability (commonly called a "deed in lieu of foreclosure"). But if your state doesn't permit deficiency judgments (called nonrecourse states), or your property is not subject to a deficiency judgment, you might benefit from fighting the foreclosure as long as possible without making any payments in the meantime.

These laws vary from state to state, which is one reason you may need to consult a real estate or bankruptcy attorney if you get a notice of foreclosure.

Renters Filing for Bankruptcy

If you're current on your rent payments and you file for either Chapter 7 or Chapter 13 bankruptcy, your bankruptcy should have no effect on your tenancy. Although your landlord might not like the idea that you filed for bankruptcy, chances are good that he or she won't even find out about it. Because you are current on your rent, you don't have to list your landlord as a creditor entitled to notice of the proceeding. Although you have to list on your bankruptcy papers any security deposits held by your landlord, you will probably be able to claim those deposits as exempt. And even if you can't, it's a rare trustee who actually will go after that money.

If You Are Behind on Your Rent When You File

Back rent is dischargeable in both Chapter 7 and Chapter 13 bankruptcies. However, if you get very far behind on your rent, your landlord will likely file an action in court to evict you. If you file for bankruptcy before the court issues a judgment for possession (an eviction order), the automatic stay will prohibit your landlord from trying to evict you on the basis of your prefiling rent default during your bankruptcy—unless the landlord files a motion to lift the stay. However, if you don't stay current on your rent after you file, the landlord is free to seek your eviction on the basis of the postfiling rent default.

> **EXAMPLE:** Aldo owes two months' back rent when he files for bankruptcy. At the time Aldo files, his landlord hasn't yet obtained a judgment of possession. The landlord can't evict him for this debt while the bankruptcy is pending unless he files a motion to lift the stay. However, if Aldo fails to pay rent on time after he files for bankruptcy, the landlord can give him a delinquency or "pay or quit" notice and file an eviction action in court if he doesn't move and the

rent isn't paid as required. Also, many states and localities give landlords the right to evict tenants for no reason at all, as long as the tenant receives adequate notice and the landlord strictly complies with the state's eviction procedures. So, even if Aldo faithfully pays his rent on time after his bankruptcy, he might still lose his apartment.

If the Landlord Already Has a Judgment

If your landlord has already obtained a judgment of possession (or "eviction") against you when you file for bankruptcy, the automatic stay won't help you (with the possible exception described below). The landlord is entitled to proceed with the eviction just as if you never filed for bankruptcy.

If the eviction order is based on your failure to pay rent, you may be able to have the automatic stay reinstated. However, this exception applies only if your state's law allows you to stay in your rental unit and "cure" (pay back) the rent delinquency after the landlord has a judgment for possession. Here's what you'll have to do to take advantage of this exception.

Step 1: As part of your bankruptcy petition, you must file a certification (a statement under oath) stating that your state's laws allow you to cure the rent delinquency after the judgment is obtained and to continue living in your rental unit. Very few states allow this. To find out whether yours is one of them, ask the sheriff or someone at legal aid (if you have legal aid in your area). In addition, when you

file your bankruptcy petition, you must deposit with the court clerk the amount of rent that will become due during the 30-day period after you file.

Once you have filed your petition containing the certification and deposited the rent, you are protected from eviction for 30 days unless the landlord successfully objects to your initial certification before the 30-day period ends. If the landlord objects to your certification, the court must hold a hearing on the objection within ten days, so theoretically you could have less than 30 days of protection if the landlord files and serves the objection immediately.

Step 2: To keep the stay in effect longer, you must, before the 30-day period runs out, file and serve a second certification showing that you have fully cured the default in the manner provided by your state's law. However, if the landlord successfully objects to this second certification, the stay will no longer be in effect and the landlord may proceed with the eviction. As in Step 1, the court must hold a hearing within ten days if the landlord objects.

 SEE AN EXPERT

If you really want to keep your apartment, talk to a lawyer. As you can see, these new rules are somewhat complicated. If you don't interpret your state's law properly, file the necessary paperwork on time, and successfully argue your side if the landlord objects, you could find yourself put out of your home. A good lawyer can tell you whether it's worth fighting an eviction—and, if so, how to go about it.

Endangering the Property or Illegal Use of Controlled Substances

Under the new bankruptcy law, an eviction action will not be stayed by your bankruptcy filing if your landlord wants you out because you endangered the property or engaged in the "illegal use of controlled substances" on the property. And your landlord doesn't have to have a judgment in hand when you file for bankruptcy: The landlord may start an eviction action against you or continue with a pending eviction action even after your filing date if the eviction is based on property endangerment or drug use.

To evict you on these grounds after you have filed for bankruptcy, your landlord must file and serve on you a certification showing that:

- the landlord has filed an eviction action against you based on property endangerment or illegal drug use on the property, or
- you have endangered the property or engaged in illegal drug use on the property during the 30-day period prior to the landlord's certification.

If your landlord files this certification, he or she can proceed with the eviction 15 days later unless, within that time, you file and serve on the landlord an objection to the truth of the statements in the landlord's certification. If you do that, the court must hold a hearing on your objection within ten days. If you prove that the statements in the certification aren't true or have been remedied, you will be protected from the eviction while your bankruptcy is pending. If the court denies your objection, the eviction may proceed immediately.

As a practical matter, you will have a very difficult time proving a negative—that is, that you weren't endangering the property or using drugs. Similarly, once allegations of property endangerment or drug use are made, it's hard to see how they would be "remedied."

CAUTION

Landlords can always ask the court to lift the automatic stay to begin or continue an eviction on any grounds. Although the automatic stay will kick in unless one of these exceptions apply, the judge can lift the stay upon the landlord's request. And many courts are willing to do so, because most evictions will have no effect on the bankruptcy estate—that is, your tenancy isn't something that the trustee can turn into money to pay your creditors. As a general rule, bankruptcy courts are inclined to let landlords exercise their property rights regardless of the tenant's debt problems.

RESOURCE

Need help with your landlord? For more information on dealing with landlords— including landlords who are trying to evict you— see *Every Tenant's Legal Guide,* by Janet Portman and Marcia Stewart (Nolo).

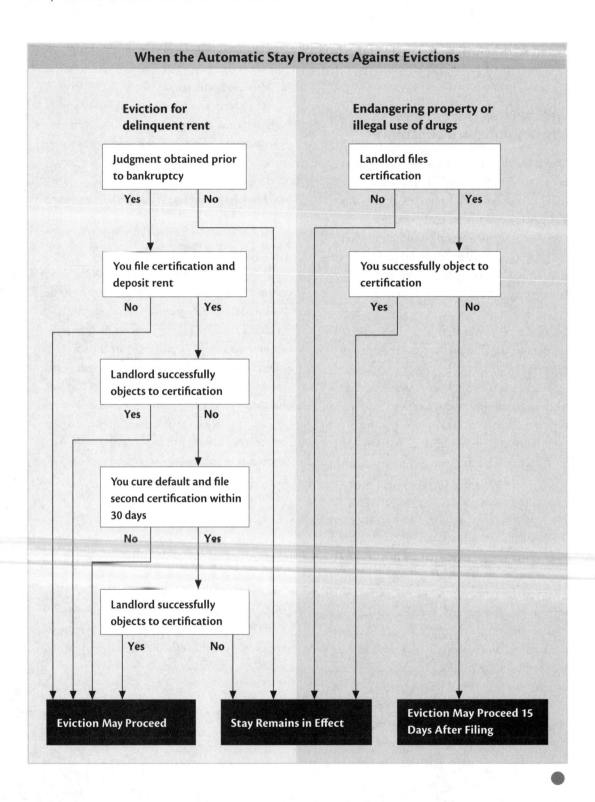

When the Automatic Stay Protects Against Evictions

What Happens to Personal Property That Secures a Loan

This chapter explains what happens to personal property you are making payments on when you file for bankruptcy—typically, a car or major household furnishings, such as living room or bedroom sets. It also covers other collateral: property you already owned that you pledged as security for a personal or business loan.

What Are Secured Debts?

Almost without exception, if you are making payments on property, you have agreed that the property will serve as collateral for repayment of the debt. This means that if you default on your payments, the creditor (or lender) can repossess the property, sell it, and obtain a court judgment against you (a deficiency judgment) for the difference between what you owe and what the property sold for. In bankruptcy, debts secured by collateral are called "secured debts."

How Secured Debts Are Handled in Chapter 7 Bankruptcy

Secured debts are treated differently in bankruptcy than other kinds of debts. Unlike a credit card debt or medical bills, a secured debt has a piece of property attached to it. Although the debt itself may be discharged in bankruptcy (and usually is), the creditor may still have a right to take the property back if you default on the payments.

A secured debt has two parts:

- **Personal liability.** You have personal liability for a secured debt just as you would for any other debt. This is what

obligates you to pay the debt to the creditor. Chapter 7 bankruptcy wipes out this personal liability if the debt is otherwise dischargeable. Once your personal liability is eliminated, the creditor cannot sue you to collect the debt.
- **Security interest.** The second part of a secured debt is the creditor's legal claim (lien or security interest) on the property that serves as collateral for the debt. The lien gives the creditor the right to repossess the property or force its sale if you do not pay the debt. And liens are not affected by the bankruptcy discharge. In other words, by failing to remain current on payments, you can lose the property, even if the debt itself is discharged. (In some cases, however, you can ask the bankruptcy court to remove the lien as part of your bankruptcy case.)

If You Are Current on Your Payments

If you are current on your payments for a secured debt when you file Chapter 7 bankruptcy, you can surrender the property and discharge the underlying debt (that is, you can walk away from the contract free and clear). Or, you can keep the property if:

- your equity in the property, if any, is protected by an applicable exemption (see below), and
- you are willing to take one of the two available options to secured debtors—reaffirmation or redemption (see below).

Does an Exemption Protect Any Equity You Have in the Property?

You have equity in property serving as collateral if it could be sold for more than you owe. For instance, if you owe $3,000 on a car loan and the car could be sold for $6,000, you have $3,000 worth of equity. This equity is part of your bankruptcy estate (see Ch. 4), which means the trustee can take it unless it's protected by an exemption. In this example, if you have $3,000 equity in your car and the exemptions available to you allow only $1,000 for motor vehicles, the trustee could sell the car, pay your secured creditor the $3,000 you still owe, give you your $1,000 exemption in cash, and distribute the remaining $2,000 (less costs of sale and the trustee's commission) to your unsecured creditors.

RELATED TOPIC

Information for homeowners. See Ch. 5 for information on computing your equity in a home.

Debtors frequently owe more on a secured loan than the property securing the debt is worth—which by definition means they have no equity in the property. Typically, the interest that is charged on a secured loan often makes your total payment much higher than it would be if you had paid cash for the property. Also, even though the value of the property decreases (depreciates) over time, your loan and accompanying interest is based on the value of the property when you bought it.

If you have no equity in the property, or if your equity is fully protected by an available

exemption, the trustee will have no interest in the property. You can either surrender it to the secured creditor or take one of the actions explained in "Redemption and Reaffirmation," just below, if you want to hold on to the property.

Redemption and Reaffirmation

Even if the trustee isn't interested in taking your property (because there is insufficient equity to produce payments to your unsecured creditors), that doesn't necessarily mean you get to keep it. The creditor still has that lien on the property, which means you might lose it to repossession unless you are current on your payments and use one of the remedies explained in this section.

Of course, you always have the option of simply giving the secured property to the creditor. Surrendering the property completely frees you from the debt, quickly and easily: The lien is satisfied by your surrender of the property, and your personal liability is discharged by the bankruptcy. The downside, obviously, is that you lose the property.

If you want to hang on to secured property, you have two options: redemption or reaffirmation.

Redeem the Property

In Chapter 7 bankruptcy, you have the right to "redeem" property—that is, to buy it back from the creditor in a lump sum, rather than have the creditor take it and sell it to someone else. Under the new bankruptcy law, if the property is used for personal, family, or household purposes, you can redeem it by paying the replacement value —the price a retail merchant would charge for property of that kind, considering the age and condition of the property at the time you redeem it. This means, for example, that you can redeem a car for the middle price listed in the *Kelley Blue Book* (www.kbb.com) or similar car valuation systems, such as www.nada.com.

At first glance, redemption doesn't seem like much of a remedy. After all, if you are filing for bankruptcy, how can you afford to buy the property outright? The answer is that all cash and other property you acquire after your bankruptcy filing date is yours to do with as you please (with the few exceptions explained in Ch. 4) and can be used to redeem property. For instance, you can sell some of your exempt property (with the trustee's permission during the time you are in bankruptcy), get a loan from family or friends, or work overtime to raise the money.

Redemption is a great option if your debt substantially exceeds the property's value. The creditor must accept the replacement value of the item as payment in full, even if you owe much more. However, you do have to come up with the replacement value of the property in a lump sum. If you can't afford to do that, you may be able to file a Chapter 13 case and pay off the property's replacement value over the life of your plan rather than through a lump sum payment.

You have the right to redeem property in a Chapter 7 bankruptcy only if all of the following are true:

- The debt is a consumer debt on goods used for personal or household purposes. This means you cannot redeem property that secures business debts or a car that you use for business purposes.
- The property is tangible personal property. "Personal property" includes everything but real estate. "Tangible property" is property you can touch, such as a car or stereo system. (Examples of intangible personal property, for comparison purposes, include investments, like stocks and bonds, or intellectual property rights, like patents, trademarks, and copyrights.)
- You have either claimed the property as exempt or the trustee has abandoned it because it has little or no equity.

Reaffirm the Debt

When you "reaffirm" a debt, you and the creditor use an official form to set out the amount you owe and the terms of the repayment. In essence, this creates a brand-new debt, although you have a right to the same terms set out in the original contract. You might even be able to negotiate better terms. In return, you get to keep the property as long as you keep current on your payments under the new agreement. If the debt is reaffirmed, both the creditor's lien on the collateral and your personal liability under the new contract survive bankruptcy.

Reaffirmation can be used when redemption is unavailable or impractical. It provides a sure way to keep property, as long as you abide by the terms of the reaffirmation agreement. But because reaffirmation leaves you personally liable, there is no way to walk away from the debt after your bankruptcy, even if the property becomes worthless or you simply decide you no longer want it. (Remember, you will have to wait eight years to file another Chapter 7 bankruptcy case.)

As a general rule, you should sign a reaffirmation agreement only if it is the sole way to keep property you can't be without, and you have good reason to believe you'll be able to pay off the balance. For example, many people use reaffirmation to keep a car, one of the few essential items of property in today's world.

Negotiate for Better Terms

There is no requirement that your reaffirmation agreement contain the same terms as your current agreement, although you have a right to reaffirm under the same terms if you can't get better terms through negotiation. While your lender ultimately has the right to hold you to the same terms, bankruptcy law gives you the right to surrender the property and walk away from the note without paying a penny. Because the lender will lose a ton of money if it has to auction off the property after you surrender it, you do have some leverage to negotiate a better deal.

Assume you are paying $350 a month on a 2009 Ford F-250 truck. When you file bankruptcy in 2011, the truck is worth $14,000 but you still owe $22,000. The lender sends you a reaffirmation agreement containing the same terms as the old note. You call the lender back and explain that you won't be able to afford $350 a month but that you are willing to reaffirm if the lender reduces the principal to the current value of the truck, and the payment from $350 to $250 a month. The lender rejects your offer but counteroffers with a plan that will require payments of $300 a month and a longer time to pay off the note. Because you really do want to keep the truck, you accept the offer and the lender sends you a new reaffirmation agreement to be signed and filed with the court.

The reaffirmation agreement form contains a number of disclosures about what you are getting into by reaffirming the debt. If you are represented by an attorney, the agreement becomes effective upon its signing unless the attorney refuses to approve the reaffirmation (perhaps because the attorney believes the payments would be a substantial hardship). If you are not represented by an attorney, or the attorney refuses to sign off on it, the agreement will become effective only after it has been filed with the court and approved by the bankruptcy judge in a court hearing near the end of your bankruptcy that you must attend.

At the hearing, the judge will look at the income and expense schedules you filed with your other bankruptcy paperwork and consider whether continuing to make payments on the debt will be a substantial hardship or interfere with your ability to get a fresh start through bankruptcy. While the judge will probably be sympathetic to your desire to keep your ride, he or she may nevertheless disapprove the reaffirmation agreement. Courts have ruled that if you do everything you are supposed to do to reaffirm—that is, agree to reaffirm in your Statement of Intention, sign and file the reaffirmation agreement in court, and appear at the reaffirmation hearing—bankruptcy law authorizes you to retain possession of the car as long as you remain current, regardless of whether the judge approves or disapproves the agreement. Oddly, you will be better off if the judge disapproves the agreement because then you won't owe a deficiency if you have to return the car after bankruptcy. But you'll be able to keep the car as long as you remain current on your payments.

TIP

Most bankruptcy judges won't approve the reaffirmation of an unsecured debt. Some debtors want to keep a credit card that has a balance and are told by the credit card company that they can do that if they agree to reaffirm the debt. While this may technically be true, very few judges would approve such a reaffirmation agreement. Why not? From the judge's viewpoint, a reaffirmation agreement on an unsecured debt provides no benefit to the bankruptcy debtor (other than the right to keep the card) and is therefore not a legal contract.

The Statement of Intention

As part of your bankruptcy case, you are required to file an official form called a "Statement of Intention," which tells your secured creditors what you plan to do with the collateral. That is, you must tell them whether you plan to surrender the collateral, redeem it, or reaffirm the debt.

If you don't file the Statement of Intention within 30 days after you file your bankruptcy petition, your creditor can repossess the property in the manner permitted by state law. Repossession may also occur if you fail to carry out your stated intention within either 30 or 45 days after your 341 hearing (the law appears to be contradictory on the time limit).

Keeping Property Without Reaffirming or Redeeming

Prior to the 2005 changes in the bankruptcy law, many bankruptcy courts allowed debtors to keep secured property without going through the reaffirmation process, provided they remained current on their payments under the contract with the creditor. If the debtor fell behind, the creditor could take the property, but the debtor's personal liability for the debt was wiped out by the bankruptcy. This method was often referred to as the "retain and pay" or "ridethrough" option.

According to recent court decisions, this remedy is no longer available under bankruptcy law. However, if the law of your state forbids creditors from enforcing a lien on your property as long as you are current under the contract, your creditors may have to let you keep the property as long as you remain current, no matter what the new bankruptcy law says. Many creditors are perfectly happy with this arrangement; they would rather have a steady payment stream on the original contract than repossess used property that has to be sold at auction.

If You Are Not Current on Your Payments

If you're behind on your payments to a secured creditor and don't have the wherewithal to get current, Chapter 7 bankruptcy probably won't prevent the creditor from repossessing the property. While your bankruptcy filing will initially stop any repossession activity, the creditor can ask the court to lift the automatic stay. If you are behind on your payments, most courts will lift the stay in order to let the creditor proceed with repossession. (For more on the automatic stay, see Ch. 1.) If you want to keep the property, you'll need to reinstate the loan outside of bankruptcy, by making up the missed payments (and fees associated with the default) and by resuming your regular payments.

If your lender has already accelerated the loan (declared the entire balance due) and won't let you reinstate it, you can file for Chapter 13 bankruptcy. You can make up the missed payments in your plan as long as you also make the regular payments called for under your original agreement. (See Ch. 2.) Also, in Chapter 13, you may be able to reduce the total amount of your payments to the property's actual value.

Eliminating Liens in Chapter 7 Bankruptcy

During your Chapter 7 bankruptcy case, you may be able to eliminate a lien on an item of secured property. If you can eliminate, or "avoid," a lien, you get to keep the property free and clear, without paying anything more to the creditor. To avoid a lien, you must be able to claim an exemption in the property that is impaired by the lien—that is, that the lien deprives you of your right to benefit from the exemption because you can't sell the property without paying off the lien. (See Ch. 4 for more on exemptions.)

For the purpose of lien avoidance, there are two types of liens: (1) judicial liens, and (2) liens you agree to have placed on property you already own in exchange for a personal loan. A judicial lien is one that was placed on your property to collect a court judgment for money. The second type of lien is called a nonpossessory, nonpurchase money lien because the lienholder doesn't possess the collateral (as would be the case if the lien were owned by a pawnbroker), and you didn't use the loan to buy the collateral.

A judicial lien may be "avoided" (wiped out) on any type of property, including real estate, to the extent the lien "impairs an exemption." A nonpossessory, nonpurchase money lien, on the other hand, may be avoided only on certain types of personal property (see below).

In most courts, lien avoidance actions are relatively simple. Most of the time, the lien owner doesn't contest the motion, so you'll just have to make sure you get the paperwork right. On occasion, however, a lien owner may object, which means you will have to participate in one or more court hearings, depending on the type of objection. (The procedural steps necessary for lien avoidance are described in more detail in Ch. 10.)

Avoiding Judicial Liens

Most judicial liens occur when:

- You've been sued for money and lost.
- The judgment creditor (the winner of the lawsuit) obtains a judgment against you for a sum of money.
- The judgment is recorded against your property in the form of a lien.

Most often, judicial liens are imposed on real estate. Judicial liens can also be imposed on business assets; almost all states provide a way to do this under the Uniform Commercial Code.

However, liens are seldom, if ever, attached to personal property, both because there are no procedures for doing so and because ownership of personal property is rarely recorded in public documents.

If paying a judicial lien would deprive you of any part of the exemption you are entitled to claim on the property, you can get rid of the lien by following the lien avoidance process outlined in Ch. 10. A few courts have ruled that you can avoid a judicial lien even if you have no equity in the property. Be sure to speak to an attorney about the possibility of avoiding the lien even if you are underwater on the mortgage.

Avoiding Nonpossessory, Nonpurchase Money Liens

A nonpossessory, nonpurchase money security lien is almost always created when a consumer obtains a personal loan from Beneficial Finance or a credit union. These liens can be avoided only on the following types of property (and only if the property is exempt without regard to your equity in the property):

- household furnishings, household goods (see the list below), clothing, appliances, books, musical instruments, or jewelry
- health aids professionally prescribed for you or a dependent
- the first $5,475 of a lien attaching to animals or crops held primarily for your personal, family, or household use, and
- the first $5,475 of a lien attaching to tools used in your trade.

Under the new bankruptcy law, the term "household goods" is limited to:

- clothing
- furniture
- appliances
- one radio
- one television
- one VCR
- linens
- china
- crockery
- kitchenware
- educational equipment and materials primarily for the use of your minor dependent children
- medical equipment and supplies
- furniture exclusively for the use of your minor children or elderly or disabled dependents
- your personal effects (including the toys and hobby equipment of your minor dependent children and your wedding rings) and those of your dependents, and
- one personal computer and related equipment.

The following are not considered to be household goods, and you cannot avoid liens on them:

- works of art (unless they are by you or a relative)
- electronic entertainment equipment with a fair market value of more than $550 in the aggregate (excluding the one television, one radio, and one VCR listed above)
- items acquired as antiques with a fair market value of more than $550 in the aggregate
- jewelry with a fair market value of more than $550 in the aggregate (excluding wedding rings), and

- a computer (excluding the computer equipment listed above), a motor vehicle (including a tractor or lawn tractor), a boat, or a motorized recreational device, conveyance vehicle, watercraft, or aircraft.

To avoid a nonpossessory, nonpurchase money lien, you must have owned the property before the lien was "fixed" on it. This will almost always be the case with this type of lien. See Ch. 10 for more on lien avoidance.

How Secured Debts Are Handled in Chapter 13 Bankruptcy

Secured debts are handled completely differently in Chapter 13 than in Chapter 7. By filing for Chapter 13 bankruptcy, you can keep property subject to a secured debt even though you are behind on your payments when you file. Under your Chapter 13 plan, you can pay off the arrearage (the defaulted payments) over the course of the plan, as long as you meet your current payment obligations during that time.

Surrendering Property

If you don't want to keep property that is subject to a secured debt, you can surrender it to the creditor and schedule what you still owe on the contract as an unsecured debt. This means that you may have to pay a portion of the debt over the life of your plan, depending on the factors described in Ch. 2, "Chapter 13 Eligibility Requirements."

Reducing Secured Debt to the Property's Value (Cramdowns)

If you want to keep property that is worth less than what you still owe on it, you can propose a plan that pays off the replacement value of the property over the life of the plan (rather than what you owe on the contract). For example, if you owe $20,000 on the property and its replacement value is $10,000, you can propose a plan that pays only $10,000. If you complete your plan, then you'll own the property free and clear. This remedy of reducing a secured debt to the replacement value of the collateral is known as a "cramdown," a most descriptive term.

You can't cram down a mortgage owned on your residence. Nor can you cram down a debt you owe on your car if you purchased the car for your personal use during the 30-month period before you filed for bankruptcy. If you use the car as part of your business, for example, you can cram down the debt without regard to the 30-month restriction. You also can't cram down a secured debt on other personal property you purchased within one year preceding your bankruptcy filing.

The purpose of these restrictions is to prevent people from purchasing cars or other property with the intent to file for bankruptcy and use the cramdown remedy. The good news is that, because you can't cram down the debt, you can surrender the vehicle and perhaps get off the hook for the entire debt. (*In re Ezell*, 338 B.R. 330 (E.D. Tenn. 2006).) However, the majority of the courts that have decided this issue require you to include the deficiency as an unsecured debt when you formulate your plan.

Continuing the Contract

If you want to continue the secured debt as before, all you have to do is provide in your proposed plan that you will remain current on the contract during the life of the plan. If you don't complete your Chapter 13 plan, but are still making payments on the secured debt, you can either convert to Chapter 7 and use one of the remedies described in "How Secured Debts Are Handled in Chapter 7 Bankruptcy," above, or continue making the payments outside of bankruptcy. If you are still in Chapter 13 and something happens to the collateral (for example, it is destroyed in an accident), it is usually possible to amend your plan and reschedule what you still owe as unsecured debt. ●

Making the Decision

The previous chapters explain how bankruptcy works in general to stop collection efforts and give you a fresh start, how the two main types of consumer bankruptcy—Chapter 7 and Chapter 13— will affect your debts and property, and how to determine your eligibility for each. It's a lot of information to absorb, especially when making the choice between chapters. It brings to mind the famous Yogi Berra aphorism, "When you get to the fork in the road, take it."

To help you sort through this information, weigh the pros and cons, and reach a decision, this chapter gives you a transcript of a consultation between a debtor and a lawyer. As you'll see, the debtor, Georgia Cox, is trying to figure out whether to file for bankruptcy under Chapter 7 or Chapter 13. She has decided to consult with a bankruptcy lawyer to help her with her decision. The questions the lawyer asks will help remind you of factors you should consider as you evaluate your own situation.

Lawyer: Good morning. What's your name?

Debtor: Georgia Cox.

Lawyer: Hi, Georgia. How can I help you today?

Debtor: Well, I've run up quite a bit of debt, and I've decided to file for bankruptcy. I know there are different types of bankruptcy,

but I think I need to learn more about them. I need some help figuring out what my options are.

Lawyer: Okay, I can help you with that. The two basic types of bankruptcy for individuals are Chapter 7 bankruptcy and Chapter 13 bankruptcy. There are a couple of major differences between them. In a Chapter 13 bankruptcy, you pay down some or all of your debts over a three- to five-year period and discharge (cancel) whatever is left over at the completion of your plan. In a Chapter 7 bankruptcy, you don't pay down any of your debt, and the entire process takes between three and four months. But you may have to give up property you own so it can be sold and the proceeds distributed to your creditors.

In either type of bankruptcy, some types of debts aren't discharged, but will survive your bankruptcy. For instance, overdue child support must be paid in full as part of a Chapter 13 bankruptcy. Also, some debts that can be discharged in Chapter 13 will survive a Chapter 7 bankruptcy. But we'll get to that later. Are you with me so far?

Debtor: Yes. I kind of already knew most of what you just told me by reading some articles on the Nolo website. Right now, I'm leaning toward Chapter 7 since it's over a lot sooner and seems like it's a lot simpler. But I wouldn't want to choose Chapter 7 if Chapter 13 would be the better choice for me.

Lawyer: Okay. Well, let's start by figuring out whether you even have a choice. Some people aren't eligible to file for Chapter 7 bankruptcy. If both options are available to you, then we can talk about which one makes more sense.

Debtor: Okay.

Lawyer: What state do you live in?

Debtor: New Hampshire.

Lawyer: Who lives with you as part of your household? That includes not only relatives and dependents, but anyone else whose income and expenses are regularly combined with yours to maintain your home.

Debtor: Just me and my two children. One is eight and the other just turned 12.

Lawyer: Okay. And do you operate a business?

Debtor: Actually, I do. What difference does that make?

Lawyer: Well, business debts are sometimes treated differently than consumer debts when it comes to deciding your eligibility for filing Chapter 7. Also, Chapter 13 is often the better type of bankruptcy for an ongoing business, because you can keep your business assets and use your business earnings to make your required payments, but we'll get to that later.

Debtor: Okay. I run my own business, repairing used electronic equipment.

Lawyer: Have you incorporated your business or is it a partnership?

Debtor: No, just me, a sole proprietor.

Lawyer: And do you have other work? In other words, do you have a regular job and operate your business on the side?

Debtor: No, just the business.

Lawyer: Is your income pretty steady?

Debtor: It was until recently. Near the end of 2008, my business dropped off and I'll be lucky to bring in half of what I was earning not too long ago. Also, I receive alimony and child support, which helps stabilize my income, but my ex told me just last week that his company is starting to lay people off and he may be next.

Lawyer: Looking at your debts as a whole, were more of them due to your business or more due to your personal needs? When making this assessment, your mortgage counts as a consumer debt and back taxes count as a business debt.

Debtor: Why are you asking?

Lawyer: If your debts were primarily incurred for your business, you wouldn't have to worry about something we call the means test— essentially a questionnaire that determines whether you can afford to pay back some of your debts in a Chapter 13 bankruptcy.

Debtor: I would say about 40% were from my business and 60% were personal.

Lawyer: Okay, too bad. That makes you a consumer debtor rather than a business debtor and we'll have to see whether you need to take the means test. For starters, how much did you earn in the last six months? That's gross earnings less your reasonable business expenses.

Debtor: About $3,000 a month after expenses for the last six months.

Lawyer: You mentioned that you receive child support and alimony. How much, and do you have any other income?

Debtor: About $1,000 a month in alimony and $800 a month for child support, and that's it.

Lawyer: Have those amounts been steady over the last six months?

Debtor: Yes, there haven't been any changes.

Lawyer: So, it looks like your average monthly earnings over the past six months are $3,000 from your business, $1,000 in alimony, and $800 for child support, for a total of $4,800. Does that sound right?

Debtor: Yes.

Lawyer: Under the bankruptcy law, if your income is less than the median annual income for a family of your size in your state, you are presumed to be eligible to file for Chapter 7 bankruptcy. You don't have to go fill out a lengthy form comparing your income to your expenses and your deductions for contractual obligations, such as a car note and mortgage. Does any of this sound familiar to you?

Debtor: Yes, I remember reading a few years ago that higher-income people won't be able to file for Chapter 7 anymore. Is that what you are talking about?

Lawyer: Yes, that's it. Also, if your income is less than the median for your state and you decide to file a Chapter 13 bankruptcy anyway, your repayment plan has to last for only three years. If, on the other hand, your income is more than the median, your plan would have to last for five years.

Debtor: I didn't know that.

Lawyer: So, let's see how these numbers work out. Your annual income based on your gross income for the last six months is $57,600. The New Hampshire median income for a household of three people is $81,134. So, you're under the median income and don't have to take the means test to prove your eligibility for Chapter 7 bankruptcy. And if you decide to use Chapter 13, you can repay your debts over three years, instead of five.

Debtor: I guess that's good news, but when it comes right down to it, I wish I earned more,

even if that meant I had to take the means test and have a Chapter 13 case last longer. Of course, if I had more money, I guess I wouldn't be talking to you about filing for bankruptcy in the first place.

Lawyer: Even though you qualify for Chapter 7 bankruptcy on the basis of your average income over the past six months, you can still be disqualified if, going forward, your actual monthly net income is substantially more than your actual monthly expenses, leaving you with some extra income every month to pay down your debt under a three-year Chapter 13 repayment plan.

Debtor: Oh dear, I wish I did have some extra income. When I recently compared my net income to my expenses, I definitely have very little, if any, money left over. Of course there are probably ways I could reduce my expenses if I had to.

Lawyer: Well, as long as your basic living expenses are more or less equal to your net income, and because your income is below the state median income, you have the option of filing for Chapter 7 bankruptcy.

Let's turn now to your residence. How long have you lived in New Hampshire?

Debtor: About three years.

Lawyer: Have you lived there continuously for the last three years, or did you live or maintain a residence somewhere else?

Debtor: I've lived here the whole time. I moved here from Vermont because of a job, but I didn't keep a home in Vermont. I vote and get my mail here.

Lawyer: Great. Because you've been living in New Hampshire for more than two years, we'll use our state's property exemptions. These will determine what property you can keep if you file a Chapter 7, and the minimum amount you'll have to pay your unsecured creditors if you file a Chapter 13 bankruptcy.

Debtor: Why do the exemptions matter in a Chapter 13 bankruptcy? I thought I could keep all of my property if I use Chapter 13.

Lawyer: Yes, you're right about that. But the law doesn't want your creditors to be worse off because you use Chapter 13. So a Chapter 13 repayment plan has to give your unsecured, nonpriority creditors at least as much they would have received had you filed a Chapter 7 bankruptcy. Roughly speaking that would equal the value of the property minus the exemption you are entitled to take, the costs of sale, and the trustee's commission.

Debtor: Okay, I guess that's fair, but I'm not sure who my nonpriority creditors are.

Lawyer: Oh, priority creditors are those who hold claims that have to be paid 100% in Chapter 13 cases, like back taxes, child support and alimony, and a portion of wages owed to employees. Nonpriority creditors are the rest of your creditors, typically credit card issuers, banks, doctors and lawyers, and holders of money judgments for repossessed and foreclosed property. For example, in your case, if you owed your employees wages or you owed contributions to a retirement plan, these would be priority debts and those creditors would be paid first in a Chapter 7 case if you have nonexempt assets. In a Chapter 13 case, priority debts must be paid in full over the life of your plan.

Debtor: Thanks for explaining that.

Lawyer: You're welcome. Now, let's figure out which of your property items is exempt. Do you own your home?

Debtor: Yes.

Lawyer: Are you making payments on a mortgage?

Debtor: Yes.

Lawyer: What's your monthly payment?

Debtor: $1,200.

Lawyer: Are you current on your payments?

Debtor: Yes.

Lawyer: What's your home worth?

Debtor: $150,000. It used to be worth $200,000 just last year.

Lawyer: And how much do you owe on it?

Debtor: About $100,000.

Lawyer: That's a total?

Debtor: Yes.

Lawyer: Okay. Under the New Hampshire homestead exemption, you are entitled to protect $100,000 of equity in your home. You have $50,000 of equity, so all of your equity is protected.

Debtor: What's a homestead exemption?

Lawyer: That's an exemption for your home. You are entitled to keep that much equity in your home, even if you file for Chapter 7 bankruptcy. If your equity exceeded the exemption, you might lose the extra equity if you filed for Chapter 7. The trustee could sell your home, pay off the mortgage, pay you your exemption, and still have money left over to distribute among your creditors. But because your equity is protected by the exemption, there wouldn't be anything left for your creditors after you got your exemption amount and the mortgage was paid. That's how exemptions work.

We already discussed how exemptions work in Chapter 13. If you have property that isn't exempt, your repayment plan has to pay at least the portion of that property's value that your unsecured creditors would have received in a Chapter 7 bankruptcy.

Debtor: I remember reading back in 2005 that the new bankruptcy law makes it harder for people to keep their homes. Will that affect me?

Lawyer: Nope. The new law puts a cap of about $137,000 on the exemption amount for people who bought their home within the 40 months before they filed for bankruptcy. So it affects only people who bought a home more recently, and then only if their state would otherwise allow them to take a higher exemption. For example, even if you bought your home in New Hampshire within the previous 40 months, the New Hampshire homestead is only $100,000, so the $137,000 cap wouldn't make any difference.

Debtor: So, I don't have to worry about that.

Lawyer: Right. Oh, your exemption might be affected if you used nonexempt property in the last ten years to buy your home in order to cheat your creditors. I guess I should ask how you got the money to pay for your home.

Debtor: I borrowed money from my parents.

Lawyer: Great. Your home equity is covered by your state's homestead exemption and you can keep it if you file for Chapter 7 bankruptcy.

Debtor: What happens to my home if I file for Chapter 13 bankruptcy?

Lawyer: As long as you keep making your mortgage payments and the other payments required by your Chapter 13 plan, there won't be a problem. However, if you fall behind on your payments, your lender could foreclose, just as if you hadn't filed bankruptcy. On the other hand, if you have reason to believe that the mortgage or foreclosure papers are defective, you can challenge the mortgage or foreclosure as part of your Chapter 13 case.

Debtor: So unless I have some basis to challenge the mortgage, I have to keep my mortgage payments current, no matter which type of bankruptcy I file?

Lawyer: That's right. What other debts do you owe?

Debtor: Mainly credit card debts. And one SBA bank loan for my business.

Lawyer: Is the SBA loan secured by any of your property?

Debtor: No, it's just a bank loan.

Lawyer: How much are you paying on that loan?

Debtor: About $300 a month.

Lawyer: And how much credit card debt do you owe?

Debtor: About $23,000.

Lawyer: What were the credit card debts for?

Debtor: About $14,000 for personal expenses and $6,000 for paying off back taxes. Also, $3,000 for a credit card charge by my husband that I assumed in our divorce.

Lawyer: Oh yeah? What period did you owe the taxes for?

Debtor: The last couple of years.

Lawyer: That's interesting. I'll come back to this later, but bankruptcy law allows you to discharge credit card charges used to pay off taxes in a Chapter 13 bankruptcy but not in a Chapter 7 bankruptcy. So, if there is no other reason to choose one type of bankruptcy over the other, you would be wise to choose Chapter 13.

So, having paid those taxes, are you now current on your taxes for the past four years?

Debtor: Yes.

Lawyer: That's good. You can't file for Chapter 13 unless you have filed your state and federal taxes for the previous four years. How much was the bank loan for?

Debtor: $40,000

Lawyer: Did anybody cosign on that loan?

Debtor: As matter of fact, my mother cosigned that loan.

Lawyer: Hmm. Even if you could get rid of that debt in bankruptcy, your mother would still be on the hook to repay it if you filed under Chapter 7. Even though you wouldn't be responsible for the debt any more, she would be.

But if you file for Chapter 13 bankruptcy, your mother won't have to repay it while your plan is in place, as long as your plan provides for payment of some or all of that debt. So, assuming your plan lasts for three years, your mother won't be on the hook during that period. However, she will still be responsible for any amount you haven't paid when your plan ends. So, again, if there is no other reason to choose one type of bankruptcy instead of the other, it looks like Chapter 13 might be a good choice.

Do you have any other debts?

Debtor: Nothing significant, maybe a total of $2,000 in miscellaneous bills. And, oh, does child support count?

Lawyer: I thought you were receiving child support.

Debtor: I am, but I also owe child support, for a child from a previous marriage. I never paid because my ex never asked, but now he's seeking current support as well as $5,000 in back support.

Lawyer: How much will you owe?

Debtor: Under the court order, $300 a month.

Lawyer: Have you started paying the support?

Debtor: No. I have to start paying it next month.

Lawyer: If you decide to file for Chapter 13, you will have to remain current on your child support payments throughout the life of your plan. If you don't, your case will be dismissed or converted to a Chapter 7 bankruptcy.

Debtor: I understand.

Lawyer: Let's talk later about the back support you owe. When were you divorced?

Debtor: A couple of years ago.

Lawyer: Did you assume any of the debts in the course of your divorce?

Debtor: Yes, I assumed the credit card charges for personal expenses in exchange for my ex-husband's share of our home.

Lawyer: Okay. How much were these charges?

Debtor: About $3,000

Lawyer: Hmmm, in a Chapter 7 bankruptcy you can discharge this debt as regards the creditor, but your ex can come after you for this debt if he is sued by the creditor. In Chapter 13 bankruptcy, the debt would be fully discharged, both in respect to the creditor and your ex.

Debtor: It sounds like I should probably file for Chapter 13.

Lawyer: Maybe, but we're not through yet. Let's talk about your other property. And this is where exemptions will become important. Other than your home, do you have any other property you would want to keep in your bankruptcy?

Debtor: Oh, yes. I have a concert piano and some copyright interests in several songs I wrote. Also, I have a car I want to hold on to and the tools I use in my business.

Lawyer: How much are the tools worth?

Debtor: About $3,000.

Lawyer: Great. New Hampshire allows you to keep up to $5,000 worth of tools for your occupation, so those are covered. How much is the car worth?

Debtor: About $4,000 according to *Kelley Blue Book.*

Lawyer: Are you making payments on it?

Debtor: Yes.

Lawyer: How much is left on your note?

Debtor: About $8,000.

Lawyer: When did you buy it?

Debtor: Three years ago.

Lawyer: If you file for Chapter 13, you can pay off the value of the car rather than what you still owe on the note. This is called a cramdown, and it's another great reason to file for Chapter 13. And it's a good thing you didn't buy your car more recently: You couldn't use this cramdown procedure if you bought the car within 2½ years of your bankruptcy filing date.

Now let's take a look at the New Hampshire exemptions to see whether your other property is covered. Remember, exemptions like the homestead exemption and the tools of your occupation exemption are laws that determine what property you can keep in your bankruptcy. As I read them, the car is covered because you owe more than it's worth, so your creditors wouldn't get anything if it were sold. Because you don't have any equity in the car, you don't need to protect it with an exemption. As for the piano and your copyright interests, there are no state exemptions that specifically cover those items.

Debtor: Does that mean I'll lose my piano?

Lawyer: Not necessarily. Remember, if you file for Chapter 13, you don't lose any property—you just have to make sure you pay your creditors at least what they would have received from a sale of the piano in a Chapter 7 bankruptcy. And even though New Hampshire doesn't specifically exempt pianos, it has a $3,500 exemption for all your furniture. So depending on your piano's value, it might be covered by the furniture exemption.

Debtor: I think my piano would sell for about $12,000 and I guess my copyrights are pretty much worthless.

Lawyer: Why do you say your copyright interests are worthless?

Debtor: Well, they belong to three songs I wrote, but I've never had the songs published, so there is no one to sell them to.

Lawyer: Okay, let's forget about the songs. We're only talking about the piano. Looking at the New Hampshire exemptions, in addition to the portion of the piano's value arguably covered by the furniture exemption—$3,500—there are also some wildcard exemptions. This type of exemption can be used to protect any property you choose. New Hampshire's wildcard exemptions will provide an additional $8,000 that you can put toward the piano: That takes into account a $1,000 straight wildcard, plus a $7,000 wildcard that you can use if you don't fully take advantage of certain other exemptions. If you use these wildcards for your piano, only about $500 of its value is not exempt. Since the costs of sale and the trustee's commission, on top of the exemptions, would more than eat up that $500, you won't have to pay any of the piano's value to your creditors in a Chapter 13 case. Of course, if you need part of the furniture exemption for other pieces of furniture, that would take away from the exemption available for your piano.

Debtor: Okay.

Lawyer: Here is a copy of the New Hampshire exemptions. (Lawyer hands Georgia a page showing the New Hampshire bankruptcy exemptions.) Other than the piano, do you have any property that exceeds the exemption limit or that isn't listed in the exemption list?

Debtor: No, the piano is the only problem. But if I use the furniture exemption for my piano, my furniture won't be exempt. It's old furniture I bought at the Goodwill. I have nothing that would be of any value.

Lawyer: Well, that's up to the trustee. If you choose to use the entire furniture exemption for your piano, you might have to place some value on your furniture equal to what it would cost you to replace it.

Debtor: That would probably be about $1,000.

Lawyer: Okay, so you may have a couple of thousand dollars in nonexempt property depending on how you use the wildcard. That's under the New Hampshire state exemptions. If your state allows it, you may choose to use a different set of exemptions set out in the bankruptcy code termed the "federal exemptions." As it turns out, New Hampshire does allow use of the federal exemptions. You can choose from the federal exemption list or from the New Hampshire state list, but you can't mix or match.

Let's take a look and see if the federal exemptions would do you any good. The federal exemptions protect only $20,000 in your home equity. You have $50,000 equity to protect, so you wouldn't want to choose the federal exemptions.

So, we know you can file for Chapter 7 bankruptcy if you wish. You could keep your home and probably your piano, even though it isn't completely exempt. The cost of collecting and storing the piano, then selling it at auction, would probably be more than $500—the nonexempt portion—which means there wouldn't be anything left after selling it to pay to your unsecured creditors. If you had to use the whole furniture exemption for other pieces of furniture, however, $4,000 of the value of your piano would be nonexempt. If that were the case, the trustee would probably take it and sell it, giving you the exempt amount and paying the rest to your unsecured creditors. Or, you could keep the piano if the trustee were willing to sell it to you for a negotiated price. Because the trustee would probably have to pay about $1,000 to sell it, you might be able to keep it by paying the trustee $3,000. But that's all in a Chapter 7 bankruptcy.

Debtor: It's still sounding to me like Chapter 13 is a good idea. But you said I have to make sure I'm eligible. What are the requirements?

Lawyer: Before we get to that, I have a couple of more questions.

Debtor: Okay.

Lawyer: During the previous year, have you made payments on any loans you owe to relatives?

Debtor: Nope.

Lawyer: Good. If you had, the trustee might require the relative to return the money so it could be added to the amount your creditors would get.

Debtor: I wouldn't want that to happen.

Lawyer: Have you given away or sold any property to anyone within the past two years?

Debtor: No.

Lawyer: That also simplifies things. If you had given away some property, or you had sold some property for less than what it was worth, the difference in value would be considered nonexempt property. You'd have to add that to the amount you have to pay under your Chapter 13 plan. But you didn't sell any property, so this rule doesn't affect you.

Debtor: Wow, there's a lot to consider here. Are we done—isn't it clear that Chapter 13 is the right route for me?

Lawyer: Bear with me, just a few more issues to consider. Chapter 13 has some limitations on how much debt you can owe. Let's see, you owe a total of $69,000 of unsecured debt: a $40,000 bank loan, $23,000 in credit card debts, $5,000 in child support arrearage, and $2,000 in other debts. You owe a total of $108,000 secured debt (your home and car). This means you fall within the eligibility guidelines, which are $1,010,650 for secured debts and $336,900 for unsecured debts.

Debtor: That's good.

Lawyer: Now let's see what debts you would have to pay in your Chapter 13 bankruptcy. Some debts have to be paid in full while others could be paid in part, depending on your income. The debts that would have to be paid in full over the life of your plan would be at least the $5,000 arrearage for your child support and the $500 for the nonexempt portion of your piano and your furniture, or $5,500 total debt payable in full over the course of your Chapter 13 plan.

Debtor: So how much would that be a month?

Lawyer: People whose average gross income for the preceding six months is less than the state median income—which is your situation—can propose a three-year repayment plan. If your income were higher than the median, you'd have to propose a five-year program.

So, when spreading out $5,000 over three years, you would have to pay at least $139 a month, plus the monthly payment on your car as modified downwards to reflect its value ($111), your current mortgage payment, and other expenses related to Chapter 13 bankruptcy, such as the trustee's fee and your attorney's fee if you use an attorney. If you don't have enough income to pay that after you subtract your living expenses (including your mortgage payment and your car payment) you won't qualify for a three-year Chapter 13 plan.

Debtor: How can I tell whether I have enough income to meet the Chapter 13 requirements?

Lawyer: If you decide to file a Chapter 13 bankruptcy, you have to fill out some forms to determine your income and your expenses. These forms will basically show whether you can afford a Chapter 13 bankruptcy. If you don't have enough income to pay all necessary debts in three years, you can ask the judge to let you propose a five-year plan, so you can pay less each month. If you still won't have enough left, after paying your expenses, to make your payments, you probably won't be able to use Chapter 13.

Debtor: So, do you suggest that I file for Chapter 7? Or should I use Chapter 13?

Lawyer: Well, before I answer that, I've saved the best for last. Let's talk about attorney fees. I charge $3,500 for a Chapter 13 and $1,000 for a Chapter 7. So, by filing a Chapter 7, you'll save at least $2,500 in legal fees. But in Chapter 13 cases, I charge only $2,000 up front; the additional $1,500 can be paid through your plan. I think you'll find that my rates are competitive. Overall, it will cost less up front for you to file a Chapter 7 bankruptcy. Also, in your case, I see no reason why you couldn't handle your own Chapter 7 bankruptcy with the help of the ABC Bankruptcy Petition Preparation Service down the street. They have the same computer program as I use, but all they do is help you complete your paperwork. They can't give you legal advice. If you are up to handling your own case, which I think you are from this conversation, you should explore the self-help option.

If you do decide to do it yourself, I would be happy to consult with you for a flat rate of $150. Under my consultation agreement you could ask me as many questions as you want, over the telephone. Unless you use my service or a good self-help book, you might miss important information that you need to have a good result in your bankruptcy.

Debtor: I want you to handle my case. I don't think I'm up for self-representation.

Lawyer: Okay, now I'm ready to answer your basic question. As long as you have enough income left over in your budget to use Chapter 13, that would be an excellent choice for you because:

- It will protect your codebtor—your mother—for the life of the plan.

- It will allow you to keep your car and pay it off at market value rather than reaffirming the current note, which is twice what it's worth.

- Unlike Chapter 7, it fully discharges the credit card debts you assumed in your divorce.

- Unlike Chapter 7, it will allow you to discharge the credit card debts you incurred to pay off your taxes.

- It will allow you to pay off your child support arrearage—that is, the back child support you owe—over the life of your plan, without worrying about wage garnishments and bank levies.

So, assuming you have enough income to propose a confirmable Chapter 13 plan, and pay my fees, I recommend Chapter 13. If you can't propose a confirmable Chapter 13 plan, even over a five-year period, or you can't afford my fees, I suggest you to with Chapter 7. ●

Your Credit Cards

What will happen to your credit cards when you file for bankruptcy depends largely on the current status of your account, and to a lesser degree on the creditor. For this discussion, most credit cards fall into three possible categories:

- cards on which you have a zero balance—that is, you're all paid up
- cards on which you have a balance but are current—that is, you make at least the minimum payment each month, and
- cards on which you are in default—that is, you haven't made any payments in a while.

The Uncertain Future of Credit Cards

The information in this chapter is based on the history of credit card practices in the United States. This history may no longer be a guide to future policies. Because millions of people with previously solid credit scores may lose some or all of their income in the coming months and years, credit card issuers may radically change their policies, as to existing credit card accounts and the issuance of new cards to people who may be considered "subprime" because of a bankruptcy, foreclosure, or other causes of bad credit.

If Your Balance Is Zero

On your bankruptcy papers, you'll have to list your creditors—all of the people and businesses to whom you currently owe money. If you have a balance of zero on a credit card, you don't currently owe the card issuer any money and you don't have to list it on your bankruptcy papers. This means you *might* come through bankruptcy—Chapter 7 or Chapter 13—still owning that credit card. But there are exceptions.

The Trustee May Take Your Card

It's possible that the bankruptcy trustee will confiscate your credit cards, ask you about the creditors with whom you have a zero balance, or demand that you write to them and tell them about your bankruptcy. This is much more likely to happen in a Chapter 13 case, where the trustee must supervise your finances for three to five years, than in a Chapter 7 case, where the trustee won't care about debts you incur after filing.

The Credit Card Issuer May Find Out About Your Bankruptcy

Most credit card companies constantly troll your credit reports for any sign of economic weakness. For example, credit card companies often raise interest rates on cards if the cardholder makes a late payment on another card or to another creditor. Even if the credit card issuer in question doesn't check your credit report, other credit card companies may notify your company of your bankruptcy—a common practice. Either way, a credit card company with which you have a zero balance may find out about your bankruptcy even though you haven't listed it as a creditor.

EXAMPLE: You file for bankruptcy and include the following debts, among others: BigBank Visa, MediumBank MasterCard, and LittleBank Visa. Your balance on your

TinyBank MasterCard is $0, so you don't include that creditor on your bankruptcy papers. TinyBank learns of your bankruptcy anyway from the credit bureaus it checks to monitor the creditworthiness of its customers.

Your Credit Card Issuer May Cancel Your Zero-Balance Card

On learning of your bankruptcy, the company that issued your credit card may decide to terminate your account, even though you don't owe that business a penny, on the ground that you are no longer a good credit risk. On the other hand, some credit card companies will be happy to continue doing business with you on the ground you are now an excellent credit risk because you won't be able to file a Chapter 7 bankruptcy again for eight years.

Even if you lose all your credit cards in your bankruptcy, don't get too worked up over it. Especially if you file for Chapter 7 bankruptcy, there are other ways to get a credit card, if you really think you need one. Although you may have trouble getting a card with a large credit balance, you will be able to obtain a check card that gives you all the advantages of a credit card, with one important exception—the amount you can charge will be limited to the amount in your bank account (unless you opt into the bank's overdraft protection program—which many consumer advocates advise against).

The Trustee Might Recover Recent Payments on Your Credit Card

It may not be wise to pay off a credit card just before you file bankruptcy. When you file for

bankruptcy, you must indicate on your papers all of your recent financial transactions. For filers whose debts are primarily consumer debts, payments of more than $600 to any one creditor in the three months prior to filing may be retroactively cancelled. For filers whose debts are primarily business debts, payments of more than $5,475 to any one creditor in the three months prior to filing may be retroactively cancelled.

These "eve of bankruptcy" payments are called "preferences." The trustee can recover preferences from the creditor you paid and use the money for the benefit of all your creditors, not just the creditor who received the payment. There are exceptions to this rule for business debtors who make the payment in the normal course of their business, and for payments made for regular ongoing expenses like your mortgage or utilities (as opposed to one-time expenses, like paying off a delinquent bill).

So the bottom line is this: If you want to pay off a credit card balance before filing bankruptcy, your debts are primarily consumer debts, and the payments total $600 or more, you must wait at least 91 days after your last payment before filing. Of course, there is still no guarantee you will get to keep the card. If you don't get to keep the card, paying off the balance will have been a waste of money.

If You Owe Money but Are Current

If you owe money on a credit card but have managed to eke out at least a minimum payment each month, you will have to list this creditor on your bankruptcy papers even though you aren't behind. Your bankruptcy—

Chapter 7 or Chapter 13—may come as a great surprise to the creditor. In fact, credit card issuers have recently lamented the increase in "surprise" bankruptcies—cases filed by people not in default.

If you file for Chapter 7 bankruptcy and want to keep your credit card, you probably can do so by offering to sign a reaffirmation agreement with the credit card issuer. In a reaffirmation agreement, you agree to repay the balance in full, as if you never filed for bankruptcy. Under the new bankruptcy law, you will have to convince the court that reaffirming the debt is in your best interest. (See Ch. 6 for more on reaffirming debts.)

Reaffirming a Credit Card Debt May Not Be a Good Idea

Before you reaffirm a credit card debt, ask yourself whether it really makes sense. For most people, it doesn't. The purpose of filing for bankruptcy is to get rid of debts, not to still owe money. Admittedly, some people choose to file, even though they know that they won't be able to eliminate certain debts. But even in that situation, it almost never makes sense to come out of bankruptcy owing a credit card balance you had before you filed. More likely, you will come out of bankruptcy still owing taxes or a student loan. If you want to have a credit card after bankruptcy, chances are very good that you'll be able to get one (but one that starts with a zero balance, not with the amount you owed before you filed). A check card will probably serve all of your needs—and won't get you back into debt.

The credit card issuer may ask you to sign a reaffirmation agreement when you file for Chapter 7 bankruptcy, even if you intend to wipe out the debt. The creditor may offer tempting terms—a reduction in the interest rate, a reduction of the balance you owe, or an increase in your line of credit. But you should resist. To sign a reaffirmation agreement would probably defeat a major, if not the sole, reason you filed— to get rid of your credit card debt. (If the creditor gets insistent or starts claiming that you incurred the credit card debt fraudulently, you still have options—see Ch. 10.)

If you file for Chapter 13 bankruptcy, your plan will propose to repay your unsecured creditors, including your credit card issuers, some percentage of what you owe. Chapter 13 plans are sometimes referred to by this percentage— for example, "this couple filed a 55% plan." (Remember that unlike credit card debts, some types of debts, including priority debts and secured debts, must be repaid in full, even in Chapter 13. For more on secured debts, see Ch. 6.) In most cases, if you propose to pay less than 100% of what you owe on a card, the creditor will cancel your account. And the Chapter 13 trustee may confiscate your card anyway. ●

Your Job, Freedom, and Self-Respect

For most people, the thought of filing for bankruptcy raises a number of troubling questions. Many of these have to do with eliminating debts. (Those are answered in Ch. 3.) Other questions concern the potential loss of property. (Those are addressed in Chs. 4, 5, and 6.)

But many of the questions go beyond debts and assets and hit at the core of what it means to be a member of our society—earning a living, bringing up your children, and keeping your freedom and self-respect.

Will You Lose Your Self-Respect?

Americans learn almost from birth that it's a good thing to buy all sorts of goods and services. A highly paid army of persuaders surrounds us with thousands of seductive messages each day that say "Buy, buy, buy." Easily available credit makes living beyond our means easy—and resisting the siren sounds of the advertisers difficult. But we're also told that if we fail to pay for it all right on time, we're miserable deadbeats. In short, much of American economic life is built on a contradiction.

Adding to this contradiction is the system of high interest and penalties employed by most credit card companies that cause our debt to soar beyond any reasonable expectation. In many cases, the interest rates are so high that the companies involved would have been prosecuted for loan sharking in the not-too-distant past—before the credit card industry systematically lobbied to do away with usury laws or to create exceptions to those laws for credit card interest rates.

Credit card companies keep this system working by encouraging us to make the minimum payment, which stimulates us to make more credit purchases and eases us into debt loads far beyond our ability to ever pay them off. We now all owe our soul to the company store. To feel guilty about being caught in this deliberately contrived economic trap is nonsense. There's much more to life than an A+ credit rating and bigger things to feel guilty about than the failure to pay bills on time—especially those owed to the credit card companies.

Fortunately, for thousands of years, it's been recognized that debts can get the better of even the most conscientious among us. From Biblical times to the present, sane societies have discouraged debtors from falling on their swords and have provided sensible ways for debt-oppressed people to start new economic lives. In the United States, this is done through bankruptcy.

Until very recently, filing bankruptcy was a dignified way to achieve a fresh start in a world filled with economic uncertainty. The law presumed that bankruptcy filers were honest citizens seeking to get rid of their debt and start over, sadder but wiser. Unfortunately, thanks to provisions written primarily by the credit card industry, the bankruptcy law of 2005 turned this presumption on its head and views each debtor as a potential bankruptcy cheat.

While this change in attitude won't prevent you from achieving a bankruptcy discharge in most cases—because you, like most other filers, are in fact honest—it does have the potential to make you feel bad about yourself. But don't fall into this trap. Bankruptcy is a truly worthy part of our legal system, based as it is on forgiveness rather than retribution. Certainly, it gives people a fresh start in our increasingly volatile economy, helps keep families together, reduces suicide rates, and keeps the ranks of the homeless from growing even larger. So, don't let the word "bankruptcy" get you down.

What About Friendly Creditors?

While you may not care about discharging your credit card debts in bankruptcy, you may feel bad about doing the same to the debts you owe to friends, family, or business creditors in your community—such as a doctor, dentist, chiropractor, pharmacist, accountant, lawyer, contractor, or hardware store. While debts you owe to these creditors will most likely be discharged in your bankruptcy—because you have to list *all* debts you know of in your bankruptcy papers—there is nothing to prevent you from voluntarily paying the debts after you file. Communicating your intent to repay to these friendly creditors will make everybody involved feel a whole lot better about your bankruptcy.

Will You Lose Your Job?

No employer—government or private—may fire you because you filed for bankruptcy. Nor may an employer discriminate against you in other terms and conditions of employment—for example, by reducing your salary, demoting you, or taking away responsibilities—because of your bankruptcy.

Termination for Other Reasons

If there are other valid reasons for taking these actions, the fact that you filed for bankruptcy won't protect you. In other words, an employer who wants to take negative action against you can do so provided there are other valid reasons to explain the action—such as tardiness, dishonesty, or incompetence. But if you are fired shortly after your bankruptcy is brought to your employer's attention, you might have a case against the employer for illegal discrimination because of your bankruptcy.

How Employers Find Out About Bankruptcy Filings

In practice, employers rarely find out about a Chapter 7 bankruptcy filing. However, if a creditor has sued you, obtained a judgment, and started garnishing your wages, your employer will get the news. The bankruptcy will stop the wage garnishment, and your employer will be notified about it. In such a situation, your employer (or at least the payroll department) already knew you were having financial problems and will probably welcome the bankruptcy as a way for you to take affirmative steps to put your problems behind you.

If you file for Chapter 13 bankruptcy, your employer is likely to learn of your bankruptcy case. If you have a regular job with regular income, the bankruptcy judge may order your Chapter 13 payments to be automatically deducted from your wages and sent to the bankruptcy court. (This is called an "income deduction order.") In effect, your employer will be pressed into service as a sort of collection agency, to make sure you honor your Chapter 13 plan.

Income Deduction Orders Work

You may not like the idea of the income deduction order, but the bankruptcy court is likely to deny your Chapter 13 plan if you refuse to comply with it. And the order will probably make it easier for you to complete your plan. The success rate of Chapter 13 cases is higher for debtors with income deduction orders than for debtors who pay the trustee themselves, for the very obvious reason that it's hard to spend money you never lay hands on.

Security Clearances

Many jobs require a security clearance. If you are a member of the armed forces or an employee of the CIA, FBI, another government agency, or a private company that contracts with the government, you may have a security clearance. Do you risk losing your security clearance if you file for bankruptcy? Probably not—in fact, the opposite may be true. According to credit counselors for the military and the CIA, a person with financial problems—particularly someone with a lot of debt—is at high risk for being blackmailed. By filing for bankruptcy and getting rid of the debts, you substantially lower that risk. Bankruptcy usually works more in your favor than to your detriment.

Effect of Bankruptcy on Job Applicants

No federal, state, or local government agency may take your bankruptcy into consideration when deciding whether to hire you. There is no corresponding rule for private employers, however, and some people find that having a bankruptcy in their past comes back to haunt them, particularly when applying for jobs that require them to deal with money (bookkeeping, accounting, payroll, and so on).

Many private employers conduct a credit check on job applicants as a matter of course and will find out about your bankruptcy from the credit report. While employers need your permission to run a credit check, employers can also refuse to hire you if you don't consent. If you're asked to give this authorization, consider speaking candidly about what the employer will find in your file. Being honest up front about problems that are truly behind you may outweigh any negative effects of the bankruptcy filing itself.

Other Forms of Discrimination Because of Bankruptcy

Federal, state, and local governmental units can't legally discriminate against you because you filed for bankruptcy.

Discrimination by Government Agencies

Governmental units may not deny, revoke, suspend, or refuse to renew a license, permit, charter, franchise, or other similar grant on the basis of your bankruptcy. Judges interpreting this law have ruled that the government cannot:

- deny or terminate public benefits
- deny or evict you from public housing
- deny or refuse to renew your state liquor license
- exclude you from participating in a state home mortgage finance program
- withhold your college transcript
- deny you a driver's license
- deny you a contract, such as a contract for a construction project, or
- exclude you from participating in a government-guaranteed student loan program.

In general, once any government-related debt has been discharged, all acts against you that arise out of that debt must also end. If, for example, you lost your driver's license because you didn't pay a civil court judgment that resulted from a car accident, you must be granted a license once the debt is discharged. If the debt isn't discharged, however, you can still be denied your license until you pay up.

Discrimination by Private Entities

Prohibitions against private discrimination aren't nearly as broad as prohibitions against government discrimination. As mentioned above, private employers may not fire you or punish you because you filed for bankruptcy. Other forms of discrimination in the private sector, however, such as denying you rental housing, a surety bond, or withholding a college transcript, are legal.

The best way to confront this type of discrimination is to build a solid credit history after bankruptcy. You can find sound strategies for getting back on your financial feet in *Credit Repair*, by Robin Leonard and Margaret Reiter (Nolo).

If a potential landlord does a credit check, sees your bankruptcy, and refuses to rent to you, there's not much you can do except try to show that you'll pay your rent and be a responsible tenant. You probably will need to go apartment hunting with a "renter's résumé" that shows you in the best possible light. Be ready to offer a cosigner, find roommates, offer to pay more rent, or even pay several months' rent up front in cash.

Effect of Bankruptcy on Child Custody

There are no reported cases from any state of a parent losing custody because he or she filed for bankruptcy. Bankruptcy and divorce (or separation) are so often related these days that one frequently follows the other. Bankruptcy judges are becoming experts on family law matters, and family law judges are becoming experts in bankruptcy. Don't worry about your bankruptcy affecting your custody status. Keep in mind, however, that bankruptcy does not relieve you of your child support and alimony obligations, past or present.

Effect of Bankruptcy on Your Freedoms

We Americans are used to some basic freedoms, and many people fear the loss of those freedoms if they file for bankruptcy. Relax. Except in some unusual cases, this is just not going to happen.

Consequences of Dishonesty

When you file for bankruptcy, you swear, under "penalty of perjury," that everything in your papers is true to the best of your knowledge. If you deliberately commit a dishonest act, such as failing to disclose property, omitting material information about your financial affairs, unloading nonexempt assets just before filing (especially if you don't disclose the transfer), or using a false Social Security number (to hide your identity as a prior filer), you can be criminally prosecuted for fraud.

While such prosecution has been rare in the past, the 2005 bankruptcy law streamlines the process by which fraud-related cases can be referred to the U.S. Attorney's office for prosecution. Also, the new law requires the government to audit one out of every 250 bankruptcy cases, which means you are more likely to face an audit than bankruptcy filers in the past. More than ever, it is important to disclose all of your property and debts in your bankruptcy papers, provide accurate answers to the questions in the Statement of Financial Affairs (see Ch. 10), and not try to hide property from the trustee or your creditors prior to filing.

Examples of criminal prosecutions under the old law abound. A debtor in Massachusetts went to jail for failing to list on his bankruptcy papers his interest in a condominium and $26,000 worth of jewelry. Another Massachusetts debtor served time for listing her home on her bankruptcy papers as worth $70,000 when it had been appraised for $116,000. An Alaska debtor was jailed for failing to disclose buried cash and diamonds. A Pennsylvania debtor omitted from her papers $50,000 from a divorce settlement and was sentenced to some time in prison.

The message is simple: Bankruptcy is geared toward the honest debtor who inadvertently gets in too deep and needs the help of the bankruptcy court to get a fresh start. A bankruptcy judge will not help someone who has played fast and loose with creditors or tries to do so with the bankruptcy court. If you lie, hide, or cheat, it may come back to haunt you in ways much worse than your current debt crisis ever could.

Moving

You are free to change your residence after you file. Just be sure to send the trustee and court a written notification of change of address if your case is still open. If your move involves selling your house and you've filed for Chapter 13 bankruptcy, the trustee may want to use proceeds of the sale to pay off your creditors (if your plan doesn't already propose full payment).

Changing Jobs

You can certainly change jobs while your bankruptcy case is pending, and after it ends. If you've filed a Chapter 13 case, be sure to tell the trustee so he or she can transfer the income deduction order.

Divorce

No one can force you to stay married, not even a bankruptcy judge. Here's how a divorce will fit (or not) into your bankruptcy.

Chapter 7. If you've filed for Chapter 7 bankruptcy and want to end your marriage, go ahead. Your bankruptcy case will probably end long before your divorce case does. However, it often makes sense to wait until a divorce is completed before filing for bankruptcy. Your property ownership and personal debt situation will be much clearer after your divorce becomes final—and your marital debts and property have been divided between you and your former spouse.

On the other hand, if you assume responsibility for debts in a divorce, you will still owe those debts after your bankruptcy to the extent that the creditor goes after your ex. For instance, if you agree in your divorce agreement to pay off a particular credit card and then you file bankruptcy, your liability to the creditor is discharged, but you are still responsible to your ex if the credit card company sues him or her for the amount owed. For this reason, it sometimes makes sense to file bankruptcy before you assume responsibility for any debt in the course of your divorce. Note that unlike the situation in Chapter 7, in Chapter 13 you are permitted to fully discharge debt you've assumed responsibility for in your divorce.

Chapter 13. If you've filed a Chapter 13 case with your spouse, you may face some complications if you want to continue your case and get divorced. Bankruptcy law states that you must be a married couple to be eligible to file a joint case. If you divorce, you are no longer eligible to file (or maintain) a joint Chapter 13 case, at least in theory. The trustee could file a motion to dismiss your case. Some trustees have been known to ignore a divorce if both spouses want to keep the Chapter 13 going and continue to make the payments. Even so, you will probably want to ask the divorce court to handle your divorce in two stages ("bifurcate," in legalese) so that your marital status changes from married to divorced, but the final division of marital property and debts is postponed until your Chapter 13 case ends. You could simplify matters by separating, but not divorcing. In either situation, be sure to let the trustee know what's happening and where to reach you if you move.

 TIP

Who's going to know? It's highly unusual for anyone to find out about your bankruptcy other than your creditors, businesses that obtain a copy of your credit report, and the people you tell. Although your bankruptcy filing will be published in a local newspaper, these notices often appear in low-circulation papers, and few people sit around reading these notices anyway. Bankruptcy filings aren't broadcast on local television or radio.

Bankruptcy Forms and Procedures

When the bankruptcy laws radically changed in 2005, lawyers and journalists alike were quick to point out that Chapter 7 bankruptcy was no longer available to many filers, primarily due to the new means test requirements and the increased costs resulting from due diligence obligations placed on bankruptcy lawyers. While it's true that lawyers' fees have doubled in many areas, Chapter 7 bankruptcy is still a straightforward process for most filers. You can look forward to smooth sailing—whether you represent yourself or are represented by a lawyer—if all of the following are true in your situation:

- Your average gross monthly income over the six-month period prior to the month you file is less than the median income for a household of your size in the state where you are filing (which fits most would-be filers).
- If you are in business for yourself: Your business has little or no assets or inventory.
- Your only real estate is your home and you have little or no equity in it.
- You have lived in the state where you are filing for at least two years.
- Your net income doesn't exceed your reasonable living expenses by more than a few hundred dollars.
- You haven't given any property away (or sold it for less than it's worth) during the previous two years.
- Property you care about keeping is clearly exempt (that is, the trustee can't take it under your state's exemption laws or, if available in your state, under the federal exemption law).
- You haven't repaid a debt owed to a relative or business associate within the previous year.

If you meet all of these criteria, it is unlikely that your case will produce any disputes that will have to be resolved by a bankruptcy judge, rather than by agreement between you and the trustee or your creditors. Your only personal appearance is likely to be at the creditors' meeting (see Ch. 1). However, if you are reaffirming a car note or other debt connected to collateral, you will have to appear at a brief hearing where the bankruptcy judge will decide whether reaffirmation is in your best interest (see Ch. 6 for more on the reaffirmation hearing). The point is, there is nothing in a simple Chapter 7 bankruptcy that would require you to be represented by a lawyer—no matter what they tell you. But, to the extent that your case is more complex— perhaps because of multiple real estate holdings, an ongoing retail business, or inappropriate prebankruptcy transfers of property—it makes good sense to hire a lawyer in order to achieve the best possible result.

Some brief descriptions of the Chapter 7 proceedings that might require some legal help are explained in this chapter. (Ch. 11 explains what type of help is available and how to find it.)

While many Chapter 7 filers successfully represent themselves, most people who file for Chapter 13 bankruptcy hire an attorney to represent them. Chapter 13 bankruptcy is usually too difficult for people to successfully complete without representation. Some of the trouble points are outlined later in this chapter.

If, after you file your bankruptcy, you want to change course and convert to another type of bankruptcy or get out of bankruptcy altogether, you'll find the rules that apply in this chapter. And, no matter what type of bankruptcy you file, you can look forward to completing plenty of paperwork. The basic forms required in both types of bankruptcy are explained in this chapter as well.

The Means Test

A single dollar's difference in your income can have a large impact on your bankruptcy plans. If your "current monthly income" (CMI, defined and described in Ch. 2) is one dollar less than your state's median income, you can:

- file for Chapter 7 bankruptcy without completing the means test (Form 22A)
- use your actual expenses (rather than the IRS's expense standards, which are often lower) to compute your disposable income (and thus your Chapter 13 plan payments), and
- propose a three-year plan if you file for Chapter 13 bankruptcy.

On the other hand, if your CMI is even one dollar more than the state's median income, you must:

- complete the means test and produce results showing that you have insufficient funds in your budget to support a Chapter 13 repayment plan
- use the IRS standards to compute your disposable income if you decide to file a Chapter 13 bankruptcy, and
- propose a five-year plan if you file for Chapter 13 bankruptcy.

For many filers, this won't be a close call: It will be fairly easy to figure out where you stand. In fact, only about 15% of bankruptcy filers don't pass the means test. But how should you proceed if a modest change in your income or expenses would put you below the median income or change the outcome of the means test?

Sometimes waiting a month or two before filing will take care of the problem. For example, if you have recently become unemployed but your income for the months prior to your unemployment put you over the top, just waiting another month might sufficiently lower your average income for the six-month period to squeeze you under the bar. Let's see how this works. Assume Denis makes an average monthly gross income of $5,000 for the five-month period of March through July 2011. He gets laid off in August and receives $1,800 in unemployment insurance payments. His average gross income for the entire six-month period (March to August) is $4,466. If Denis files bankruptcy in September, his average monthly gross income for the preceding six-month period will exceed the median income or a family of his size ($4,000). However, if Denis waits another month to file, his average income for the six-month period preceding his filing date will decrease to $3,933, putting him under the median income level applicable to his case.

If waiting to file bankruptcy won't solve the problem, the stakes may well be worth the cost of a consultation with a bankruptcy attorney who will be familiar with the categories and definitions of income and expenses. In addition to appreciating the nuances contained within the means test, attorneys in close cases can raise novel arguments on behalf of their clients. These arguments result in court decisions that a bankruptcy attorney can use to suggest legal ways to decrease your income or increase your expenses to achieve a more desirable outcome. For example, some courts allow you to claim an ownership expense for your car even though you own it outright, while other courts don't allow this expense. In 2011, this issue will be decided by the U.S. Supreme Court in *Ransom v. MBNA (American Bank)*. Only an attorney familiar with your local court's practices would know how to handle this issue. Also, in some courts you can file a Chapter 13 bankruptcy and then later convert the case to Chapter 7 without having to take the means test. This might not be the most direct route to your objective—a Chapter 7 discharge—but it would still get the job done.

Challenges for Abuse

Bankruptcy law describes two kinds of abuse that can sink your Chapter 7 filing:

- failure to pass the means test (known as presumptive abuse because the trustee will presume that you aren't entitled to file under Chapter 7 if you flunk the means test), and
- abuse under the totality of the circumstances (general abuse).

If abuse is presumed because you fail the means test, you may not be allowed to proceed with your Chapter 7 bankruptcy unless you can rebut the presumption by showing special circumstances (see "Defending a Motion to Dismiss or Convert," below). If you are accused of abuse under the totality of the circumstances, however, the party bringing the charge (usually the U.S. Trustee) has the burden of proving abuse. Needless to say, you are much more likely to be barred from Chapter 7 when abuse is presumed than when it must be proved.

 TIP

Abuse laws apply only to consumer cases. The law on abuse, both general and presumed, applies only to filers with primarily consumer debts. Filers who have primarily business debts are not subject to abuse motions on either general or presumptive grounds. Your debts are primarily business debts if more than half of the total value of your debt arises from the operation of a business.

If you file under Chapter 7, you won't know for sure whether your bankruptcy filing will be challenged on abuse grounds until the trustee (or in some cases, a creditor) asks for a court hearing to dismiss or convert your case.

Presumed Abuse

If your bankruptcy paperwork demonstrates that you don't pass the means test, you can expect the U.S. Trustee to file a motion to dismiss your case or (with your consent) convert the case to Chapter 13. The regular trustee or any creditor can also file a motion to dismiss or convert your case on the grounds of abuse, but the U.S. Trustee will probably be the one bringing the motion. The U.S. Trustee is legally responsible for assessing your eligibility for Chapter 7 bankruptcy and otherwise seeing that the bankruptcy laws are complied with.

General Abuse

As mentioned, even if you pass—or don't have to take—the means test, your Chapter 7 filing can still be challenged for general abuse.

If You Pass the Means Test

If you were subject to the means test but passed it on the face of your paperwork, the court, U.S. Trustee, regular trustee, or a creditor can still file a motion to dismiss your bankruptcy or convert it to Chapter 13 if the totality of the circumstances demonstrates abuse. For example, the new bankruptcy law indicates that you could be subject to an abuse motion if you seek to reject a personal services contract—a contract in which you've agreed to provide services to another person or business—without adequate financial justification. For instance, if you sign a three-year recording contract and then file for Chapter 7 bankruptcy just to get out of it, your case could be challenged on general abuse grounds.

If Your Income Is Less Than Your State's Median Income

If your average monthly income (calculated according to the formula explained in Ch. 2, "Calculating Your Income Status") is less than the state's median income, you aren't subject to the means test and your filing won't be presumed to be abusive. Your Chapter 7 filing can still be challenged on the ground of general abuse, but only if the judge or U.S. Trustee files the motion; no creditors allowed at this party. Again, absent the presumption, the court or U.S. Trustee must prove abuse.

The U.S. Trustee is likely to challenge your Chapter 7 bankruptcy filing on general abuse grounds if you could easily propose a feasible Chapter 13 plan, even though you weren't subject to the means test. For instance, if you otherwise qualify for Chapter 13 and can pay $10,950 or more over a five-year period toward a Chapter 13 plan—or you could pay at least 25% of your unsecured, nonpriority debt—you might be facing an abuse motion.

For example, during the previous six months, suppose Julian and Edna's combined average monthly gross income is $7,000, which is $1,500 a month over the median income for a similarly sized family. They pass the means test because they have a number of large deductions, including $1,000 a month for two car notes and $3,500 for their mortgage. As it turns out, shortly before filing, Julian gets a large raise, and his and Edna's actual monthly net income exceeds their actual living expenses by $700 (well over the $10,950 for a five-year period). The U.S. Trustee files a motion to dismiss or convert the bankruptcy on the ground that a Chapter 7 filing would constitute an abuse under all the circumstances. His reasoning is that there is enough excess actual income to fund a Chapter 13 plan, and because Julian and Edna are spending more for their car notes and mortgage than is reasonable in their particular situation. Following other cases decided by courts in his district, the bankruptcy judge grants the motion, giving Julian and Edna 15 days to either convert their case to Chapter 13 or have it dismissed.

Motions to Dismiss for Abuse Under All the Circumstances

As we've explained, it's possible to have your case dismissed if it appears that your Chapter 7 filing is an abuse of the bankruptcy code under all the circumstances. Motions to dismiss for this reason tend to focus primarily on whether the debtor's expenses are unnecessarily extravagant. For example, an Ohio bankruptcy court ruled that a mortgage expense on a $400,000 home and an expense for repayment of a 401(k) loan should not be allowed. Without those expenses, the debtors had adequate income to fund a Chapter 13 plan, which made their case an abuse under all the circumstances. (*In Re Felske*, 385 B.R. 649 (N.D. Ohio 2008).)

The grounds for dismissal don't necessarily have to exist when you file for bankruptcy. One appellate court ruled that a motion to dismiss for abuse may be brought on the basis of events occurring anytime before the discharge. (*In re Cortez*, 457 F.3d 448 (5th Cir. 2006).) So if you get a new job or win the lottery, or some other event happens while your case is pending that would enable you to proceed under Chapter 13, you may face a challenge to your Chapter 7 case. (See also *In re Henebury*, 361 B.R. 595 (S.D. Fla. 2007).)

If you face dismissal on this ground, you will need to explain why it's unlikely you could complete a Chapter 13 bankruptcy, or why expenses that are challenged by the trustee are really necessary for you to get a fresh start. There is no clear test of what constitutes abuse under all the circumstances. As with obscenity, the judges will know it when they see it. Fortunately, the U.S. Trustee (usually the party bringing these motions) has the burden of proving the abuse. If you pass the means test, your eligibility for Chapter 7 bankruptcy is presumed and the trustee has to overcome that presumption.

Charitable Contributions

Assuming you have a record of making set charitable contributions to a qualified religious or charitable entity or organization, a court many not consider these contributions as part of your disposable income. In other words, the trustee cannot argue that you should pay your money into a Chapter 13 repayment plan rather than to the charity of your choice.

EXAMPLE: You pass the means test but the U.S. Trustee files a motion to dismiss your case for abuse because you give 25% of your income to your church (and have over a substantial period of time). The U.S. Trustee argues that if you only tithed (gave 10% of your income), you could propose a feasible Chapter 13 repayment plan. Following this new law, the court dismisses the U.S. Trustee's motion and allows your Chapter 7 bankruptcy to proceed.

Court Procedures

If you fail the means test, the U.S. Trustee must file a statement indicating whether your filing should be considered an abuse within ten days after your meeting of creditors. (See Ch. 1 for more on this meeting.) Five days after the U.S. Trustee's statement is filed, the court must send the notice to all of your creditors, to let them know about the U.S. Trustee's assessment and to give them an opportunity to file their own motion to dismiss or convert on abuse grounds, if they desire.

Within 30 days after filing this statement, the U.S. Trustee must either:

- file a motion to dismiss or convert your case on grounds of abuse, or
- explain why a motion to convert or dismiss isn't appropriate (for example, because you passed the means test).

If your income is below the state median income, the U.S. Trustee doesn't have to file either statement, because abuse will not be presumed. However, your filing can still be challenged for general abuse, as explained earlier.

Note that these duties and time limits apply only to the U.S. Trustee. If your income is more than the state median, your creditors can file a motion to dismiss or convert anytime after you file, but no later than 60 days after the first date set for your creditors' meeting.

Defending a Motion to Dismiss or Convert

If the U.S. Trustee (or the trustee or a creditor in appropriate circumstances) files a motion to dismiss or convert your case, you are entitled to notice of the hearing at least 20 days in advance. You will receive papers in the mail explaining the grounds for the motion and what you need to do to respond. If the motion to dismiss or convert is based on presumed abuse, the burden is on you to prove that your filing is not abusive. If the motion is based on general abuse, you only have to show up at the hearing to argue that it should be denied. However, it's a good idea to also file an opposition to the motion, at least five days before the hearing.

Presumed Abuse

If the motion to dismiss or convert is based on your failure to pass the means test, your only defense is to show "special circumstances." However, it's not enough to show that these circumstances exist: You must also show that they justify additional expenses or adjustments of current monthly income "for which there is no reasonable alternative."

In order to establish special circumstances, you must itemize each additional expense or adjustment of income and provide:

- documentation for the expense or adjustment, and
- a detailed explanation of the special circumstances that make the expense or adjustment necessary and reasonable.

You will win only if the additional expenses or adjustments to income enable you to pass the means test.

EXAMPLE: Maureen and Ralph have a child (Sarah) with severe autism. Sarah is making remarkable progress in her private school, for which Maureen and Ralph pay $1,000 a month. No equivalent school is available at a lower tuition. Under the means test guidelines, Maureen and Ralph are entitled to deduct only $1,650 a year from their income for private school expenses. If Maureen and Ralph were allowed to deduct the full $1,000 monthly tuition, they would easily pass the means test. By documenting Sarah's condition, the necessity for the extra educational expense, and the fact that moving her to a less expensive school would greatly undermine her progress, Maureen and Ralph would have a good chance of

convincing the court to allow the $1,000 expense, which would in turn rebut the presumption of abuse.

Bankruptcy courts have issued written decisions on a variety of special circumstance claims. If you need to prove special circumstances to pass the mean test, you will definitely want to check with a local attorney or do your own research to find out how bankruptcy court or the courts in your state have treated the special circumstances you're claiming.

A frequently addressed issue is whether payments on nondischargeable student loans can be considered a special circumstance. While a few courts have held that they can be, more courts have gone the other way and ruled that student loan payments do not constitute special circumstances. (See, for example, *In re Champagne*, 389 B.R. 191 (Bkrtcy Kan. 2008) and *In re Pageau*, 383 B.R. 281 (S.D. Ind. 2008).)

Here are some cases in which the court has allowed a particular special circumstances claim, but remember that courts in your area may see the issue differently:

- unusually high transportation expenses (*In re Batzkiel,* 349 B.R. 581 (Bkrtcy N.D. Iowa 2006); *In re Turner,* 376 B.R. 370 (Bkrtcy D. N.H. 2007))
- mandatory repayment of 401(k) loan (*In re Lenton,* 358 B.R. 651 (Bkrtcy E.D. Pa. 2006))
- reduction in income (*In re Martin,* 371 B.R. 347 (Bkrtcy C.D. Ill. 2007) (diminished future availability of overtime hours); *In re Tamez,* No. 07-60047 (Bkrtcy W.D. Tex. 2007) (reduction in income due to voluntary job changes))

- wife's pregnancy in a joint case (*In re Martin,* 371 B.R. 347 (Bkrtcy C.D. Ill. 2007))
- joint debtors who have two separate households (*In re Graham*, 363 B.R. 844 (Bkrtcy S.D. Ohio 2007); *In re Armstrong*, No. 06-31414 (Bkrtcy N.D. Ohio 2007))
- unusually high rent expenses (*In re Scarafiotti*, 375 B.R. 618 (Bkrtcy D. Colorado 2007)), and
- court-ordered child support payments (*In re Littman,* 370 B.R. 820 (Bkrtcy D. Idaho 2007)).

In addition, the U.S. Trustee's office recently provided some guidance on this issue, noting that it may consider as special circumstances the following:

- job loss or reduction in income for which there is no reasonable alternative
- a one-time "bump" in prepetition income that is not likely to happen again
- the debtors have separate households due to pending divorce or job relocation, and have filed a joint bankruptcy petition, and
- a postpetition household size increase due to pregnancy or a reasonable need to support an additional person.

General Abuse

If your filing is challenged for general abuse, the party bringing the motion to dismiss or convert has the burden of proof. If the motion is based on your ability to fund a Chapter 13 plan (even though you passed the means test), you can raise any special expense you have—for example, necessary private tuition, extraordinary child care expenses, or legal fees associated with a continuing legal action—to demonstrate your inability to fund a Chapter 13 plan.

Valuation Hearings

There are two situations when you may need to ask the court to assign a value to a car or other personal property. In a Chapter 7 bankruptcy, you may need a valuation if you propose to redeem property that you are making payments on. (See Ch. 6 for more on redemption.) If the property's replacement value (what the property could be purchased for in a retail market, considering its age and condition) is less than the debt, you can pay the replacement value in a lump sum and own the property outright.

In a Chapter 13 bankruptcy, you may want the court to determine the replacement value of property that is collateral for a secured debt. If the replacement value is less than the debt, your repayment plan can pay the replacement value. This is called a "cramdown." For example, suppose you owe $13,000 on your car, and its replacement value is $8,000. You can propose to pay $8,000 in equal payments over the life of your plan and then own the car outright once you obtain a discharge. If you fail to complete your Chapter 13 plan, the cramdown is cancelled and you must pay the full balance of your debt before obtaining title.

There are three important exceptions to the cramdown rule. First, you can't cram down a debt owed on a motor vehicle purchased within 30 months of your filing date. Second, you can't cram down a debt owed on other personal property purchased within a year of your filing date. Third, you can't cram down a mortgage that is used exclusively for your primary residence.

RESOURCE

Getting evidence of value. For cars, *Kelley Blue Book* appraisals are a good start (www.kbb.com). Another good place to look is the website of the National Automobile Dealers Association, www.nada.com, which is recommended by the courts. However, you and the creditor may disagree about the car's value because of its condition, something these websites can't shed much light on. In that case, a private appraisal would be persuasive.

To get a valuation hearing, you or a creditor must file a motion. These motions are handled in the same way as the other motions discussed in "Common Chapter 7 Motions and Proceedings," just below. If you or a creditor requests a valuation hearing in Chapter 13, the court will either postpone your confirmation hearing or hold the valuation hearing immediately before the confirmation hearing.

Common Chapter 7 Motions and Proceedings

In very simple Chapter 7 cases, you will probably have to attend only one official proceeding: the creditors' meeting, supervised by the trustee. But if your Chapter 7 case involves issues that must be decided by a bankruptcy judge—for example, if you are facing a motion to dismiss or convert for abuse—you, or someone helping you, must know the required court procedures. You will have to either take the time to learn how to represent yourself or consult an attorney who already knows what needs to be done. You can also get help from bankruptcy petition preparers, but they are allowed only to fill in the bankruptcy

forms in accordance with your instructions— they can't give you legal advice or appear for you in court. (See Ch. 11 for more information on bankruptcy petition preparers.)

This section briefly describes some of the more common court proceedings that might be required in a Chapter 7 bankruptcy (in addition to the abuse motion to dismiss or convert discussed above). This will give you an idea of what you'll be facing if one of these issues pops up in your case.

RESOURCE

Use Nolo resources to help you through the litigation maze. Nolo's *How to File for Chapter 7 Bankruptcy*, by Stephen R. Elias, Albin Renauer, and Robin Leonard, provides guidance for some of these procedures. *Represent Yourself in Court*, by Paul Bergman and Sara J. Berman (Nolo), also has an excellent chapter on litigating in bankruptcy court. For a plain-English guide to making your way through law books and other resources, see *Legal Research: How to Find & Understand the Law*, by Stephen R. Elias and Susan Levinkind (Nolo).

Hearing on Relief From Stay

A creditor who wants to collect from you directly may request relief from the automatic stay in order to do so. This is called a "relief from stay" hearing. (For more on the automatic stay, see Ch. 1.) This could come up, for example, if you are behind on your mortgage or car payments.

The creditor asks for this type of hearing by filing a motion in the bankruptcy case. The creditor doesn't need to file a separate lawsuit, as it would with some other types of disputes within a bankruptcy case. The work you have to do to oppose the request and get your side of the case heard in court is not all that difficult. However, you may need to do a little legal research.

CAUTION

Always follow the rules when giving notice. When a debtor is required to give a creditor notice, the notice must contain the debtor's Social Security number and be sent to the contact address and account number that is listed on at least two written communications received from the creditor within the 180 days prior to the bankruptcy filing (or just the two most recent communications, if the debtor hasn't received two in the previous 180 days). If you don't provide notice in this way, the creditor may not be fined if it violates the automatic stay because it did not receive notice (see Ch. 1).

Common Motion Procedures

There are many types of motions. The two main varieties are called "ex parte" motions and "noticed" motions. Ex parte motions are easier to bring because you don't have to send formal notice to all of the parties or schedule a court hearing. These are used primarily for administrative issues that are not controversial, such as a request to reopen a case or to get permission to shorten the required time for giving notice.

Noticed motions are more complex. One party files the motion and sends notice of what is requested to the appropriate parties (this is called "serving" the parties). The notice is accompanied by a legal argument (points and authorities) and a declaration—a sworn statement that sets out the facts of the case under penalty of perjury.

The notice typically includes the date and time at which the court will hear the motion. Sometimes, the notice states that a hearing will be set only if the party served with the motion wants to oppose it. If a hearing is set, all parties must receive notice at least 20 days in advance.

The party against whom the motion is brought typically can file a written opposition to the motion at any time up to five days before the hearing. Other parties in all bankruptcy motion proceedings are the U.S. Trustee and the regular trustee.

The bankruptcy judge will hear argument on the motion and either rule right then and there (from the bench) or take the matter under submission (take it back to his or her chambers and think about it for a while). When the judge makes a decision, he or she typically issues a written decision and orders the prevailing party to prepare a formal order.

Either party may appeal the motion to a U.S. District Court or a Bankruptcy Appellate Panel (if one has been established in the district where the case is heard). Notice of appeal must usually be filed with the bankruptcy court *within ten days* of the date the court's decision or order is "entered." If you don't file this notice on time, you will almost surely lose your right to appeal.

Dischargeability Hearing

Ch. 3 explains that some types of debts survive your bankruptcy only if the creditor comes into court and challenges the proposed discharge of the debt. In addition, student loans and certain other types of debts will be discharged only if you (the debtor) file a separate action in the bankruptcy court against the creditor and convince the judge that the debt should be discharged. These court procedures that determine whether debts survive a bankruptcy are called "dischargeability" actions.

Debtors are most likely to bring dischargeability actions to discharge a student loan on the basis of hardship, or to cancel a tax debt on the basis that it meets the requirements for discharge under the bankruptcy code. Creditors are most likely to bring a dischargeability action alleging that a debtor incurred a debt through fraudulent means or caused personal injury through drunk driving or a willful and malicious act.

To start a dischargeability action, a creditor (or you) must file a separate complaint in the bankruptcy court, formally serve the complaint on the other party, and move the case forward to trial before the bankruptcy judge. This requires considerable research and knowledge of court rules. You are likely to have one or two false starts, in which the clerk returns your paperwork or the court tells you to try again. Dealing with formal court procedures can be quite frustrating for self-represented people. On the other hand, if there is enough money at stake, it may be worth your while to spend the time and deal with the frustration that comes with formal court litigation.

Of course, you can hire a bankruptcy attorney just for this part of your case, if there is enough at stake to justify paying the attorney's fees and you are able to find an attorney willing to provide limited services. (See Ch. 11.)

Reaffirmation Hearing

If you aren't represented by an attorney and have agreed with a creditor to "reaffirm" a debt (to recommit yourself to personal liability for the car note or other secured debt, despite your bankruptcy discharge), you will have to attend a hearing at which the judge will warn you of the consequences of reaffirmation: You'll continue to owe the full debt, you may lose the collateral if you default on your payments, and in many states, the creditor can sue you for any balance due after the property is sold at auction.

In some cases, the court will decide (on the basis of the debtor's income and expenses) that making the payments would be too much of a hardship to the debtor after bankruptcy, and will disallow the reaffirmation agreement.

The bankruptcy laws state that you have to enter into an agreement with the lender (assuming the lender requires it), but say nothing about what happens if the judge disallows the agreement. Courts have ruled that you are entitled to keep your vehicle if the only reason the car note is not reaffirmed is that the judge wouldn't allow it. Along this line, when disapproving reaffirmation agreements, some judges order lenders to refrain from repossessing cars as long as debtors are current on their payments. As a general rule, you are better off having the judge disapprove the reaffirmation agreement, since you'll then be able to keep the vehicle as long as you remain current, but you won't owe the car note if you have to give the car back sometime after your bankruptcy is over.

Lien Avoidance Motions

Ch. 6 explains that certain types of liens can be removed from your property in a Chapter 7 bankruptcy case. To do this, you need to file a motion to "avoid" the lien. As with other motions, you must mail the lienholder a written explanation of what you want (to avoid the lien) and why you are entitled to it. You must also provide the lien owner with a notice explaining what the lien owner must do to respond (in order to keep the lien). If there is no response, you can obtain an order to avoid the lien by default. If the creditor responds, you can set the matter for hearing. Sometimes, you set the matter for hearing in your initial notice—it all depends on the rules for your bankruptcy court's district.

Converting From One Chapter to Another

The bankruptcy law allows you to change your bankruptcy from one chapter to another in most circumstances. This process is called conversion. If you want to remain in bankruptcy and you convert, you won't have to pay another filing fee and your creditors are still prevented from taking action against you.

Conversions From Chapter 7

You may voluntarily convert a Chapter 7 case into a Chapter 11 (usually only businesses do this), Chapter 12 (for farmers), or Chapter 13 bankruptcy *at any time* unless you already converted to your Chapter 7 case from one of the other chapters. Some cases have held that a court may deny permission to convert if the conversion is made in bad faith, while other courts have upheld the plain language of the statute, which doesn't mention such a condition.

Upon a creditor's request, after notice and hearing, the court can convert a Chapter 7 case to a Chapter 11 case at any time. The court can convert your Chapter 7 case to a Chapter 13 case only if you consent. For example, as explained earlier, if you file for Chapter 7 and your filing is found to be abusive, the court can convert the case to Chapter 13 if you consent. If you don't consent, the court will dismiss your case outright.

Your case cannot be converted unless you qualify for relief under the new chapter. For example, you can't convert to Chapter 13 unless you fall within the debt guidelines for that chapter (secured debts not exceeding $1,010,650 and unsecured debts not exceeding $336,900).

Conversions From Chapter 13

Just like a Chapter 7 bankruptcy, you can convert your Chapter 13 case to another chapter, but only if you qualify for relief under that chapter. And your Chapter 13 case can also be converted against your wishes, in some situations.

Voluntary Conversion

You may convert your Chapter 13 case into a Chapter 7 case at any time, as long as you qualify to file for Chapter 7 under the rules discussed in Ch. 2. As I mentioned earlier, some courts don't require you to take the Chapter 7 means test upon such a conversion.

Involuntary Conversion

The U.S. Trustee, the trustee, or a creditor may request that the court, after notice and hearing, dismiss your Chapter 13 case or convert it to Chapter 7, whichever is in the best interest of your creditors. Your case might be converted to Chapter 7 rather than dismissed if you have valuable nonexempt property that the trustee could seize for the benefit of your creditors. If, on the other hand, you have no nonexempt property, the creditors would benefit more from an outright dismissal.

The court may order the dismissal of your Chapter 13 case, or convert it to Chapter 7, only for cause, such as your:

- unreasonable delay that is prejudicial to your creditors
- nonpayment of any court fees or charges
- failure to file a repayment plan in a timely manner
- failure to start making your plan payments on time
- failure to comply with your plan
- failure to file your bankruptcy papers on time
- failure to stay current on your alimony or child support payments after your filing date, or
- failure to file your state and federal tax returns with the court.

Any time prior to confirming the Chapter 13 plan, the court, after notice and hearing, may order your case converted to Chapter 11 or 12 upon request by the U.S. Trustee, the trustee, or a creditor. If you are a farmer, the court may not order a conversion to Chapter 7, 11, or 12 unless you request it. As with Chapter 7, no conversion may be ordered to another chapter unless you qualify for relief under that chapter.

Effect of Conversion From Chapter 13 to Chapter 7

One issue that often arises in the course of a conversion from Chapter 13 to Chapter 7 is how you treated your property between your filing date and your conversion date. As explained in Ch. 4, the trustee technically owns all of the property in your bankruptcy estate—which is essentially everything you own when you file, except pensions. If you start out in Chapter 13 and sell some of your nonexempt property, then convert to Chapter 7, what happens to the property you got rid of? Not a problem. When you convert from Chapter 13 to Chapter 7, the property of the estate is the property that remains in your possession or under your control on the date of conversion.

If you are able to cram down a debt in Chapter 13, the lien remains on the property until you complete the plan or the claim is paid in full without regard to the cramdown. If you don't complete the plan, the cramdown becomes ineffective and you will still owe the entire debt with lien attached, less money you have paid to the creditor during your Chapter 13 plan. In Chapter 7, you'll have the opportunity to surrender or redeem the property

Potential Problems in Chapter 13

As with Chapter 7 cases, there are some potential bumps in the road in Chapter 13 cases. These typically come up in the context of the confirmation hearing, where the judge approves or rejects your proposed repayment plan.

Confirmation Hearing

Unlike Chapter 7, a Chapter 13 bankruptcy requires at least one appearance before a bankruptcy judge—the confirmation hearing. At the confirmation hearing, the court approves or rejects your proposed repayment plan. (Rejecting a plan is also called "denial of confirmation.")

Under the new law, the confirmation hearing must be held between 20 days and 45 days after your meeting of creditors. However, the hearing can be held earlier if no one objects.

Although a judge technically presides over the confirmation hearing, the trustee usually runs the show. If the trustee tells the judge that he or she has no objection to your plan, and no creditor shows up to convince the judge that your plan is unfair, the judge will most likely approve the plan without a further hearing. But if the trustee has some problems with your plan, or a creditor raises issues of fairness, the judge will most likely send you back to the drawing board and reschedule ("continue," in legalese) the confirmation hearing to another date, when you will have to submit a modified plan. Each time you submit a modified plan, you must notify all of your creditors (typically, by using the mailing matrix prepared by the court).

If it becomes obvious that Chapter 13 bankruptcy isn't realistic for you—for example, you earn very little money to pay into a plan—the judge will order that your case be dismissed unless you can convert it to Chapter 7 bankruptcy before the date set for the dismissal.

Objections to Your Plan

The trustee (or a creditor) may raise objections to your proposed plan. (See Ch. 2, "Chapter 13 Eligibility Requirements.")

Listed below are some objections you might face in Chapter 13.

The plan was not submitted in good faith. The bankruptcy law explicitly requires you to file for Chapter 13 in good faith. In determining whether you filed in "good faith," courts will look to see whether your proposed plan has any purpose other than sincerely trying for a fresh start. For example, one bankruptcy court ruled that a Chapter 13 filing was not in good faith because the debtor filed for the sole purpose of getting around a judge's decision in an ongoing state court case. If you are filing your papers with the honest intention of getting back on your feet, and you really can make the payments required by the plan, you probably will be able to overcome a "good-faith" objection.

Most bankruptcy courts will look at the following factors:

- How often you have filed for bankruptcy. Filing and then dismissing multiple bankruptcies does not, in itself, show bad faith. However, if you've filed and dismissed two or more other bankruptcy cases within one year, the court may find lack of good faith if there are inconsistencies in your papers or you can't show that your circumstances have changed since the previous dismissal.
- The accuracy of your bankruptcy papers and oral statements. The court is likely to find a lack of good faith if you misrepresent your income, debts, expenses, or assets, or if you lie at the creditors' meeting.

- Your efforts to repay your debts. If your plan will pay your unsecured creditors a small percentage of what you owe, or nothing at all, you may have to show the court that you are stretching as much as you can. The court will want to see that you are not living luxuriously and that you are making substantial efforts to pay your unsecured creditors, even if it means trading in your fancy new car for a used model.

The plan is not feasible. Probably the most common objection is that your plan is not feasible—that is, you won't be able to make the required payments or comply with the other terms of the plan. To overcome this type of objection, your monthly income must exceed your monthly expenses by at least enough to allow you to make the payments required under Chapter 13 bankruptcy. For instance, a debtor who owes a $50,000 tax arrearage as well as $25,000 in credit card debts must propose a plan that, at a minimum, pays the $50,000 in full over the life of the plan (because taxes are usually a priority debt and must be paid in full).

The trustee or a creditor might also question your job stability, the likelihood that you'll incur extraordinary expenses, and whether you have any outside sources of money. If your plan seems to reflect too much wishful thinking, and your sources of money are uncertain, the court will probably reject the plan on the ground that it isn't feasible. Possible scenarios leading the court to find that your plan isn't feasible include:

- You have a business that has been failing, but you've predicted a rebound and intend to use business income to make your plan payments.

- You propose making plan payments from the proceeds of the sale of certain property, but nothing points to the likelihood of a sale.
- Your plan includes a balloon payment (a large payment at the end), but you have not identified a source of money from which the payment will be made.
- You've been convicted of a crime, and you haven't convinced the bankruptcy court that you will stay out of jail.

The plan fails to promote the "best interest" of the creditors. Under your Chapter 13 repayment plan, you must pay your unsecured creditors at least as much as they would have received had you filed for Chapter 7 bankruptcy—that is, the value of your nonexempt property less the costs of sale and the trustee's commission. (Exemptions are discussed in Ch. 4 and the method for determining what the creditors would have received in a Chapter 7 bankruptcy is explained in Ch. 2.) This is called the "best interest of the creditors" test.

If the trustee or a creditor raises this objection, you will have to provide documents showing the values of the potentially nonexempt portions of your property, such as a recent appraisal of a home in which your equity is equal to or exceeds your state's homestead exemption, or a publication stating the value of an automobile of the same make, model, and year as yours. In determining property value, keep in mind that costs of sale also take into consideration the fact that at an auction (the means used by trustees to liquidate property in a Chapter 7 bankruptcy), property sells for about 60% of wholesale.

The plan unfairly discriminates. Chapter 13 bankruptcy is intended to treat all unsecured creditors fairly, relative to each other. You might be inclined to pay some unsecured creditors more than others—for example, you might propose to pay 100% of a student loan (which isn't dischargeable anyway) but only 35% of your credit card debts (which are dischargeable). In this situation, the trustee or the credit card issuers are likely to object to your plan on the ground that they are unfairly being discriminated against.

The plan doesn't provide adequate protection for collateral. Plans must provide that payments to secured creditors on property serving as collateral will be distributed in equal monthly amounts and will be sufficient to provide the creditor with adequate protection of its interest in the collateral.

Filling Out the Bankruptcy Forms

When you file bankruptcy, you'll need to complete a large number of official forms. Fortunately, although there are, as you know, several types (chapters) of bankruptcy, the same forms are used for all the chapters. In other words, if you file a simple Chapter 7 bankruptcy, you'll be using the same forms that big corporations use when filing under Chapter 11 and that individuals with surplus income use to file Chapter 13. This of course means that lots of questions on the forms will concern non-Chapter 7 bankruptcies, and they won't apply to you. You'll just enter "N.A." or "None" in these blanks.

You have several options for completing the forms. You can:

- download the forms from the Internet and fill them in yourself
- hire a bankruptcy petition preparer to complete the forms under your direction (see Ch. 11)
- get limited telephonic advice from a lawyer (see, for example, my limited-scope bankruptcy advice service at www.affordableattorneyadvice.com—this service is currently only available to people in California using bankruptcy petition preparers), or
- hire an attorney to handle everything.

If you use an attorney, the papers will be filed electronically in most courts. If you represent yourself, you will mail the forms to the court or file them in person.

Chapter 7 Documents

There are a number of documents you will have to file in a Chapter 7 case.

The Voluntary Petition

You start a Chapter 7 case by filing a "Voluntary Petition," the official court form that asks for some basic information, including:

- your name(s), address, and the last four digits of your Social Security number
- whether you have lived, maintained a residence, maintained a business, or had assets in the district for the better part of 180 days prior to filing (this establishes your right to file in a particular district)
- the type of bankruptcy you are filing (Chapter 7, 11, 12, or 13)

- the type of debtor you are (individual, corporation, partnership, and so on)
- whether your debts are primarily consumer or business
- if you are a business debtor, the type of business
- how you will be paying your filing fee (at filing, in installments, or not at all because of a fee waiver)
- the estimated number of creditors
- the estimated amount of your debts
- the estimated value of your property
- whether you have nonexempt assets
- whether a judgment for eviction has been entered against you
- whether you are aware of some bankruptcy basics
- your history of bankruptcy filings within the past eight years, if any, and
- whether you have completed your debt counseling or obtained a waiver.

Additional Documents

A number of additional documents must be filed within 14 days after filing the petition. The best practice is to file all the documents when you file your petition, to keep your case under control (and make sure you don't miss the 14-day deadline).

Here are the documents you must provide:

- a list of all of your creditors, including their name, mailing address, and account number (this is called the "creditor matrix")
- lists of your assets (Schedules A (real property) and B (personal property))

- a schedule of liabilities (Schedules D (secured creditors), E (priority creditors), and F (unsecured creditors))
- a statement of your financial affairs for the two years prior to your filing date
- a schedule of your current income (Schedule I) and current expenditures (Schedule J)
- a certificate stating that you have received a notice explaining your duties under the bankruptcy law and the consequences of being untruthful or providing incomplete information
- wage stubs for the 60 days prior to filing
- a statement of your average monthly gross income over the previous six months, and a means test calculation if your income exceeds the median income for a similarly sized family in your state
- a certificate showing that you received credit counseling from an authorized provider within the six months prior to filing
- a copy of any debt repayment plan you developed during your mandatory credit counseling
- a form showing that you received counseling in personal financial management from an authorized provider during the course of your bankruptcy case; this is due before you receive your discharge
- a copy of your most recent tax return or a transcript of the return obtained from the IRS (due to the bankruptcy trustee seven days prior to the creditors' meeting)
- a schedule indicating which assets you are claiming as exempt (Schedule C)

- a schedule of any executory contracts (contracts that are still in force and require action by one or both parties) and leases you have signed (Schedule G)
- a schedule of your codebtors, if any (Schedule H)
- a form called Chapter 7 Individual Debtor's Statement of Intention, in which you tell your secured creditors how you plan to deal with your secured debt (see Ch. 6)
- if you are being evicted and want your bankruptcy filing to hold the eviction off, the certification and rent described in Ch. 5, and
- a form setting out your full Social Security number.

Chapter 13 Documents

Almost all of the documents required for a Chapter 7 bankruptcy are also required in a Chapter 13 bankruptcy, with the exception of the Chapter 7 Individual Debtor's Statement of Intention.

In addition to these documents, you must file a proposed Chapter 13 repayment plan and a form that you use to calculate your disposable income available to repay your unsecured creditors. You must also provide evidence that you have filed tax returns (or transcripts from the IRS) for the previous four tax years, prior to the creditors' meeting. The trustee can keep the creditors' meeting open for 120 days after the first date for which it is scheduled to allow you extra time to obtain and file your returns. And the court can give you 30 additional days, if necessary.

While your Chapter 13 case is pending, you must also file with the court:

- any new tax returns and amendments that you file with the IRS
- a statement under oath of your income and expenditures for each tax year, and
- a statement of your monthly income that shows how income, expenditures, and monthly income are calculated.

These statements must show:

- the amount and sources of your income
- the identity of any person who is responsible (along with you) for the support of any of your dependents, and
- the identity of any person who contributed, and the amount contributed, to your household.

Upon request, you must provide the tax returns to your creditors, the U.S. Trustee, and the regular trustee.

Basic Requirements for Completing Bankruptcy Documents

Whether you file on your own or with the help of a professional, you have a duty to make sure that your papers meet these requirements:

- **You must be ridiculously thorough.** Always err on the side of giving too much information rather than too little.
- **You must respond to every question.** If a question doesn't apply to you, check the "none" box. If there isn't one, you will have to type "N/A" for "not applicable." Make sure to list and value all of your property, even if you think it has no value. List the property, and either put zero for its value, or check

the "unknown" box. Then be prepared to explain your answer at the creditors' meeting.

- **You must be willing to repeat yourself.** Sometimes different forms—or different questions on the same form—ask for the same or overlapping information. You will have to provide the same information multiple times.

- **You must be scrupulously honest.** You must swear, under penalty of perjury, that you've been truthful on your bankruptcy forms. The most likely consequence for failing to be scrupulously honest is a dismissal of your bankruptcy case, but you could be prosecuted for perjury if it's evident that you deliberately lied.

RESOURCE

Finding the forms. You can find samples of the basic forms described in this section in Appendix C. You can also view the current official forms online at www.uscourts.gov/bkforms. These forms can be filled in online, but you can't save them (which means you should download the forms, make drafts, and then fill in and print each form based on your draft, one form at a time).

At first glance, you might think that there's no way you can deal with all of this paperwork. However, especially in Chapter 7 cases, it really isn't as difficult as it looks. Nolo publishes excellent, up-to-date, line-by-line guides for the forms, and you'll only need to complete the parts of the forms that apply to your personal situation. To paraphrase the old saying, just take it one document at a time.

Getting Help With Your Bankruptcy

Y ou will have three sources of outside help if you wish to file for bankruptcy:

- a debt relief agency (as both lawyers and nonlawyer bankruptcy petition preparers are now called)
- a book that gives you step-by-step instructions on how to file for bankruptcy (such as those published by Nolo), or
- a combination of bankruptcy books, Internet sites, lawyer consultants, and bankruptcy petition preparers (the best bang for your buck in many cases).

Debt Relief Agencies

Under the new bankruptcy law, any person or entity that you pay or otherwise compensate for help with your bankruptcy is considered a debt relief agency. The two main types of debt relief agencies are lawyers and bankruptcy petition preparers (BPPs). Credit counseling agencies and budget counseling agencies are not debt relief agencies. Nor are any of the following:

- employers or employees of debt relief agencies
- nonprofit organizations that have federal 501(c)(3) tax-exempt status
- any creditor who works with you to restructure your debt
- banks, credit unions, and other deposit institutions, or
- an author, publisher, distributor, or seller of works subject to copyright protection when acting in that capacity (in other words, Nolo and the stores that sell its books aren't debt relief agencies).

Lawyers and BPPs are covered separately below. This section explains what the new bankruptcy law requires of debt relief agencies generally.

Lawyers Are Debt Relief Agencies

In *Milavetz v. United States*, 559 U.S. __ (2010), the Supreme Court ruled that lawyers may be considered debt relief agencies under the bankruptcy code and therefore are subject to the various notice and contract requirements imposed on all debt relief agencies. As to the rule which prohibits debt relief agencies from advising clients to undertake new debts, the Supreme Court said this section only prohibits lawyers from advising their clients to load up on debt that could later be discharged—and therefore did not infringe on lawyers' free speech rights.

Mandatory Contract

Within five days after a debt relief agency assists you, it (or he or she) must enter into a contract with you that explains, clearly and conspicuously:

- what services the agency will provide you
- what the agency will charge for the services, and
- the terms of payment.

The agency must give you a copy of the completed, signed contract.

Mandatory Disclosures and Notices

The debt relief agency must inform you, in writing, that:

- All information you are required to provide in your bankruptcy papers must be complete, accurate, and truthful.
- You must completely and accurately disclose your assets and liabilities in the documents you file to begin your case.
- You must undertake a reasonable inquiry to establish the replacement value of any item you plan to keep, before you provide that value on your forms.
- Your current monthly income, the amounts you provide in the means test, and your computation of projected disposable income (in a Chapter 13 case), as stated in your bankruptcy papers, must be based on a reasonable inquiry into their accuracy.
- Your case may be audited, and your failure to cooperate in the audit may result in dismissal of your case or some other sanction, including a possible criminal penalty.

In addition to these stark warnings, a debt relief agency must also give you a general notice regarding some basic bankruptcy requirements and your options for help in filing and pursuing your case. The notice that you can expect to receive from any debt relief agency within three business days after the agency first offers to provide you with services is shown below. Failure to give you this notice can land the agency in big trouble.

Restrictions on Debt Relief Agencies

Under the new law, a debt relief agency may not:

- fail to perform any service that the agency informed you it would perform in connection with your bankruptcy case

- counsel you to make any statement in a document that is untrue and misleading or that the agency should have known was untrue or misleading, or
- advise you to incur more debt in order to pay for the agency's services.

Any contract that doesn't comply with the new requirements on debt relief agencies may not be enforced against you. A debt relief agency is liable to you for costs and fees, including legal fees, if the agency negligently or intentionally:

- fails to comply with the new law's restrictions on debt relief agencies, or
- fails to file a document that results in dismissal of your case or conversion to another chapter.

In sum, debt relief agencies are on the hook if they are negligent in performing the services required by the bankruptcy law or other services they have agreed to provide.

Bankruptcy Petition Preparers

Even though you should be able to handle routine bankruptcy procedures yourself, you may want someone familiar with the bankruptcy forms and courts in your area to use a computer to enter your data in the official forms and print them out for filing with the court. For this level of assistance—routine form preparation and organization—consider using a bankruptcy petition preparer (BPP).

What a Bankruptcy Petition Preparer Can Do for You

BPPs are very different from lawyers. BPPs are legally prohibited from giving you legal advice, which includes information such as:

IMPORTANT INFORMATION ABOUT BANKRUPTCY ASSISTANCE SERVICES FROM AN ATTORNEY OR BANKRUPTCY PETITION PREPARER

If you decide to seek bankruptcy relief, you can represent yourself, you can hire an attorney to represent you, or you can get help in some localities from a bankruptcy petition preparer who is not an attorney. THE LAW REQUIRES AN ATTORNEY OR BANKRUPTCY PETITION PREPARER TO GIVE YOU A WRITTEN CONTRACT SPECIFYING WHAT THE ATTORNEY OR BANKRUPTCY PETITION PREPARER WILL DO FOR YOU AND HOW MUCH IT WILL COST. Ask to see the contract before you hire anyone.

The following information helps you understand what must be done in a routine bankruptcy case to help you evaluate how much service you need. Although bankruptcy can be complex, many cases are routine. Before filing a bankruptcy case, either you or your attorney should analyze your eligibility for different forms of debt relief available under the Bankruptcy Code and which form of relief is most likely to be beneficial for you. Be sure you understand the relief you can obtain and its limitations.

To file a bankruptcy case, documents called a Petition, Schedules, and Statement of Financial Affairs, as well as in some cases a Statement of Intention, need to be prepared correctly and filed with the bankruptcy court. You will have to pay a filing fee to the bankruptcy court. Once your case starts, you will have to attend the required first meeting of creditors where you may be questioned by your creditors.

If you choose to file a Chapter 7 case, you may be asked by a creditor to reaffirm a debt. You may want help deciding whether to do so. A creditor is not permitted to coerce you into reaffirming your debts.

If you choose to file a Chapter 13 case in which you repay your creditors what you can afford over three to five years, you may also want help with preparing your Chapter 13 plan and with the confirmation hearing on your plan which will be before a bankruptcy judge.

If you select another type of relief under the Bankruptcy Code other than Chapter 7 or Chapter 13, you will want to find out what should be done from someone familiar with that type of relief.

Your bankruptcy case may also involve litigation. You are generally permitted to represent yourself in litigation in bankruptcy court, but only attorneys, not bankruptcy petition preparers, can give you legal advice.

- whether to file a bankruptcy petition or which chapter (7, 11, 12, or 13) is appropriate
- whether your debts will be discharged under a particular chapter
- whether you will be able to hang on to your home or other property if you file under a particular chapter (that is, which exemptions you should choose)
- information about the tax consequences of a case brought under a particular chapter or whether tax claims in your case can be discharged
- whether you should offer to repay or agree to reaffirm a debt
- how to characterize the nature of your interest in property or debts, and
- information about bankruptcy procedures and rights.

Fees

All fees charged by debt relief agencies are reviewed by the U.S. Trustee for reasonableness. However, unlike lawyers' fees, which can vary widely according to the circumstances, a BPP's fees are subject to a strict cap, somewhere between $100 and $200, depending on the district. The rationale offered by the U.S. Trustee for this cap—and by the courts that have upheld it—is that BPP fees can be set according to what general typists charge per page in the community. Because BPPs aren't supposed to be doing anything other than "typing" the forms, the argument goes, they shouldn't be able to charge rates for professional services.

Rates allowed for BPPs are far less than lawyers charge. For that reason, BPPs are a good choice for people who want some help getting their forms typed and organized in a way that will sail past the court clerk and satisfy the trustee.

How Bankruptcy Petition Preparers Are Regulated

Anyone can be a BPP. Yes, anyone. There is nothing in the bankruptcy code that requires BPPs to have any particular level of education, training, or experience. Unlike most other jobs, a prison record is no handicap to becoming a BPP. How, then, are BPPs regulated? Regulation is provided by the U.S. Trustee's office, which reviews all bankruptcy petitions prepared by BPPs. BPPs must provide their name, address, telephone number, and Social Security number on bankruptcy petitions, as well as on every other bankruptcy document they prepare. The U.S. Trustee uses this information to keep tabs on BPPs.

BPPs are also regulated at the creditors' meeting, where the bankruptcy trustee can ask you about the manner in which the BPP conducts his or her business. For instance, if you are representing yourself, the trustee might ask how you got the information necessary to choose your exemptions (see Ch. 4) or how you decided which bankruptcy chapter to use.

If the BPP provided you with this information, the trustee may refer the case to the U.S. Trustee's office and the BPP will be hauled into court to explain why he or she violated the rules against giving legal advice. The BPP may be forced to return the fee you paid and may even be banned from practicing as a BPP, if it's not the first offense. None of this will have any effect on your case, however, other than the inconvenience of being dragged into court.

Can BPPs Give You Written Information?

Under the Bankruptcy Code, BPPs are supposed to prepare your bankruptcy forms under your direction. This means you are supposed to tell the BPP what exemptions to choose, whether to file under Chapter 7 or Chapter 13, what approach to take in respect to your secured debts (car note, mortgage), and what values to place on your property. That's fine in theory, but unless you have the benefit of this book or another source of legal information, there is no way you would have adequate bankruptcy expertise to tell the BPP how to proceed. In an attempt to bridge this gap, many BPPs hand their customers written materials that contain all the information their customers need to direct the case. Unfortunately, providing a customer with written legal information about bankruptcy has itself been held to be the unauthorized practice of law in many states (California is an important exception). Whether these holdings will continue under the new bankruptcy law remains to be seen.

- using the word legal or any similar term in advertisements, or advertising under a category that includes such terms, and
- accepting court filing fees from you.
  You must pay the filing fee to the court yourself or, in some districts, give the BPP a cashier's check made out to the court.

Finally, under the new law, BPPs must submit a statement under oath with each petition they prepare stating how much you paid them in the previous 12 months and any fees that you owe them but haven't yet paid them. If they charge more than they are permitted, they will be ordered to return the excess fees to you.

If a BPP engages in any fraudulent act in regard to your case or fails to comply with the rules governing their behavior listed above, they may be required to return your entire fee as well as pay a $500 fine for each transgression. If they engage in serious fraud, they may be fined up to $2,000 and three times your fee, and even be ordered to cease providing BPP services. Simply put, fraudulent BPPs (those who would take your money without providing promised services or counsel you to play fast and loose with the bankruptcy system) are likely to be weeded out in a hurry.

BPPs can be fined for certain actions and inactions spelled out in the Bankruptcy Code (11 U.S.C. § 110). These are:

- failing to put their name, address, and Social Security number on your bankruptcy petition
- failing to give you a copy of your bankruptcy documents when you sign them

How to Find Bankruptcy Petition Preparers

BPP services are springing up all over the country to help people who don't want or can't afford to hire a lawyer, but you're still more likely to find a BPP if you live on the West Coast. The best way to find a reputable BPP in your area is to get a recommendation from someone who has used a particular BPP and has been satisfied with his or her work.

BPPs sometimes advertise in classified sections of local newspapers and in the yellow pages. You may have to look hard to spot their ads, however, because they go by different names in different states. In California, your best bet is to find a legal document assistant (the official name given to independent paralegals in California) who also provides BPP services. Check the website maintained by the California Association of Legal Document Assistants (www.calda.org). In Arizona, hunt for a legal document preparer. In other states, especially Florida, search for paralegals who directly serve the public (often termed independent paralegals or legal technicians). In many states, an independent paralegal franchise called We the People offers BPP services. You can also look for BPPs in your area at www.legalconsumer.com.

Combining Lawyers and Bankruptcy Petition Preparers

In California and some other parts of the country, it is possible to use a BPP to grind out your paperwork, and a lawyer to provide you with all the legal savvy you need to direct your own case. Under this arrangement, you are still representing yourself, but you are combining legal and secretarial resources to get the job done. This is what is known as unbundled legal services, where you hire an attorney for a discrete task (legal advice in this case) rather than for the whole enchilada we know as "legal representation." For example, the Affordable Attorney Advice services operated by Stephen Elias (this book's author) provides legal information and advice over the phone to bankruptcy filers, for a one-time flat fee. For more information on this service, go to www.bankruptcylawproject.com/aaa.html.

A Bankruptcy Petition Preparer Cannot Represent You

If you decide to use a BPP, remember that you are representing yourself and are responsible for the outcome of your case. This means not only learning about your rights under the bankruptcy law and understanding the proper procedures to be followed, but also accepting responsibility for correctly and accurately filling in the bankruptcy petition and schedules. If, for example, you lose your home because it turned out to be worth much more than you thought, and the homestead exemption available to you didn't cover your equity, you can't blame the BPP. Nor can you blame the BPP if other property is taken from you because you didn't get the necessary information—from a lawyer or from this book—to properly claim your exemptions. The point is, unless you hire a lawyer to represent you, you are solely responsible for acquiring the information necessary to competently pursue your case.

Bankruptcy Lawyers

Bankruptcy lawyers (a type of debt relief agency under the new law) are regular lawyers who specialize in handling bankruptcy cases. Under the old law, it was usually possible to find an affordable bankruptcy lawyer who would provide at least a minimal level of representation throughout your case. However, for the reasons discussed below, lawyers are charging a lot more to represent clients in bankruptcies filed under the new law.

When You May Need a Lawyer

Most Chapter 7 bankruptcies sail through without a hitch. However, there are some situations in which you may need some help from a bankruptcy lawyer:

- Your average income during the six months before you file is more than your state's median income, and it looks like you won't be able to pass the means test. (See Ch. 2 for more information on these calculations.)

- You want to hold onto a house or motor vehicle and the information we provide on these subjects doesn't adequately address your situation or answer all of your questions.

- You want to get rid of a student loan or income tax debt that won't be wiped out in bankruptcy unless you convince a court that it should be discharged.

- A creditor files a lawsuit in the bankruptcy court claiming that one of your debts should survive your bankruptcy because you incurred it through fraud or other misconduct.

- The bankruptcy trustee (the court official in charge of your case) seeks to have your whole bankruptcy dismissed because you didn't give honest and complete answers to questions about your assets, liabilities, and economic transactions.

- The U.S. Trustee asks the court to dismiss your case—or force you into Chapter 13—because your income is high enough to fund a Chapter 13 repayment plan, or because the trustee believes that your filing is an abuse of the Chapter 7 bankruptcy process for other reasons.

- You have recently given away or sold valuable property for less than it is worth.

- You went on a recent buying spree with your credit card (especially if you charged more than $550 on luxury goods within the past 90 days).

- You want help negotiating with a creditor or the bankruptcy court, and the amount involved justifies hiring a bankruptcy lawyer to assist you.

- You have a large lien on your property because of a court judgment against you, and you want to remove the lien in your bankruptcy case.

- A creditor is asking the court to allow it to proceed with its collection action despite your bankruptcy filing (for instance, a creditor wants to foreclose on your house because you are behind on your mortgage payments).

- You are being evicted by your landlord because you have fallen behind on your rent.

Even if you aren't facing one of these complications, you may still want a lawyer's help. If you find the thought of going through the process overwhelming, a lawyer can take charge of your case and relieve you of the responsibility to get everything done. The lawyer can accompany you to the creditor's meeting, work with you to make sure that your documents are complete and accurate, get all your paperwork filed on time, and generally handle all of the little details that go into a successful bankruptcy case. Although representation comes at a price—which can be considerable—you will have the peace of mind of knowing that someone is watching your back. While we obviously believe that many people can handle their own Chapter 7 bankruptcies, it isn't right for everyone, especially if you have other significant sources of stress in your life or simply don't feel up to handling it all by yourself.

Full-Service Lawyer Representation

In a general sense, you are represented by a lawyer if you contract with the lawyer to handle some or all of your bankruptcy case for you. More specifically, there are two types of representation—the type where you hire a lawyer to assume complete responsibility for your bankruptcy and the type where you represent yourself but hire a lawyer to handle one particular aspect of your bankruptcy case. We refer to the first type of representation as "full-service representation" and the second type of representation as unbundled services (discussed below).

When providing full-service representation, a bankruptcy lawyer is responsible for making sure that all of your paperwork is filed on time and that the information in your paperwork is accurate. These duties require the lawyer to review various documents—for instance, your credit report, tax returns, and home value appraisal—both to assure the accuracy of your paperwork and to make sure that you are filing for bankruptcy under the appropriate chapter. Under the new law, if your paperwork is inaccurate or you filed under Chapter 7 when you should have filed under Chapter 13, the lawyer can be fined a hefty amount and be required to return your fees.

In exchange for their basic fee, full-service bankruptcy lawyers typically are also responsible for appearing on your behalf at the creditors' meeting, representing you if a creditor opposes the discharge of a debt, and eliminating any liens

that the bankruptcy laws allow to be stripped from your property.

Sometimes, a case appears to be simple at the beginning but turns out to be complicated later on. In that event, you might start out representing yourself but later decide to hire an attorney to handle a tricky issue that arises.

Because full-service lawyer duties for even a simple bankruptcy case have drastically increased under the new bankruptcy law, typical lawyer fees have gone way up. For this reason, many people who would have used lawyers in the past will now be forced to represent themselves— with or without the help of outside resources. And many readers of this book are likely to find themselves in this boat.

Unbundled Services

As mentioned earlier, the recent changes in bankruptcy law mean that many people who would have hired a full-service lawyer in the past will now have to represent themselves. However, this doesn't mean that they can't get a lawyer to help out with some aspect of the case. Since the 1990s, lawyers have been increasingly willing to offer their services on a piecemeal basis and provide legal advice over the telephone and Internet to help people who are representing themselves. In bankruptcy cases, lawyers are increasingly willing to step in and handle a particular matter, such as stripping liens from your property or handling a dischargeability action brought by you or a creditor.

When lawyers do specific jobs at a client's request but don't contract for full-service representation in the underlying case, they are said to be providing an unbundled service. For example, you may be able to hire an attorney to handle a specific procedure—such as to defend against a motion for relief from stay—while you handle the main part of the bankruptcy yourself.

Few court cases discuss the boundaries of unbundled services. Some courts have held that attorneys can't "ghostwrite" legal documents for nonlawyers—because that would be a type of fraud on the court—but the issue has not been decided by most courts. Also, nothing prevents a lawyer from appearing for you in a limited capacity and putting his or her own name on associated documents.

Lawyers providing unbundled services usually charge an hourly fee. As a general rule, you should bring an attorney into the case for an unbundled service only if a dispute involves something valuable enough to justify the attorney's fees. If a creditor objects to the discharge of a $500 debt, and it will cost you $400 to hire an attorney, you may be better off trying to handle the matter yourself, even though this increases the risk that the creditor will win. If, however, the dispute is worth $1,000 and the attorney will cost you $200, hiring the attorney makes better sense.

Unfortunately, many bankruptcy attorneys do not like to appear or do paperwork on a piecemeal basis. Justified or not, these attorneys believe that by doing a little work for you, they might be on the hook if something goes wrong in another part of your case—that is, if they are in for a penny, they are in for a pound. Also, the bar associations of some states frown on unbundled services on ethical grounds. On the other hand, a number of other state bar associations are starting to encourage their attorneys to offer unbundled services simply because so many people—even middle-income people—are unable to afford full representation.

Bankruptcy Consultants

Under the old bankruptcy law, many people were able to represent themselves with a Nolo book as their main source of information. Bankruptcy under the new law is more complex, but in many cases, it's still just a matter of knowing what to put in the forms and what forms to file. For many people, however, a book just won't do the trick, no matter how well written and complete: They want to talk to a human being. Because of unauthorized practice laws and restrictions in the bankruptcy law, however, there is only one kind of human being who is authorized to answer your questions about bankruptcy law and procedure: a lawyer.

Fortunately, there are lawyers who provide bankruptcy consultations (a category of unbundled service) for a transaction fee (for example, a $100 flat rate) or a fee based on the amount of time your call takes (for example, $3 a minute). There are also free consultations offered by private attorneys and bar associations. Similar services—free and paid—are available on the Internet. To find a telephonic or online consultation service, in addition to those mentioned here, go to Google or another search engine and look for "bankruptcy legal advice telephone or Internet."

Even if you use a BPP to prepare your paperwork and are using this book, you may wish to talk to a lawyer to get the information you need to make your own choices and tell the BPP what you want in your papers. For instance, a BPP can't choose your exemptions for you, because that would be considered the practice of law—something only lawyers can do. However, a lawyer can help you decide which exemptions to pick so you can tell the BPP what to put in the form that lists your exemptions.

As with other debt relief agencies, lawyers offering telephonic services are considered debt relief agencies and will have to offer you a contract detailing their services and provide the other notices described above.

How to Find a Bankruptcy Lawyer

Where there's a bankruptcy court, there are bankruptcy lawyers. They're listed in the yellow pages under "Attorneys," and often advertise in newspapers. You should use an experienced bankruptcy lawyer, not a general practitioner, to handle or advise you on matters associated with bankruptcy.

There are several ways to find the best bankruptcy lawyer for your job:

- **Personal referrals.** This is your best approach. If you know someone who was pleased with the services of a bankruptcy lawyer, call that lawyer first.
- **Bankruptcy petition preparers.** If there's a BPP in your area, he or she may know some bankruptcy attorneys who are both competent and sympathetic to self-helpers. It is here that you are most likely to find a good referral to attorneys who are willing to deliver unbundled services, including advice over the telephone.
- **Legal Aid.** Legal Aid offices are partially funded by the federal Legal Services Corporation and offer legal assistance in many areas. A few offices may do bankruptcies, although most do not. To qualify for Legal Aid, you must have a very low income.
- **Legal clinic.** Many law schools sponsor legal clinics and provide free legal advice to consumers. Some legal clinics have

the same income requirements as Legal Aid; others offer free services to low- and moderate-income people.

- **Group legal plans.** If you're a member of a plan that provides free or low-cost legal assistance and the plan covers bankruptcies, make that your first stop in looking for a lawyer.
- **Lawyer-referral panels.** Most county bar associations will give you the names of bankruptcy attorneys who practice in your area. But bar associations may not provide much screening. Take the time to check out the credentials and experience of the person to whom you're referred.
- **Internet directories.** Both bar associations and private companies provide lists of bankruptcy lawyers on the Internet, with a lot more information about the lawyer than you're likely to get in a yellow pages ad. A good place to start is Nolo's Lawyer Directory, at www.nolo.com (click on "Find a Lawyer").

Fees

For a routine Chapter 7 bankruptcy, a full-service lawyer will likely charge you somewhere between $1,000 and $2,000 (plus the $299 filing fee). In most situations, you will have to pay the attorney in full before the attorney will file your case. Once you file your Chapter 7 bankruptcy, any money you owe the attorney is discharged along with your other dischargeable unsecured debts.

On your bankruptcy papers, you must state the amount you are paying your bankruptcy lawyer. Because every penny you pay to a bankruptcy lawyer is a penny not available to your creditors (at least in theory), the court has the legal authority to make the attorney justify his or her fee. This rarely happens, however, because attorneys know the range of fees generally allowed by local bankruptcy judges, and set their fees accordingly. This means that you probably won't find much variation in the amounts charged by lawyers in your area (although it never hurts to shop around).

The scope and range of services that the attorney promises you in return for your initial fee will be listed in what's called a "Rule 2016 Attorney Fee Disclosure Form." This form is filed as part of your bankruptcy papers. In the typical Chapter 7 case, the attorney's fee will include the routine tasks associated with a bankruptcy filing: counseling, preparing bankruptcy and reaffirmation forms, and attendance at the creditors' meeting. Any task not included in the Rule 2016 disclosure form is subject to a separate fee.

If your case will likely require more attorney time, you may—and probably will—be charged extra, according to the attorney's hourly fee or other criteria he or she uses. A typical bankruptcy attorney charges between $200 and $300 an hour (rural and urban) and would charge a minimum of roughly $400 to $600 for a court appearance. Some attorneys will add these fees to their standard fee and require you to pay it all in advance. For instance, if the attorney's standard fee is $1,000, but the attorney sees extra work down the line, you may be charged $1,500 or even $2,000 in anticipation of the extra work.

Other attorneys will happily just charge you their standard fee up front and wait until after you file to charge you for the extra work. Because these fees are earned after your bankruptcy filing, they won't be discharged in your bankruptcy

and the attorney need not collect them up front. However the attorney charges you, you are protected against fee gouging. An attorney must file a supplemental Rule 2016 form to obtain the court's permission for any postfiling fees.

What to Look for in a Lawyer

No matter how you find a lawyer, these three suggestions will help you make sure you have the best possible working relationship.

First, fight any urge you may have to surrender to, or be intimidated by, the lawyer. You should be the one who decides what you feel comfortable doing about your legal and financial affairs. Keep in mind that you're hiring the lawyer to perform a service for you, so shop around if the price or personality isn't right.

Second, make sure you have good "chemistry" with any lawyer you hire. When making an appointment, ask to talk directly to the lawyer. If you can't, this may give you a hint as to how accessible he or she is. Of course, if you're told that a paralegal will be handling the routine aspects of your case under the supervision of a lawyer, you may be satisfied with that arrangement. If you do talk directly, ask some specific questions. Do you get clear, concise answers? If not, try someone else. Also, pay attention to how the lawyer responds to your knowledge. If you've read this book, you're already better informed than most clients (and some lawyers are threatened by clients who have done their homework).

Finally, once you find a lawyer you like, make an hour-long appointment to discuss your situation fully. The lawyer or a paralegal in the lawyer's office will tell you what to bring to the meeting, if anything (if not, be sure to ask ahead of time). Some lawyers will want to see a recent credit report and tax return, while others will send you a questionnaire to complete prior to your visit. Depending on the circumstances, you may also be asked to bring your bills and documents pertaining to your home and other real estate you own. Some lawyers prefer not to deal with details during the first visit, and will simply ask you to come as you are.

Your main goal at the initial conference is to find out what the lawyer recommends in your particular case and how much it will cost. Go home and think about the lawyer's suggestions. If they don't make sense or you have other reservations, call someone else.

TIP

Look for a member of the National Association of Consumer Bankruptcy Attorneys. Because of the massive changes enacted by the new bankruptcy law, you will want to find an attorney who has a means of keeping up to date and communicating with other bankruptcy lawyers. Membership in the National Association of Consumer Bankruptcy Attorneys (NACBA) is a good sign that your lawyer will be tuned in to the nuances of the new law and the court interpretations of the law that are sure to come.

Legal Research

Legal research can vary from the very simple to the hopelessly complex. In this section, we are staying on the simple side. If you would like to learn more about legal research or if you find that our suggestions come up a bit short in your particular case, we recommend that you obtain a copy of *Legal Research: How to Find & Understand the Law*, by Stephen Elias (Nolo), which provides a plain-English tutorial on legal research in the law library and on the Internet.

Sources of Bankruptcy Law

Bankruptcy law comes from a variety of sources:
- federal bankruptcy statutes passed by Congress
- federal rules about bankruptcy procedure issued by a federal judicial agency
- local rules issued by individual bankruptcy courts
- federal and bankruptcy court cases applying bankruptcy laws to specific disputes
- laws (statutes) passed by state legislatures that define the property you can keep in bankruptcy, and
- state court cases interpreting state exemption statutes.

Not so long ago, you would have had to visit a law library to find these resources. Now you can find most of them on the Internet. However, if you are able to visit a decent-sized law library, your research will be the better for it. Using actual books allows you to more easily find and read relevant court interpretations of the underlying statutes and rules—which are crucial to getting a clear picture of what the laws and rules really mean.

There is another important reason to visit the law library, if possible. While you can find superficial discussions and overviews of various aspects of bankruptcy on the Internet, you'll find in-depth encyclopedias and treatises in the law library that delve into every aspect of bankruptcy. In other words, you can find not only the law itself, but also what the experts have to say about all the picky little issues that have arisen over the years. Also, books in a law library are almost always subjected to a rigorous quality control process—as is this book—whereas you never know what you're getting on the Internet. To avoid getting lost in cyberspace, follow our suggestions below for researching bankruptcy law online and avoid the temptation to settle for the first hit in a Google search.

Below, we show you how to get to the resources you'll most likely be using, whether you are doing your research on the Internet or in the law library.

Bankruptcy Background Materials: Overviews, Encyclopedias, and Treatises

Before digging into the primary law sources (statutes, rules, cases, and so on that we discuss below), you may want to do some background reading to get a firm grasp of your issue or question.

The Internet

A number of Internet sites contain large collections of articles written by experts about various aspects of bankruptcy. Good starting places are Nolo's website, www.nolo.com, and www.legalconsumer.com, which offer lots of information and resources. Our next favorite jumping-off site for this type of research is The Bankruptcy Law Trove page at www.lawtrove. com/bankruptcy. You might also want to visit www.bankruptcyfinder.com, a comprehensive site that provides links to hundreds of bank-ruptcy articles, reference materials, statutes, and more.

The Law Library

Providing you with a good treatise or encyclopedia discussion of bankruptcy is where the law library shines. This type of resource is not typically available online unless you find a way to access the expensive legal databases—Westlaw and Lexis—marketed almost exclusively to lawyers.

Collier on Bankruptcy

It's a good idea to get an overview of your subject before trying to find a precise answer to a precise question. The best way to do this is to find a general commentary on your subject by a bankruptcy expert. For example, if you want to find out whether a particular debt is nondischargeable, you should start by reading a general discussion about the type of debt you're dealing with. Or, if you don't know whether you're entitled to claim certain property as exempt, a good overview of your state's exemptions would get you started on the right track.

The most complete source of this type of background information is a set of books known as *Collier on Bankruptcy*, by Lawrence P. King, et al (Matthew Bender). It's available in virtually all law libraries. *Collier* is both incredibly thorough and meticulously up to date; semiannual supplements, with all the latest developments, are in the front of each volume. In addition to comments on every aspect of bankruptcy law, *Collier* contains the bankruptcy statutes, rules, and exemption lists for every state.

Collier is organized according to the bank-ruptcy statutes. This means that the quickest way to find information in it is to know what statute you're looking for. (See the Bankruptcy Code sections set out below.) If you still can't figure out the governing statute, start with the *Collier* subject matter index. Be warned, however, that the index can be difficult to use because it contains a lot of bankruptcy jargon you may be unfamiliar with. A legal dictionary will be available in the library.

Foreclosure Resources

If you are facing foreclosure, you'll definitely want to look at *The Foreclosure Survival Guide,* by Stephen Elias (Nolo). This book explains the options available to you, then walks you through the necessary steps for handling your particular situation. If you are looking for a more comprehensive resource written primarily for lawyers, you can't do better than *Foreclosures,* by John Rao, Odette Williamson, and Tara Twomey (National Consumer Law Center). While the book is pricey ($110), it is cheap compared to the consequences of losing your home or hiring a lawyer to represent you. Even if you do hire a lawyer, you can benefit from having your own independent source of information. You can order a copy online at www.nclc.org.

Other Background Resources

For general discussions of bankruptcy issues, there are several other good places to start. An excellent all-around resource is called *Consumer Bankruptcy Law and Practice.* This volume, published by the National Consumer Law Center, is updated every year. It contains a complete discussion of Chapter 7 bankruptcy procedures, the official bankruptcy forms, and a marvelous bibliography.

How to Use Law Libraries

Law libraries that are open to the public are most often found in and around courthouses. Law schools also frequently admit the public at least some of the time (not, typically during exam time, over the summer, or during other breaks in the academic year).

If you're using a library as a member of the public, find a way to feel at home, even if it seems that the library is run mostly to serve members of the legal community. Almost without exception, law libraries come with law librarians. The law librarians will be helpful as long as you ask them the right questions. For example, the law librarians will help you find specific library resources (for instance, where you can find the federal bankruptcy statutes or rules), but they normally won't teach you the ins and outs of legal research. Nor will they give an opinion about what a law means, how you should deal with the court, or how your particular question should be answered. For instance, if you want to find a state case interpreting a particular exemption, the law librarian will show you where your state code is located on the shelves and may even point out the volumes that contain the exemptions. The librarian won't, however, help you interpret the exemption, apply the exemption to your specific facts, or tell you how to raise the exemption in your bankruptcy case. Nor is the librarian likely to tell you what additional research steps you can or should take. When it comes to legal research in the law library, self-help is the order of the day.

Another good treatise is a legal encyclopedia called *American Jurisprudence*, 2nd Series. Almost all law libraries carry it. The article on bankruptcy has an extensive table of contents, and the entire encyclopedia has an index. Between these two tools, you should be able to zero in on helpful material. Finally, some large and well-stocked law libraries carry a looseleaf publication known as the Commerce Clearing House (CCH) *Bankruptcy Law Reporter* (BLR). In this publication, you can find all three primary source materials relating to bankruptcy: statutes, rules, and cases.

If you are looking for information on adversary proceedings (such as how to defend against a creditor's challenge to the dischargeability of a debt), turn to *Represent Yourself in Court,* by Paul Bergman and Sara J. Berman (Nolo). It has an entire chapter on representing yourself in adversary proceedings in bankruptcy court. If you need information on court procedures or the local rules of a specific court, consult the *Collier Bankruptcy Practice Manual.*

Finding Federal Bankruptcy Statutes

Title 11 of the United States Code contains all the statutes that govern your bankruptcy.

The Internet

If you are using the Internet, click www.lawtrove.com/bankruptcy or go to the Legal Information Institute of Cornell University Law School, www.law.cornell.edu. Cornell lets you browse laws by subject matter and also offers a keyword search. To help you in your browsing, below is a table setting out the various subject matter sections of the U.S. Code that apply to bankruptcy.

The Law Library

Virtually every law library has at least one complete set of the annotated United States Code ("annotated" means that each statute is followed by citations and summaries of cases interpreting that provision). If you already have a citation to the statute you are seeking, you can use the citation to find the statute. However, if you have no citation—which is frequently the case—you can use either the index to Title 11 (the part of the Code that applies to bankruptcy) or the table we set out just below, which matches various issues that are likely to interest you with specific sections of Title 11.

Once you have found and read the statute, you can browse the one-paragraph summaries of written opinions issued by courts that have interpreted that particular statute. You will be looking to see whether a court has addressed your particular issue. If so, you can find and read the entire case in the law library. Reading what a judge has had to say about the statute regarding facts similar to yours is an invaluable guide to understanding how a judge is likely to handle the issue in your case, although when and where the case was decided may be important.

Finding the Federal Rules of Bankruptcy Procedure (FRBP)

The Federal Rules of Bankruptcy Procedure govern what happens if an issue is contested in the bankruptcy court. They also apply to certain routine bankruptcy procedures, such as deadlines for filing paperwork. Because most cases sail through the court without any need for the bankruptcy judge's intervention, you may not need to be familiar with these rules.

Bankruptcy Code Sections (11 U.S.C.)

§ 101 Definitions

§ 109 Who May File for Which Type of Bankruptcy; Credit Counseling Requirements

§ 110 Rules for Bankruptcy Petition Preparers

§ 111 Budget and Credit Counseling Agencies

§ 302 Who Can File Joint Cases

§ 326 How Trustees Are Compensated

§ 332 Consumer Privacy Ombudsmen

§ 341 Meeting of Creditors

§ 342 Notice of Creditors' Meeting; Informational Notice to Debtors; Requirements for Notice by Debtors

§ 343 Examination of Debtor at Creditors' Meeting

§ 348 Converting From One Type of Bankruptcy to Another

§ 349 Dismissing a Case

§ 350 Closing and Reopening a Case

§ 362 The Automatic Stay

§ 365 How Leases and Executory Contracts Are Treated in Bankruptcy

§ 366 Continuing or Reconnecting Utility Service

§ 501 Filing of Creditors' Claims

§ 506 Allowed Secured Claims and Lien Avoidance

§ 507 Priority Claims

§ 521 Paperwork Requirements and Deadlines

§ 522 Exemptions; Residency Requirements for Homestead Exemption; Stripping Liens From Property

§ 523 Nondischargeable Debts

§ 524 Effect of Discharge and Reaffirmation of Debts

§ 525 Prohibited Postbankruptcy Discrimination

§ 526 Restrictions on Debt Relief Agencies

§ 527 Required Disclosures by Debt Relief Agencies

§ 528 Requirements for Debt Relief Agencies

§ 541 What Property Is Part of the Bankruptcy Estate

§ 547 Preferences

§ 548 Fraudulent Transfers

§ 554 Trustee's Abandonment of Property in the Bankruptcy Estate

§ 707 The Means Test; Dismissal for Abuse; Conversion From Chapter 7 to Chapter 13

§ 722 Redemption of Liens on Personal Property

§ 727 Chapter 7 Discharge; Financial Management Counseling Requirements

§ 1301 Stay of Action Against Codebtor

§ 1302 Duties of the Chapter 13 Trustee

§ 1304 Rights of Chapter 13 Debtor Engaged in Business

§ 1305 Property of the Chapter 13 Bankruptcy Estate

§ 1307 Conversion of Chapter 13 to Another Title and Dismissal

§ 1308 Pre-petition Tax Return Filing Requirement

§ 1322 Required Contents of Chapter 13 Plan

§ 1323 Modification of Plan Before Confirmation

§ 1324 Timing of Confirmation Hearing

§ 1325 Requirements for Confirmation of Plan

§ 1326 Chapter 13 Plan Payments

§ 1327 Effect of Confirmation

§ 1328 Requirements for, and Effect of, Chapter 13 Discharge

§ 1329 Modification of Chapter 13 Plan After Confirmation

However, certain types of creditor actions in the bankruptcy court must proceed by way of a regular lawsuit conducted under both these rules and the Federal Rules of Civil Procedure—for example, complaints to determine dischargeability of a debt. If you are representing yourself in such a lawsuit, you'll want to know these rules and look at the cases interpreting them. Any law library will have these rules. Your bankruptcy court's website will also have a link to the rules, as does www.law.cornell.edu.

Finding Local Court Rules

Every bankruptcy court operates under a set of local rules that govern how it does business and what is expected of the parties who use it. Throughout this book, we have cautioned you to read the rules for your particular court so that your dealings with the court will go smoothly—and so you won't end up getting tossed out of court if you become involved in litigation, such as an action to determine the dischargeability of a debt or a creditor's motion to lift the automatic stay.

Your bankruptcy court clerk's office will have the local rules available for you. Most courts also post their local rules on their own websites. To find the website for your court, take these steps.

Step 1:   Go to www.uscourts.gov/links.html.

Step 2:   Click the number on the map that is closest to where you live.

Step 3:   Browse the list until you find your court and click on it.

Step 4:   Click on the local rules link.

Court websites usually contain other helpful information as well, including case information, official and local bankruptcy forms, court guidelines (in addition to the local rules), information

for lawyers and BPPs, information about the court and its judges, and the court calendar.

At the law library, the *Collier Bankruptcy Practice Manual* has the local rules for most (if not all) of the nation's bankruptcy courts.

Finding Federal Court Bankruptcy Cases

Court opinions are vital to understanding how a particular law might apply to your individual case. The following levels of federal courts issue bankruptcy-related opinions:

- the U.S. Supreme Court
- the U.S. Courts of Appeals
- the Bankruptcy Appellate Panels
- the U.S. District Courts, and
- the bankruptcy courts.

Most bankruptcy-related opinions are, not surprisingly, issued by the bankruptcy courts. By comparison, very few bankruptcy opinions come out of the U.S. Supreme Court. The other courts are somewhere in the middle.

The Internet

Depending on the date the case was decided, U.S. Supreme Court decisions and U.S. Court of Appeals decisions are available for free on the Internet. For $13.95 a month you can also subscribe to VersusLaw (at www.versuslaw. com), which provides U.S. Court of Appeals cases for an earlier period than you can get for free—often back to 1950. VersusLaw doesn't require you to sign a long-term contract. So, one payment of $13.95 gets you a month's worth of research. Not too shabby. VersusLaw also publishes many U.S. District Court cases on its website. Opinions by the bankruptcy courts

The Structure of the Court System for Bankruptcy Cases

Bankruptcy court decisions play a role in the overall bankruptcy law. Every state has at least one bankruptcy court and most states have several. Each of these courts is called on to decide contested issues arising in the bankruptcy cases filed in that court. Many of these decisions are published in the Bankruptcy Reporter, published by West Publishing Co.

If a party doesn't like the outcome of the bankruptcy court's decision, and can afford it, it can appeal the case (ask a higher court to review the decision) to the U.S District Court in the area where the bankruptcy court is located. In many parts of the country, the party may opt instead to appeal to the Bankruptcy Appellate Panel, or BAP, in the judicial circuit in which the bankruptcy court is located. U.S. District Court decisions do not have to be followed by other courts that decide the same issue, but the opinions by the BAP must be followed by the bankruptcy courts in the same judicial circuit

unless they conflict with a higher circuit court (see below). These decisions are routinely published in volumes covering the U.S. District Court and the U.S. Court of Appeals.

If a party doesn't like the decision issued by a U.S. District Court or BAP, it can appeal the decision to the U.S. Court of Appeals in the appropriate judicial circuit. (This would be the second appeal.) A decision by the Court of Appeals supersedes decisions by the U.S. District Court or BAP and becomes law for that circuit. These decisions are also published alongside other Court of Appeal decisions.

Finally, a party to a U.S. Court of Appeals decision can appeal that decision to the U.S. Supreme Court (called petitioning for certiorari). The U.S. Supreme Court can decide to hear the case, or not. Decisions by the U.S. Supreme Court are the last word on any particular issue. These decisions are published along with other U.S. Supreme Court decisions.

are generally not yet available over the Internet, unless you subscribe to Lexis or Westlaw, both of which are extremely pricey.

U.S. Supreme Court. To find a Supreme Court case, go to Nolo's Supreme Court Center (at www.nolo.com, look in the Legal Research Center under FAQs). You can search by case citation, case name, or words related to your legal issue.

U.S. Court of Appeals. Google has federal appeals cases going back to 1925. Under "Advanced Search" on the Google home page, choose "Google Scholar." Then simply select

"Legal opinions and journals" and type in a case name.

U.S. District Court and Bankruptcy Court. Cases reported by the bankruptcy courts are generally not available online unless you subscribe to Westlaw or Lexis. However, if you know the name of a particular case and the court that decided it, a Google search might lead you to a court's website, where some judges post their decisions. Still, you will probably have to take a trip to a law library if you want to know what the judges are doing in these courts—where the legal rubber meets the judicial road.

The Law Library

U.S. Supreme Court cases are published in three different book series:

- *Supreme Court Reports*
- *Supreme Court Reporter*, and
- *Supreme Court Lawyer's Edition*.

Some law libraries carry all three of these publications; others have only one. The cases are the same, but each series has different editorial enhancements.

U.S. Court of Appeals cases are published in the *Federal Reporter* (abbreviated simply as "F."). Most law libraries, large and small, carry this series.

Many U.S. District Court cases are published in the *Federal Supplement* (F.Supp.), a series available in most law libraries.

Written opinions of bankruptcy judges, and related appeals, are published in the *Bankruptcy Reporter* (B.R.), available in most mid- to large-sized libraries. To accurately understand how your bankruptcy court is likely to interpret the laws in your particular case, sooner or later you will need access to the *Bankruptcy Reporter*.

State Statutes

The secret to understanding what property you can keep frequently lies in the exemptions that your state allows you to claim. These exemptions are found in your state's statutes.

The Internet

Every state has its statutes online, including its exemption statutes. This means that you can read your state's exemption statutes for yourself. Follow these steps:

Step 1: Go to Appendix A. At the top of your state's exemption table, you'll see a general reference to the collection of state laws for your state that contain the exemption statutes.

Step 2: Go to www.nolo.com.

Step 3: Click "Site Map" at the bottom of the page.

Step 4: Select "State Statutes" under the "Legal Research" heading.

Step 5: Click on your state.

Step 6: Locate the collection of statutes mentioned in Appendix A.

Step 7: Use the exemption citation to the far right of your state's exemption table to search for the statute.

The Law Library

Your law library will have your state's statutes in book form, usually referred to as your state's code, annotated statutes, or compiled laws. Use Appendix A in this book to find a reference to the exemption statute you want to read, then use that reference to locate the exemption statute in the code. Once you find and read the statute, you can browse the summaries of court opinions interpreting the statute and, if you wish, read the cases in their entirety.

Alternatively, if your library has a copy of *Collier on Bankruptcy* (see above), you can find the exemptions for your state, accompanied by annotations summarizing state court interpretations.

State Court Cases

State courts are sometimes called on to interpret exemption statutes. If a court has interpreted the statute in which you are interested, you'll definitely want to chase down the relevant case and read it for yourself.

The Internet

All states make their more recent cases available free on the Internet—usually back to about 1996. To find these cases for your state:

Step 1: Go to www.law.cornell.edu/opinions. html#state.

Step 2: Click on your state.

Step 3: Locate the link to the court opinions for your state. This may be one link, or there may be separate links for your state's supreme court and your state's courts of appeal (the lower trial courts seldom publish their opinions, so you probably won't be able to find them).

If you want to go back to an earlier case, consider subscribing to VersusLaw at www.versuslaw.com. As mentioned earlier, you don't have to sign a long-term contract.

The Law Library

Your law library will have a collection of books that contain opinions issued by your state's courts. If you have a citation, you can go right to the case. If you don't have a citation, you'll need to use a digest to find relevant bankruptcy cases. Finding cases by subject matter is a little too advanced for this brief summary. See *Legal Research: How to Find & Understand the Law,* by Stephen Elias and Susan Levinkind (Nolo), for more help.

Other Helpful Resources

The Office of the United States Trustee's website, at www.usdoj.gov/ust, provides lists of approved credit and financial management counseling agencies, median income figures for every state, the IRS national, regional, and local expenses you will need to complete the means test, and all of the forms you will need to file, in a fill-in-the-blanks PDF format. You can also download official bankruptcy forms from www.uscourts. gov/bkforms/index.html. However, this site doesn't include required local forms; for those, you'll have to visit your court or its website.

As part of the bankruptcy process, you are required to give the replacement (retail) value for all of the property you list in Schedule A (real property) and Schedule B (personal property). These figures are also the key to figuring out which of your property is exempt. Here are some tips on finding these values:

- **Cars.** Use the *Kelley Blue Book*, at www. kbb.com, or the website of the National Auto Dealers Association, www.nada.com.
- **Other personal property.** Check prices on eBay, www.ebay.com.
- **Homes.** Check the prices for which comparable homes have sold in the recent past. For a modest fee, you can get details on comparable homes, including sales history, number of bedrooms and baths, square footage, and property tax information, at www.smarthomebuy.com. Less-detailed information (purchase price, sales date, and address) is available free from sites like www.zillow.com, www. homevalues.com, www.domania.com, www.homeradar.com, and http://list. realestate.yahoo.com/re/homevalues. ●

Alternatives to Bankruptcy

After reading the previous 11 chapters, you should have a pretty good idea of what filing a consumer Chapter 7 or a Chapter 13 bankruptcy will involve—and what you can hope to get out of it. Before you decide whether either type of bankruptcy is the right solution, however, consider the other options described in this chapter. Although bankruptcy is the only sensible remedy for some people with debt problems, an alternative course of action makes better sense for others.

Do Nothing

Surprisingly, the best approach for some people who are deeply in debt is to take no action at all. You can't be thrown in jail for not paying your debts (except in the unusual situations described in Ch. 7), and your creditors can't collect money from you that you just don't have.

Creditors Must Sue to Collect

Except for taxing agencies and student loan creditors, creditors must first sue you in court and get a money judgment before they can go after your income and property. The big exception to this general rule is that a creditor can take back collateral—repossess a car or furniture, for example—when you default on a debt that's secured by that collateral. (If you're worried about foreclosure on a house, see Ch. 5.)

Under the typical security agreement (a contract involving collateral), the creditor can repossess the property without first going to court. But the creditor will not be able to go after your other property and income for any "deficiency" (the difference between what you

owe and what the repossessed property fetches at auction) without first going to court for a money judgment.

Much of Your Property Is Protected

Even if creditors get a money judgment against you, they can't take away such essentials as:

- basic clothing
- ordinary household furnishings
- personal effects
- food
- Social Security or SSI payments
- unemployment benefits
- public assistance
- bank accounts with direct deposits from government benefit programs, and
- 75% of your wages (but child support judgments can grab a larger share).

The state exemptions described in Ch. 4 (and listed in Appendix A) apply whether or not you file for bankruptcy. Even creditors who get a money judgment against you can't seize these protected items to satisfy the judgment. (However, neither the federal bankruptcy exemptions nor the California System 2 exemptions described in Ch. 4 apply if a creditor sues you. Those are bankruptcy-only exemptions.)

What It Means to Be Judgment Proof

If all of the property you own is exempt, you are what is commonly referred to as "judgment proof." Whoever sues you and wins will be holding a useless piece of paper (at least temporarily), simply because you don't have anything that can legally be taken. While money judgments last a long time—typically ten years—and can be renewed, this won't make any difference unless your fortunes change for the better. If that happens, you might reconsider bankruptcy at that time.

If your creditors know that their chances of collecting a judgment from you any time soon are slim, they probably won't sue you in the first place. Instead, they'll simply write off your debt and treat it as a deductible business loss for income tax purposes. After some years have passed (usually between four and ten), the debt will become legally uncollectable, under state laws known as statutes of limitation.

Although statutes of limitation periods won't apply if the creditor sues you in time, lawsuits typically cost thousands of dollars in legal fees. If a creditor decides, on the basis of your economic profile, not to go to court at the present time, it is unlikely to seek a judgment down the line to extend its claims. In short, because creditors are reluctant to throw good money after bad, your poor economic circumstances might shield you from trouble.

> **CAUTION**
>
> **Watch out for later liens, even if you don't currently own real estate.** Even though you may technically be judgment proof because you don't own any real estate, a lien recorded in your county may cause problems later on if you buy a house. This is because in some states (including California) creditors can record liens even if you don't own any property. If you later buy property, the lien will "pop up" and attach to the property, meaning you'll have to deal with it. If this happens after you've completed a bankruptcy, you may be

able to reopen the bankruptcy and file a motion to avoid the lien (See Ch. 10).

> **CAUTION**
>
> **Don't restart the clock.** The statute of limitations can be renewed if you revive an old debt by, for example, admitting that you owe it or making a payment. As soon as you acknowledge a debt, the clock starts all over again. Savvy creditors are aware of this loophole and may try to trick you into admitting the debt so they can sue to collect it. Sometimes, it might be a good idea to try to repay a debt, particularly one to a local merchant with whom you wish to continue doing business. But unless you are planning to make good on the debt or try to negotiate a new payment schedule, you should avoid any admissions. (You'll find a sample letter that avoids admitting a debt below.)

Stopping Bill Collector Harassment

Many people are moved to file for bankruptcy to stop their creditors from making harassing telephone calls and writing threatening letters. (See Ch. 1 for more on the automatic stay.) Fortunately, there is another way to get annoying creditors off your back. Federal law forbids collection agencies from threatening you, lying about what they can do to you, or invading your privacy. And many state laws prevent original creditors from taking similar actions.

Under the federal law, you can legally force collection agencies to stop phoning or writing you by simply demanding that they stop, even if you owe them a bundle and can't pay a cent. (The law is the federal Fair Debt Collections Practices

Act, 15 U.S.C. §§ 1692 and following.) For more information, see *Solve Your Money Troubles*, by Robin Leonard and Margaret Reiter (Nolo). Below is a sample letter asking a creditor to stop contacting the debtor.

Negotiate With Your Creditors

If you have some income, or you have assets you're willing to sell, you may be better off negotiating with your creditors than filing for bankruptcy. Negotiation may buy you some time to get back on your feet, or you and your creditors may agree to settle your debts for less than the amount you owe.

Creditors hate it when debtors don't pay their debts. They don't like the hassle of instituting collection proceedings, or the fact that these proceedings tend to turn debt-owing customers into former customers. To avoid the collection process and to keep customers, creditors sometimes will reduce the debtor's expected payments, extend the time to pay, drop their demands for late fees, and make similar adjustments. They're most likely to be lenient if they believe you are making an honest effort to deal with your debt problems.

As soon as it becomes clear to you that you're going to have trouble paying a bill, write to the creditor. Explain the problem—whether it's an accident, job layoff, divorce, emergency expense for your child, unexpected tax bill, or something else. Mention any development that points to an improving financial condition, such as job prospects. Also, consider sending a token payment every month (the more the better, of course). This tells the creditor that you are continuing to be serious about paying the full debt but just can't afford to right now.

Sample Letter to Collection Agency

November 11, 20xx
Sasnak Collection Service
49 Pirate Place
Topeka, Kansas 69000

Attn: Marc Mist

Re: Lee Anne Ito
     Account No. 88-90-92

Dear Mr. Mist:

For the past three months, I have received several phone calls and letters from you concerning an overdue Rich's Department Store account.

This is my formal notice to you under 15 U.S.C. § 1692c to cease all further communications with me except for the reasons specifically set forth in the federal law.

This letter is not meant in any way to be an acknowledgment that I owe this money.

Very truly yours,

Lee Anne Ito

Lee Anne Ito

Token payments make a big difference, especially to local creditors. And if you want to keep that credit or that business relationship, paying even a small amount might help. On the other hand, if it's been a long time since you've made any payments, you might want to hold off on your token payment until you've checked on the "statute of limitations" for that debt (the state time limit after which the debt goes away if no court action has been filed to collect it). Your payment might have the unfortunate effect of starting up a new limitations period.

Your success in getting creditors to give you time to pay will depend on the types of debts you have, how far behind you are, and the creditors' policies toward debts that are in arrears.

If you are not yet behind on your bills, be aware that a number of creditors have a ridiculous policy that requires you to default—and in some cases, become at least 90 days past due—before they will negotiate with you for better repayment terms. If any creditor makes this a condition of negotiating, find out from the creditor how you can keep the default out of your credit report.

Some creditors simply refuse to negotiate with debtors. Despite the fact that creditors get at least something when they negotiate settlements, many ignore debtors' pleas for help, continue to make telephone calls demanding payment (unless you assert your right under federal law to not receive the calls—see "Stopping Bill Collector Harassment," above) and leave debtors with few options other than to file for bankruptcy. In fact, a majority of my clients who contact me about bankruptcy do so because of the unreasonableness of their creditors or the collection agencies hired by their creditors.

To help your creditors see the wisdom of settling with you on reasonable terms, it often won't hurt to mention the fact that you're thinking of filing for bankruptcy. Creditors know that they are very likely to get nothing in a bankruptcy case and may settle for a very few cents on the dollar. This being said, don't be surprised if a creditor tells you to "go ahead and file." More than a few creditors stand on what they take to be principle.

Legal Remedies for Unreasonable Creditor Actions

Creditors often violate federal laws preventing unfair collection practices—such as contacting you when you've made it clear you don't intend to repay a debt. These laws allow you to sue a law-breaking creditor in federal court and recover damages—including damages for emotional distress. If you become seriously irked by an overzealous collector and want to know whether a legal line has been crossed, take a look at *Solve Your Money Troubles: Debt, Credit & Bankruptcy,* by Robin Leonard and Margaret Reiter (Nolo). You can also consult a consumer bankruptcy attorney, using your local yellow pages or the referral list on the National Association of Consumer Bankruptcy Attorneys website, at www.nacba.org.

Get Outside Help to Design a Repayment Plan

Many people have trouble negotiating with creditors, either because they don't have the skills and negotiating experience to do a good job or because they find the whole process exceedingly unpleasant. Because the ability to negotiate is an art, many people benefit from outside help.

If you don't want to negotiate with your creditors, you can turn to a lawyer or to a credit counseling agency. These agencies come in two basic varieties: nonprofit and for profit. They all work on the same basic principle: A repayment plan is negotiated with all of your unsecured creditors. You make one monthly payment to the agency, which distributes the payment to your creditors as provided in the plan. As long as you make the payments, the creditors will not take any action against you. And, if you succeed in completing the plan, one or more of your creditors may be willing to offer you new credit on reasonable terms.

The nonprofit agencies tend to be funded primarily by the major creditors (in the form of a commission for each repayment plan they negotiate) and by moderate fees charged the user (roughly $20–$25 per plan negotiated). The for-profit agencies are funded by the same sources but tend to charge much higher fees.

The big downside to entering into one of the repayment plans is that if you fail to make a payment, the creditors may pull the plug on the deal and come after you, regardless of how faithful you've been in the past. When that happens, you may find that you would have been better off filing for bankruptcy in the first place. For more on the pros and cons of repayment plans, see *Solve Your Money Troubles*, by Robin Leonard and Margaret Reiter (Nolo).

Credit Counseling Agencies

As explained above, bankruptcy filers are required to get credit counseling. You must get this counseling from a nonprofit agency that meets a number of requirements and has been approved by the U.S. Trustee. If you decide to get help with a repayment plan, you would do well to choose one of these agencies—the U.S. Trustee's office oversees their operation, which gives you some protection against fraudulent practices. You can find a list of approved agencies at the U.S. Trustee's website, at www.usdoj.gov/ust.

How Debt Management Typically Works

To use a credit counseling agency to help you pay your debts, you must have some steady income. A counselor will contact your creditors to let them know that you've sought assistance and need more time to pay. Based on your income and debts, the counselor, with your creditors, will decide how much you must pay and for how long. You must then make one payment each month to the counseling agency, which in turn will pay your creditors. The agency will ask the creditors to return a small percentage of the money received to the agency office, in order to fund its work. This arrangement is generally referred to as a "debt management program."

Some creditors will make overtures to help you when you're participating in a debt management program, such as reducing interest, waiving minimum payments, and forgiving late charges. But many creditors will not make interest concessions, such as waiving a portion of the accumulated interest to help you repay the principal portion of the debt. More likely, you'll get the late fees dropped and the opportunity to reinstate your credit if you successfully complete a debt management program.

Disadvantages of Debt Management

Participating in a credit counseling agency's debt management program is a little bit like filing for Chapter 13 bankruptcy. But working with a credit or debt counseling agency has one big advantage: No bankruptcy will appear on your credit record. On the other hand, a debt management program has two disadvantages when compared to Chapter 13 bankruptcy. First, if you miss a plan payment, Chapter 13 will often provide a way for you to make it up and continue to protect you from creditors who would otherwise start collection actions. A debt management program has no such protection, so any one creditor can pull the plug on your plan. Also, a debt management program plan usually requires you to pay your unsecured debts in full, over time. In Chapter 13, you often are only required to pay a small fraction of your nonpriority unsecured debts (if any), such as credit card and medical debts.

Critics of credit counseling agencies point out that the counselors tilt toward signing people up for a repayment plan in circumstances where bankruptcy would be in their best interest—so the agency will get a commission from the creditors that isn't available for cases that end up in bankruptcy. However, credit counseling agencies approved by the Office of the U.S. Trustee have a number of requirements placed on them to protect against undue influence by creditors and are required to make a number of disclosures that should prevent you from being ripped off. (See Ch. 2 for more on these rules.)

File for Chapter 11 Bankruptcy

Chapter 11 bankruptcy is ordinarily used by financially struggling businesses to reorganize their affairs. However, it is also available to individuals. Individuals who consider Chapter 11 bankruptcy usually have debts in excess of one or both of the Chapter 13 bankruptcy limits—$336,900 of unsecured debts and $1,010,650 of secured debts—or substantial nonexempt assets, such as several pieces of real estate.

The initial filing fee is currently $839, compared to $299 for Chapter 7 or $274 for Chapter 13 bankruptcy. In addition, you must pay a quarterly fee, based on a percentage of the disbursements made to pay your debts. The fee runs from $250 a quarter when the disbursements total less than $15,000, to $10,000 a quarter when disbursements total $5,000,000 or more. The fee must be paid until your reorganization plan is either approved or dismissed, or your case is converted to Chapter 7 bankruptcy. Most attorneys require a minimum $10,000 retainer fee to handle a Chapter 11 bankruptcy case. Add to that the Chapter 11 bankruptcy court fees, which in one year could run from $1,000 to $10,000, and you can see that Chapter 11 isn't for everyone.

You'll need a lawyer to file for Chapter 11 bankruptcy. A Chapter 11 bankruptcy typically turns into a long, expensive, lawyer-infested mess, and many Chapter 11 filings are converted to Chapter 7 (and the business is dissolved) once legal fees gobble up the business assets. Chapter 11 small business bankruptcy is even more difficult in that all documents must be filed within 30 days of the filing of the petition. Even to file a "fast-track" Chapter 11 bankruptcy for small businesses with debts up to $2 million, you will need an attorney.

File for Chapter 12 Bankruptcy

Chapter 12 bankruptcy is like Chapter 13 bankruptcy in many respects. However, only people and entities that meet the definition of family farmer may use it. To qualify as a family farmer:

- your debts cannot exceed $3,544,525
- 50% or more of your debt must have arisen from the farming operation, not including a purchase money mortgage
- 50% or more of your income must have been earned from the farming operation in the year preceding the filing of the petition, and
- your income must be "sufficiently stable and regular" to enable payments under a Chapter 12 plan.

Like Chapter 13, you must file a schedule of assets and liabilities and a statement of financial affairs. Even though a trustee is appointed to supervise the plan, the farm debtor remains in possession of the farm assets and actions by creditors are automatically stayed upon filing the petition.

As in Chapter 13, you must file a plan that meets Chapter 12 requirements. The plan must provide that all unsecured debts are paid in full or, alternatively, all disposable income is used to pay down the unsecured debt over the ensuing three-year period (which can be extended to five years with court permission). Plan payments must pay unsecured creditors at least what they would have received in a Chapter 7 bankruptcy. After completion of the plan, all are discharged except debts that wouldn't be dischargeable in Chapter 7.

Chapter 12 has several advantages over Chapter 13 bankruptcy. The court has unrestricted authority to modify (cram down) secured debts, such as mortgages and car notes, so the debt matches the market value of the property. (See Ch. 6 for more on cramdowns.) This is different from Chapter 13, where cramdowns cannot be used for home mortgages and recent car loans. Another advantage of Chapter 12—secured debts that extend beyond the plan period can be modified without having to pay them all off in the plan. That is, payments can extend beyond the plan until the debt is paid off in the normal course of time. And unlike Chapter 13, priority debts do not have to be paid in full so long as all disposable income over a five-year period is devoted to the plan.

If you are interested in Chapter 12 bankruptcy, consult with a lawyer.

Glossary

341 meeting. See "meeting of creditors."

341 notice. A notice sent to the debtor and the debtor's creditors announcing the date, time, and place for the first meeting of creditors. The 341 notice is sent along with the notice of bankruptcy filing and information about important deadlines by which creditors have to take certain actions, such as filing objections.

342 notice. A notice that the court clerk is required to give to debtors pursuant to Section 342 of the Bankruptcy Code, to inform them of their obligations as bankruptcy debtors and the consequences of not being completely honest in their bankruptcy case.

707(b) action. An action taken by the U.S. Trustee, the regular trustee, or any creditor, under authority of Section 707(b) of the Bankruptcy Code, to dismiss a debtor's Chapter 7 filing on the ground of abuse.

Abuse. Misuse of the Chapter 7 bankruptcy remedy. This term is typically applied to Chapter 7 bankruptcy filings that should have been filed under Chapter 13 because the debtor appears to have enough disposable income to fund a Chapter 13 repayment plan.

Accounts receivable. Money or other property that one person or business owes to another for goods or services. Accounts receivable most often refer to the debts owed to a business by its customers.

Administrative expenses. The trustee's fee, the debtor's attorney fee, and other costs of bringing a bankruptcy case that a debtor must pay in full in a Chapter 13 repayment plan. Administrative costs are typically 10% of the debtor's total payments under the plan.

Administrative Office of the United States Courts. The federal government agency that issues court rules and forms to be used by the federal courts, including bankruptcy courts.

Adversary action. Any lawsuit that begins with the filing of a formal complaint and formal service of process on the parties being sued. In a bankruptcy case, adversary actions are often brought to determine the dischargeability of a debt or to recover property transferred by the debtor shortly before filing for bankruptcy.

Affidavit. A written statement of facts, signed under oath in front of a notary public.

Allowed secured claim. A debt that is secured by collateral or a lien against the debtor's property, for which the creditor has filed a proof of claim with the bankruptcy court. The claim is secured only to the extent of the value of the property—for example, if a debtor owes $5,000 on a note for a car that is worth only $3,000, the remaining $2,000 is an unsecured claim.

Amendment. A document filed by the debtor that changes one or more documents previously filed with the court. A debtor often files an amendment because the trustee requires changes to the debtor's paperwork based on the testimony at the meeting of creditors.

Animals. An exemption category in many states. Some states specifically exempt pets or livestock and poultry. If your state simply allows you to exempt "animals," you may include livestock, poultry, or pets. Some states exempt only domestic animals, which are usually considered to be all animals except pets.

Annuity. A type of insurance policy that pays out during the life of the insured, unlike life insurance, which pays out at the insured's death. Once the insured reaches the age specified in the policy, he or she receives monthly payments until death.

Appliance. A household apparatus or machine, usually operated by electricity, gas, or propane. Examples include refrigerators, stoves, washing machines, dishwashers, vacuum cleaners, air conditioners, and toasters.

Arms and accoutrements. Arms are weapons (such as pistols, rifles, and swords); accoutrements are the furnishings of a soldier's outfit, such as a belt or pack, but not clothes or weapons.

Arms-length creditor. A creditor with whom the debtor deals in the normal course of business, as opposed to an insider (a friend, relative, or business partner).

Articles of adornment. See "jewelry."

Assessment benefits. See "stipulated insurance."

Assisted person. Any person contemplating or filing for bankruptcy who receives bankruptcy assistance, whose debts are primarily consumer debts, and whose nonexempt property is valued at less than $150,000. A person or entity that offers help to an assisted person is called a "debt relief agency."

Automatic stay. An injunction automatically issued by the bankruptcy court when a debtor files for bankruptcy. The automatic stay prohibits most creditor collection activities, such as filing or continuing lawsuits, making written requests for payment, or notifying credit reporting bureaus of an unpaid debt.

Avails. Any amount available to the owner of an insurance policy other than the actual proceeds of the policy. Avails include dividend payments, interest, cash or surrender value (the money you'd get if you sold your policy back to the insurance company), and loan value (the amount of cash you can borrow against the policy).

Bankruptcy Abuse Prevention and Reform Act of 2005. The formal name of the new bankruptcy law that took effect on October 17, 2005.

Bankruptcy administrator. The official responsible for supervising the administration of bankruptcy cases, estates, and trustees in Alabama and North Carolina, where there is no U.S. Trustee.

Bankruptcy Appellate Panel. A specialized court that hears appeals of bankruptcy court decisions (available only in some regions).

Bankruptcy assistance. Goods or services provided to an "assisted person" for the purpose of providing information, advice, counsel, document preparation or filing, or attendance at a creditors' meeting; appearing in a case or proceeding on behalf of another person; or providing legal representation.

Bankruptcy Code. The federal law that governs the creation and operation of the bankruptcy courts and establishes bankruptcy procedures. (You can find the Bankruptcy Code in Title 11 of the United States Code.)

Bankruptcy estate. All of the property you own when you file for bankruptcy, except for most pensions and educational trusts. The trustee technically takes control of your bankruptcy estate for the duration of your case.

Bankruptcy lawyer. A lawyer who specializes in bankruptcy and is licensed to practice law in the federal courts.

Bankruptcy petition preparer. Any non-lawyer who helps someone with his or her bankruptcy. Bankruptcy petition preparers (BPPs) are a special type of debt relief agency, regulated by the U.S. Trustee. Because they are not lawyers, BPPs can't represent anyone in bankruptcy court or provide legal advice.

Bankruptcy Petition Preparer Fee Declaration. An official form bankruptcy petition preparers must file with the bankruptcy court to disclose their fees.

Bankruptcy Petition Preparer Notice to Debtor. A written notice that bankruptcy petition preparers must provide to debtors who use their services. The Notice explains that bankruptcy petition preparers aren't attorneys and that they are permitted to perform only certain acts, such as entering information in the bankruptcy petition and schedules under the direction of their clients.

Benefit or benevolent society benefits. See "fraternal benefit society benefits."

Building materials. Items, such as lumber, brick, stone, iron, paint, and varnish, that are used to build or improve a structure.

Burial plot. A cemetery plot.

Business bankruptcy. A bankruptcy in which the debts arise primarily from the operation of a business, including bankruptcies filed by corporations, limited liability companies, and partnerships.

Certification. The act of signing a document under penalty of perjury. (The document that is signed is also called a certification.)

Chapter 7 bankruptcy. A liquidation bankruptcy, in which the trustee sells the debtor's nonexempt property and distributes the proceeds to the debtor's creditors. At the end of the case, the debtor receives a discharge of all remaining debts, except those that cannot legally be discharged.

Chapter 9 bankruptcy. A type of bankruptcy restricted to governmental units.

Chapter 11 bankruptcy. A type of bankruptcy intended to help businesses reorganize their debt load in order to remain in business. A Chapter 11 bankruptcy is typically much more expensive than a Chapter 7 or 13 bankruptcy because all of the lawyers must be paid out of the bankruptcy estate.

Chapter 12 bankruptcy. A type of bankruptcy designed to help small farmers reorganize their debts.

Chapter 13 bankruptcy. A type of consumer bankruptcy designed to help individuals reorganize their debts and pay all or a portion of them over three to five years.

Chapter 13 plan. A document filed in a Chapter 13 bankruptcy in which the debtor shows how all of his or her projected disposable income will be used over a three- to five-year period to pay all mandatory debts—for example, back child support, taxes, and mortgage arrearages—as well as some or all unsecured, nonpriority debts, such as medical and credit card bills.

Claim. A creditor's assertion that the bankruptcy filer owes it a debt or obligation.

Clothing. As an exemption category, the everyday clothes you and your family need for work, school, household use, and protection from the elements. In many states, luxury items and furs are not included in the clothing exemption category.

Codebtor. A person who assumes an equal responsibility, along with the debtor, to repay a debt or loan.

Collateral. Property pledged by a borrower as security for a loan.

Common law property states. States that don't use a community property system to classify marital property.

Community property. Certain property owned by married couples in Arizona, California, Idaho, Louisiana, New Mexico, Nevada, Texas, Washington, Wisconsin, and, if both spouses agree, Alaska. Very generally, all property acquired during the marriage is considered community property, belonging equally to both spouses, except for gifts and inheritances by one spouse. Similarly, all debts incurred during the marriage are considered community debts, owed equally by both spouses, with limited exceptions.

Complaint. A formal document that initiates a lawsuit.

Complaint to determine dischargeablity. A complaint initiating an adversary action in bankruptcy court that asks the court to decide whether a particular debt should be discharged at the end of the debtor's bankruptcy case.

Condominium. A building or complex in which separate units, such as townhouses or apartments, are owned by individuals, and the common areas (lobby, hallways, stairways, and so on) are jointly owned by the unit owners.

Confirmation. The bankruptcy judge's ruling approving a Chapter 13 plan.

Confirmation hearing. A court hearing conducted by a bankruptcy judge in which the judge decides whether a debtor's proposed Chapter 13 plan appears to be feasible and meets all applicable legal requirements.

Consumer bankruptcy. A bankruptcy in which a preponderance of the debt was incurred for personal, family, or household purposes.

Consumer debt. A debt incurred by an individual for personal, family, or household purposes.

Contingent debts. Debts that may be owed if certain events happen or conditions are satisfied.

Contingent interests in the estate of a decedent. The right to inherit property if one or more conditions to the inheritance are satisfied. For example, a debtor who will inherit property only if he survives his brother has a contingent interest.

Conversion. When a debtor who has filed one type of bankruptcy switches to another type—as when a Chapter 7 debtor converts to a Chapter 13 bankruptcy, or vice versa.

Cooperative housing. A building or other residential structure that is owned by a corporation formed by the residents. In exchange for purchasing stock in the corporation, the residents have the right to live in particular units.

Cooperative insurance. Compulsory employment benefits provided by a state or federal government, such as old age, survivors, disability, and health insurance, to assure a minimum standard of living for lower- and middle-income people. Also called social insurance.

Court clerk. The court employee who is responsible for accepting filings and other documents, and generally maintaining an accurate and efficient flow of paper and information in the court.

Cram down. In a Chapter 13 bankruptcy, the act of reducing a secured debt to the replacement value of the collateral securing the debt.

Credit counseling. Counseling that explores the possibility of repaying debts outside of bankruptcy and educates the debtor about credit, budgeting, and financial management. Under the new bankruptcy law, a debtor must undergo credit counseling with an approved provider before filing for bankruptcy.

Credit insurance. An insurance policy that covers a borrower for an outstanding loan. If the borrower dies or becomes disabled before paying off the loan, the policy will pay off the balance due.

Creditor. A person or institution to whom money is owed.

Creditor committee. In a Chapter 11 bankruptcy, a committee that represents the unsecured debtors in reorganization proceedings.

Creditor matrix. A specially formatted list of creditors that a debtor must file with the bankruptcy petition. The matrix helps the court notify creditors of the bankruptcy filing and the date and time set for the first meeting of creditors.

Creditors' meeting. See "meeting of creditors."

Crops. Products of the soil or earth that are grown and raised annually and gathered in a single season. Thus, oranges (on the tree or harvested) are crops; an orange tree isn't.

Current market value. What property could be sold for. This is how a debtor's property was previously valued for purposes of determining whether the property is protected by an applicable exemption. Under the new bankruptcy law, property must be valued at its "replacement cost."

Current monthly income. As defined by the new bankruptcy law, a bankruptcy filer's total gross income (whether taxable or not), averaged over the six-month period immediately preceding the month in which the bankruptcy is filed. The current monthly income is used to determine whether the debtor can file for Chapter 7 bankruptcy, among other things.

Debt. An obligation of any type, including a loan, credit, or promise to perform a contract or lease.

Debt relief agency. An umbrella term for any person or agency—including lawyers and bankruptcy petition preparers, but excluding banks, nonprofit and government agencies, and employees of debt relief agencies—that provides "bankruptcy assistance" to an "assisted person."

Debtor. Someone who owes money to another person or business. Also, the generic term used to refer to anyone who files for bankruptcy.

Declaration. A written statement that is made under oath but not witnessed by a notary public.

Declaration of homestead. A form filed with the county recorder's office to put on record your right to a homestead exemption. In most states, the homestead exemption is automatic—that is, you are not required to record a homestead declaration in order to claim the homestead exemption. A few states do require such a recording, however.

Disability benefits. Payments made under a disability insurance or retirement plan when the insured is unable to work (or retires early) because of disability, accident, or sickness.

Discharge. A court order, issued at the conclusion of a Chapter 7 or Chapter 13 bankruptcy case, which legally relieves the debtor of personal liability for debts that can be discharged in that type of bankruptcy.

Discharge exceptions. Debts that are not discharged in a bankruptcy case. The debtor continues to owe these debts even after the bankruptcy is concluded.

Discharge hearing. A hearing conducted by a bankruptcy court to explain the discharge, urge the debtor to stay out of debt, and review reaffirmation agreements to make sure they are feasible and fair.

Dischargeability action. An adversary action brought by a party who asks the court to determine whether a particular debt qualifies for discharge.

Dischargeable debt. A debt that is wiped out at the conclusion of a bankruptcy case, unless the judge decides that it should not be.

Dismissal. When the court orders a case to be closed without providing the relief available under the bankruptcy laws. For example, a Chapter 13 case might be dismissed because the debtor fails to propose a feasible plan; a Chapter 7 case might be dismissed for abuse.

Disposable income. The difference between a debtor's "current monthly income" and allowable expenses. This is the amount that the bankruptcy law deems available to pay into a Chapter 13 plan.

Domestic animals. See "animals."

Domestic support obligation. An obligation to pay alimony or child support to a spouse, child, or government entity pursuant to an order by a court or other governmental unit.

Doubling. The ability of married couples to double the amount of certain property exemptions when filing for bankruptcy together. The federal bankruptcy exemptions allow doubling. State laws vary—some permit doubling and some do not.

Education Individual Retirement Account. A type of account to which a person can contribute a certain amount of tax-deferred funds every year for the educational benefit of the debtor or certain relatives. Such an account is not part of the debtor's bankruptcy estate.

Emergency bankruptcy filing. An initial bankruptcy filing that includes only the petition and the creditor matrix, filed right away because the debtor needs the protection of the automatic stay to prevent a creditor from taking certain action, such as a foreclosure. An emergency filing case will be dismissed if the other required documents and forms are not filed in a timely manner.

Endowment insurance. An insurance policy that gives an insured who lives for a specified time (the endowment period) the right to receive the face value of the policy (the amount paid at death). If the insured dies sooner, the beneficiary named in the policy receives the proceeds.

Equity. The amount you get to keep if you sell property—typically the property's market value, less the costs of sale and the value of any liens on the property.

ERISA-qualified benefits. Pensions that meet the requirements of the Employee Retirement Income Security Act (ERISA), a federal law that sets minimum standards for such plans and requires beneficiaries to receive certain notices.

Executory contract. A contract in which one or both parties still have a duty to carry out one or more of the contract's terms.

Exempt property. Property described by state and federal laws (exemptions) that a debtor is entitled to keep in a Chapter 7 bankruptcy. Exempt property cannot be taken and sold by the trustee for the benefit of the debtor's unsecured creditors.

Exemptions. State and federal laws specifying the types of property creditors are not entitled to take to satisfy a debt, and the bankruptcy trustee is not entitled to take and sell for the benefit of the debtor's unsecured creditors.

Farm tools. Tools used by a person whose primary occupation is farming. Some states limit farm tools of the trade to items that can be held in the hand, such as hoes, axes, pitchforks, shovels, scythes, and the like. In other states, farm tools also include plows, harnesses, mowers, reapers, and so on.

Federal exemptions. A list of exemptions contained in the federal Bankruptcy Code. Some states give debtors the option of using the federal exemptions rather than the state exemptions.

Federal Rules of Bankruptcy Procedure. A set of rules issued by the Administrative Office of the United States Courts, which govern bankruptcy court procedures.

Filing date. The date a bankruptcy petition in a particular case is filed. With few exceptions, debts incurred after the filing date are not discharged. Similarly, property owned before the filing date is part of the bankruptcy estate, while property acquired after the filing date is not.

Fines, penalties, and restitution. Debts owed to a court or a victim as a result of a sentence in a criminal matter. These debts are generally not dischargeable in bankruptcy.

Foreclosure. The process by which a creditor with a lien on real estate forces a sale of the property in order to collect on the lien. Foreclosure typically occurs when a homeowner defaults on a mortgage.

Fraternal benefit society benefits. Benefits, often group life insurance, paid for by fraternal societies, such as the Elks, Masons, Knights of Columbus, or the Knights of Maccabees, for their members. Also called benefit society, benevolent society, or mutual aid association benefits.

Fraud. Generally, an act that is intended to mislead another for the purpose of financial gain. In a bankruptcy case, fraud is any writing or representation intended to mislead creditors for the purpose of obtaining a loan or credit, or any act intended to mislead the bankruptcy court or the trustee.

Fraudulent transfer. In a bankruptcy case, a transfer of property to another for less than the property's value for the purpose of hiding the property from the bankruptcy trustee— for instance, when a debtor signs a car over to a relative to keep it out of the bankruptcy estate. Fraudulently transferred property can be recovered and sold by the trustee for the benefit of the creditors.

Fraudulently concealed assets. Property that a bankruptcy debtor deliberately fails to disclose as required by the bankruptcy rules.

Furnishings. An exemption category recognized in many states, which includes furniture, fixtures in your home (such as a heating unit, furnace, or built-in lighting), and other items with which a home is furnished, such as carpets and drapes.

Good faith. In a Chapter 13 case, when a debtor files for bankruptcy with the sincere purpose of paying off debts over the period of time required by law rather than for manipulative purposes—such as to prevent a foreclosure that by all rights should be allowed to proceed.

Goods and chattels. See "personal property."

Group life or group health insurance. A single insurance policy covering individuals in a group (for example, employees) and their dependents.

Head of household. A person who supports and maintains, in one household, one or more people who are closely related to the person by blood, marriage, or adoption. Also referred to as "head of family."

Health aids. Items needed to maintain their owner's health, such as a wheelchair, crutches, prosthesis, or a hearing aid. Many states require that health aids be prescribed by a physician.

Health benefits. Benefits paid under health insurance plans, such as Blue Cross/Blue Shield, to cover the costs of health care.

Heirloom. An item with special monetary or sentimental value, which is passed down from generation to generation.

Home equity loan. A loan made to a homeowner on the basis of the equity in the home—and secured by the home in the same manner as a mortgage.

Homestead. A state or federal exemption applicable to property where the debtor lives when he or she files bankruptcy—usually including boats and mobile homes.

Homestead declaration. See "declaration of homestead."

Household good. As an exemption category, an item of permanent nature (as opposed to items consumed, like food or cosmetics) used in or about the house. This includes linens, dinnerware, utensils, pots and pans, and small electronic equipment like radios. Many state laws specifically list the types of household goods that fall within this exemption, as do the federal bankruptcy laws.

Householder. A person who supports and maintains a household, with or without other people. Also called a "housekeeper."

Impairs an exemption. When a lien, in combination with any other liens on the property and the amount the debtor is entitled to claim as exempt, exceeds the value of the property the debtor could claim in the absence of any liens. For example, if property is worth $15,000, there are $5,000 worth of liens on the property, and the debtor is entitled to a $5,000 exemption in the property, a lien that exceeded $5,000 would impair the debtor's exemption. Certain types of liens that impair an exemption may be removed (avoided) by the debtor if the court so orders.

Implement. As an exemption category, an instrument, tool, or utensil used by a person to accomplish his or her job.

In lieu of homestead (or burial) exemption. Designates an exemption that is available only if you don't claim the homestead (or burial) exemption.

Individual Debtor's Statement of Intention. An official bankruptcy form that debtors with secured debts must file to indicate what they want to do with the property that secures the debt. For instance, a debtor with a car note must indicate whether he or she wants to keep the car and continue the debt (reaffirmation), pay off the car note at a reduced price (redemption), or give the car back to the creditor and cancel the debt.

Injunction. A court order prohibiting a person or entity from taking specified actions—for example, the automatic stay (in reality an automatic injunction), which prevents most creditors from trying to collect their debts.

Insider creditor. A creditor with whom the debtor has a personal relationship, such as a relative, friend, or business partner.

Intangible property. Property that cannot be physically touched, such as an ownership share in a corporation or a copyright. Documents—such as a stock certificate—may provide evidence of intangible property.

Involuntary dismissal. When a bankruptcy judge dismisses a case because the debtor fails to carry out his or her duties—such as filing papers in a timely manner and cooperating with the trustee—or because the debtor files the bankruptcy in bad faith or engages in abuse by wrongfully filing for Chapter 7 when he or she should have filed for Chapter 13.

Involuntary lien. A lien that is placed on the debtor's property without the debtor's consent—for instance, when the IRS places a lien on property for back taxes.

IRS expenses. A table of national and regional expense estimates published by the IRS. Debtors whose "current monthly income" is more than their state's "median family income" must use the IRS expenses to calculate their average net income in a Chapter 7 case, or their disposable income in a Chapter 13 case.

Jewelry. Items created for personal adornment; usually includes watches. Also called "articles of adornment."

Joint debtors. Married people who file for bankruptcy together and pay a single filing fee.

Judgment proof. A description of a person whose income and property are such that a creditor can't (or won't) seize them to enforce a money judgment—for example, a dwelling protected by a homestead exemption or a bank account containing only a few dollars.

Judicial lien. A lien created by the recording of a court money judgment against the debtor's property—usually real estate.

Lease. A contract that governs the relationship between an owner of property and a person who wishes to use the property for a specific period of time—as in car and real estate leases.

Lien. A legal claim against property that must be paid before title to the property can be transferred. Liens can also often be collected through repossession (personal property) or foreclosure (real estate), depending on the type of lien.

Lien avoidance. A bankruptcy procedure in which certain types of liens can be removed from certain types of property. Liens that are not avoided survive the bankruptcy even though the underlying debt may be cancelled—for instance, a lien remains on a car even if the debt evidenced by the car note is discharged in the bankruptcy.

Life estate. The right to live in, but not own, a specific home until your death.

Life insurance. A policy that provides for the payment of money to an individual (called the beneficiary) in the event of the death of another (called the insured). The policy matures (becomes payable) only when the insured dies.

Lifting the stay. When a bankruptcy court allows a creditor to continue with debt collection or other activities that are otherwise banned by the automatic stay. For instance, the court might allow a landlord to proceed with an eviction or a lender to repossess a car because the debtor has defaulted on the note.

Liquid assets. Cash or items that are easily convertible into cash, such as a money market account, stock, U.S. Treasury bill, or bank deposit.

Liquidated debt. An existing debt for a specified amount arising out of a contract or court judgment. In contrast, an unliquidated debt is a claim for an as-yet uncertain amount, such as for injuries suffered in a car accident before the case goes to court.

Lost future earnings. The portion of a lawsuit judgment intended to compensate an injured person for the money he or she won't be able to earn in the future because of the injury. Also called lost earnings payments or recoveries.

Luxuries. In bankruptcy, goods or services purchased by the debtor that a court decides were not appropriate in light of the debtor's insolvency. This might include vacations, jewelry, costly cars, or frequent meals at expensive restaurants.

Mailing matrix. See "creditor matrix."

Marital debts. Debts owed jointly by a married couple.

Marital property. Property owned jointly by a married couple.

Marital settlement agreement. An agreement between a divorcing couple that sets out who gets what percentage (or what specific items) of the marital property, who pays what marital debts, and who gets custody and pays child support if there are children of the marriage.

Materialmen's and mechanics' liens. Liens imposed by statute on real estate when suppliers of materials, labor, and contracting services used to improve the real estate are not properly compensated.

Matured life insurance benefits. Insurance benefits that are currently payable because the insured person has died.

Means test. A formula that uses predefined income and expense categories to determine whether a debtor whose income is more than the median family income for his or her state should be allowed to file a Chapter 7 bankruptcy.

Median family income. An annual income figure for which there are as many families with incomes below that level as there are above that level. The U.S. Census Bureau publishes median family income figures for each state and for different family sizes. In bankruptcy, the median family income is used as a basis for determining whether a debtor must pass the means test to file Chapter 7 bankruptcy, and whether a debtor filing a Chapter 13 bankruptcy must commit all his or her projected disposable income to a five year repayment plan.

Meeting of creditors. A meeting that the debtor is required to attend in a bankruptcy case, at which the trustee and creditors may ask the debtor questions about his or her property, information in the documents and forms he or she filed, and his or her debts.

Mortgage. A contract in which a loan to purchase real estate is secured by the real estate as collateral. If the borrower defaults on loan payments, the lender can foreclose on the property.

Motion. A formal legal procedure in which the bankruptcy judge is asked to rule on a dispute in the bankruptcy case. To bring a motion, a party must file a document explaining what relief is requested, the facts of the dispute, and the legal reasons why the court should grant the relief. The party bringing the motion must mail these documents to all affected parties and let them know when the court will hear argument on the motion.

Motion to avoid judicial lien on real estate. A motion brought by a bankruptcy debtor that asks the bankruptcy court to remove a judicial lien on real estate because the lien impairs the debtor's homestead exemption.

Motion to lift stay. A motion in which a creditor asks the court for permission to continue a court action or collection activities in spite of the automatic stay.

Motor vehicle. A self-propelled vehicle suitable for use on a street or road. This includes a car, truck, motorcycle, van, and moped. See also "tools of the trade."

Musical instrument. An instrument having the capacity, when properly operated, to produce a musical sound. Pianos, guitars, drums, drum machines, synthesizers, and harmonicas are all musical instruments.

Mutual aid association benefits. See "fraternal benefit society benefits."

Mutual assessment or mutual life. See "stipulated insurance."

Necessities. Articles needed to sustain life, such as food, clothing, medical care, and shelter.

Newly discovered creditors. Creditors who the debtor discovers after the bankruptcy is filed. If the case is still open, the debtor can amend the list to include the creditor; if the case is closed, it usually can be reopened to accommodate the amendment.

Nonbankruptcy federal exemptions. Federal laws that allow a debtor who has not filed for bankruptcy to keep creditors away from certain property. The debtor can also use these exemptions in bankruptcy if the debtor is using a state exemption system.

Nondischargeable debt. Debt that survives bankruptcy, such as back child support and most student loans.

Nonexempt property. Property in the bankruptcy estate that is unprotected by the exemption system available to the debtor (this is typically—but not always—the exemption system in the state where the debtor files bankruptcy). In a Chapter 7 bankruptcy, the trustee may sell it for the benefit of the debtor's unsecured creditors. In a Chapter 13 bankruptcy, debtors must propose a plan that pays their unsecured creditors at least the value of their unsecured property.

Nonpossessory, nonpurchase money lien. A lien placed on property that is already owned by the debtor and is used as collateral for the loan without being possessed by the lender. In contrast, a nonpurchase money, possessory lien exists on collateral that is held by a pawnshop.

Nonpriority debt. A type of debt that is not entitled to be paid first in bankruptcy, as priority debts are. Nonpriority debts do not have to be paid in full in a Chapter 13 case.

Nonpriority, unsecured claim. A claim that is not for a priority debt (such as child support) and is not secured by collateral or other property. Typical examples include credit card debt, medical bills, and student loans.

In a Chapter 13 repayment plan, nonpriority, unsecured claims are paid only after all other debts are paid.

Notice of appeal. A form that must be filed with a court when a party wishes to appeal a judgment or order issued by the court. Often, the notice of appeal must be filed within ten days of the date the order or judgment is entered in the court's records.

Objection. A document one party files to oppose a proposed action by another party—for instance, when a creditor or trustee files an objection to a bankruptcy debtor's claim of exemption.

Order for relief. The court's automatic injunction against certain collection and other activities that might negatively affect the bankruptcy estate. Another name for the "automatic stay."

Oversecured debt. A debt that is secured by collateral that is worth more than the amount of the debt.

PACER. An online, fee-based database containing bankruptcy court dockets (records of proceedings in bankruptcy cases) and federal court documents, such as court rules and recent appellate court decisions.

Pain and suffering damages. The portion of a court judgment intended to compensate for past, present, and future mental and physical pain, suffering, impairment of ability to work, and mental distress caused by an injury.

Partially secured debt. A debt secured by collateral that is worth less than the debt itself—for instance, when a person owes $15,000 on a car that is worth only $10,000.

Party in interest. Any person or entity that has a financial interest in the outcome of a bankruptcy case, including the trustee, the debtor, and all creditors.

Pension. A fund into which payments are made to provide an employee income after retirement. Typically, the beneficiary can't access the account without incurring a significant penalty, usually a tax. There are many types of pensions, including defined benefit pensions provided by many large corporations and individual pensions (such as 401(k) and IRA accounts). In bankruptcy, most pensions are not considered part of the bankruptcy estate and are therefore not affected by a bankruptcy filing.

Personal financial responsibility counseling. Under the new bankruptcy law, a two-hour class intended to teach good budget management. Every consumer bankruptcy filer must attend such a class in order to obtain a discharge in Chapter 7, Chapter 12, or Chapter 13 bankruptcy.

Personal injury cause of action. The right to seek compensation for physical and mental suffering, including injury to body, reputation, or both. For example, someone who is hit and injured by a car might have a personal injury cause of action against the driver.

Personal injury recovery. The portion of a lawsuit judgment or insurance settlement that is intended to compensate someone for physical and mental suffering, including physical injury, injury to reputation, or both. Bankruptcy exemptions usually do not apply to compensation for pain or suffering or punitive damages—in other words, that part of the recovery can be taken by the trustee in a Chapter 7 case.

Personal property. All property not classified as real property, including tangible items such as cars and jewelry, and intangible property such as stocks and pensions.

Petition. The document a debtor files to officially begin a bankruptcy case and ask for relief. Other documents and schedules must be filed to support the petition at the time it is filed, or shortly afterwards.

Pets. See "animals."

Preference. A payment made by a debtor to a creditor within a defined period prior to filing for bankruptcy—within three months for arms-length creditors (regular commercial creditors) and one year for insider creditors (friends, family, business associates). Because a preference gives that debtor an edge over other debtors in the bankruptcy case, the trustee can recover the preference and distribute it among all of the creditors.

Prepetition. Any time prior to the moment the bankruptcy petition is filed.

Prepetition counseling. Debt or credit counseling that occurs before the bankruptcy petition is filed—as opposed to personal financial management counseling, which occurs after the petition is filed.

Presumed abuse. In a Chapter 7 bankruptcy, when the debtor has a current monthly income in excess of the family median income for the state where the debtor lives, and has sufficient income to propose a Chapter 13 plan under the "means test." If abuse is presumed, the debtor has to prove that his or her Chapter 7 filing is not abusive in order to proceed further.

Primarily business debts. When the majority of debt owed by a bankruptcy debtor—in dollar terms—arises from debts incurred to operate a business.

Primarily consumer debts. When the majority of debt owed by a bankruptcy debtor—in dollar terms—arises from debts incurred for personal or family purposes.

Priority claim. See "priority debt."

Priority creditor. A creditor who has filed a Proof of Claim showing that the debtor owes it a priority debt.

Priority debt. A type of debt that is paid first if there are distributions to be made from the bankruptcy estate. Priority debts include alimony and child support, fees owed to the trustee and attorneys in the case, and wages owed to employees. With one exception (back child support obligations assigned to government entities), priority claims must be paid in full in a Chapter 13 bankruptcy.

Proceeds for damaged exempt property. Money received through insurance coverage, arbitration, mediation, settlement, or a lawsuit to pay for exempt property that has been damaged or destroyed. For example, if a debtor had the right to use a $30,000 homestead exemption, but his or her home was destroyed by fire, the debtor can instead exempt $30,000 of the insurance proceeds.

Projected disposable income. The amount of income a debtor will have left over each month, after deducting allowable expenses, payments on mandatory debts, and administrative expenses from his or her current monthly income. This is the amount the debtor must pay toward his or her unsecured nonpriority debts in a Chapter 13 plan.

Proof of Claim. A formal document filed by bankruptcy creditors in a bankruptcy case to assert their right to payments from the bankruptcy estate, if any payments are made.

Proof of service. A document signed under penalty of perjury by the person serving a document showing how the service was made, who made it, and when.

Property of the estate. See "bankruptcy estate."

Purchase money loans. Loans that are made to purchase specific property items, and that use the property as collateral to assure repayment, such as car loans and mortgages.

Purchase money security interest. A claim on property owned by the holder of a loan that was used to purchase the property and that is secured by the property (as collateral).

Reaffirmation. An agreement entered into after a bankruptcy filing (postpetition) between the debtor and a creditor in which the debtor agrees to repay all or part of a prepetition debt after the bankruptcy is over. For instance, a debtor makes an agreement with the holder of a car note that the debtor can keep the car and must continue to pay the debt after bankruptcy.

Real property. Real estate (land and buildings on the land, usually including mobile homes attached to a foundation).

Reasonable investigation. A bankruptcy attorney's obligation, under the new bankruptcy law, to look into the information provided to them by their clients.

Redemption. In a Chapter 7 bankruptcy, when the debtor obtains legal title to collateral for a secured debt by paying the secured creditor the replacement value of the collateral in a lump sum. For example, a debtor may redeem a car note by paying the lender the replacement value of the car (what a retail vendor would charge for the car, considering its age and condition).

Reopen a case. To open a closed bankruptcy case—usually for the purpose of adding an overlooked creditor or filing a motion to avoid an overlooked lien. A debtor must request that the court reopen the case.

Repayment plan. An informal plan to repay creditors most or all of what they are owed outside of bankruptcy. Also refers to the plan proposed by a debtor in a Chapter 13 case.

Replacement cost. What it would cost to replace a particular item by buying it from a retail vendor, considering its age and condition—for instance, when buying a car from a used car dealer, furniture from a used furniture shop, or electronic equipment on eBay.

Repossession. When a secured creditor takes property used as collateral because the debtor has defaulted on the loan secured by the collateral.

Request to lift the stay. A written request filed in bankruptcy court by a creditor, which seeks permission to engage in debt collection activity otherwise prohibited by the automatic stay.

Schedule A. The official bankruptcy form a debtor must file to describe all of his or her real property.

Schedule B. The official bankruptcy form a debtor must file to describe all personal property owned by the debtor, including tangible property such as jewelry and vehicles, and intangible property such as investments and accounts receivable.

Schedule C. The official bankruptcy form a debtor must file to describe the property the debtor is claiming as exempt, and the legal basis for the claims of exemption.

Schedule D. The official bankruptcy form a debtor must file to describe all secured debts owed by the debtor, such as car notes and mortgages.

Schedule E. The official bankruptcy form a debtor must file to describe all priority debts owed by the debtor, such as back child support and taxes.

Schedule F. The official bankruptcy form a debtor must file to describe all nonpriority, unsecured debts owed by the debtor, such as most credit card and medical bills.

Schedule G. The official bankruptcy form a debtor must file to describe any leases and executory contracts (contracts under which one or both parties still have obligations) to which the debtor is a party.

Schedule H. The official bankruptcy form a debtor must file to describe all codebtors that might be affected by the bankruptcy.

Schedule I. The official bankruptcy form a debtor must file to describe the debtor's income.

Schedule J. The official bankruptcy form a debtor must file to describe the debtor's actual monthly expenses.

Schedules. Official bankruptcy forms a debtor must file, detailing the debtor's property, debts, income, and expenses.

Second deed of trust. A loan against real estate made after the original mortgage (or first deed of trust). Most home equity loans are second deeds of trust.

Secured claim. A debt secured by collateral under a written agreement (for instance, a mortgage or car note) or by operation of law—such as a tax lien.

Secured creditor. The owner of a secured claim.

Secured debt. A debt secured by collateral.

Secured interest. A claim to property used as collateral. For instance, a lender on a car note retains legal title to the car until the loan is paid off.

Secured property. Property that is collateral for a secured debt.

Serial bankruptcy filing. A practice used by some debtors to file and dismiss one bankruptcy after another to obtain the protection of the automatic stay, even though the bankruptcies themselves offer no debt relief—for instance, when a debtor files successive Chapter 13 cases to prevent foreclosure of his or her home even though there are no debts to repay.

Sickness benefits. See "disability benefits."

State exemptions. State laws that specify the types of property creditors are not entitled to take to satisfy a debt, and the bankruptcy trustee is not entitled to take and sell for the benefit of the debtor's unsecured creditors.

Statement of Affairs. The official bankruptcy form a debtor must file to describe the debtor's legal, economic, and business transactions for the several years prior to filing, including gifts, preferences, income, closing of deposit accounts, lawsuits, and other information that the trustee needs to assess the legitimacy of the bankruptcy and the true extent of the bankruptcy estate.

Statement of Current Monthly Income and Disposable Income Calculation. The official bankruptcy form a debtor must file in a Chapter 13 case, setting out the debtor's current monthly income and calculating the debtor's projected disposable income that will determine how much will be paid to the debtor's unsecured creditors.

Statement of Current Monthly Income and Means Test Calculation. The official bankruptcy form a debtor must file in a Chapter 7 filing that shows the debtor's current monthly income, calculates whether the debtor's income is higher than the state's median family income, and, if so, uses the means test to determine whether a Chapter 7 bankruptcy would constitute abuse.

Statement of Intention. The official bankruptcy form a debtor must file in a Chapter 7 case to tell the court and secured creditors how the debtor plans to treat his or her secured debts—that is, reaffirm the debt, redeem the debt, or surrender the property and discharge the debt.

Statement of Social Security Number. The official bankruptcy form a debtor must file to disclose the debtor's complete Social Security number.

Statutory lien. A lien imposed on property by law, such as tax liens and mechanics' liens, as opposed to voluntary liens (such as mortgages) and liens arising from court judgments (judicial liens).

Stay. See "automatic stay."

Stipulated insurance. An insurance policy that allows the insurance company to assess an amount on the insured, above the standard premium payments, if the company experiences losses worse than had been calculated into the standard premium. Also called assessment, mutual assessment, or mutual life insurance.

Stock options. A contract between a corporation and an employee that gives the employee the right to purchase corporate stock at a specific price mentioned in the contract (the strike price).

Stripdown of lien. In a Chapter 13 bankruptcy, when the amount of a lien on collateral is reduced to the collateral's replacement value. See "cramdown."

Student loan. A type of loan made for educational purposes by nonprofit or commercial lenders with repayment and interest terms dictated by federal law. Student loans are not dischargeable in bankruptcy unless the debtor can show that repaying the loan would impose an "undue hardship."

Substantial abuse. Under the old bankruptcy law, filing a Chapter 7 bankruptcy when a Chapter 13 bankruptcy was feasible.

Suits, executions, garnishments, and attachments. Activities engaged in by creditors to enforce money judgments, typically involving the seizure of wages and bank accounts.

Summary of Schedules. The official bankruptcy form a debtor must file to summarize the property and debt information contained in a debtor's schedules

Surrender value. See "avails."

Surrendering collateral. In Chapter 7 bankruptcy, the act of returning collateral to a secured lender in order to discharge the underlying debt—for example, returning a car to discharge the car note.

Tangible personal property. See "tangible property" and "personal property."

Tangible property. Property that may be physically touched. Examples include money, furniture, cars, jewelry, artwork, and houses. Compare "Intangible property."

Tax lien. A statutory lien imposed on property to secure payment of back taxes—typically income and property taxes.

Tenancy by the entirety. A way that married couples can hold title to property in about half of the states. When one spouse dies, the surviving spouse automatically owns 100% of the property. In most cases, this type of property is not part of the bankruptcy estate if only one spouse files.

To ____ acres. A limitation on the size of a homestead that may be exempted.

Tools of the trade. Items needed to perform a line of work that you are currently doing and relying on for support. For a mechanic, plumber, or carpenter, for example, tools of trade are the implements used to repair, build, and install. Traditionally, tools of the trade were limited to items that could be held in the hand. Most states, however, now embrace a broader definition, and a debtor may be able to fit many items under a tool of trade exemption.

Transcript of tax return. A summary of a debtor's tax return provided by the IRS upon the debtor's request, usually acceptable as a substitute for the return in the instances when a return must be filed under the new bankruptcy law.

Trustee. An official appointed by the bankruptcy court to carry out the administrative tasks associated with a bankruptcy and to seize and sell nonexempt property in the bankruptcy estate for the benefit of the debtor's unsecured creditors.

U.S. Trustee. An official employed by Office of the U.S. Trustee (a division of the U.S. Department of Justice) who is responsible for overseeing the bankruptcy trustees, regulating credit and personal financial management counselors, regulating bankruptcy petition preparers, auditing bankruptcy cases, ferreting out fraud, and generally making sure that the bankruptcy laws are obeyed.

Undersecured debt. A debt secured by collateral that is worth less than the debt.

Undue hardship. The conditions under which a debtor may discharge a student loan—for example, when the debtor has no income and little chance of earning enough to repay the loan in the future.

Unexpired lease. A lease that is still in effect.

Unmatured life insurance. A policy that is not yet payable because the insured is still alive.

Unscheduled debt. A debt that is not included in the schedules accompanying a bankruptcy filing, perhaps because it was overlooked or intentionally left out.

Unsecured priority claims. Priority claims that aren't secured by collateral, such as back child support or taxes for which no lien has been placed on the debtor's property.

Valuation of property. The act of determining the replacement value of property for the purpose of describing it in the bankruptcy schedules, determining whether it is protected by an applicable exemption, redeeming secured property, or cramming down a lien in Chapter 13 bankruptcy.

Voluntary dismissal. When a bankruptcy debtor dismisses his or her Chapter 7 or Chapter 13 case on his or her own, without coercion by the court.

Voluntary lien. A lien agreed to by the debtor, as when the debtor signs a mortgage, car note, or second deed of trust.

Weekly net earnings. The earnings a debtor has left after mandatory deductions, such as income tax, mandatory union dues, and Social Security contributions, have been subtracted from his or her gross income.

Wildcard exemption. A dollar value that the debtor can apply to any type of property to make it—or more of it—exempt. In some states, filers may use the unused portion of a homestead exemption as a wildcard exemption.

Willful and malicious act. An act done with the intent to cause harm. In a Chapter 7 bankruptcy, a debt arising from the debtor's willful and malicious act is not discharged if the victim proves to the bankruptcy court's satisfaction that the act occurred.

Willful or malicious act resulting in a civil judgment. A bad act that was careless or reckless, but was not necessarily intended to cause harm. In a Chapter 13 case, a debt arising from the debtor's act that was either willful or malicious is not discharged if it is part of a civil judgment.

Wrongful death cause of action. The right to seek compensation for having to live without a deceased person. Usually only the spouse and children of the deceased have a wrongful death cause of action.

Wrongful death recoveries. The portion of a lawsuit judgment intended to compensate a plaintiff for having to live without a deceased person. The compensation is intended to cover the earnings and the emotional comfort and support the deceased would have provided.

Federal and State Exemption Tables

Confirm the Information in the Exemption Charts Before Relying on It

The exemptions in the following charts were current when this book went to press, but your state may have changed the law since then. In addition, states often carve out *exceptions* to the exemptions, which are far too detailed to list here. For instance, even if an item is listed as exempt in one of these charts, you might have to give it up to pay a child support or tax debt.

Before relying on any particular exemption, consider:

- reading the exemption statute yourself, using the research information in Ch. 10, and
- cross-checking the chart's information against the exemptions for your state listed on www.legalconsumer.com.

Last, but certainly not least, consult a bankruptcy lawyer.

CAUTION

Some courts might not allow "bankruptcy specific" exemptions. Eight states have exemption schemes that apply only in bankruptcy (which means debtors cannot use them against judgment creditors). A few courts over the years have determined that such "bankruptcy specific" exemption schemes are unconstitutional. The Sixth Circuit will be reviewing this issue in 2011 (*In Re: Sharon Kay Pontius*). Any decision it makes will be binding on courts in that circuit only.

Although the majority of bankruptcy courts in states with bankruptcy specific exemption schemes allow debtors to use these exemptions, you may wish to consult with an attorney if you live in one of these states to find out what exemptions are permitted in your local bankruptcy court. These states are: California, Colorado, Georgia, Michigan, Montana, New York, Ohio, and West Virginia.

Alabama

Federal bankruptcy exemptions not available. All law references are to Alabama Code unless otherwise noted.

ASSET	EXEMPTION	LAW
homestead	Real property or mobile home to $5,000; property cannot exceed 160 acres	6-10-2
	Must record homestead declaration before attempted sale of home	6-10-20
insurance	Annuity proceeds or avails to $250 per month	27-14-32
	Disability proceeds or avails to an average of $250 per month	27-14-31
	Fraternal benefit society benefits	27-34-27
	Life insurance proceeds or avails	6-10-8; 27-14-29
	Life insurance proceeds or avails if clause prohibits proceeds from being used to pay beneficiary's creditors	27-15-26
	Mutual aid association benefits	27-30-25
pensions	Tax-exempt retirement accounts, including 401(k)s, 403(b)s, profit-sharing and money purchase plans, SEP and SIMPLE IRAs, and defined-benefit plans	11 U.S.C. § 522(b)(3)(C)
	Traditional and Roth IRAs to $1,171,650 per person	11 U.S.C. § 522(b)(3)(C); (n)
	IRAs & other retirement accounts	19-3B-508
	Judges (only payments being received)	12-18-10(a),(b)
	Law enforcement officers	36-21-77
	Spendthrift trusts (with exceptions)	19-3B-501 to 503
	State employees	36-27-28
	Teachers	16-25-23
personal property	Books of debtor & family	6-10-6
	Burial place for self & family	6-10-5
	Church pew for self & family	6-10-5
	Clothing of debtor & family	6-10-6
	Family portraits or pictures	6-10-6
public benefits	Aid to blind, aged, disabled, & other public assistance	38-4-8
	Crime victims' compensation	15-23-15(e)
	Southeast Asian War POWs' benefits	31-7-2
	Unemployment compensation	25-4-140
	Workers' compensation	25-5-86(b)
tools of trade	Arms, uniforms, equipment that state military personnel are required to keep	31-2-78
wages	With respect to consumer loans, consumer credit sales, & consumer leases, 75% of weekly net earnings or 30 times the federal minimum hourly wage; all other cases, 75% of earned but unpaid wages; bankruptcy judge may authorize more for low-income debtors	5-19-15; 6-10-7
wildcard	$3,000 of any personal property, except wages	6-10-6

Alaska

Alaska law states that only the items found in Alaska Statutes §§ 9.38.010, 9.38.015(a), 9.38.017, 9.38.020, 9.38.025, and 9.38.030 may be exempted in bankruptcy. In *In re McNutt*, 87 B.R. 84 (9th Cir. 1988), however, an Alaskan debtor used the federal bankruptcy exemptions. All law references are to Alaska Statutes unless otherwise noted.

Alaska exemption amounts are adjusted regularly by administrative order. Current amounts are found at 8 Alaska Admin. Code tit. 8, § 95.030.

ASSET	EXEMPTION	LAW
homestead	$70,200 (joint owners may each claim a portion, but total can't exceed $70,200)	09.38.010(a)
insurance	Disability benefits	09.38.015(b); 09.38.030(e)(1),(5)
	Fraternal benefit society benefits	21.84.240
	Life insurance or annuity contracts, total avails to $100,000	09.38.025
	Medical, surgical, or hospital benefits	09.38.015(a)(3)
miscellaneous	Alimony, to extent wages exempt	09.38.030(e)(2)
	Child support payments made by collection agency	09.38.015(b)
	Liquor licenses	09.38.015(a)(7)
	Property of business partnership	09.38.100(b)
pensions	Tax-exempt retirement accounts, including 401(k)s, 403(b)s, profit-sharing and money purchase plans, SEP and SIMPLE IRAs, and defined-benefit plans	11 U.S.C. § 522(b)(3)(C)
	Traditional and Roth IRAs to $1,171,650 per person	11 U.S.C. § 522(b)(3)(C); (n)
	Elected public officers (only benefits building up)	09.38.015(b)
	ERISA-qualified benefits deposited more than 120 days before filing bankruptcy	09.38.017
	Judicial employees (only benefits building up)	09.38.015(b)
	Public employees (only benefits building up)	09.38.015(b); 39.35.505
	Roth & traditional IRAs, medical savings accounts	09.38.017(e)(3)
	Teachers (only benefits building up)	09.38.015(b)
	Other pensions, to extent wages exempt (only payments being received)	09.38.030(e)(5)
personal property	Books, musical instruments, clothing, family portraits, household goods, & heirlooms to $3,900 total	09.38.020(a)
	Building materials	34.35.105
	Burial plot	09.38.015(a)(1)
	Cash or other liquid assets to $1,930; for sole wage earner in household, $2,860 (restrictions apply—see *wages*)	09.38.030(b)
	Deposit in apartment or condo owners' association	09.38.010(e)
	Health aids needed	09.38.015(a)(2)
	Jewelry to $1,300	09.38.020(b)
	Money held in mortgage escrow accounts after July 1, 2008	09.38.015(e)
	Motor vehicle to $3,900; vehicle's market value can't exceed $26,000	09.38.020(e)
	Personal injury recoveries, to extent wages exempt	09.38.030(e)(3)
	Pets to $1,300	09.38.020(d)
	Proceeds for lost, damaged, or destroyed exempt property	09.38.060
	Tuition credits under an advance college tuition payment contract	09.38.015(a)(8)
	Wrongful death recoveries, to extent wages exempt	09.38.030(e)(3)

public benefits	Adult assistance to elderly, blind, disabled	47.25.550
	Alaska benefits for low-income seniors	09.38.015(a)(11)
	Alaska longevity bonus	09.38.015(a)(5)
	Crime victims' compensation	09.38.015(a)(4)
	Federally exempt public benefits paid or due	09.38.015(a)(6)
	General relief assistance	47.25.210
	Senior care (prescription drug) benefits	09.38.015(a)(10)
	20% of permanent fund dividends	43.23.065
	Unemployment compensation	09.38.015(b); 23.20.405
	Workers' compensation	23.30.160
tools of trade	Implements, books, & tools of trade to $3,640	09.38.020(c)
wages	Weekly net earnings to $456; for sole wage earner in a household, $716; if you don't receive weekly or semimonthly pay, you can claim $1,820 in cash or liquid assets paid any month; for sole wage earner in household, $2,860	9.38.030(a),(b); 9.38.050(b)
wildcard	None	

Arizona

Federal bankruptcy exemptions not available. All law references are to Arizona Revised Statutes unless otherwise noted.

ASSET	EXEMPTION	LAW
homestead	Real property, an apartment, or mobile home you occupy to $150,000; sale proceeds exempt 18 months after sale or until new home purchased, whichever occurs first (spouses may not double)	33-1101(A)
	May record homestead declaration to clarify which one of multiple eligible parcels is being claimed as homestead	33-1102
insurance	Fraternal benefit society benefits	20-877
	Group life insurance policy or proceeds	20-1132
	Health, accident, or disability benefits	33-1126(A)(4)
	Life insurance cash value or proceeds, or annuity contract if owned at least two years and beneficiary is dependent family member	33-1126(A)(6); 20-1131(D)
	Life insurance proceeds to $20,000 if beneficiary is spouse or child	33-1126(A)(1)
miscellaneous	Alimony, child support needed for support	33-1126(A)(3)
	Minor child's earnings, unless debt is for child	33-1126(A)(2)
pensions *see also wages*	Tax-exempt retirement accounts, including 401(k)s, 403(b)s, profit-sharing and money purchase plans, SEP and SIMPLE IRAs, and defined-benefit plans	11 U.S.C. § 522(b)(3)(C)
	Traditional and Roth IRAs to $1,171,650 per person	11 U.S.C. § 522(b)(3)(C); (n)
	Board of regents members, faculty & administrative officers under board's jurisdiction	15-1628(I)
	District employees	48-227
	ERISA-qualified benefits deposited over 120 days before filing	33-1126(B)
	IRAs & Roth IRAs	33-1126(B); *In re Herrscher*, 121 B.R. 29 (D. Ariz. 1989)
	Firefighters	9-968
	Police officers	9-931
	Public Safety Personnel Retirement System	38-850(c)
	Rangers	41-955
	State employees' retirement & disability	38-792; 38-797.11

personal property *spouses may double all personal property*	2 beds & bedding; 1 living room chair per person; 1 dresser, table, lamp; kitchen table; dining room table & 4 chairs (1 more per person); living room carpet or rug; couch; 3 lamps; 3 coffee or end tables; pictures, paintings, personal drawings, family portraits; refrigerator, stove, washer, dryer, vacuum cleaner; TV, radio, stereo, alarm clock to $4,000 total	33-1123
	Bank deposit to $150 in one account	33-1126(A)(9)
	Bible; bicycle; sewing machine; typewriter; burial plot; rifle, pistol, or shotgun to $500 total	33-1125
	Books to $250; clothing to $500; wedding & engagement rings to $1,000; watch to $100; pets, horses, milk cows, & poultry to $500; musical instruments to $250	33-1125
	Food & fuel to last 6 months	33-1124
	Funeral deposits to $5,000	32-1391.05(4)
	Health aids	33-1125(9)
	Motor vehicle to $5,000 ($10,000, if debtor is physically disabled)	33-1125(8)
	Prepaid rent or security deposit to $1,000 or 1½ times your rent, whichever is less, in lieu of homestead	33-1126(C)
	Proceeds for sold or damaged exempt property	33-1126(A)(5),(8)
	Wrongful death awards	12-592
public benefits	Unemployment compensation	23-783(A)
	Welfare benefits	46-208
	Workers' compensation	23-1068(B)
tools of trade *husband & wife may double*	Arms, uniforms, & accoutrements of profession or office required by law	33-1130(3)
	Farm machinery, utensils, seed, instruments of husbandry, feed, grain, & animals to $2,500 total	33-1130(2)
	Library & teaching aids of teacher	33-1127
	Tools, equipment, instruments, & books to $2,500	33-1130(1)
wages	75% of earned but unpaid weekly net earnings or 30 times the federal minimum hourly wage; 50% of wages for support orders; bankruptcy judge may authorize more for low-income debtors	33-1131
wildcard	None	

Arkansas

Federal bankruptcy exemptions available. All law references are to Arkansas Code Annotated unless otherwise noted.

Note: *In re Holt*, 894 F.2d 1005 (8th Cir. 1990), held that Arkansas residents are limited to exemptions in the Arkansas Constitution. Statutory exemptions can still be used within Arkansas for nonbankruptcy purposes, but they cannot be claimed in bankruptcy.

ASSET	EXEMPTION	LAW
homestead *choose Option 1 or 2*	1. For married person or head of family: unlimited exemption on real or personal property used as residence to ¼ acre in city, town, or village, or 80 acres elsewhere; if property is between ¼ and 1 acre in city, town, or village, or 80 to 160 acres elsewhere, additional limit is $2,500; homestead may not exceed 1 acre in city, town, or village, or 160 acres elsewhere (spouses may not double)	Constitution 9-3; 9-4, 9-5; 16-66-210; 16-66-218(b)(3), (4); *In re Stevens*, 829 F.2d 693 (8th Cir. 1987)
	2. Real or personal property used as residence to $800 if single; $1,250 if married	16-66-218(a)(1)

insurance	Annuity contract	23-79-134
	Disability benefits	23-79-133
	Fraternal benefit society benefits	23-74-403
	Group life insurance	23-79-132
	Life, health, accident, or disability cash value or proceeds paid or due to $500	16-66-209; Constitution 9-1, 9-2; *In re Holt*, 894 F.2d 1005 (8th Cir. 1990)
	Life insurance proceeds if clause prohibits proceeds from being used to pay beneficiary's creditors	23-79-131
	Life insurance proceeds or avails if beneficiary isn't the insured	23-79-131
	Mutual assessment life or disability benefits to $1,000	23-72-114
	Stipulated insurance premiums	23-71-112
pensions	Tax-exempt retirement accounts, including 401(k)s, 403(b)s, profit-sharing and money purchase plans, SEP and SIMPLE IRAs, and defined-benefit plans	11 U.S.C. § 522(b)(3)(C)
	Traditional and Roth IRAs to $1,171,650 per person	11 U.S.C. § 522(b)(3)(C); (n)
	Disabled firefighters	24-11-814
	Disabled police officers	24-11-417
	Firefighters	24-10-616
	IRA deposits to $20,000 if deposited over 1 year before filing for bankruptcy	16-66-218(b)(16)
	Police officers	24-10-616
	School employees	24-7-715
	State police officers	24-6-205; 24-6-223
personal property	Burial plot to 5 acres, if choosing federal homestead exemption (Option 2)	16-66-207; 16-66-218(a)(1)
	Clothing	Constitution 9-1, 9-2
	Motor vehicle to $1,200	16-66-218(a)(2)
	Prepaid funeral trusts	23-40-117
	Wedding rings	16-66-219
public benefits	Crime victims' compensation	16-90-716(e)
	Unemployment compensation	11-10-109
	Workers' compensation	11-9-110
tools of trade	Implements, books, & tools of trade to $750	16-66-218(a)(4)
wages	Earned but unpaid wages due for 60 days; in no event less than $25 per week	16-66-208; 16-66-218(b)(6)
wildcard	$500 of any personal property if married or head of family; $200 if not married	Constitution 9-1, 9-2; 16-66-218(b)(1),(2)

California—System 1

Federal bankruptcy exemptions not available. California has two systems; you must select one or the other. All law references are to California Code of Civil Procedure unless otherwise noted. Many exemptions do not apply to claims for child support.

Note: California's exemption amounts are no longer updated in the statutes themselves. California Code of Civil Procedure Section 740.150 deputized the California Judicial Council to update the exemption amounts every three years. (The next revision will be in 2013.) As a result, the amounts listed in this chart will not match the amounts that appear in the cited statutes. The current exemption amounts can be found on the California Judicial Council website, www.courtinfo.ca.gov/forms/exemptions.htm.

ASSET	EXEMPTION	LAW
homestead	Real or personal property you occupy including mobile home, boat, stock cooperative, community apartment, planned development, or condo to $75,000 if single & not disabled; $100,000 for families if no other member has a homestead (if only one spouse files, may exempt one-half of amount if home held as community property & all of amount if home held as tenants in common); $175,000 if 65 or older, or physically or mentally disabled; $175,000 if 55 or older, single, & earn gross annual income under $15,000 or married & earn gross annual income under $20,000 & creditors seek to force the sale of your home; forced sale proceeds received exempt for 6 months after (spouses may not double); separated married debtor may claim homestead in community property homestead occupied by other spouse	704.710; 704.720; 704.730; *In re McFall*, 112 B.R. 336 (9th Cir. BAP 1990)
	May file homestead declaration to protect exemption amount from attachment of judicial liens and to protect proceeds of voluntary sale for 6 months	704.920
insurance	Disability or health benefits	704.130
	Fidelity bonds	Labor 404
	Fraternal benefit society benefits	704.170
	Fraternal unemployment benefits	704.120
	Homeowners' insurance proceeds for 6 months after received, to homestead exemption amount	704.720(b)
	Life insurance proceeds if clause prohibits proceeds from being used to pay beneficiary's creditors	Ins. 10132; Ins. 10170; Ins. 10171
	Matured life insurance benefits needed for support	704.100(c)
	Unmatured life insurance policy cash surrender value completely exempt; loan value exempt to $11,475	704.100(b)
miscellaneous	Business or professional licenses	695.060
	Inmates' trust funds to $1,425 (spouses may not double)	704.090
	Property of business partnership	Corp. 16501-04
pensions	Tax-exempt retirement accounts, including 401(k)s, 403(b)s, profit-sharing and money purchase plans, SEP and SIMPLE IRAs, and defined-benefit plans	11 U.S.C. § 522(b)(3)(C)
	Traditional and Roth IRAs to $1,171,650 per person	11 U.S.C. § 522(b)(3)(C); (n)
	County employees	Gov't 31452
	County firefighters	Gov't 32210
	County peace officers	Gov't 31913
	Private retirement benefits, including IRAs & Keoghs	704.115
	Public employees	Gov't 21255
	Public retirement benefits	704.110

personal property	Appliances, furnishings, clothing, & food	704.020
	Bank deposits from Social Security Administration to $2,875 ($4,300 for husband & wife); unlimited if SS funds are not commingled with other funds	704.080
	Bank deposits of other public benefits to $1,425 ($2,150 for husband & wife)	
	Building materials to repair or improve home to $2,875 (spouses may not double)	704.030
	Burial plot	704.200
	Funds held in escrow	Fin. 17410
	Health aids	704.050
	Jewelry, heirlooms, & art to $7,175 total (spouses may not double)	704.040
	Motor vehicles to $2,725, or $2,725 in auto insurance for loss or damages (spouses may not double)	704.010
	Personal injury & wrongful death causes of action	704.140(a); 704.150(a)
	Personal injury & wrongful death recoveries needed for support; if receiving installments, at least 75%	704.140(b),(c),(d); 704.150(b),(c)
public benefits	Aid to blind, aged, disabled; public assistance	704.170
	Financial aid to students	704.190
	Relocation benefits	704.180
	Unemployment benefits	704.120
	Union benefits due to labor dispute	704.120(b)(5)
	Workers' compensation	704.160
tools of trade	Tools, implements, materials, instruments, uniforms, one commercial vehicle, books, furnishings, & equipment to $7,175 total ($14,350 total if used by both spouses in same occupation)	704.060
	Commercial vehicle (Vehicle Code § 260) to $4,850 ($9,700 total if used by both spouses in same occupation) (this counts toward total tools of trade exemption)	704.060
wages	Minimum 75% of wages paid within 30 days prior to filing	704.070
	Public employees' vacation credits; if receiving installments, at least 75%	704.113
wildcard	None	

California—System 2

Refer to the notes for California—System 1, above.

Note: Married couples may not double any exemptions. (*In re Talmadge*, 832 F.2d 1120 (9th Cir. 1987); *In re Baldwin*, 70 B.R. 612 (9th Cir. BAP 1987).)

One court has argued that System 2 exemptions are not available to debtors in bankruptcy. To date, the vast majority of (if not all) California bankruptcy courts accept System 2 exemptions. However, you may wish check with a bankruptcy attorney to find out which exemptions are acceptable in your local court. See, "Some courts might not allow 'bankruptcy specific' exemptions," at the beginning of this appendix for more information.

ASSET	EXEMPTION	LAW
homestead	Real or personal property, including co-op, used as residence to $22,075; unused portion of homestead may be applied to any property	703.140(b)(1)
insurance	Disability benefits	703.140(b)(10)(C)
	Life insurance proceeds needed for support of family	703.140(b)(11)(C)
	Unmatured life insurance contract accrued avails to $11,800	703.140(b)(8)
	Unmatured life insurance policy other than credit	703.140(b)(7)

miscellaneous	Alimony, child support needed for support	703.140(b)(10)(D)
pensions	Tax-exempt retirement accounts, including 401(k)s, 403(b)s, profit-sharing and money purchase plans, SEP and SIMPLE IRAs, and defined-benefit plans	11 U.S.C. § 522(b)(3)(C)
	Traditional and Roth IRAs to $1,171,650 per person	11 U.S.C. § 522(b)(3)(C); (n)
	ERISA-qualified benefits needed for support	703.140(b)(10)(E)
personal property	Animals, crops, appliances, furnishings, household goods, books, musical instruments, & clothing to $550 per item	703.140(b)(3)
	Burial plot to $22,075, in lieu of homestead	703.140(b)(1)
	Health aids	703.140(b)(9)
	Jewelry to $1,425	703.140(b)(4)
	Motor vehicle to $3,525	703.140(b)(2)
	Personal injury recoveries to $22,075 (not to include pain & suffering; pecuniary loss)	703.140(b)(11)(D),(E)
	Wrongful death recoveries needed for support	703.140(b)(11)(B)
public benefits	Crime victims' compensation	703.140(b)(11)(A)
	Public assistance	703.140(b)(10)(A)
	Social Security	703.140(b)(10)(A)
	Unemployment compensation	703.140(b)(10)(A)
	Veterans' benefits	703.140(b)(10)(B)
tools of trade	Implements, books, & tools of trade to $2,200	703.140(b)(6)
wages	None (use federal nonbankruptcy wage exemption)	
wildcard	$1,175 of any property	703.140(b)(5)
	Unused portion of homestead or burial exemption of any property	703.140(b)(5)

Colorado

Federal bankruptcy exemptions not available. All law references are to Colorado Revised Statutes unless otherwise noted.

Some of the exemptions in this table may not be available to you in some bankruptcy courts. Before filing bankruptcy, check with a bankruptcy attorney to find out which exemptions are acceptable in your court. See, "Some courts might not allow 'bankruptcy specific' exemptions," at the beginning of this appendix for more information.

ASSET	EXEMPTION	LAW
homestead	Real property, mobile home, manufactured home, or house trailer you occupy to $60,000; $90,000 if owner, spouse, or dependent is disabled or at least 60 years old; sale proceeds exempt 2 years after received	38-41-201; 38-41-201.6; 38-41-203; 38-41-207; *In re Pastrana*, 216 B.R. 948 (D. Colo., 1998)
	Spouse or child of deceased owner may claim homestead exemption	38-41-204
insurance	Disability benefits to $200 per month; if lump sum, entire amount exempt	10-16-212
	Fraternal benefit society benefits	10-14-403
	Group life insurance policy or proceeds	10-7-205
	Homeowners' insurance proceeds for 1 year after received, to homestead exemption amount	38-41-209
	Life insurance cash surrender value to $50,000, except contributions to policy within past 48 months	13-54-102(1)(l)
	Life insurance proceeds if clause prohibits proceeds from being used to pay beneficiary's creditors	10-7-106

miscellaneous	Child support or domestic support obligation	13-54-102(u) 13-54-102.5
	Property of business partnership	7-60-125
pensions *see also wages*	Tax-exempt retirement accounts, including 401(k)s, 403(b)s, profit-sharing and money purchase plans, SEP and SIMPLE IRAs, and defined-benefit plans	11 U.S.C. § 522(b)(3)(C)
	Traditional and Roth IRAs to $1,171,650 per person	11 U.S.C. § 522(b)(3)(C); (n)
	ERISA-qualified benefits, including IRAs & Roth IRAs	13-54-102(1)(s)
	Firefighters & police officers	31-30.5-208; 31-31-203
	Public employees' pensions, deferred compensation, & defined contribution plans	24-51-212
	Teachers	22-64-120
	Veteran's pension for veteran, spouse, or dependents if veteran served in war or armed conflict	13-54-102(1)(h); 13-54-104
personal property	1 burial plot per family member	13-54-102(1)(d)
	Clothing to $1,500	13-54-102(1)(a)
	Food & fuel to $600	13-54-102(1)(f)
	Health aids	13-54-102(1)(p)
	Household goods to $3,000	13-54-102(1)(e)
	Jewelry & articles of adornment to $2,000	13-54-102(1)(b)
	Motor vehicles or bicycles used for work to $5,000; $10,000 if used by a debtor or by a dependent who is disabled or 60 or over	13-54-102(j)(I), (II)
	Personal injury recoveries	13-54-102(1)(n)
	Family pictures & books to $1,500	13-54-102(1)(c)
	Proceeds for damaged exempt property	13-54-102(1)(m)
	Security deposits	13-54-102(1)(r)
public benefits	Aid to blind, aged, disabled; public assistance	26-2-131
	Crime victims' compensation	13-54-102(1)(q); 24-4.1-114
	Disability benefits to $3,000	13-54-102(v)
	Earned income tax credit or refund	13-54-102(1)(o)
	Unemployment compensation	8-80-103
	Veteran's benefits for veteran, spouse, or child if veteran served in war or armed conflict	13-54-102(1)(h)
	Workers' compensation	8-42-124
tools of trade	Livestock or other animals, machinery, tools, equipment, & seed of person engaged in agriculture, to $50,000 total	13-54-102(1)(g)
	Professional's library to $3,000 (if not claimed under other tools of trade exemption)	13-54-102(1)(k)
	Stock in trade, supplies, fixtures, tools, machines, electronics, equipment, books, & other business materials, to $20,000 total	13-54-102(1)(i)
	Military equipment personally owned by members of the National Guard	13-54-102(1)(h.5)
wages	Minimum 75% of weekly net earnings or 30 times the federal or state minimum wage, whichever is greater, including pension & insurance payments	13-54-104
wildcard	None	

Connecticut

Federal bankruptcy exemptions available. All law references are to Connecticut General Statutes Annotated unless otherwise noted.

ASSET	EXEMPTION	LAW
homestead	Owner-occupied real property, including co-op or mobile manufactured home, to $75,000; applies only to claims arising after 1993, but to $125,000 in the case of a money judgment arising out of services provided at a hospital	52-352a(e); 52-352b(t)
insurance	Disability benefits paid by association for its members	52-352b(p)
	Fraternal benefit society benefits	38a-637
	Health or disability benefits	52-352b(e)
	Life insurance proceeds if clause prohibits proceeds from being used to pay beneficiary's creditors	38a-454
	Life insurance proceeds or avails	38a-453
	Unmatured life insurance policy avails to $4,000 if beneficiary is dependent	52-352b(s)
miscellaneous	Alimony, to extent wages exempt	52-352b(n)
	Child support	52-352b(h)
	Farm partnership animals & livestock feed reasonably required to run farm where at least 50% of partners are members of same family	52-352d
pensions	Tax-exempt retirement accounts, including 401(k)s, 403(b)s, profit-sharing and money purchase plans, SEP and SIMPLE IRAs, and defined-benefit plans	11 U.S.C. § 522(b)(3)(C)
	Traditional and Roth IRAs to $1,171,650 per person	11 U.S.C. § 522(b)(3)(C); (n)
	ERISA-qualified benefits, including IRAs, Roth IRAs, & Keoghs, to extent wages exempt	52-321a; 52-352b(m)
	Medical savings account	52-321a
	Municipal employees	7-446
	State employees	5-171; 5-192w
	Teachers	10-183q
personal property	Appliances, food, clothing, furniture, bedding	52-352b(a)
	Burial plot	52-352b(c)
	Health aids needed	52-352b(f)
	Motor vehicle to $1,500	52-352b(j)
	Proceeds for damaged exempt property	52-352b(q)
	Residential utility & security deposits for 1 residence	52-352b(l)
	Spendthrift trust funds required for support of debtor & family	52-321(d)
	Transfers to a licensed debt adjuster	52-352b(u)
	Tuition savings accounts	52-321a(E)
	Wedding & engagement rings	52-352b(k)
public benefits	Crime victims' compensation	52-352b(o); 54-213
	Public assistance	52-352b(d)
	Social Security	52-352b(g)
	Unemployment compensation	31-272(c); 52-352b(g)
	Veterans' benefits	52-352b(g)
	Workers' compensation	52-352b(g)

tools of trade	Arms, military equipment, uniforms, musical instruments of military personnel	52-352b(i)
	Tools, books, instruments, & farm animals needed	52-352b(b)
wages	Minimum 75% of earned but unpaid weekly disposable earnings, or 40 times the state or federal hourly minimum wage, whichever is greater	52-361a(f)
wildcard	$1,000 of any property	52-352b(r)

Delaware

Federal bankruptcy exemptions not available. All law references are to Delaware Code Annotated (in the form title number-section number) unless otherwise noted.

Note: A single person may exempt no more than $25,000 total in all exemptions (not including retirement plans and principal residence); a husband & wife may exempt no more than $50,000 total (10-4914).

ASSET	EXEMPTION	LAW
homestead	Real property or manufactured home used as principal residence to $75,000 in 2010, $100,000 in 2011, and $125,000 in 2012; $125,000 for working or married persons where one spouse is 65 or older (spouses may not double)	10-4914(c)
	Property held as tenancy by the entirety may be exempt against debts owed by only one spouse	*In re Kelley*, 289 B.R. 38 (Bankr. D. Del. 2003)
insurance	Annuity contract proceeds to $350 per month	18-2728
	Fraternal benefit society benefits	18-6218
	Group life insurance policy or proceeds	18-2727
	Health or disability benefits	18-2726
	Life insurance proceeds if clause prohibits proceeds from being used to pay beneficiary's creditors	18-2729
	Life insurance proceeds or avails	18-2725
pensions	Tax-exempt retirement accounts, including 401(k)s, 403(b)s, profit-sharing and money purchase plans, SEP and SIMPLE IRAs, and defined-benefit plans	11 U.S.C. § 522(b)(3)(C)
	Traditional and Roth IRAs to $1,171,650 per person	11 U.S.C. § 522(b)(3)(C); (n)
	IRAs, Roth IRAs, & any other retirement plans	10-4915
	Kent County employees	9-4316
	Police officers	11-8803
	State employees	29-5503
	Volunteer firefighters	16-6653
personal property	Bible, books, & family pictures	10-4902(a)
	Burial plot	10-4902(a)
	Church pew or any seat in public place of worship	10-4902(a)
	Clothing, includes jewelry	10-4902(a)
	College investment plan account (limit for year before filing is $5,000 or average of past two years' contribution, whichever is more)	10-4916
	Principal and income from spendthrift trusts	12-3536
	Pianos & leased organs	10-4902(d)
	Sewing machines	10-4902(c)

public benefits	Aid to blind	31-2309
	Aid to aged, disabled; general assistance	31-513
	Crime victims' compensation	11-9011
	Unemployment compensation	19-3374
	Workers' compensation	19-2355
tools of trade	Tools of trade and/or vehicle necessary for employment to $15,000 each	10-4914(c)
	Tools, implements, & fixtures to $75 in New Castle & Sussex Counties; to $50 in Kent County	10-4902(b)
wages	85% of earned but unpaid wages	10-4913
wildcard	$500 of any personal property, except tools of trade, if head of family	10-4903

District of Columbia

Federal bankruptcy exemptions available. All law references are to District of Columbia Code unless otherwise noted.

ASSET	EXEMPTION	LAW
homestead	Any property used as a residence or co-op that debtor or debtor's dependent uses as a residence	15-501(a)(14)
	Property held as tenancy by the entirety may be exempt against debts owed by only one spouse	*Estate of Wall*, 440 F.2d 215 (D.C. Cir. 1971)
insurance	Disability benefits	15-501(a)(7); 31-4716.01
	Fraternal benefit society benefits	31-5315
	Group life insurance policy or proceeds	31-4717
	Life insurance payments	15-501(a)(11)
	Life insurance proceeds if clause prohibits proceeds from being used to pay beneficiary's creditors	31-4719
	Life insurance proceeds or avails	31-4716
	Other insurance proceeds to $200 per month, maximum 2 months, for head of family; else $60 per month	15-503
	Unmatured life insurance contract other than credit life insurance	15-501(a)(5)
miscellaneous	Alimony or child support	15-501(a)(7)
pensions *see also wages*	Tax-exempt retirement accounts, including 401(k)s, 403(b)s, profit-sharing and money purchase plans, SEP and SIMPLE IRAs, and defined-benefit plans	11 U.S.C. § 522(b)(3)(C)
	Traditional and Roth IRAs to $1,171,650 per person	11 U.S.C. § 522(b)(3)(C); (n)
	ERISA-qualified benefits, IRAs, Keoghs, etc. to maximum deductible contribution	15-501(b)(9)
	Any stock bonus, annuity, pension, or profit-sharing plan	15-501(a)(7)
	Judges	11-1570(f)
	Public school teachers	38-2001.17; 38-2021.17
personal property	Appliances, books, clothing, household furnishings, goods, musical instruments, pets to $425 per item or $8,625 total	15-501(a)(2)
	Cemetery & burial funds	43-111
	Cooperative association holdings to $50	29-928
	Food for 3 months	15-501(a)(12)
	Health aids	15-501(a)(6)
	Higher education tuition savings account	47-4510
	Residential condominium deposit	42-1904.09

personal property (continued)	All family pictures; all the family library to $400	15-501(a)(8)
	Motor vehicle to $2,575	15-501(a)(1)
	Payment, including pain & suffering, for loss of debtor or person depended on	15-501(a)(11)
	Uninsured motorist benefits	31-2408.01(h)
	Wrongful death damages	15-501(a)(11); 16-2703
public benefits	Aid to blind, aged, disabled; general assistance	4-215.01
	Crime victims' compensation	4-507(e); 15-501(a)(11)
	Social Security	15-501(a)(7)
	Unemployment compensation	51-118
	Veterans' benefits	15-501(a)(7)
	Workers' compensation	32-1517
tools of trade	Library, furniture, tools of professional or artist to $300	15-501(a)(13)
	Tools of trade or business to $1,625	15-501(a)(5)
	Mechanic's tools to $200	15-503(b)
	Seal & documents of notary public	1-1206
wages	Minimum 75% of earned but unpaid wages, pension payments; bankruptcy judge may authorize more for low-income debtors	16-572
	Nonwage (including pension & retirement) earnings to $200 per month for head of family; else $60 per month for a maximum of two months	15-503
	Payment for loss of future earnings	15-501(e)(11)
wildcard	Up to $850 in any property, plus up to $8,075 of unused homestead exemption	15-501(a)(3)

Florida

Federal bankruptcy exemptions not available. All law references are to Florida Statutes Annotated unless otherwise noted.

ASSET	EXEMPTION	LAW
homestead	Real or personal property including mobile or modular home to unlimited value; cannot exceed half acre in municipality or 160 acres elsewhere; spouse or child of deceased owner may claim homestead exemption	222.01; 222.02; 222.03; 222.05; Constitution 10-4 *In re Colwell*, 196 F.3d 1225 (11th Cir. 1999)
	May file homestead declaration	222.01
	Property held as tenancy by the entirety may be exempt against debts owed by only one spouse	*Havoco of America, Ltd. v. Hill*, 197 F.3d 1135 (11th Cir. 1999)
insurance	Annuity contract proceeds; does not include lottery winnings	222.14; *In re Pizzi*, 153 B.R. 357 (S.D. Fla. 1993)
	Death benefits payable to a specific beneficiary, not the deceased's estate	222.13
	Disability or illness benefits	222.18
	Fraternal benefit society benefits	632.619
	Life insurance cash surrender value	222.14
miscellaneous	Alimony, child support needed for support	222.201
	Damages to employees for injuries in hazardous occupations	769.05

pensions *see also wages*	Tax-exempt retirement accounts, including 401(k)s, 403(b)s, profit-sharing and money purchase plans, SEP and SIMPLE IRAs, and defined-benefit plans	11 U.S.C. § 522(b)(3)(C)
	Traditional and Roth IRAs to $1,171,650 per person	11 U.S.C. § 522(b)(3)(C); (n)
	County officers, employees	122.15
	ERISA-qualified benefits, including IRAs & Roth IRAs	222.21(2)
	Firefighters	175.241
	Police officers	185.25
	State officers, employees	121.131
	Teachers	238.15
personal property	Any personal property to $1,000 (husband & wife may double); to $4,000 if no homestead claimed	Constitution 10-4; *In re Hawkins*, 51 B.R. 348 (S.D. Fla. 1985)
	Federal income tax refund or credit	222.25
	Health aids	222.25
	Motor vehicle to $1,000	222.25
	Pre-need funeral contract deposits	497.56(8)
	Prepaid college education trust deposits	222.22(1)
	Prepaid hurricane savings accounts	222.22(4)
	Prepaid medical savings account deposits	222.22(2)
public benefits	Crime victims' compensation, unless seeking to discharge debt for treatment of injury incurred during the crime	960.14
	Public assistance	222.201
	Social Security	222.201
	Unemployment compensation	222.201; 443.051(2),(3)
	Veterans' benefits	222.201; 744.626
	Workers' compensation	440.22
tools of trade	None	
wages	100% of wages for heads of family up to $750 per week either unpaid or paid & deposited into bank account for up to 6 months	222.11
	Federal government employees' pension payments needed for support & received 3 months prior	222.21
wildcard	See personal property	

Georgia

Federal bankruptcy exemptions not available. All law references are to the Official Code of Georgia Annotated unless otherwise noted.

Some of the exemptions in this table may not be available to you in some bankruptcy courts. Before filing bankruptcy, check with a bankruptcy attorney to find out which exemptions are acceptable in your court. See, "Some courts might not allow 'bankruptcy specific' exemptions," at the beginning of this appendix for more information.

ASSET	EXEMPTION	LAW
homestead	Real or personal property, including co-op, used as residence to $10,000 (to $20,000 if married and debtor spouse is sole owner); up to $5,000 of unused portion of homestead may be applied to any property	44-13-100(a)(1); 44-13-100(a)(6); *In re Burnett*, 303 B.R. 684 (M.D. Ga. 2003)

insurance	Annuity & endowment contract benefits	33-28-7
	Disability or health benefits to $250 per month	33-29-15
	Fraternal benefit society benefits	33-15-62
	Group insurance	33-30-10
	Proceeds & avails of life insurance	33-26-5; 33-25-11
	Life insurance proceeds if policy owned by someone you depended on, needed for support	44-13-100(a)(11)(C)
	Unmatured life insurance contract	44-13-100(a)(8)
	Unmatured life insurance dividends, interest, loan value, or cash value to $2,000 if beneficiary is you or someone you depend on	44-13-100(a)(9)
miscellaneous	Alimony, child support needed for support	44-13-100(a)(2)(D)
pensions	Tax-exempt retirement accounts, including 401(k)s, 403(b)s, profit-sharing and money purchase plans, SEP and SIMPLE IRAs, and defined-benefit plans	11 U.S.C. § 522(b)(3)(C)
	Traditional and Roth IRAs to $1,171,650 per person	11 U.S.C. § 522(b)(3)(C); (n)
	Employees of nonprofit corporations	44-13-100(a)(2.1)(B)
	ERISA-qualified benefits & IRAs	18-4-22
	Public employees	44-13-100(a)(2.1)(A); 47-2-332
	Payments from IRA necessary for support	44-13-100(a)(2)(F)
	Other pensions needed for support	18-4-22; 44-13-100(a)(2)(E); 44-13-100(a)(2.1)(C)
personal property	Animals, crops, clothing, appliances, books, furnishings, household goods, musical instruments to $300 per item, $5,000 total	44-13-100(a)(4)
	Burial plot, in lieu of homestead	44-13-100(a)(1)
	Compensation for lost future earnings needed for support to $7,500	44-13-100(a)(11)(E)
	Health aids	44-13-100(a)(10)
	Jewelry to $500	44-13-100(a)(5)
	Motor vehicles to $3,500	44-13-100(a)(3)
	Personal injury recoveries to $10,000	44-13-100(a)(11)(D)
	Wrongful death recoveries needed for support	44-13-100(a)(11)(B)
public benefits	Aid to blind	49-4-58
	Aid to disabled	49-4-84
	Crime victims' compensation	44-13-100(a)(11)(A)
	Local public assistance	44-13-100(a)(2)(A)
	Old age assistance	49-4-35
	Social Security	44-13-100(a)(2)(A)
	Unemployment compensation	44-13-100(a)(2)(A)
	Veterans' benefits	44-13-100(a)(2)(B)
	Workers' compensation	34-9-84
tools of trade	Implements, books, & tools of trade to $1,500	44-13-100(a)(7)
wages	Minimum 75% of earned but unpaid weekly disposable earnings, or 30 times the state or federal hourly minimum wage, whichever is greater, for private & federal workers; bankruptcy judge may authorize more for low-income debtors	18-4-20; 18-4-21
wildcard	$600 of any property	44-13-100(a)(6)
	Unused portion of homestead exemption to $5,000	44-13-100(a)(6)

Hawaii

Federal bankruptcy exemptions available. All law references are to Hawaii Revised Statutes unless otherwise noted.

ASSET	EXEMPTION	LAW
homestead	Head of family or over 65 to $30,000; all others to $20,000; property cannot exceed 1 acre; sale proceeds exempt for 6 months after sale (spouses may not double)	651-91; 651-92; 651-96
	Property held as tenancy by the entirety may be exempt against debts owed by only one spouse	*Security Pacific Bank v. Chang*, 818 F.Supp. 1343 (D. Haw. 1993)
insurance	Annuity contract or endowment policy proceeds if beneficiary is insured's spouse, child, or parent	431:10-232(b)
	Accident, health, or sickness benefits	431:10-231
	Fraternal benefit society benefits	432:2-403
	Group life insurance policy or proceeds	431:10-233
	Life insurance proceeds if clause prohibits proceeds from being used to pay beneficiary's creditors	431:10D-112
	Life or health insurance policy for spouse or child	431:10-234
miscellaneous	Property of business partnership	425-125
pensions	Tax-exempt retirement accounts, including 401(k)s, 403(b)s, profit-sharing and money purchase plans, SEP and SIMPLE IRAs, and defined-benefit plans	11 U.S.C. § 522(b)(3)(C)
	Traditional and Roth IRAs to $1,171,650 per person	11 U.S.C. § 522(b)(3)(C); (n)
	IRAs, Roth IRAs, and ERISA-qualified benefits deposited over 3 years before filing bankruptcy	651-124
	Firefighters	88-169
	Police officers	88-169
	Public officers & employees	88-91; 653-3
personal property	Appliances & furnishings	651-121(1)
	Books	651-121(1)
	Burial plot to 250 sq. ft. plus tombstones, monuments, & fencing	651-121(4)
	Clothing	651-121(1)
	Jewelry, watches, & articles of adornment to $1,000	651-121(1)
	Motor vehicle to wholesale value of $2,575	651-121(2)
	Proceeds for sold or damaged exempt property, sale proceeds exempt for 6 months after sale	651-121(5)
public benefits	Crime victims' compensation & special accounts created to limit commercial exploitation of crimes	351-66; 351-86
	Public assistance paid by Department of Health Services for work done in home or workshop	346-33
	Temporary disability benefits	392-29
	Unemployment compensation	383-163
	Unemployment work relief funds to $60 per month	653-4
	Workers' compensation	386-57
tools of trade	Tools, implements, books, instruments, uniforms, furnishings, fishing boat, nets, motor vehicle, & other property needed for livelihood	651-121(3)

wages	Prisoner's wages held by Department of Public Safety (except for restitution, child support, & other claims)	353-22.5
	Unpaid wages due for services of past 31 days	651-121(6)
wildcard	None	

Idaho

Federal bankruptcy exemptions not available. All law references are to Idaho Code unless otherwise noted.

ASSET	EXEMPTION	LAW
homestead	Real property or mobile home to $100,000; sale proceeds exempt for 6 months (spouses may not double)	55-1003; 55-1113
	Must record homestead exemption for property that is not yet occupied	55-1004
insurance	Annuity contract proceeds to $1,250 per month	41-1836
	Death or disability benefits	11-604(1)(a); 41-1834
	Fraternal benefit society benefits	41-3218
	Group life insurance benefits	41-1835
	Homeowners' insurance proceeds to amount of homestead exemption	55-1008
	Life insurance proceeds if clause prohibits proceeds from being used to pay beneficiary's creditors	41-1930
	Life insurance proceeds or avails for beneficiary other than the insured	11-604(d); 41-1833
	Medical, surgical, or hospital care benefits & amount in medical savings account	11-603(5)
	Unmatured life insurance contract, other than credit life insurance, owned by debtor	11-605(9)
	Unmatured life insurance contract interest or dividends to $5,000 owned by debtor or person debtor depends on	11-605(10)
miscellaneous	Alimony, child support	11-604(1)(b)
	Liquor licenses	23-514
pension see also wages	Tax-exempt retirement accounts, including 401(k)s, 403(b)s, profit-sharing and money purchase plans, SEP and SIMPLE IRAs, and defined-benefit plans	11 U.S.C. § 522(b)(3)(C)
	Traditional and Roth IRAs to $1,171,650 per person	11 U.S.C. § 522(b)(3)(C); (n)
	ERISA-qualified benefits	55-1011
	Firefighters	72-1422
	Government & private pensions, retirement plans, IRAs, Roth IRAs, Keoghs, etc.	11-604A
	Police officers	50-1517
	Public employees	59-1317
personal property	Appliances, furnishings, books, clothing, pets, musical instruments, 1 firearm, family portraits, & sentimental heirlooms to $750 per item, $7,500 total	11-605(1)
	Building materials	45-514
	Burial plot	11-603(1)
	College savings program account	11-604A(4)(b)
	Crops cultivated on maximum of 50 acres, to $1,000; water rights to 160 inches	11-605(6) and (7)
	Health aids	11-603(2)
	Jewelry to $1,000	11-605(2)
	Motor vehicle to $7,000	11-605(3)
	Personal injury recoveries	11-604(1)(c)

personal property (continued)	Proceeds for damaged exempt property for 3 months after proceeds received	11-606
	Wrongful death recoveries	11-604(1)(c)
public benefits	Aid to blind, aged, disabled	56-223
	Federal, state, & local public assistance	11-603(4)
	General assistance	56-223
	Social Security	11-603(3)
	Unemployment compensation	11-603(6)
	Veterans' benefits	11-603(3)
	Workers' compensation	72-802
tools of trade	Arms, uniforms, & accoutrements that peace officer, National Guard, or military personnel is required to keep	11-605(5)
	Implements, books, & tools of trade to $2,500	11-605(3)
wages	Minimum 75% of earned but unpaid weekly disposable earnings, or 30 times the federal hourly minimum wage, whichever is greater; pension payments; bankruptcy judge may authorize more for low-income debtors	11-207
wildcard	$800 in any tangible personal property	11-605(11)

Illinois

Federal bankruptcy exemptions not available. All law references are to Illinois Compiled Statutes Annotated unless otherwise noted.

ASSET	EXEMPTION	LAW
homestead	Real or personal property including a farm, lot, & buildings, condo, co-op, or mobile home to $15,000; sale proceeds exempt for 1 year	735-5/12-901; 735-5/12-906
	Spouse or child of deceased owner may claim homestead exemption	735-5/12-902
	Illinois recognizes tenancy by the entirety, with limitations	750-65/22; 765-1005/1c; *In re Gillissie*, 215 B.R. 370 (Bankr. N.D. Ill. 1998); *Great Southern Co. v. Allard*, 202 B.R. 938 (N.D. Ill. 1996).
insurance	Fraternal benefit society benefits	215-5/299.1a
	Health or disability benefits	735-5/12-1001(g)(3)
	Homeowners' proceeds if home destroyed, to $15,000	735-5/12-907
	Life insurance, annuity proceeds, or cash value if beneficiary is insured's child, parent, spouse, or other dependent	215-5/238; 735-5/12-1001(f)
	Life insurance proceeds to a spouse or dependent of debtor to extent needed for support	735-5/12-1001(f),(g)(3)
miscellaneous	Alimony, child support	735-5/12-1001(g)(4)
	Property of business partnership	805-205/25
pensions	Tax-exempt retirement accounts, including 401(k)s, 403(b)s, profit-sharing and money purchase plans, SEP and SIMPLE IRAs, and defined-benefit plans	11 U.S.C. § 522(b)(3)(C)
	Traditional and Roth IRAs to $1,171,650 per person	11 U.S.C. § 522(b)(3)(C); (n)
	Civil service employees	40-5/11-223

pensions (continued)	County employees	40-5/9-228
	Disabled firefighters; widows & children of firefighters	40-5/22-230
	IRAs and ERISA-qualified benefits	735-5/12-1006
	Firefighters	40-5/4-135; 40-5/6-213
	General Assembly members	40-5/2-154
	House of correction employees	40-5/19-117
	Judges	40-5/18-161
	Municipal employees	40-5/7-217(a); 40-5/8-244
	Park employees	40-5/12-190
	Police officers	40-5/3-144.1; 40-5/5-218
	Public employees	735-5/12-1006
	Public library employees	40-5/19-218
	Sanitation district employees	40-5/13-805
	State employees	40-5/14-147
	State university employees	40-5/15-185
	Teachers	40-5/16-190; 40-5/17-151
personal property	Bible, family pictures, schoolbooks, & clothing	735-5/12-1001(a)
	Health aids	735-5/12-1001(e)
	Illinois College Savings Pool accounts invested more than 1 year before filing if below federal gift tax limit, or 2 years before filing if above	735-5/12-1001(j)
	Motor vehicle to $2,400	735-5/12-1001(c)
	Personal injury recoveries to $15,000	735-5/12-1001(h)(4)
	Pre-need cemetery sales funds, care funds, & trust funds	235-5/6-1; 760-100/4; 815-390/16
	Prepaid tuition trust fund	110-979/45(g)
	Proceeds of sold exempt property	735-5/12-1001
	Wrongful death recoveries	735-5/12-1001(h)(2)
public benefits	Aid to aged, blind, disabled; public assistance	305-5/11-3
	Crime victims' compensation	735-5/12-1001(h)(1)
	Restitution payments on account of WWII relocation of Aleuts & Japanese Americans	735-5/12-1001(12)(h)(5)
	Social Security	735-5/12-1001(g)(1)
	Unemployment compensation	735-5/12-1001(g)(1),(3)
	Veterans' benefits	735-5/12-1001(g)(2)
	Workers' compensation	820-305/21
	Workers' occupational disease compensation	820-310/21
tools of trade	Implements, books, & tools of trade to $1,500	735-5/12-1001(d)
wages	Minimum 85% of earned but unpaid weekly wages or 45 times the federal minimum hourly wage (or state minimum hourly wage, if higher); bankruptcy judge may authorize more for low-income debtors	740-170/4
wildcard	$4,000 of any personal property (does not include wages)	735-5/12-1001(b)

Indiana

Federal bankruptcy exemptions not available. All law references are to Indiana Statutes Annotated unless otherwise noted.

ASSET	EXEMPTION	LAW
homestead *see also* *wildcard*	Real or personal property used as residence to $17,600	34-55-10-2(c)(1)
	Property held as tenancy by the entirety may be exempt against debts incurred by only one spouse	34-55-10-2(c)(5); 32-17-3-1
insurance	Employer's life insurance policy on employee	27-1-12-17.1
	Fraternal benefit society benefits	27-11-6-3
	Group life insurance policy	27-1-12-29
	Life insurance policy, proceeds, cash value, or avails if beneficiary is insured's spouse or dependent	27-1-12-14
	Life insurance proceeds if clause prohibits proceeds to be used to pay beneficiary's creditors	27-2-5-1
	Mutual life or accident proceeds needed for support	27-8-3-23; *In re Stinnet*, 321 B.R. 477 (S.D. Ind. 2005)
miscellaneous	Property of business partnership	23-4-1-25
pensions	Tax-exempt retirement accounts, including 401(k)s, 403(b)s, profit-sharing and money purchase plans, SEP and SIMPLE IRAs, and defined-benefit plans	11 U.S.C. § 522(b)(3)(C)
	Traditional and Roth IRAs to $1,171,650 per person	11 U.S.C. § 522(b)(3)(C); (n)
	Firefighters	36-8-7-22 36-8-8-17
	Police officers	36-8-8-17; 10-12-2-10
	Public employees	5-10.3-8-9
	Public or private retirement benefits & contributions	34-55-10-2(c)(6)
	Sheriffs	36-8-10-19
	State teachers	5-10.4-5-14
personal property	Health aids	34-55-10-2(c)(4)
	Money in medical care savings account	34-55-10-2(c)(7)
	Spendthrift trusts	30-4-3-2
	$350 of any intangible personal property, except money owed to you	34-55-10-2(c)(3)
public benefits	Crime victims' compensation, unless seeking to discharge the debts for which the victim was compensated	5-2-6.1-38
	Unemployment compensation	22-4-33-3
	Workers' compensation	22-3-2-17
tools of trade	National Guard uniforms, arms, & equipment	10-16-10-3
wages	Minimum 75% of earned but unpaid weekly disposable earnings, or 30 times the federal hourly minimum wage; bankruptcy judge may authorize more for low-income debtors	24-4.5-5-105
wildcard	$9,350 of any real estate or tangible personal property	34-55-10-2(c)(2)

Iowa

Federal bankruptcy exemptions not available. All law references are to Iowa Code Annotated unless otherwise noted.

ASSET	EXEMPTION	LAW
homestead	May record homestead declaration	561.4
	Real property or an apartment to an unlimited value; property cannot exceed ½ acre in town or city, 40 acres elsewhere (spouses may not double)	499A.18; 561.2; 561.16
insurance	Accident, disability, health, illness, or life proceeds or avails	627.6(6)
	Disability or illness benefit	627.6(8)(c)
	Employee group insurance policy or proceeds	509.12
	Fraternal benefit society benefits	512B.18
	Life insurance proceeds if clause prohibits proceeds from being used to pay beneficiary's creditors	508.32
	Life insurance proceeds paid to spouse, child, or other dependent (limited to $10,000 if acquired within 2 years of filing for bankruptcy)	627.6(6)
	Upon death of insured, up to $15,000 total proceeds from all matured life, accident, health, or disability policies exempt from beneficiary's debts contracted before insured's death	627.6(6)
miscellaneous	Alimony, child support needed for support	627.6(8)(d)
	Liquor licenses	123.38
pensions *see also wages*	Tax-exempt retirement accounts, including 401(k)s, 403(b)s, profit-sharing and money purchase plans, SEP and SIMPLE IRAs, and defined-benefit plans	11 U.S.C. § 522(b)(3)(C)
	Traditional and Roth IRAs to $1,171,650 per person	11 U.S.C. § 522(b)(3)(C); (n)
	Disabled firefighters, police officers (only payments being received)	410.11
	Federal government pension	627.8
	Firefighters	411.13
	Other pensions, annuities, & contracts fully exempt; however, contributions made within 1 year prior to filing for bankruptcy not exempt to the extent they exceed normal & customary amounts	627.6(8)(e)
	Peace officers	97A.12
	Police officers	411.13
	Public employees	97B.39
	Retirement plans, Keoghs, IRAs, Roth IRAs, ERISA-qualified benefits	627.6(8)(f)
personal property	Bibles, books, portraits, pictures, & paintings to $1,000 total	627.6(3)
	Burial plot to 1 acre	627.6(4)
	Clothing & its storage containers, household furnishings, appliances, musical instruments, and other personal property to $7,000	627.6(5)
	Health aids	627.6(7)
	Jewelry to $2,000	627.6(1)(6)
	Residential security or utility deposit, or advance rent, to $500	627.6(14)
	Rifle or musket; shotgun	627.6(2)
	One motor vehicle to $7,000	627.6(9)
	Wedding or engagement rings, limited to $7,000 if purchased after marriage and within last two years	627.6(1)(a)
	Wrongful death proceeds and awards needed for support of debtor and dependents	627.6(15)

public benefits	Adopted child assistance	627.19
	Aid to dependent children	239B.6
	Any public assistance benefit	627.6(8)(a)
	Social Security	627.6(8)(a)
	Unemployment compensation	627.6(8)(a)
	Veterans' benefits	627.6(8)(b)
	Workers' compensation	627.13
tools of trade	Farming equipment; includes livestock, feed to $10,000	627.6(11)
	National Guard articles of equipment	29A.41
	Nonfarming equipment to $10,000	627.6(10)
wages	Expected annual earnings / Amount NOT exempt per year	642.21
	$0 to $12,000 — $250	
	$12,000 to $16,000 — $400	
	$16,000 to $24,000 — $800	
	$24,000 to $35,000 — $1,000	
	$35,000 to $50,000 — $2,000	
	More than $50,000 — 10%	
	Not exempt from spousal or child support	
	Wages or salary of a prisoner	356.29
wildcard	$1,000 of any personal property, including cash	627.6(14)

Kansas

Federal bankruptcy exemptions not available. All law references are to Kansas Statutes Annotated unless otherwise noted.

ASSET	EXEMPTION	LAW
homestead	Real property or mobile home you occupy or intend to occupy to unlimited value; property cannot exceed 1 acre in town or city, 160 acres on farm	60-2301; Constitution 15-9
insurance	Cash value of life insurance; not exempt if obtained within 1 year prior to bankruptcy with fraudulent intent	60-2313(a)(7); 40-414(b)
	Disability & illness benefits	60-2313(a)(1)
	Fraternal life insurance benefits	60-2313(a)(8)
	Life insurance proceeds	40-414(a)
miscellaneous	Alimony, maintenance, & support	60-2312(b)
	Liquor licenses	60-2313(a)(6); 41-326
pensions	Tax-exempt retirement accounts, including 401(k)s, 403(b)s, profit-sharing and money purchase plans, SEP and SIMPLE IRAs, and defined-benefit plans	11 U.S.C. § 522(b)(3)(C)
	Traditional and Roth IRAs to $1,171,650 per person	11 U.S.C. § 522(b)(3)(C); (n)
	Elected & appointed officials in cities with populations between 120,000 & 200,000	13-14a10
	ERISA-qualified benefits	60-2308(b)
	Federal government pension needed for support & paid within 3 months of filing for bankruptcy (only payments being received)	60-2308(a)
	Firefighters	12-5005(e); 14-10a10
	Judges	20-2618
	Police officers	12-5005(e); 13-14a10

pensions (continued)	Public employees	74-4923; 74-49,105
	State highway patrol officers	74-4978g
	State school employees	72-5526
	Payment under a stock bonus, pension, profit-sharing, annuity, or similar plan or contract on account of illness, disability, death, age, or length of service, to the extent reasonably necessary for support	60-2312(b)
personal property	Burial plot or crypt	60-2304(d)
	Clothing to last 1 year	60-2304(a)
	Food & fuel to last 1 year	60-2304(a)
	Funeral plan prepayments	60-2313(a)(10); 16-310(d)
	Furnishings & household equipment	60-2304(a)
	Jewelry & articles of adornment to $1,000	60-2304(b)
	Motor vehicle to $20,000; if designed or equipped for disabled person, no limit	60-2304(c)
public benefits	Crime victims' compensation	60-2313(a)(7); 74-7313(d)
	General assistance	39-717(c)
	Social Security	60-2312(b)
	Unemployment compensation	60-2313(a)(4); 44-718(c)
	Veterans' benefits	60-2312(b)
	Workers' compensation	60-2313(a)(3); 44-514
tools of trade	Books, documents, furniture, instruments, equipment, breeding stock, seed, grain, & stock to $7,500 total	60-2304(e)
	National Guard uniforms, arms, & equipment	48-245
wages	Minimum 75% of disposable weekly wages or 30 times the federal minimum hourly wage per week, whichever is greater; bankruptcy judge may authorize more for low-income debtors	60-2310
wildcard	None	

Kentucky

Federal bankruptcy exemptions available. All law references are to Kentucky Revised Statutes unless otherwise noted.

ASSET	EXEMPTION	LAW
homestead	Real or personal property used as residence to $5,000; sale proceeds exempt	427.060; 427.090
insurance	Annuity contract proceeds to $350 per month	304.14-330
	Cooperative life or casualty insurance benefits	427.110(1)
	Fraternal benefit society benefits	427.110(2)
	Group life insurance proceeds	304.14-320
	Health or disability benefits	304.14-310
	Life insurance policy if beneficiary is a married woman	304.14-340
	Life insurance proceeds if clause prohibits proceeds from being used to pay beneficiary's creditors	304.14-350
	Life insurance proceeds or cash value if beneficiary is someone other than insured	304.14-300
miscellaneous	Alimony, child support needed for support	427.150(1)
pensions	Tax-exempt retirement accounts, including 401(k)s, 403(b)s, profit-sharing and money purchase plans, SEP and SIMPLE IRAs, and defined-benefit plans	11 U.S.C. § 522(b)(3)(C)
	Traditional and Roth IRAs to $1,171,650 per person	11 U.S.C. § 522(b)(3)(C); (n)

pensions (continued)	ERISA-qualified benefits, including IRAs, SEPs, & Keoghs deposited more than 120 days before filing	427.150
	Firefighters	67A.620; 95.878
	Police officers	427.120; 427.125
	State employees	61.690
	Teachers	161.700
	Urban county government employees	67A.350
personal property	Burial plot to $5,000, in lieu of homestead	427.060
	Clothing, jewelry, articles of adornment, & furnishings to $3,000 total	427.010(1)
	Health aids	427.010(1)
	Lost earnings payments needed for support	427.150(2)(d)
	Medical expenses paid & reparation benefits received under motor vehicle reparation law	304.39-260
	Motor vehicle to $2,500	427.010(1)
	Personal injury recoveries to $7,500 (not to include pain & suffering or pecuniary loss)	427.150(2)(c)
	Prepaid tuition payment fund account	164A.707(3)
	Wrongful death recoveries for person you depended on, needed for support	427.150(2)(b)
public benefits	Aid to blind, aged, disabled; public assistance	205.220(c)
	Crime victims' compensation	427.150(2)(a)
	Unemployment compensation	341.470(4)
	Workers' compensation	342.180
tools of trade	Library, office equipment, instruments, & furnishings of minister, attorney, physician, surgeon, chiropractor, veterinarian, or dentist to $1,000	427.040
	Motor vehicle of auto mechanic, mechanical, or electrical equipment servicer, minister, attorney, physician, surgeon, chiropractor, veterinarian, or dentist to $2,500	427.030
	Tools, equipment, livestock, & poultry of farmer to $3,000	427.010(1)
	Tools of nonfarmer to $300	427.030
wages	Minimum 75% of disposable weekly earnings or 30 times the federal minimum hourly wage per week, whichever is greater; bankruptcy judge may authorize more for low-income debtors	427.010(2),(3)
wildcard	$1,000 of any property	427.160

Louisiana

Federal bankruptcy exemptions not available. All law references are to Louisiana Revised Statutes Annotated unless otherwise noted.

ASSET	EXEMPTION	LAW
homestead	Property you occupy to $25,000 (if debt is result of catastrophic or terminal illness or injury, limit is full value of property as of 1 year before filing); cannot exceed 5 acres in city or town, 200 acres elsewhere (spouses may not double)	20:1(A)(1),(2),(3)
	Spouse or child of deceased owner may claim homestead exemption; spouse given home in divorce gets homestead	20:1(B)
insurance	Annuity contract proceeds & avails	22:647
	Fraternal benefit society benefits	22:558
	Group insurance policies or proceeds	22:649
	Health, accident, or disability proceeds or avails	22:646

insurance (continued)	Life insurance proceeds or avails; if policy issued within 9 months of filing, exempt only to $35,000	22:647
miscellaneous	Property of minor child	13:3881(A)(3); Civil Code Art. 223
pensions	Tax-exempt retirement accounts, including 401(k)s, 403(b)s, profit-sharing and money purchase plans, SEP and SIMPLE IRAs, and defined-benefit plans	11 U.S.C. § 522(b)(3)(C)
	Traditional and Roth IRAs to $1,171,650 per person	11 U.S.C. § 522(b)(3)(C); (n)
	Assessors	11:1403
	Court clerks	11:1526
	District attorneys	11:1583
	ERISA-qualified benefits, including IRAs, Roth IRAs, & Keoghs, if contributions made over 1 year before filing for bankruptcy	13:3881; 20:33(1)
	Firefighters	11:2263
	Gift or bonus payments from employer to employee or heirs whenever paid	20:33(2)
	Judges	11:1378
	Louisiana University employees	11:952.3
	Municipal employees	11:1735
	Parochial employees	11:1905
	Police officers	11:3513
	School employees	11:1003
	Sheriffs	11:2182
	State employees	11:405
	Teachers	11:704
	Voting registrars	11:2033
personal property	Arms, military accoutrements; bedding; dishes, glassware, utensils, silverware (nonsterling); clothing, family portraits, musical instruments; bedroom, living room, & dining room furniture; poultry, 1 cow, household pets; heating & cooling equipment, refrigerator, freezer, stove, washer & dryer, iron, sewing machine	13:3881(A)(4)
	Cemetery plot, monuments	8:313
	Disaster relief insurance proceeds	13:3881(A)(7)
	Engagement & wedding rings to $5,000	13:3881(A)(5)
	Motor vehicle to $7,500	13:3881(A)(7)
	Motor vehicle modified for disability to $7,500	13:3881(A)(8)
	Spendthrift trusts	9:2004
public benefits	Aid to blind, aged, disabled; public assistance	46:111
	Crime victims' compensation	46:1811
	Earned income tax credit	13:3881 (A)(6)
	Unemployment compensation	23:1693
	Workers' compensation	23:1205
tools of trade	Tools, instruments, books, $7,500 of equity in a motor vehicle, one firearm to $500, needed to work	13:3881(A)(2)
wages	Minimum 75% of disposable weekly earnings or 30 times the federal minimum hourly wage per week, whichever is greater; bankruptcy judge may authorize more for low-income debtors	13:3881(A)(1)
wildcard	None	

Maine

Federal bankruptcy exemptions not available. All law references are to Maine Revised Statutes Annotated, in the form title number-section number, unless otherwise noted.

ASSET	EXEMPTION	LAW
homestead	Real or personal property (including cooperative) used as residence to $47,500; if debtor has minor dependents in residence, to $95,000; if debtor over age 60 or physically or mentally disabled, $95,000; proceeds of sale exempt for six months	14-4422(1)
insurance	Annuity proceeds to $450 per month	24-A-2431
	Death benefit for police, fire, or emergency medical personnel who die in the line of duty	25-1612
	Disability or health proceeds, benefits, or avails	14-4422(13)(A),(C); 24-A-2429
	Fraternal benefit society benefits	24-A-4118
	Group health or life policy or proceeds	24-A-2430
	Life, endowment, annuity, or accident policy, proceeds or avails	14-4422(14)(C); 24-A-2428
	Life insurance policy, interest, loan value, or accrued dividends for policy from person you depended on, to $4,000	14-4422(11)
	Unmatured life insurance policy, except credit insurance policy	14-4422(10)
miscellaneous	Alimony & child support needed for support	14-4422(13)(D)
pensions	Tax-exempt retirement accounts, including 401(k)s, 403(b)s, profit-sharing and money purchase plans, SEP and SIMPLE IRAs, and defined-benefit plans	11 U.S.C. § 522(b)(3)(C)
	Traditional and Roth IRAs to $1,171,650 per person	11 U.S.C. § 522(b)(3)(C); (n)
	ERISA-qualified benefits	14-4422(13)(E)
	Judges	4-1203
	Legislators	3-703
	State employees	5-17054
personal property	Animals, crops, musical instruments, books, clothing, furnishings, household goods, appliances to $200 per item	14-4422(3)
	Balance due on repossessed goods; total amount financed can't exceed $2,000	9-A-5-103
	Burial plot in lieu of homestead exemption	14-4422(1)
	Cooking stove; furnaces & stoves for heat	14-4422(6)(A),(B)
	Food to last 6 months	14-4422(7)(A)
	Fuel not to exceed 10 cords of wood, 5 tons of coal, or 1,000 gal. of heating oil	14-4422(6)(C)
	Health aids	14-4422(12)
	Jewelry to $750; no limit for one wedding & one engagement ring	14-4422(4)
	Lost earnings payments needed for support	14-4422(14)(F)
	Military clothes, arms, & equipment	37-B-262
	Motor vehicle to $5,000	14-4422(2)
	Personal injury recoveries to $12,500	14-4422(14)(D)
	Seeds, fertilizers, & feed to raise & harvest food for 1 season	14-4422(7)(B)
	Tools & equipment to raise & harvest food	14-4422(7)(C)
	Wrongful death recoveries needed for support	14-4422(14)(B)
public benefits	Maintenance under the Rehabilitation Act	26-1411-H
	Crime victims' compensation	14-4422(14)(A)

public benefits (continued)	Federal, state, or local public assistance benefits; earned income and child tax credits	14-4422(13)(A); 22-3180, 22-3766
	Social Security	14-4422(13)(A)
	Unemployment compensation	14-4422(13)(A),(C)
	Veterans' benefits	14-4422(13)(B)
	Workers' compensation	39-A-106
tools of trade	Books, materials, & stock to $5,000	14-4422(5)
	Commercial fishing boat, 5-ton limit	14-4422(9)
	One of each farm implement (& its maintenance equipment needed to harvest & raise crops)	14-4422(8)
wages	None (use federal nonbankruptcy wage exemption)	
wildcard	Unused portion of exemption in homestead to $6,000; or unused exemption in animals, crops, musical instruments, books, clothing, furnishings, household goods, appliances, tools of the trade, & personal injury recoveries	14-4422(16)
	$400 of any property	14-4422(15)

Maryland

Federal bankruptcy exemptions not available. All law references are to Maryland Code of Courts & Judicial Proceedings unless otherwise noted. New Maryland homestead exemption is indexed for inflation by matching the federal homestead amount.

ASSET	EXEMPTION	LAW
homestead	Owner-occupied residential property to $21,625 (spouses may not double). Property held as tenancy by the entirety is exempt against debts owed by only one spouse	11-504(f); *In re Birney*, 200 F.3d 225 (4th Cir. 1999)
insurance	Disability or health benefits, including court awards, arbitrations, & settlements	11-504(b)(2)
	Fraternal benefit society benefits	Ins. 8-431; Estates & Trusts 8-115
	Life insurance or annuity contract proceeds or avails if beneficiary is insured's dependent, child, or spouse	Ins. 16-111(a); Estates & Trusts 8-115
	Medical insurance benefits deducted from wages plus medical insurance payments to $145 per week or 75% of disposable wages	Commercial Law 15-601.1(3)
miscellaneous	Child support	11-504(b)(6)
	Alimony to same extent wages are exempt	11-504(b)(7)
pensions	Tax-exempt retirement accounts, including 401(k)s, 403(b)s, profit-sharing and money purchase plans, SEP and SIMPLE IRAs, and defined-benefit plans	11 U.S.C. § 522(b)(3)(C)
	Traditional and Roth IRAs to $1,171,650 per person	11 U.S.C. § 522(b)(3)(C); (n)
	ERISA-qualified benefits, including IRAs, Roth IRAs, & Keoghs	11-504(h)(1), (4)
	State employees	State Pers. & Pen. 21-502
personal property	Appliances, furnishings, household goods, books, pets, & clothing to $1,000 total	11-504(b)(4)
	Burial plot	Bus. Reg. 5-503
	Health aids	11-504(b)(3)
	Perpetual care trust funds	Bus. Reg. 5-603
	Prepaid college trust funds	Educ. 18-1913
	Lost future earnings recoveries	11-504(b)(2)

public benefits	Baltimore Police death benefits	Code of 1957 art 24 16 103
	Crime victims' compensation	Crim. Proc. 11-816(b)
	Unemployment compensation	Labor & Employment 8-106
	Workers' compensation	Labor & Employment 9-732
tools of trade	Clothing, books, tools, instruments, & appliances to $5,000	11-504(b)(1)
wages	Earned but unpaid wages, the greater of 75% or $145 per week; in Kent, Caroline, Queen Anne's, & Worcester Counties, the greater of 75% or 30 times federal minimum hourly wage	Commercial Law 15-601.1
wildcard	$6,000 in cash or any property, if claimed within 30 days of attachment or levy	11-504(b)(5)
	An additional $5,000 in real or personal property	11-504(f)

Massachusetts

Federal bankruptcy exemptions available. All law references are to Massachusetts General Laws Annotated, in the form title number-section number, unless otherwise noted.

ASSET	EXEMPTION	LAW
homestead	If statement of homestead is not in title to property, must record homestead declaration before filing bankruptcy	188-2
	Property held as tenancy by the entirety may be exempt against debt for nonnecessity owed by only one spouse	209-1
	Property you occupy or intend to occupy (including mobile home) to $500,000 (special rules if over 65 or disabled) (co-owners may not double)	188-1; 188-1A
	Spouse or children of deceased owner may claim homestead exemption	188-4
insurance	Disability benefits to $400 per week	175-110A
	Fraternal benefit society benefits	176-22
	Group annuity policy or proceeds	175-132C
	Group life insurance policy	175-135
	Life insurance or annuity contract proceeds if clause prohibits proceeds from being used to pay beneficiary's creditors	175-119A
	Life insurance policy if beneficiary is a married woman	175-126
	Life or endowment policy, proceeds, or cash value	175-125
	Medical malpractice self-insurance	175F-15
miscellaneous	Property of business partnership	108A-25
pensions *see also wages*	Tax-exempt retirement accounts, including 401(k)s, 403(b)s, profit-sharing and money purchase plans, SEP and SIMPLE IRAs, and defined-benefit plans	11 U.S.C. § 522(b)(3)(C)
	Traditional and Roth IRAs to $1,171,650 per person	11 U.S.C. § 522(b)(3)(C); (n)
	Credit union employees	171-84
	ERISA-qualified benefits, including IRAs & Keoghs to specified limits	235-34A; 246-28
	Private retirement benefits	32-41
	Public employees	32-19
	Savings bank employees	168-41; 168-44
personal property	Bank deposits to $125	235-34
	Beds & bedding; heating unit; clothing	235-34
	Bibles & books to $200 total; sewing machine to $200	235-34

personal property (continued)	Burial plots, tombs, & church pew	235-34
	Cash for fuel, heat, water, or light to $75 per month	235-34
	Cash to $200 per month for rent, in lieu of homestead	235-34
	Cooperative association shares to $100	235-34
	Food or cash for food to $300	235-34
	Furniture to $3,000; motor vehicle to $700	235-34
	Moving expenses for eminent domain	79-6A
	Trust company, bank, or credit union deposits to $500	246-28A
	2 cows, 12 sheep, 2 swine, 4 tons of hay	235-34
public benefits	Aid to families with dependent children	118-10
	Public assistance	235-34
	Unemployment compensation	151A-36
	Veterans' benefits	115-5
	Workers' compensation	152-47
tools of trade	Arms, accoutrements, & uniforms required	235-34
	Fishing boats, tackle, & nets to $500	235-34
	Materials you designed & procured to $500	235-34
	Tools, implements, & fixtures to $500 total	235-34
wages	Earned but unpaid wages to $125 per week	246-28
wildcard	None	

Michigan

Federal bankruptcy exemptions available. All law references are to Michigan Compiled Laws Annotated unless otherwise noted.

Under Michigan law, bankruptcy exemption amounts are adjusted for inflation every three years (starting in 2005) by the Michigan Department of Treasury. These amounts have already been adjusted, so the amounts listed in the statutes are not current. You can find the current amounts at www.michigan.gov documents/BankruptcyExemptions2005_141050_7.pdf or by searching Google for "Property Debtor in Bankruptcy May Exempt, Inflation Adjusted Amounts."

Some of the exemptions in this table may not be available to you in some bankruptcy courts. Before filing bankruptcy, check with a bankruptcy attorney to find out which exemptions are acceptable in your court. See, "Some courts might not allow 'bankruptcy specific' exemptions," at the beginning of this appendix for more information.

ASSET	EXEMPTION	LAW
homestead	Property held as tenancy by the entirety may be exempt against debts owed by only one spouse	600.5451(1)(o)
	Real property including condo to $34,450 ($51,650 if over 65 or disabled); property cannot exceed 1 lot in town, village, city, or 40 acres elsewhere; spouse or children of deceased owner may claim homestead exemption; spouses or unmarried co-owners may not double	600.5451(1)(n); *Vinson v. Dakmak*, 347 B.R. 620 (E.D. Mich. 2006)
insurance	Disability, mutual life, or health benefits	600.5451(1)(j)
	Employer-sponsored life insurance policy or trust fund	500.2210
	Fraternal benefit society benefits	500.8181
	Life, endowment, or annuity proceeds if clause prohibits proceeds from being used to pay beneficiary's creditors	500.4054
	Life insurance	500.2207
miscellaneous	Property of business partnership	449.25

pensions	Tax-exempt retirement accounts, including 401(k)s, 403(b)s, profit-sharing and money purchase plans, SEP and SIMPLE IRAs, and defined-benefit plans	11 U.S.C. § 522(b)(3)(C)
	Traditional and Roth IRAs to $1,171,650 per person	11 U.S.C. § 522(b)(3)(C); (n)
	ERISA-qualified benefits, except contributions within last 120 days	600.5451(1)(m)
	Firefighters, police officers	38.559(6); 38.1683
	IRAs & Roth IRAs, except contributions within last 120 days	600.5451(1)(l)
	Judges	38.2308; 38.1683
	Legislators	38.1057; 38.1683
	Probate judges	38.2308; 38.1683
	Public school employees	38.1346; 38.1683
	State employees	38.40; 38.1683
personal property	Appliances, utensils, books, furniture, & household goods to $525 each, $3,450 total	600.5451(1)(c)
	Building & loan association shares to $1,150 par value, in lieu of homestead	600.5451(1)(k)
	Burial plots, cemeteries	600.5451(1)(a)(vii)
	Church pew, slip, seat for entire family to $575	600.5451(1)(d)
	Clothing; family pictures	600.5451(1)(a)
	Food & fuel to last family for 6 months	600.5451(1)(b)
	Crops, animals, and feed to $2,300	600.5451(1)(e)
	1 motor vehicle to $3,175	600.5451(1)(g)
	Computer & accessories to $575	600.5451(1)(h)
	Household pets to $575	600.5451(1)(f)
	Professionally prescribed health aids	600.5451(a)
public benefits	Crime victims' compensation	18.362
	Social welfare benefits	400.63
	Unemployment compensation	421.30
	Veterans' benefits for Korean War veterans	35.977
	Veterans' benefits for Vietnam veterans	35.1027
	Veterans' benefits for WWII veterans	35.926
	Workers' compensation	418.821
tools of trade	Arms & accoutrements required	600.6023(1)(a)
	Tools, implements, materials, stock, apparatus, or other things needed to carry on occupation to $2,300 total	600.5451(1)(i)
wages	Head of household may keep 60% of earned but unpaid wages (no less than $15/week), plus $2/week per nonspouse dependent; if not head of household may keep 40% (no less than $10/week)	600.5311
wildcard	None	

Minnesota

Federal bankruptcy exemptions available. All law references are to Minnesota Statutes Annotated, unless otherwise noted.

Note: Section 550.37(4)(a) requires certain exemptions to be adjusted for inflation on July 1 of even-numbered years; this table includes all changes made through July 1, 2008. Exemptions are published on or before the May 1 issue of the Minnesota State Register, www.comm.media.state.mn.us/bookstore/stateregister.asp, or call the Minnesota Dept. of Commerce at 651-296-7977.

ASSET	EXEMPTION	LAW
homestead	Home & land on which it is situated to $360,000; if homestead is used for agricultural purposes, $900,000; cannot exceed ½ acre in city, 160 acres elsewhere (spouses may not double)	510.01; 510.02
	Manufactured home to an unlimited value	550.37 subd. 12
insurance	Accident or disability proceeds	550.39
	Fraternal benefit society benefits	64B.18
	Life insurance proceeds to $44,000 if beneficiary is spouse or child of insured, plus $11,000 per dependent	550.37 subd. 10
	Police, fire, or beneficiary association benefits	550.37 subd. 11
	Unmatured life insurance contract dividends, interest, or loan value to $8,800 if insured is debtor or person debtor depends on	550.37 subd. 23
miscellaneous	Earnings of minor child	550.37 subd. 15
pensions	Tax-exempt retirement accounts, including 401(k)s, 403(b)s, profit-sharing and money purchase plans, SEP and SIMPLE IRAs, and defined-benefit plans	11 U.S.C. § 522(b)(3)(C)
	Traditional and Roth IRAs to $1,171,650 per person	11 U.S.C. § 522(b)(3)(C); (n)
	ERISA-qualified benefits if needed for support, up to $66,000 in present value	550.37 subd. 24
	IRAs or Roth IRAs needed for support, up to $66,000 in present value	550.37 subd. 24
	Public employees	353.15; 356.401
	State employees	352.965 subd. 8; 356.401
	State troopers	352B.071; 356.401
personal property	Appliances, furniture, jewelry, radio, phonographs, & TV to $9,900 total	550.37 subd. 4(b)
	Bible & books	550.37 subd. 2
	Burial plot; church pew or seat	550.37 subd. 3
	Clothing, one watch, food, & utensils for family	550.37 subd. 4(a)
	Motor vehicle to $4,400 (up to $44,000 if vehicle has been modified for disability)	550.37 subd. 12(a)
	Personal injury recoveries	550.37 subd. 22
	Proceeds for damaged exempt property	550.37 subds. 9, 16
	Wedding rings to $2,695	550.37 subd. 4(c)
	Wrongful death recoveries	550.37 subd. 22
public benefits	Crime victims' compensation	611A.60
	Public benefits	550.37 subd. 14
	Unemployment compensation	268.192 subd. 2
	Veterans' benefits	550.38
	Workers' compensation	176.175

tools of trade	Farm machines, implements, livestock, produce, & crops	550.37 subd. 3
total (except teaching materials) can't exceed $13,000	Teaching materials of college, university, public school, or public institution teacher	550.37 subd. 8
	Tools, machines, instruments, stock in trade, furniture, & library to $11,000 total	550.37 subd. 6
wages	Minimum 75% of weekly disposable earnings or 40 times federal minimum hourly wage, whichever is greater	571.922
	Wages deposited into bank accounts for 20 days after depositing	550.37 subd. 13
	Wages paid within 6 months of returning to work after receiving welfare or after incarceration; includes earnings deposited in a financial institution in the last 60 days	550.37 subd. 14
wildcard	None	

Note: In cases of suspected fraud, the Minnesota constitution permits courts to cap exemptions that would otherwise be unlimited. (*In re Tveten*, 402 N.W.2d 551 (Minn. 1987); *In re Medill*, 119 B.R. 685 (Bankr. D. Minn. 1990); *In re Sholdan*, 217 F.3d 1006 (8th Cir. 2000).)

Mississippi

Federal bankruptcy exemptions not available. All law references are to Mississippi Code unless otherwise noted.

ASSET	EXEMPTION	LAW
homestead	May file homestead declaration	85-3-27; 85-3-31
	Mobile home does not qualify as homestead unless you own land on which it is located (*see personal property*)	*In re Cobbins*, 234 B.R. 882 (S.D. Miss. 1999)
	Property you own & occupy to $75,000; if over 60 & married or widowed may claim a former residence; property cannot exceed 160 acres; sale proceeds exempt	85-3-1(b)(i); 85-3-21; 85-3-23
insurance	Disability benefits	85-3-1(b)(ii)
	Fraternal benefit society benefits	83-29-39
	Homeowners' insurance proceeds to $75,000	85-3-23
	Life insurance proceeds if clause prohibits proceeds from being used to pay beneficiary's creditors	83-7-5; 85-3-11
pensions	Tax-exempt retirement accounts, including 401(k)s, 403(b)s, profit-sharing and money purchase plans, SEP and SIMPLE IRAs, and defined-benefit plans	11 U.S.C. § 522(b)(3)(C)
	Traditional and Roth IRAs to $1,171,650 per person	11 U.S.C. § 522(b)(3)(C); (n)
	ERISA-qualified benefits, IRAs, Keoghs deposited over 1 year before filing bankruptcy	85-3-1(e)
	Firefighters (includes death benefits)	21-29-257; 45-2-1
	Highway patrol officers	25-13-31
	Law enforcement officers' death benefits	45-2-1
	Police officers (includes death benefits)	21-29-257; 45-2-1
	Private retirement benefits to extent tax-deferred	71-1-43
	Public employees retirement & disability benefits	25-11-129
	State employees	25-14-5
	Teachers	25-11-201(1)(d)
	Volunteer firefighters' death benefits	45-2-1

personal property	Mobile home to $30,000	85-3-1(d)
	Personal injury judgments to $10,000	85-3-17
	Sale or insurance proceeds for exempt property	85-3-1(b)(i)
	State health savings accounts	85-3-1(g)
	Tangible personal property to $10,000: any items worth less than $200 each; furniture, dishes, kitchenware, household goods, appliances, 1 radio, 1 TV, 1 firearm, 1 lawn-mower, clothing, wedding rings, motor vehicles, tools of the trade, books, crops, health aids, domestic animals (does not include works of art, antiques, jewelry, or electronic entertainment equipment)	85-3-1(a)
	Tax-qualified § 529 education savings plans, including those under the Mississippi Prepaid Affordable College Tuition Program	85-3-1(f)
public benefits	Assistance to aged	43-9-19
	Assistance to blind	43-3-71
	Assistance to disabled	43-29-15
	Crime victims' compensation	99-41-23(7)
	Federal income tax refund to $5,000; earned income tax credit to $5,000; state tax refunds to $5,000	85-3-1(h); (i); (j); (k)
	Social Security	25-11-129
	Unemployment compensation	71-5-539
	Workers' compensation	71-3-43
tools of trade	*See personal property*	
wages	Earned but unpaid wages owed for 30 days; after 30 days, minimum 75% of earned but unpaid weekly disposable earnings or 30 times the federal hourly minimum wage, whichever is greater; bankruptcy judge may authorize more for low-income debtors	85-3-4
wildcard	$50,000 of any property, including deposits of money, available to Mississippi resident who is at least 70 years old; *also see personal property*	85-3-1(h)

Missouri

Federal bankruptcy exemptions not available. All law references are to Annotated Missouri Statutes unless otherwise noted.

ASSET	EXEMPTION	LAW
homestead	Property held as tenancy by the entirety may be exempt against debts owed by only one spouse	*In re Eads*, 271 B.R. 371 (Bankr. W.D. Mo. 2002)
	Real property to $15,000 or mobile home to $5,000 (joint owners may not double)	513.430(6); 513.475 *In re Smith*, 254 B.R. 751 (Bankr. W.D. Mo. 2000)
insurance	Assessment plan or life insurance proceeds	377.090
	Disability or illness benefits	513.430(10)(c)
	Fraternal benefit society benefits to $5,000, bought over 6 months before filing	513.430(8)
	Life insurance dividends, loan value, or interest to $150,000, bought over 6 months before filing	513.430(8)
	Stipulated insurance premiums	377.330
	Unmatured life insurance policy	513.430(7)
miscellaneous	Alimony, child support to $750 per month	513.430(10)(d)
	Property of business partnership	358.250

pensions	Tax-exempt retirement accounts, including 401(k)s, 403(b)s, profit-sharing and money purchase plans, SEP and SIMPLE IRAs, and defined-benefit plans	11 U.S.C. § 522(b)(3)(C)
	Traditional and Roth IRAs to $1,171,650 per person	11 U.S.C. § 522(b)(3)(C); (n)
	Employee benefit spendthrift trust	456.014
	Employees of cities with 100,000 or more people	71.207
	ERISA-qualified benefits, IRAs, Roth IRAs, & other retirement accounts needed for support	513.430(10)(e), (f)
	Firefighters	87.090; 87.365; 87.485
	Highway & transportation employees	104.250
	Police department employees	86.190; 86.353; 86.1430
	Public officers & employees	70.695; 70.755
	State employees	104.540
	Teachers	169.090
personal property	Appliances, household goods, furnishings, clothing, books, crops, animals, & musical instruments to $3,000 total	513.430(1)
	Burial grounds to 1 acre or $100	214.190
	Health aids	513.430(9)
	Motor vehicle to $3,000	513.430(5)
	Wedding ring to $1,500 & other jewelry to $500	513.430(2)
	Wrongful death recoveries for person you depended on	513.430(11)
public benefits	Crime victim's compensation	595.025
	Public assistance	513.430(10)(a)
	Social Security	513.430(10)(a)
	Unemployment compensation	288.380(10)(l); 513.430(10)(c)
	Veterans' benefits	513.430(10)b)
	Workers' compensation	287.260
tools of trade	Implements, books, & tools of trade to $3,000	513.430(4)
wages	Minimum 75% of weekly earnings (90% of weekly earnings for head of family), or 30 times the federal minimum hourly wage, whichever is more; bankruptcy judge may authorize more for low-income debtors	525.030
	Wages of servant or common laborer to $90	513.470
wildcard	$1,250 of any property if head of family, else $600; head of family may claim additional $350 per child	513.430(3); 513.440

Montana

Federal bankruptcy exemptions not available. All law references are to Montana Code Annotated unless otherwise noted.

Some of the exemptions in this table may not be available to you in some bankruptcy courts. Before filing bankruptcy, check with a bankruptcy attorney to find out which exemptions are acceptable in your court. See, "Some courts might not allow 'bankruptcy specific' exemptions," at the beginning of this appendix for more information.

ASSET	EXEMPTION	LAW
homestead	Must record homestead declaration before filing for bankruptcy	70-32-105
	Real property or mobile home you occupy to $250,000; sale, condemnation, or insurance proceeds exempt for 18 months	70-32-104; 70-32-201; 70-32-213

insurance	Annuity contract proceeds to $350 per month	33-15-514
	Disability or illness proceeds, avails, or benefits	25-13-608(1)(d); 33-15-513
	Fraternal benefit society benefits	33-7-522
	Group life insurance policy or proceeds	33-15-512
	Hail insurance benefits	80-2-245
	Life insurance proceeds if clause prohibits proceeds from being used to pay beneficiary's creditors	33-20-120
	Medical, surgical, or hospital care benefits	25-13-608(1)(f)
	Unmatured life insurance contracts	25-13-608(1)(k)
miscellaneous	Alimony, child support	25-13-608(1)(g)
pensions	Tax-exempt retirement accounts, including 401(k)s, 403(b)s, profit-sharing and money purchase plans, SEP and SIMPLE IRAs, and defined-benefit plans	11 U.S.C. § 522(b)(3)(C)
	Traditional and Roth IRAs to $1,171,650 per person	11 U.S.C. § 522(b)(3)(C); (n)
	IRAs & ERISA-qualified benefits deposited over 1 year before filing bankruptcy or up to 15% of debtor's gross annual income	31-2-106
	Firefighters	19-18-612(1)
	IRA & Roth IRA contributions & earnings made before judgment filed	25-13-608(1)(e)
	Police officers	19-19-504(1)
	Public employees	19-2-1004; 25-13-608(i)
	Teachers	19-20-706(2); 25-13-608(j)
	University system employees	19-21-212
personal property	Appliances, household furnishings, goods, animals with feed, crops, musical instruments, books, firearms, sporting goods, clothing, & jewelry to $600 per item, $4,500 total	25-13-609(1)
	Burial plot	25-13-608(1)(h)
	Cooperative association shares to $500 value	35-15-404
	Health aids	25-13-608(1)(a)
	Motor vehicle to $2,500	25-13-609(2)
	Proceeds from sale or for damage or loss of exempt property for 6 months after received	25-13-610
public benefits	Aid to aged, disabled needy persons	53-2-607
	Crime victims' compensation	53-9-129
	Local public assistance	25-13-608(1)(b)
	Silicosis benefits	39-73-110
	Social Security	25-13-608(1)(b)
	Subsidized adoption payments to needy persons	53-2-607
	Unemployment compensation	31-2-106(2); 39-51-3105
	Veterans' benefits	25-13-608(1)(c)
	Vocational rehabilitation to blind needy persons	53-2-607
	Workers' compensation	39-71-743
tools of trade	Implements, books, & tools of trade to $3,000	25-13-609(3)
	Uniforms, arms, & accoutrements needed to carry out government functions	25-13-613(b)
wages	Minimum 75% of earned but unpaid weekly disposable earnings, or 30 times the federal hourly minimum wage, whichever is greater; bankruptcy judge may authorize more for low-income debtors	25-13-614
wildcard	None	

Nebraska

Federal bankruptcy exemptions not available. All law references are to Revised Statutes of Nebraska unless otherwise noted.

ASSET	EXEMPTION	LAW
homestead	$60,000 for head of family or an unmarried person age 65 or older; cannot exceed 2 lots in city or village, 160 acres elsewhere; sale proceeds exempt 6 months after sale (spouses may not double)	40-101; 40-111; 40-113
	May record homestead declaration	40-105
insurance	Fraternal benefit society benefits to $100,000 loan value unless beneficiary convicted of a crime related to benefits	44-1089
	Life insurance proceeds and avails to $100,000	44-371
pensions *see also wages*	Tax-exempt retirement accounts, including 401(k)s, 403(b)s, profit-sharing and money purchase plans, SEP and SIMPLE IRAs, and defined-benefit plans	11 U.S.C. § 522(b)(3)(C)
	Traditional and Roth IRAs to $1,171,650 per person	11 U.S.C. § 522(b)(3)(C); (n)
	County employees	23-2322
	Deferred compensation of public employees	48-1401
	ERISA-qualified benefits including IRAs & Roth IRAs needed for support	25-1563.01
	Military disability benefits	25-1559
	School employees	79-948
	State employees	84-1324
personal property	Burial plot	12-517
	Clothing	25-1556(2)
	Crypts, lots, tombs, niches, vaults	12-605
	Furniture, household goods & appliances, household electronics, personal computers, books, & musical instruments to $1,500	25-1556(3)
	Health aids	25-1556(5)
	Medical or health savings accounts to $25,000	8-1, 131(2)(b)
	Perpetual care funds	12-511
	Personal injury recoveries	25-1563.02
	Personal possessions	25-1556
public benefits	Aid to disabled, blind, aged; public assistance	68-1013
	General assistance to poor persons	68-148
	Unemployment compensation	48-647
	Workers' compensation	48-149
tools of trade	Equipment or tools including a vehicle used in or for commuting to principal place of business to $2,400 (husband & wife may double)	25-1556(4); *In re Keller,* 50 B.R. 23 (D. Neb. 1985)
wages	Minimum 85% of earned but unpaid weekly disposable earnings or pension payments for head of family; minimum 75% of earned but unpaid weekly disposable earnings or 30 times the federal hourly minimum wage, whichever is greater, for all others; bankruptcy judge may authorize more for low-income debtors	25-1558
wildcard	$2,500 of any personal property except wages, in lieu of homestead	25-1552

Nevada

Federal bankruptcy exemptions not available. All law references are to Nevada Revised Statutes Annotated unless otherwise noted.

ASSET	EXEMPTION	LAW
homestead	Must record homestead declaration before filing for bankruptcy	115.020
	Real property or mobile home to $550,000 Spouses may not double	115.010; 21.090(1)(m)
insurance	Annuity contract proceeds to $350 per month	687B.290
	Fraternal benefit society benefits	695A.220
	Group life or health policy or proceeds	687B.280
	Health proceeds or avails	687B.270
	Life insurance policy or proceeds if annual premiums not over $1,000	21.090(1)(k); *In re Bower*, 234 B.R. 109 (Nev. 1999)
	Life insurance proceeds if you're not the insured	687B.260
miscellaneous	Alimony & child support	21.090(1)(s)
	Property of some business partnerships	87.250
	Security deposits for a rental residence, except landlord may enforce terms of lease or rental agreement	21.090(1)(n)
pensions	Tax-exempt retirement accounts, including 401(k)s, 403(b)s, profit-sharing and money purchase plans, SEP and SIMPLE IRAs, and defined-benefit plans	11 U.S.C. § 522(b)(3)(C)
	Traditional and Roth IRAs to $1,171,650 per person	11 U.S.C. § 522(b)(3)(C); (n)
	ERISA-qualified benefits, deferred compensation, SEP IRA, Roth IRA, or IRA to $500,000	21.090(1)(r)
	Public employees	286.670
personal property	Appliances, household goods, furniture, home & yard equipment to $12,000 total	21.090(1)(b)
	Books, works of art, musical instruments, & jewelry to $5,000	21.090(1)(a)
	Burial plot purchase money held in trust	689.700
	Funeral service contract money held in trust	689.700
	Health aids	21.090(1)(q)
	Interests in qualifying trusts	21.090(1)(cc)
	Keepsakes & pictures	21.090(1)(a)
	Metal-bearing ores, geological specimens, art curiosities, or paleontological remains; must be arranged, classified, cataloged, & numbered in reference books	21.100
	Mortgage impound accounts	645B.180
	Motor vehicle to $15,000; no limit on vehicle equipped for disabled person	21.090(1)(f),(o)
	1 gun	21.090(1)(i)
	Personal injury compensation to $16,500	21.090(1)(u)
	Restitution received for criminal act	21.090(1)(x)
	Stock in certain closely held corporations	21.090(1)(bb)
	Tax refunds derived from the earned income credit	21.090(1)(aa)
	Wrongful death awards to survivors	21.090(1)(v)
public benefits	Aid to blind, aged, disabled; public assistance	422.291
	Crime victim's compensation	21.090
	Industrial insurance (workers' compensation)	616C.205
	Public assistance for children	432.036
	Social Security retirement, disability, SSI, survivor benefits	21.090(1)(y)
	Unemployment compensation	612.710
	Vocational rehabilitation benefits	615.270

tools of trade	Arms, uniforms, & accoutrements you're required to keep	21.090(1)(j)
	Cabin or dwelling of miner or prospector; mining claim, cars, implements, & appliances to $4,500 total (for working claim only)	21.090(1)(e)
	Farm trucks, stock, tools, equipment, & seed to $4,500	21.090(1)(c)
	Library, equipment, supplies, tools, inventory, & materials to $10,000	21.090(1)(d)
wages	Minimum 75% of disposable weekly earnings or 30 times the federal minimum hourly wage per week, whichever is more; bankruptcy judge may authorize more for low-income debtors	21.090(1)(g)
wildcard	$1,000 of any personal property	21.090(1)(z)

New Hampshire

Federal bankruptcy exemptions available. All law references are to New Hampshire Revised Statutes Annotated unless otherwise noted.

ASSET	EXEMPTION	LAW
homestead	Real property or manufactured housing (& the land it's on if you own it) to $100,000	480:1
insurance	Firefighters' aid insurance	402:69
	Fraternal benefit society benefits	418:17
	Homeowners' insurance proceeds to $5,000	512:21(VIII)
miscellaneous	Jury, witness fees	512:21(VI)
	Property of business partnership	304-A:25
	Wages of minor child	512:21(III)
pensions	Tax-exempt retirement accounts, including 401(k)s, 403(b)s, profit-sharing and money purchase plans, SEP and SIMPLE IRAs, and defined-benefit plans	11 U.S.C. § 522(b)(3)(C)
	Traditional and Roth IRAs to $1,171,650 per person	11 U.S.C. § 522(b)(3)(C); (n)
	ERISA-qualified retirement accounts including IRAs & Roth IRAs	512:2 (XIX)
	Federally created pension (only benefits building up)	512:21(IV)
	Firefighters	102:23
	Police officers	103:18
	Public employees	100-A:26
personal property	Beds, bedding, & cooking utensils	511:2(II)
	Bibles & books to $800	511:2(VIII)
	Burial plot, lot	511:2(XIV)
	Church pew	511:2(XV)
	Clothing	511:2(I)
	Cooking & heating stoves, refrigerator	511:2(IV)
	Domestic fowl to $300	511:2(XIII)
	Food & fuel to $400	511:2(VI)
	Furniture to $3,500	511:2(III)
	Jewelry to $500	511:2(XVII)
	Motor vehicle to $4,000	511:2(XVI)
	Proceeds for lost or destroyed exempt property	512:21(VIII)
	Sewing machine	511:2(V)
	1 cow, 6 sheep & their fleece, 4 tons of hay	511:2(XI); (XII)
	1 hog or pig or its meat (if slaughtered)	511:2(X)

public benefits	Aid to blind, aged, disabled; public assistance	167:25
	Unemployment compensation	282-A:159
	Workers' compensation	281-A:52
tools of trade	Tools of your occupation to $5,000	511:2(IX)
	Uniforms, arms, & equipment of military member	511:2(VII)
	Yoke of oxen or horse needed for farming or teaming	511:2(XII)
wages	50 times the federal minimum hourly wage per week	512:21(II)
	Deposits in any account designated a payroll account	512:21(XI)
	Earned but unpaid wages of spouse	512:21(III)
wildcard	$1,000 of any property	511:2(XVIII)
	Unused portion of bibles & books, food & fuel, furniture, jewelry, motor vehicle, & tools of trade exemptions to $7,000	511:2(XVIII)

New Jersey

Federal bankruptcy exemptions available. All law references are to New Jersey Statutes Annotated unless otherwise noted.

ASSET	EXEMPTION	LAW
homestead	None, but survivorship interest of a spouse in property held as tenancy by the entirety is exempt from creditors of a single spouse	*Freda v. Commercial Trust Co. of New Jersey,* 570 A.2d 409 (N.J. 1990)
insurance	Annuity contract proceeds to $500 per month	17B:24-7
	Disability benefits	17:18-12
	Disability, death, medical, or hospital benefits for civil defense workers	App. A:9-57.6
	Disability or death benefits for military member	38A:4-8
	Group life or health policy or proceeds	17B:24-9
	Health or disability benefits	17:18-12; 17B:24-8
	Life insurance proceeds if clause prohibits proceeds from being used to pay beneficiary's creditors	17B:24-10
	Life insurance proceeds or avails if you're not the insured	17B:24-6b
pensions	Tax-exempt retirement accounts, including 401(k)s, 403(b)s, profit-sharing and money purchase plans, SEP and SIMPLE IRAs, and defined-benefit plans	11 U.S.C. § 522(b)(3)(C)
	Traditional and Roth IRAs to $1,171,650 per person	11 U.S.C. § 522(b)(3)(C); (n)
	Alcohol beverage control officers	43:8A-20
	City boards of health employees	43:18-12
	Civil defense workers	App. A:9-57.6
	County employees	43:10-57; 43:10-105
	ERISA-qualified benefits for city employees	43:13-9
	Firefighters, police officers, traffic officers	43:16-7; 43:16A-17
	IRAs	*In re Yuhas,* 104 F.3d 612 (3d Cir. 1997)
	Judges	43:6A-41
	Municipal employees	43:13-44
	Prison employees	43:7-13
	Public employees	43:15A-53
	School district employees	18A:66-116

pensions (continued)	State police	5JIL 0 05
	Street & water department employees	43:19-17
	Teachers	18A:66-51
	Trust containing personal property created pursuant to federal tax law, including 401(k) plans, IRAs, Roth IRAs, & higher education (529) savings plans	25:2-1; *In re Yuhas*, 104 F.3d 612 (3d Cir. 1997)
personal property	Burial plots	45:27-21
	Clothing	2A:17-19
	Furniture & household goods to $1,000	2A:26-4
	Personal property & possessions of any kind, stock or interest in corporations to $1,000 total	2A:17-19
public benefits	Old age, permanent disability assistance	44:7-35
	Unemployment compensation	43:21-53
	Workers' compensation	34:15-29
tools of trade	None	
wages	90% of earned but unpaid wages if annual income is less than 250% of federal poverty level; 75% if annual income is higher	2A:17-56
	Wages or allowances received by military personnel	38A:4-8
wildcard	None	

New Mexico

Federal bankruptcy exemptions available. All law references are to New Mexico Statutes Annotated unless otherwise noted.

ASSET	EXEMPTION	LAW
homestead	$60,000	42-10-9
insurance	Benevolent association benefits to $5,000	42-10-4
	Fraternal benefit society benefits	59A-44-18
	Life, accident, health, or annuity benefits, withdrawal or cash value, if beneficiary is a New Mexico resident	42-10-3
	Life insurance proceeds	42-10-5
miscellaneous	Ownership interest in unincorporated association	53-10-2
	Property of business partnership	54-1A-501
pensions	Tax-exempt retirement accounts, including 401(k)s, 403(b)s, profit-sharing and money purchase plans, SEP and SIMPLE IRAs, and defined-benefit plans	11 U.S.C. § 522(b)(3)(C)
	Traditional and Roth IRAs to $1,171,650 per person	11 U.S.C. § 522(b)(3)(C); (n)
	Pension or retirement benefits	42-10-1; 42-10-2
	Public school employees	22-11-42A
personal property	Books & furniture	42-10-1; 42-10-2
	Building materials	48-2-15
	Clothing	42-10-1; 42-10-2
	Cooperative association shares, minimum amount needed to be member	53-4-28
	Health aids	42-10-1; 42-10-2
	Jewelry to $2,500	42-10-1; 42-10-2
	Materials, tools, & machinery to dig, drill, complete, operate, or repair oil line, gas well, or pipeline	70-4-12
	Motor vehicle to $4,000	42-10-1; 42-10-2

public benefits	Crime victims' compensation	31-22-15
	General assistance	27-2-21
	Occupational disease disablement benefits	52-3-37
	Unemployment compensation	51-1-37
	Workers' compensation	52-1-52
tools of trade	$1,500	42-10-1; 42-10-2
wages	Minimum 75% of disposable earnings or 40 times the federal hourly minimum wage, whichever is more; bankruptcy judge may authorize more for low-income debtors	35-12-7
wildcard	$500 of any personal property	42-10-1
	$5,000 of any real or personal property, in lieu of homestead	42-10-10

New York

Federal bankruptcy exemptions are available. All references are to Consolidated Laws of New York unless otherwise noted; Civil Practice Law & Rules are abbreviated C.P.L.R.

Some of the exemptions in this table may not be available to you in some bankruptcy courts. Before filing bankruptcy, check with a bankruptcy attorney to find out which exemptions are acceptable in your court. See, "Some courts might not allow 'bankruptcy specific' exemptions," at the beginning of this appendix for more information.

ASSET	EXEMPTION	LAW
homestead	Real property including co-op, condo, or mobile home, to $75,000, $125,000, or $250,000, depending on the county	C.P.L.R. 5206(a); *In re Pearl*, 723 F.2d 193 (2nd Cir. 1983)
insurance	Annuity contract benefits due the debtor, if debtor paid for the contract; $5,000 limit if purchased within 6 months prior to filing & not tax-deferred	Ins. 3212(d); Debt. & Cred. 283(1)
	Disability or illness benefits to $400 per month	Ins. 3212(c)
	Life insurance proceeds & avails if the beneficiary is not the debtor, or if debtor's spouse has taken out policy	Ins. 3212(b)
	Life insurance proceeds left at death with the insurance company, if clause prohibits proceeds from being used to pay beneficiary's creditors	Est. Powers & Trusts 7-1.5(a) (2)
miscellaneous	Alimony, child support	C.P.L.R. 5205 (d)(3); Debt. & Cred. 282(2)(d)
	Property of business partnership	Partnership 51
pensions	Tax-exempt retirement accounts, including 401(k)s, 403(b)s, profit-sharing and money purchase plans, SEP and SIMPLE IRAs, and defined-benefit plans	11 U.S.C. § 522(b)(3)(C)
	Traditional and Roth IRAs to $1,171,650 per person	11 U.S.C. § 522(b)(3)(C); (n)
	ERISA-qualified benefits, IRAs, Roth IRAs, & Keoghs, & income needed for support	C.P.L.R. 5205(c); Debt. & Cred. 282(2)(e)
	Public retirement benefits	Ins. 4607
	State employees	Ret. & Soc. Sec. 10
	Teachers	Educ. 524
	Village police officers	Unconsolidated 5711-o
	Volunteer ambulance workers' benefits	Vol. Amb. Wkr. Ben. 23
	Volunteer firefighters' benefits	Vol. Firefighter Ben. 23

personal property	Religious texts, schoolbooks, other books to $500; pictures; clothing; church pew or seat; sewing machine, refrigerator, TV, radio; furniture, cooking utensils & tableware, dishes; food to last 120 days; stoves with fuel to last 120 days; domestic animal with food to last 120 days, to $1,000; wedding ring; watch, jewelry, art to $1,000; exemptions may not exceed $10,000 total (including tools of trade & limited annuity)	C.P.L.R. 5205(a)(1)-(6); Debt. & Cred. 283(1)
	Burial plot without structure to ¼ acre	C.P.L.R. 5206(f)
	Cash (including savings bonds, tax refunds, bank & credit union deposits) to $5,000, or to $10,000 after exemptions for personal property taken, whichever amount is less (for debtors who do not claim homestead)	Debt. & Cred. 283(2)
	College tuition savings program trust fund	C.P.L.R. 5205(j)
	Electronic deposits of exempt property into bank account in last 45 days	C.P.L.R. 5205(l)(1)
	Health aids, including service animals with food	C.P.L.R. 5205(h)
	Lost future earnings recoveries needed for support	Debt. & Cred. 282(3)(iv)
	Motor vehicle to $4,000; $10,000 if equipped for disabled person (except if municipality is creditor)	Debt. & Cred. 282(1); *In re Miller*, 167 B.R. 782 (S.D. N.Y. 1994)
	Personal injury recoveries up to 1 year after receiving	Debt. & Cred. 282(3)(iii)
	Recovery for injury to exempt property up to 1 year after receiving	C.P.L.R. 5205(b)
	Savings & loan savings to $600	Banking 407
	Security deposit to landlord, utility company	C.P.L.R. 5205(g)
	Spendthrift trust fund principal, 90% of income if not created by debtor	C.P.L.R. 5205(c),(d)
	Wrongful death recoveries for person you depended on	Debt. & Cred. 282(3)(ii)
public benefits	Aid to blind, aged, disabled	Debt. & Cred. 282(2)(c)
	Crime victims' compensation	Debt. & Cred. 282(3)(i)
	Home relief, local public assistance	Debt. & Cred. 282(2)(a)
	Public assistance	Soc. Serv. 137
	Social Security	Debt. & Cred. 282(2)(a)
	Unemployment compensation	Debt. & Cred. 282(2)(a)
	Veterans' benefits	Debt. & Cred. 282(2)(b)
	Workers' compensation	Debt. & Cred. 282(2)(c); Work. Comp. 33, 218
tools of trade	Farm machinery, team, & food for 60 days; professional furniture, books, & instruments to $3,000 total	C.P.L.R. 5205(a),(b)
	Uniforms, medal, emblem, equipment, horse, arms, & sword of member of military	C.P.L.R. 5205(e)
wages	90% of earned but unpaid wages received within 60 days before & anytime after filing	C.P.L.R. 5205(d)
	90% of earnings from dairy farmer's sales to milk dealers	C.P.L.R. 5205(f)
	100% of pay of noncommissioned officer, private, or musician in U.S. or N.Y. state armed forces	C.P.L.R. 5205(e)
wildcard	None	

North Carolina

Federal bankruptcy exemptions not available. All law references are to General Statutes of North Carolina unless otherwise noted.

ASSET	EXEMPTION	LAW
homestead	Property held as tenancy by the entirety may be exempt against debts owed by only one spouse	*In re Chandler*, 148 B.R. 13 (E.D. N.C. 1992)
	Real or personal property, including co-op, used as residence to $35,000; $60,000 if 65 or older, property owned with spouse as tenants by the entirely or joint tenants with right of survivorship, and spouse has died; up to $5,000 of unused portion of homestead may be applied to any property	1C-1601(a)(1),(2)
insurance	Employee group life policy or proceeds	58-58-165
	Fraternal benefit society benefits	58-24-85
	Life insurance on spouse or children	1C-1601(a)(6); Const. Art. X § 5
miscellaneous	Alimony, support, separate maintenance, and child support necessary for support of debtor and dependents	1C-1601(a)(12)
	Property of business partnership	59-55
	Support received by a surviving spouse for 1 year, up to $10,000	30-15
pensions	Tax-exempt retirement accounts, including 401(k)s, 403(b)s, profit-sharing and money purchase plans, SEP and SIMPLE IRAs, and defined-benefit plans	11 U.S.C. § 522(b)(3)(C)
	Traditional and Roth IRAs to $1,171,650 per person	11 U.S.C. § 522(b)(3)(C); (n)
	Firefighters & rescue squad workers	58-86-90
	IRAs & Roth IRAs	1C-1601(a)(9)
	Law enforcement officers	143-166.30(g)
	Legislators	120-4.29
	Municipal, city, & county employees	128-31
	Retirement benefits from another state to extent exempt in that state	1C-1601(a)(11)
	Teachers & state employees	135-9; 135-95
	Animals, crops, musical instruments, books, clothing, appliances, household goods & furnishings to $5,000 total; may add $1,000 per dependent, up to $4,000 total additional (all property must have been purchased at least 90 days before filing)	1C-1601(a)(4),(d)
personal property	Burial plot to $18,500, in lieu of homestead	1C-1601(a)(1)
	College savings account established under 26 U.S.C. § 529 to $25,000, excluding certain contributions within prior year	1C-1601(a)(10)
	Health aids	1C-1601(a)(7)
	Motor vehicle to $3,500	1C-1601(a)(3)
	Personal injury & wrongful death recoveries for person you depended on	1C-1601(a)(8)
public benefits	Aid to blind	111-18
	Crime victims' compensation	15B-17
	Public adult assistance under Work First program	108A-36
	Unemployment compensation	96-17
	Workers' compensation	97-21
tools of trade	Implements, books, & tools of trade to $2,000	1C-1601(a)(5)
wages	Earned but unpaid wages received 60 days before filing for bankruptcy, needed for support	1-362
wildcard	$5,000 of unused homestead or burial exemption	1C-1601(a)(2)
	$500 of any personal property	Constitution Art. X § 1

North Dakota

Federal bankruptcy exemptions not available. All law references are to North Dakota Century Code unless otherwise noted.

ASSET	EXEMPTION	LAW
homestead	Real property, house trailer, or mobile home to $100,000 (spouses may not double)	28-22-02(10); 47-18-01
insurance	Fraternal benefit society benefits Any unmatured life insurance contract, other than credit life insurance	26.1-15.1-18; 26.1-33-40; 28-22-03.1(4)
	Life insurance proceeds payable to deceased's estate, not to a specific beneficiary	26.1-33-40
	Life insurance surrender value to $8,000 per policy, if beneficiary is insured's dependent & policy was owned over 1 year before filing for bankruptcy; limit does not apply if more needed for support	28-22-03.1(5)
miscellaneous	Child support payments	14-09-09.31; 28-22-03.1(8)(d)
pensions	Tax-exempt retirement accounts, including 401(k)s, 403(b)s, profit-sharing and money purchase plans, SEP and SIMPLE IRAs, and defined-benefit plans	11 U.S.C. § 522(b)(3)(C)
	Traditional and Roth IRAs to $1,171,650 per person	11 U.S.C. § 522(b)(3)(C); (n)
	Disabled veterans' benefits, except military retirement pay	28-22-03.1(4)(d)
	ERISA-qualified benefits, IRAs, Roth IRAs, & Keoghs to $100,000 per plan; no limit if more needed for support; total of all accounts cannot exceed $200,000	28-22-03.1(7)
	Public employees deferred compensation	54-52.2-06
	Public employees pensions	28-22-19(1)
personal property	One Bible or other religious text; schoolbooks; other books	28-22-02(4)
	Burial plots, church pew	28-22-02(2),(3)
	Wearing apparel to $5,000 and all clothing & family pictures	28-22-02(1),(5)
	Crops or grain raised by debtor on 160 acres where debtor resides	28-22-02(8)
	Food & fuel to last 1 year	28-22-02(6)
	Health aids	28-22-03.1(6)
	Insurance proceeds for exempt property	28-22-02(9)
	One motor vehicle to $2,950 (or $32,000 for vehicle that has been modified to accommodate owner's disability)	28-22-03.1(2)
	Personal injury recoveries to $15,000	28-22-03.1(4)(b)
	Wrongful death recoveries to $15,000	28-22-03.1(4)(a)
	Head of household not claiming crops or grain may claim $5,000 of any personal property	28-22-03
	Unmarried with no dependents not claiming crops or grain may claim $3,750 of any personal property	28-22-05
public benefits	Crime victims' compensation	28-22-03.1(4); 28-22-19(2)
	Old age & survivor insurance program benefits	52-09-22
	Public assistance	28-22-19(3)
	Social Security	28-22-03.1(8)(a)
	Unemployment compensation	52-06-30
	Veteran's disability benefits	28-22-03.1(8)(b)
	Workers' compensation	65-05-29
tools of trade	Books, tools, & implements of trade to $1,500	28-22-03.1(3)
wages	Minimum 75% of disposable weekly earnings or 40 times the federal minimum wage, whichever is more; bankruptcy judge may authorize more for low-income debtors	32-09.1-03
wildcard	$7,500 of any property in lieu of homestead	28-22-03.1(1)

Ohio

Federal bankruptcy exemptions not available. All law references are to Ohio Revised Code unless otherwise noted. Amounts are adjusted for inflation by tracking federal exemption amounts.

Some of the exemptions in this table may not be available to you in some bankruptcy courts. Before filing bankruptcy, check with a bankruptcy attorney to find out which exemptions are acceptable in your court. See, "Some courts might not allow 'bankruptcy specific' exemptions," at the beginning of this appendix for more information.

ASSET	EXEMPTION	LAW
homestead	Property held as tenancy by the entirety may be exempt against debts owed by only one spouse	In re Pernus, 143 B.R. 856 (N.D. Ohio 1992)
	Real or personal property used as residence to $21,625	2329.66(A)(1)(b)
insurance	Benevolent society benefits to $5,000	2329.63; 2329.66(A)(6)(a)
	Disability benefits needed for support	2329.66(A)(6)(e); 3923.19
	Fraternal benefit society benefits	2329.66(A)(6)(d); 3921.18
	Group life insurance policy or proceeds	2329.66(A)(6)(c); 3917.05
	Life, endowment, or annuity contract avails for your spouse, child, or dependent	2329.66(A)(6)(b); 3911.10
	Life insurance proceeds for a spouse	3911.12
	Life insurance proceeds if clause prohibits proceeds from being used to pay beneficiary's creditors	3911.14
miscellaneous	Alimony, child support needed for support	2329.66(A)(11)
	Property of business partnership	1775.24; 2329.66(A)(14)
pensions	Tax-exempt retirement accounts, including 401(k)s, 403(b)s, profit-sharing and money purchase plans, SEP and SIMPLE IRAs, and defined-benefit plans	11 U.S.C. § 522(b)(3)(C)
	Traditional and Roth IRAs to $1,171,650 per person	11 U.S.C. § 522(b)(3)(C); (n)
	ERISA-qualified benefits needed for support	2329.66(A)(10)(b)
	Firefighters, police officers	742.47
	IRAs, Roth IRAs, & Keoghs needed for support	2329.66(A)(10)(c), (a)
	Public employees	145.56
	Public safety officers' death benefit	2329.66(A)(10)(a)
	Public school employees	3309.66
	State highway patrol employees	5505.22
	Volunteer firefighters' dependents	146.13
personal property	Animals, crops, books, musical instruments, appliances, household goods, furnishings, firearms, hunting & fishing equipment to $525 per item; jewelry to $1,450 for 1 or more items; $11,525 total	2329.66(A)(4)(b),(c),(d); In re Szydlowski, 186 B.R. 907 (N.D. Ohio 1995)
	Burial plot	517.09; 2329.66(A)(8)
	Cash, money due within 90 days, tax refund, bank, security, & utility deposits to $400 total	2329.66(A)(3); In re Szydlowski, 186 B.R. 907 (N.D. Ohio 1995)
	Compensation for lost future earnings needed for support, received during 12 months before filing	2329.66(A)(12)(d)
	Health aids (professionally prescribed)	2329.66(A)(7)
	Motor vehicle to $3,450	2329.66(A)(2)(b)
	Personal injury recoveries to $21,625, received during 12 months before filing	2329.66(A)(12)(c)
	Tuition credit or payment	2329.66(A)(16)
	Wrongful death recoveries for person debtor depended on, needed for support, received during 12 months before filing	2329.66(A)(12)(b)

public benefits	Crime victim's compensation, received during 12 months before filing	2329.66(A)(12)(a); 2743.66(D)
	Disability assistance payments	2329.66(A)(9)(f); 5115.07
	Public assistance	2329.66(A)(9)(d); (e); 5107.75; 5108.08
	Unemployment compensation	2329.66(A)(9)(c); 4141.32
	Vocational rehabilitation benefits	2329.66(A)(9)(a); 3304.19
	Workers' compensation	2329.66(A)(9)(b); 4123.67
tools of trade	Implements, books, & tools of trade to $2,175	2329.66(A)(5)
wages	Minimum 75% of disposable weekly earnings or 30 times the federal hourly minimum wage, whichever is higher; bankruptcy judge may authorize more for low-income debtors	2329.66(A)(13)
wildcard	$1,150 of any property	2329.66(A)(18)

Oklahoma

Federal bankruptcy exemptions not available. All law references are to Oklahoma Statutes Annotated (in the form title number-section number), unless otherwise noted.

ASSET	EXEMPTION	LAW
homestead	Real property or manufactured home to unlimited value; property cannot exceed 1 acre in city, town, or village, or 160 acres elsewhere; $5,000 limit if more than 25% of total sq. ft. area used for business purposes; okay to rent homestead as long as no other residence is acquired	31-1(A)(1); 31-1(A)(2); 31-2
insurance	Annuity benefits & cash value	36-3631.1
	Assessment or mutual benefits	36-2410
	Fraternal benefit society benefits	36-2718.1
	Funeral benefits prepaid & placed in trust	36-6125
	Group life policy or proceeds	36-3632
	Life, health, accident, & mutual benefit insurance proceeds & cash value, if clause prohibits proceeds from being used to pay beneficiary's creditors	36-3631.1
	Limited stock insurance benefits	36-2510
miscellaneous	Alimony, child support	31-1(A)(19)
	Beneficiary's interest in a statutory support trust	6-3010
	Liquor license	37-532
	Property of business partnership	54-1-504
pensions	Tax-exempt retirement accounts, including 401(k)s, 403(b)s, profit-sharing and money purchase plans, SEP and SIMPLE IRAs, and defined-benefit plans	11 U.S.C. § 522(b)(3)(C)
	Traditional and Roth IRAs to $1,171,650 per person	11 U.S.C. § 522(b)(3)(C); (n)
	County employees	19-959
	Disabled veterans	31-7
	ERISA-qualified benefits, IRAs, Roth IRAs, Education IRAs, & Keoghs	31-1(A)(20), (24)
	Firefighters	11-49-126
	Judges	20-1111
	Law enforcement employees	47-2-303.3
	Police officers	11-50-124
	Public employees	74-923

pensions (continued)	Tax-exempt benefits	60-328
	Teachers	70-17-109
personal property	Books, portraits, & pictures	31-1(A)(6)
	Burial plots	31-1(A)(4); 8-7
	Clothing to $4,000	31-1(A)(7)
	College savings plan interest	31-1A(24)
	Deposits in an IDA (Individual Development Account)	31-1A(22)
	Federal earned income tax credit	31-1(A)(23)
	Food & seed for growing to last 1 year	31-1(A)(17)
	Guns for household use to $2,000	31-1A(14)
	Health aids (professionally prescribed)	31-1(A)(9)
	Household & kitchen furniture; personal computer and related equipment	31-1(A)(3)
	Livestock for personal or family use: 5 dairy cows & calves under 6 months; 100 chickens; 20 sheep; 10 hogs; 2 horses, bridles, & saddles; forage & feed to last 1 year	31-1(A)(10),(11), (12),(15),(16),(17)
	Motor vehicle to $7,500	31-1(A)(13)
	Personal injury & wrongful death recoveries to $50,000	31-1(A)(21)
	Prepaid funeral benefits	36-6125(H)
	War bond payroll savings account	51-42
	Wedding and anniversary rings to $3,000	31-1(A)(8)
public benefits	Crime victims' compensation	21-142.13
	Public assistance	56-173
	Social Security	56-173
	Unemployment compensation	40-2-303
	Workers' compensation	85-48
tools of trade	Implements needed to farm homestead; tools, books, & apparatus to $10,000 total	31-1(A)(5); 31-1(C)
wages	75% of wages earned in 90 days before filing bankruptcy; bankruptcy judge may allow more if you show hardship	12-1171.1; 31-1(A)(18); 31-1.1
wildcard	None	

Oregon

Federal bankruptcy exemptions not available. All law references are to Oregon Revised Statutes unless otherwise noted.

ASSET	EXEMPTION	LAW
homestead	Prepaid rent & security deposit for renter's dwelling	*In re Casserino*, 379 F.3d 1069 (9th Cir. 2004)
	Real property of a soldier or sailor during time of war	408.440
	Real property you occupy or intend to occupy to $40,000 ($50,000 for joint owners); property cannot exceed 1 block in town or city or 160 acres elsewhere; sale proceeds exempt 1 year from sale if you intend to purchase another home or use sale proceeds for rent	18.395; 18.402; *In re Wynn*, 369 B.R. 605 (D. Or. 2007)
	Tenancy by entirety not exempt, but subject to survivorship rights of nondebtor spouse	*In re Pletz*, 225 B.R. 206 (D. Or. 1997)
insurance	Annuity contract benefits to $500 per month	743.049
	Fraternal benefit society benefits to $7,500	748.207; 18.348

insurance (continued)	Group life policy or proceeds not payable to insured	743.047
	Health or disability proceeds or avails	743.050
	Life insurance proceeds or cash value if you are not the insured	743.046; 743.047
miscellaneous	Alimony, child support needed for support	18.345(1)(i)
	Liquor licenses	471.292 (1)
pensions	Tax-exempt retirement accounts, including 401(k)s, 403(b)s, profit-sharing and money purchase plans, SEP and SIMPLE IRAs, and defined-benefit plans	11 U.S.C. § 522(b)(3)(C)
	Traditional and Roth IRAs to $1,171,650 per person	11 U.S.C. § 522(b)(3)(C); (n)
	ERISA-qualified benefits, including IRAs & SEPs; & payments to $7,500	18.358; 18.348
	Public officers', employees' pension payments to $7,500	237.980; 238.445; 18.348(2)
personal property	Bank deposits to $7,500; cash for sold exempt property	18.348; 18.345(2)
	Books, pictures, & musical instruments to $600 total	18.345(1)(a)
	Building materials for construction of an improvement	87.075
	Burial plot	65.870
	Clothing, jewelry, & other personal items to $1,800 total	18.345(1)(b)
	Compensation for lost earnings payments for debtor or someone debtor depended on, to extent needed	18.345(1)(L),(3)
	Domestic animals, poultry, & pets to $1,000 plus food to last 60 days	18.345(1)(e)
	Federal earned income tax credit	18.345(1)(n)
	Food & fuel to last 60 days if debtor is householder	18.345(1)(f)
	Furniture, household items, utensils, radios, & TVs to $3,000 total	18.345(1)(f)
	Health aids	18.345(1)(h)
	Higher education savings account to $7,500	348.863; 18.348(1)
	Motor vehicle to $3,000	18.345(1)(d),(3)
	Personal injury recoveries to $10,000	18.345(1)(k),(3)
	Pistol; rifle or shotgun (owned by person over 16) to $1,000	18.362
public benefits	Aid to blind to $7,500	411.706; 411.760; 18.348
	Aid to disabled to $7,500	411.706; 411.760; 18.348
	Civil defense & disaster relief to $7,500	401.405; 18.348
	Crime victims' compensation	18.345(1)(j)(A),(3); 147.325
	General assistance to $7,500	411.760; 18.348
	Injured inmates' benefits to $7,500	655.530, 18.348
	Medical assistance to $7,500	414.095; 18.348
	Old-age assistance to $7,500	411.706; 411.760; 18.348
	Unemployment compensation to $7,500	657.855; 18.348
	Veterans' benefits & proceeds of Veterans loans	407.125; 407.595; 18.348(m)
	Vocational rehabilitation to $7,500	344.580; 18.348
	Workers' compensation to $7,500	656.234; 18.348
tools of trade	Tools, library, team with food to last 60 days, to $3,000	18.345(1)(c),(3)
wages	75% of disposable wages or $170 per week, whichever is greater; bankruptcy judge may authorize more for low-income debtors	18.385
	Wages withheld in state employee's bond savings accounts	292.070
wildcard	$400 of any personal property not already covered by existing exemption	18.348(1)(o)

Pennsylvania

Federal bankruptcy exemptions available. All law references are to Pennsylvania Consolidated Statutes Annotated unless otherwise noted.

ASSET	EXEMPTION	LAW
homestead	None; however, property held as tenancy by the entirety may be exempt against debts owed by only one spouse	*In re Martin*, 269 B.R. 119 (M.D. Pa. 2001)
insurance	Accident or disability benefits	42-8124(c)(7)
	Fraternal benefit society benefits	42-8124(c)(1),(8)
	Group life policy or proceeds	42-8124(c)(5)
	Insurance policy or annuity contract payments where insured is the beneficiary, cash value or proceeds to $100 per month	42-8124(c)(3)
	Life insurance & annuity proceeds if clause prohibits proceeds from being used to pay beneficiary's creditors	42-8214(c)(4)
	Life insurance annuity policy cash value or proceeds if beneficiary is insured's dependent, child or spouse	42-8124(c)(6)
	No-fault automobile insurance proceeds	42-8124(c)(9)
miscellaneous	Property of business partnership	15-8342
pensions	Tax-exempt retirement accounts, including 401(k)s, 403(b)s, profit-sharing and money purchase plans, SEP and SIMPLE IRAs, and defined-benefit plans	11 U.S.C. § 522(b)(3)(C)
	Traditional and Roth IRAs to $1,171,650 per person	11 U.S.C. § 522(b)(3)(C); (n)
	City employees	53-13445; 53-23572; 53-39383; 42-8124(b)(1)(iv)
	County employees	16-4716
	Municipal employees	53-881.115; 42-8124(b)(1)(vi)
	Police officers	53-764; 53-776; 53-23666; 42-8124(b)(1)(iii)
	Private retirement benefits to extent tax-deferred, if clause prohibits proceeds from being used to pay beneficiary's creditors; exemption limited to deposits of $15,000 per year made at least 1 year before filing (limit does not apply to rollovers from other exempt funds or accounts)	42-8124(b)(1)(vii), (viii),(ix)
	Public school employees	24-8533; 42-8124(b)(1)(i)
	State employees	71-5953; 42-8124(b)(1)(ii)
personal property	Bibles & schoolbooks	42-8124(a)(2)
	Clothing	42-8124(a)(1)
	Military uniforms & accoutrements	42-8124(a)(4); 51-4103
	Sewing machines	42-8124(a)(3)
public benefits	Crime victims' compensation	18-11.708
	Korean conflict veterans' benefits	51-20098
	Unemployment compensation	42-8124(a)(10); 43-863
	Veterans' benefits	51-20012; 20048; 20098; 20127
	Workers' compensation	42-8124(c)(2)
tools of trade	Seamstress's sewing machine	42-8124(a)(3)

wages	Earned but unpaid wages	42 0123
	Prison inmate's wages	61-3704
	Wages of victims of abuse	42-8127(f)
wildcard	$300 of any property, including cash, real property, securities, or proceeds from sale of exempt property	42-8123

Rhode Island

Federal bankruptcy exemptions available. All law references are to General Laws of Rhode Island unless otherwise noted.

ASSET	EXEMPTION	LAW
homestead	$300,000 in land & buildings you occupy or intend to occupy as a principal residence (spouses may not double)	9-26-4.1
insurance	Accident or sickness proceeds, avails, or benefits	27-18-24
	Fraternal benefit society benefits	27-25-18
	Life insurance proceeds if clause prohibits proceeds from being used to pay beneficiary's creditors	27-4-12
	Temporary disability insurance	28-41-32
miscellaneous	Earnings of a minor child	9-26-4(9)
	Property of business partnership	7-12-36
pensions	Tax-exempt retirement accounts, including 401(k)s, 403(b)s, profit-sharing and money purchase plans, SEP and SIMPLE IRAs, and defined-benefit plans	11 U.S.C. § 522(b)(3)(C)
	Traditional and Roth IRAs to $1,171,650 per person	11 U.S.C. § 522(b)(3)(C); (n)
	ERISA-qualified benefits	9-26-4(12)
	Firefighters	9-26-5
	IRAs & Roth IRAs	9-26-4(11)
	Police officers	9-26-5
	Private employees	28-17-4
	State & municipal employees	36-10-34
personal property	Beds, bedding, furniture, household goods, & supplies, to $9,600 total (spouses may not double)	9-26-4(3); *In re Petrozella*, 247 B.R. 591 (R.I. 2000)
	Bibles & books to $300	9-26-4(4)
	Burial plot	9-26-4(5)
	Clothing	9-26-4(1)
	Consumer cooperative association holdings to $50	7-8-23
	Debt secured by promissory note or bill of exchange	9-26-4(7)
	Jewelry to $2,000	9-26-4 (14)
	Motor vehicles to $12,000	9-26-4 (13)
	Prepaid tuition program or tuition savings account	9-26-4 (15)
public benefits	Aid to blind, aged, disabled; general assistance	40-6-14
	Crime victims' compensation	12-25.1-3(b)(2)
	Family assistance benefits	40-5.1-15
	State disability benefits	28-41-32
	Unemployment compensation	28-44-58
	Veterans' disability or survivors' death benefits	30-7-9
	Workers' compensation	28-33-27

tools of trade	Library of practicing professional	9-26-4(2)
	Working tools to $1,500	9-26-4(2)
wages	Earned but unpaid wages due military member on active duty	30-7-9
	Earned but unpaid wages due seaman	9-26-4(6)
	Earned but unpaid wages to $50	9-26-4(8)(iii)
	Wages of any person who had been receiving public assistance are exempt for 1 year after going off of relief	9-26-4(8)(ii)
	Wages of spouse & minor children	9-26-4(9)
	Wages paid by charitable organization or fund providing relief to the poor	9-26-4(8)(i)
wildcard	$5,000	9-26-4(16)

South Carolina

Federal bankruptcy exemptions not available. All law references are to Code of Laws of South Carolina unless otherwise noted. (Amounts adjusted for inflation in 2010 (15-41-30(B).)

ASSET	EXEMPTION	LAW
homestead	Real property, including co-op, to $53,375 (single owner); $106,750 (multiple owners)	15-41-30(A)(1)
insurance	Accident & disability benefits	38-63-40(D)
	Benefits accruing under life insurance policy after death of insured, where proceeds left with insurance company pursuant to agreement; benefits not exempt from action to recover necessaries if parties agree	38-63-50
	Disability or illness benefits	15-41-30(A)(10)(C)
	Fraternal benefit society benefits	38-38-330
	Group life insurance proceeds; cash value to $50,000	38-63-40(C); 38-65-90
	Life insurance avails from policy for person you depended on to $4,275	15-41-30(A)(8)
	Life insurance proceeds from policy for person you depended on, needed for support	15-41-30(A)(12)(C)
	Proceeds & cash surrender value of life insurance payable to beneficiary other than insured's estate & for the express benefit of insured's spouse, children, or dependents (must be purchased 2 years before filing)	38-63-40(A)
	Proceeds of life insurance or annuity contract	38-63-40(B)
	Unmatured life insurance contract, except credit insurance policy	15-41-30(A)(8)
miscellaneous	Alimony, child support	15-41-30(A)(10)(D)
	Property of business partnership	33-41-720
pensions	Tax-exempt retirement accounts, including 401(k)s, 403(b)s, profit-sharing and money purchase plans, SEP and SIMPLE IRAs, and defined-benefit plans	11 U.S.C. § 522(b)(3)(C)
	Traditional and Roth IRAs to $1,171,650 per person	11 U.S.C. § 522(b)(3)(C); (n)
	ERISA-qualified benefits; your share of the pension plan fund	15-41-30(10)(E),(13)
	Firefighters	9-13-230
	General assembly members	9-9-180
	IRAs & Roth IRAs needed for support	15-41-30(A)(12)
	Judges, solicitors	9-8-190
	Police officers	9-11-270
	Public employees	9-1-1680

personal property	Animals, crops, appliances, books, clothing, household goods, furnishings, musical instruments to $4,275 total	15-41-30(A)(3)
	Burial plot to $50,000, in lieu of homestead	15-41-30(1)
	Cash & other liquid assets to $5,350, in lieu of burial or homestead exemption	15-41-30(A)(5)
	College investment program trust fund	59-2-140
	Health aids	15-41-30(A)(10)
	Jewelry to $1,075	15-41-30(A)(4)
	Motor vehicle to $5,350	15-41-30(A)(2)
	Personal injury & wrongful death recoveries for person you depended on for support	15-41-30(A)(12)
public benefits	Crime victims' compensation	15-41-30(A)(12); 16-3-1300
	General relief; aid to aged, blind, disabled	43-5-190
	Local public assistance	15-41-30(A)(11)
	Social Security	15-41-30(A)(11)
	Unemployment compensation	15-41-30(A)(11)
	Veterans' benefits	15-41-30(A)(11)
	Workers' compensation	42-9-360
tools of trade	Implements, books, & tools of trade to $1,600	15-41-30(A)(6)
wages	None (use federal nonbankruptcy wage exemption)	15-41-30(A)(7)
wildcard	Up to $5,350 for any property from unused exemption amounts	

South Dakota

Federal bankruptcy exemptions not available. All law references are to South Dakota Codified Law unless otherwise noted.

ASSET	EXEMPTION	LAW
homestead	Gold or silver mine, mill, or smelter not exempt	43-31-5
	May file homestead declaration	43-31-6
	Real property to unlimited value or mobile home (larger than 240 sq. ft. at its base & registered in state at least 6 months before filing) to unlimited value; property cannot exceed 1 acre in town or 160 acres elsewhere; sale proceeds to $30,000 ($170,000 if over age 70 or widow or widower who hasn't remarried) exempt for 1 year after sale (spouses may not double)	43-31-1; 43-31-2; 43-31-3; 43-31-4; 43-45-3
	Spouse or child of deceased owner may claim homestead exemption	43-31-13
insurance	Annuity contract proceeds to $250 per month	58-12-6; 58-12-8
	Endowment, life insurance, policy proceeds to $20,000; if policy issued by mutual aid or benevolent society, cash value to $20,000	58-12-4
	Fraternal benefit society benefits	58-37A-18
	Health benefits to $20,000	58-12-4
	Life insurance proceeds, if clause prohibits proceeds from being used to pay beneficiary's creditors	58-15-70
	Life insurance proceeds to $10,000, if beneficiary is surviving spouse or child	43-45-6
pensions	Tax-exempt retirement accounts, including 401(k)s, 403(b)s, profit-sharing and money purchase plans, SEP and SIMPLE IRAs, and defined-benefit plans	11 U.S.C. § 522(b)(3)(C)
	Traditional and Roth IRAs to $1,171,650 per person	11 U.S.C. § 522(b)(3)(C); (n)
	City employees	9-16-47
	ERISA-qualified benefits, limited to income & distribution on $1,000,000	43-45-16
	Public employees	3-12-115

personal property	Bible, schoolbooks; other books to $200	43-45-2(4)
	Burial plots, church pew	43-45-2(2),(3)
	Cemetery association property	47-29-25
	Clothing	43-45-2(5)
	Family pictures	43-45-2(1)
	Food & fuel to last 1 year	43-45-2(6)
public benefits	Crime victim's compensation	23A-28B-24
	Public assistance	28-7A-18
	Unemployment compensation	61-6-28
	Workers' compensation	62-4-42
tools of trade	None	
wages	Earned wages owed 60 days before filing bankruptcy, needed for support of family	15-20-12
	Wages of prisoners in work programs	24-8-10
wildcard	Head of family may claim $6,000, or nonhead of family may claim $4,000 of any personal property	43-45-4

Tennessee

Federal bankruptcy exemptions not available. All law references are to Tennessee Code Annotated unless otherwise noted.

ASSET	EXEMPTION	LAW
homestead	$5,000; $7,500 for joint owners; $25,000 if at least one dependent is a minor child (if 62 or older, $12,500 if single; $20,000 if married; $25,000 if spouse is also 62 or older)	26-2-301
	2–15-year lease	26-2-303
	Life estate	26-2-302
	Property held as tenancy by the entirety may be exempt against debts owed by only one spouse, but survivorship right is not exempt	*In re Arango*, 136 B.R. 740 aff'd, 992 F.2d 611 (6th Cir. 1993); *In re Arwood*, 289 B.R. 889 (Bankr. E.D. Tenn. 2003)
	Spouse or child of deceased owner may claim homestead exemption	26-2-301
insurance	Accident, health, or disability benefits for resident & citizen of Tennessee	26-2-110
	Disability or illness benefits	26-2-111(1)(C)
	Fraternal benefit society benefits	56-25-1403
	Life insurance or annuity	56-7-203
miscellaneous	Alimony, child support owed for 30 days before filing for bankruptcy	26-2-111(1)(E)
	Educational scholarship trust funds & prepayment plans	49-4-108; 49-7-822
pensions	Tax-exempt retirement accounts, including 401(k)s, 403(b)s, profit-sharing and money purchase plans, SEP and SIMPLE IRAs, and defined-benefit plans	11 U.S.C. § 522(b)(3)(C)
	Traditional and Roth IRAs to $1,171,650 per person	11 U.S.C. § 522(b)(3)(C); (n)
	ERISA-qualified benefits, IRAs, & Roth IRAs	26-2-111(1)(D)
	Public employees	8-36-111
	State & local government employees	26-2-105
	Teachers	49-5-909
personal property	Bible, schoolbooks, family pictures, & portraits	26-2-104
	Burial plot to 1 acre	26-2-305; 46-2-102
	Clothing & storage containers	26-2-104

personal property (continued)	Health aids	26-2-111(5)
	Health savings accounts	26-2-105
	Lost future earnings payments for you or person you depended on	26-2-111(3)
	Personal injury recoveries to $7,500; wrongful death recoveries to $10,000 ($15,000 total for personal injury, wrongful death, & crime victims' compensation)	26-2-111(2)(B),(C)
	Wages of debtor deserting family, in hands of family	26-2-109
public benefits	Aid to blind	71-4-117
	Aid to disabled	71-4-1112
	Crime victims' compensation to $5,000 (*see personal property*)	26-2-111(2)(A); 29-13-111
	Local public assistance	26-2-111(1)(A)
	Old-age assistance	71-2-216
	Relocation assistance payments	13-11-115
	Social Security	26-2-111(1)(A)
	Unemployment compensation	26-2-111(1)(A)
	Veterans' benefits	26-2-111(1)(B)
	Workers' compensation	50-6-223
tools of trade	Implements, books, & tools of trade to $1,900	26-2-111(4)
wages	Minimum 75% of disposable weekly earnings or 30 times the federal minimum hourly wage, whichever is more, plus $2.50 per week per child; bankruptcy judge may authorize more for low-income debtors	26-2-106,107
wildcard	$10,000 of any personal property including deposits on account with any bank or financial institution	26-2-103

Texas

Federal bankruptcy exemptions available. All law references are to Texas Revised Civil Statutes Annotated unless otherwise noted.

ASSET	EXEMPTION	LAW
homestead	Unlimited; property cannot exceed 10 acres in town, village, city or 100 acres (200 for families) elsewhere; sale proceeds exempt for 6 months after sale (renting okay if another home not acquired, Prop. 41.003)	Prop. 41.001; 41.002; Const. Art. 16 §§ 50, 51
	Must file homestead declaration, or court will file it for you & charge you for doing so	Prop. 41.005(f), 41.021 to 41.023
insurance	Church benefit plan benefits	1407a(6)
	Fraternal benefit society benefits	Ins. 885.316
	Life, health, accident, or annuity benefits, monies, policy proceeds, & cash values due or paid to beneficiary or insured	Ins. 1108.051
	Texas employee uniform group insurance	Ins. 1551.011
	Texas public school employees group insurance	Ins. 1575.006
	Texas state college or university employee benefits	Ins. 1601.008
miscellaneous	Alimony & child support	Prop. 42.001(b)(3)
	Higher education savings plan trust account	Educ. 54.709(e)
	Liquor licenses & permits	Alco. Bev. Code 11.03
	Prepaid tuition plans	Educ. 54.639
	Property of business partnership	6132b-5.01

pensions	Tax-exempt retirement accounts, including 401(k)s, 403(b)s, profit-sharing and money purchase plans, SEP and SIMPLE IRAs, and defined-benefit plans	11 U.S.C. § 522(b)(3)(C)
	Traditional and Roth IRAs to $1,171,650 per person	11 U.S.C. § 522(b)(3)(C); (n)
	County & district employees	Gov't. 811.006
	ERISA-qualified government or church benefits, including Keoghs & IRAs	Prop. 42.0021
	Firefighters	6243e(5); 6243a-1(8.03); 6243b(15); 6243e(5); 6243e.1(1.04)
	Judges	Gov't. 831.004
	Law enforcement officers, firefighters, emergency medical personnel survivors	Gov't. 615.005
	Municipal employees & elected officials, state employees	6243h(22); Gov't. 811.005
	Police officers	6243d-1(17); 6243j(20); 6243a-1(8.03); 6243b(15); 6243d-1(17)
	Retirement benefits to extent tax-deferred	Prop. 42.0021
	Teachers	Gov't. 821.005
personal property *to $60,000 total for family, $30,000 for single adult (include tools of trade in these aggregate limits)*	Athletic & sporting equipment, including bicycles	Prop. 42.002(a)(8)
	Bible or other book containing sacred writings of a religion (doesn't count toward $30,000 or $60,000 total)	Prop. 42.001(b)(4)
	Burial plots (exempt from total)	Prop. 41.001
	Clothing & food	Prop. 42.002(a)(2),(5)
	Health aids (exempt from total)	Prop. 42.001(b)(2)
	Health savings accounts	Prop. 42.0021
	Home furnishings including family heirlooms	Prop. 42.002(a)(1)
	Jewelry (limited to 25% of total exemption)	Prop. 42.002(a)(6)
	Pets & domestic animals plus their food: 2 horses, mules, or donkeys & tack; 12 head of cattle; 60 head of other livestock; 120 fowl	Prop. 42.002(a)(10),(11)
	1 two-, three- or four-wheeled motor vehicle per family member or per single adult who holds a driver's license; or, if not licensed, who relies on someone else to operate vehicle	Prop. 42.002(a)(9)
	2 firearms	Prop. 42.002(a)(7)
public benefits	Crime victims' compensation	Crim. Proc. 56.49
	Medical assistance	Hum. Res. 32.036
	Public assistance	Hum. Res. 31.040
	Unemployment compensation	Labor 207.075
	Workers' compensation	Labor 408.201
tools of trade *included in aggregate dollar limits for personal property*	Farming or ranching vehicles & implements	Prop. 42.002(a)(3)
	Tools, equipment (includes boat & motor vehicles used in trade), & books	Prop. 42.002(a)(4)
wages	Earned but unpaid wages	Prop. 42.001(b)(1)
	Unpaid commissions not to exceed 25% of total personal property exemptions	Prop. 42.001(d)
wildcard	None	

Utah

Federal bankruptcy exemptions not available. All law references are to Utah Code unless otherwise noted.

ASSET	EXEMPTION	LAW
homestead	Must file homestead declaration before attempted sale of home	78B-5-504
	Real property, mobile home, or water rights to $20,000 if primary residence; $5,000 if not primary residence	78-23-3(1),(2),(4)
	Sale proceeds exempt for 1 year	78B-5-503(5)(b)
insurance	Disability, illness, medical, or hospital benefits	78B-5-505(1)(a)(iii)
	Fraternal benefit society benefits	31A-9-603
	Life insurance policy cash surrender value, excluding payments made on the contract within the prior year	78B-5-505(i)(a)(xiii)
	Life insurance proceeds if beneficiary is insured's spouse or dependent, as needed for support	78B-5-505(i)(a)(xi)
	Medical, surgical, & hospital benefits	78B-5-505(1)(a)(iv)
miscellaneous	Alimony needed for support	78B-5-505(a)(vi),(vii)
	Child support	78B-5-505(1) (f),(k)
	Property of business partnership	48-1-22
pensions	Tax-exempt retirement accounts, including 401(k)s, 403(b)s, profit-sharing and money purchase plans, SEP and SIMPLE IRAs, and defined-benefit plans	11 U.S.C. § 522(b)(3)(C)
	Traditional and Roth IRAs to $1,171,650 per person	11 U.S.C. § 522(b)(3)(C); (n)
	ERISA-qualified benefits, IRAs, Roth IRAs, & Keoghs (benefits that have accrued & contributions that have been made at least 1 year prior to filing)	78B-5-505(1)(a)(xiv)
	Other pensions & annuities needed for support	78-23-6(3)
	Public employees	49-11-612
personal property	Animals, books, & musical instruments to $500	78B-5-506(1)(c)
	Artwork depicting, or done by, a family member	78B-5-505(1)(a)(ix)
	Bed, bedding, carpets	78B-5-505(1)(a)(viii)
	Burial plot	78B-5-505(1)(a)(i)
	Clothing (cannot claim furs or jewelry)	78B-5-505(1)(a)(viii)
	Dining & kitchen tables & chairs to $500	78B-5-505(1)(b)
	Food to last 12 months	78B-5-505(1)(a)(viii)
	Health aids	78B-5-505(1)(a)(ii)
	Heirlooms to $500	78B-5-505(1)(d)
	Motor vehicle to $2,500	78B-5-506(3)
	Personal injury, wrongful death recoveries for you or person you depended on	78B-5-505(1)(a)(x)
	Proceeds for sold, lost, or damaged exempt property	78B-5-507
	Refrigerator, freezer, microwave, stove, sewing machine, washer & dryer	78B-5-505(1)(a)(viii)
	Sofas, chairs, & related furnishings to $500	78B-5-506(1)(a)
public benefits	Crime victims' compensation	63-25a-421(4)
	General assistance	35A-3-112
	Occupational disease disability benefits	34A-3-107
	Unemployment compensation	35A-4-103(4)(b)
	Veterans' benefits	78B-5-505(1)(a)(v)
	Workers' compensation	34A-2-422

tools of trade	Implements, books, & tools of trade to $3,500	78B-5-506(2)
	Military property of National Guard member	39-1-47
wages	Minimum 75% of disposable weekly earnings or 30 times the federal hourly minimum wage, whichever is more; bankruptcy judge may authorize more for low-income debtors	70C-7-103
wildcard	None	

Vermont

Federal bankruptcy exemptions available. All law references are to Vermont Statutes Annotated unless otherwise noted.

ASSET	EXEMPTION	LAW
homestead	Property held as tenancy by the entirety may be exempt against debts owed by only one spouse	*In re McQueen*, 21 B.R. 736 (D. Ver. 1982)
	Real property or mobile home to $75,000; may also claim rents, issues, profits, & outbuildings	27-101
	Spouse of deceased owner may claim homestead exemption	27-105
insurance	Annuity contract benefits to $350 per month	8-3709
	Disability benefits that supplement life insurance or annuity contract	8-3707
	Disability or illness benefits needed for support	12-2740(19)(C)
	Fraternal benefit society benefits	8-4478
	Group life or health benefits	8-3708
	Health benefits to $200 per month	8-4086
	Life insurance proceeds for person you depended on	12-2740(19)(H)
	Life insurance proceeds if clause prohibits proceeds from being used to pay beneficiary's creditors	8-3705
	Life insurance proceeds if beneficiary is not the insured	8-3706
	Unmatured life insurance contract other than credit	12-2740(18)
miscellaneous	Alimony, child support	12-2740(19)(D)
pensions	Tax-exempt retirement accounts, including 401(k)s, 403(b)s, profit-sharing and money purchase plans, SEP and SIMPLE IRAs, and defined-benefit plans	11 U.S.C. § 522(b)(3)(C)
	Traditional and Roth IRAs to $1,171,650 per person	11 U.S.C. § 522(b)(3)(C); (n)
	Municipal employees	24-5066
	Other pensions	12-2740(19)(J)
	Self-directed accounts (IRAs, Roth IRAs, Keoghs); contributions must be made 1 year before filing	12-2740(16)
	State employees	3-476
	Teachers	16-1946
personal property	Appliances, furnishings, goods, clothing, books, crops, animals, musical instruments to $2,500 total	12-2740(5)
	Bank deposits to $700	12-2740(15)
	Cow, 2 goats, 10 sheep, 10 chickens, & feed to last 1 winter; 3 swarms of bees plus honey; 5 tons coal or 500 gal. heating oil, 10 cords of firewood; 500 gal. bottled gas; growing crops to $5,000; yoke of oxen or steers, plow & ox yoke; 2 horses with harnesses, halters, & chains	12-2740(6), (9)-(14)
	Health aids	12-2740(17)
	Jewelry to $500; wedding ring unlimited	12-2740(3),(4)

personal property (continued)	Motor vehicles to $2,500	12-2740(1)
	Personal injury, lost future earnings, wrongful death recoveries for you or person you depended on	12-2740(19)(F), (G),(I)
	Stove, heating unit, refrigerator, freezer, water heater, & sewing machines	12-2740(8)
public benefits	Aid to blind, aged, disabled; general assistance	33-124
	Crime victims' compensation needed for support	12-2740(19)(E)
	Social Security needed for support	12-2740(19)(A)
	Unemployment compensation	21-1367
	Veterans' benefits needed for support	12-2740(19)(B)
	Workers' compensation	21-681
tools of trade	Books & tools of trade to $5,000	12-2740(2)
wages	Entire wages, if you received welfare during 2 months before filing	12-3170
	Minimum 75% of weekly disposable earnings or 30 times the federal minimum hourly wage, whichever is greater; bankruptcy judge may authorize more for low-income debtors	12-3170
wildcard	Unused exemptions for motor vehicle, tools of trade, jewelry, household furniture, appliances, clothing, & crops to $7,000	12-2740(7)
	$400 of any property	12-2740(7)

Virginia

Federal bankruptcy exemptions not available. All law references are to Code of Virginia unless otherwise noted.

ASSET	EXEMPTION	LAW
homestead	$5,000 plus $500 per dependent; rents & profits; sale proceeds exempt to $5,000 (unused portion of homestead may be applied to any personal property); exemption is $10,000 if over 65	*Cheeseman v. Nachman*, 656 F.2d 60 (4th Cir. 1981); 34-4; 34-18; 34-20
	May include mobile home	*In re Goad*, 161 B.R. 161 (W.D. Va. 1993)
	Must file homestead declaration before filing for bankruptcy	34-6
	Property held as tenancy by the entirety may be exempt against debts owed by only one spouse	*In re Bunker*, 312 F.3d 145 (4th Cir. 2002)
	Surviving spouse may claim $15,000; if no surviving spouse, minor children may claim exemption	64.1-151.3
insurance	Accident or sickness benefits	38.2-3406
	Burial society benefits	38.2-4021
	Cooperative life insurance benefits	38.2-3811
	Fraternal benefit society benefits	38.2-4118
	Group life or accident insurance for government officials	51.1-510
	Group life insurance policy or proceeds	38.2-3339
	Industrial sick benefits	38.2-3549
	Life insurance proceeds	38.2-3122
miscellaneous	Property of business partnership	50-73.108
pensions *see also wages*	Tax-exempt retirement accounts, including 401(k)s, 403(b)s, profit-sharing and money purchase plans, SEP and SIMPLE IRAs, and defined-benefit plans	11 U.S.C. § 522(b)(3)(C)
	Traditional and Roth IRAs to $1,171,650 per person	11 U.S.C. § 522(b)(3)(C); (n)

pensions (continued)	City, town, & county employees	51.1-802
	ERISA-qualified benefits to same extent permitted by federal bankruptcy law	34-34
	Judges	51.1-300
	State employees	51.1-124.4(A)
	State police officers	51.1-200
personal property	Bible	34-26(1)
	Burial plot	34-26(3)
	Clothing to $1,000	34-26(4)
	Family portraits & heirlooms to $5,000 total	34-26(2)
	Health aids	34-26(6)
	Household furnishings to $5,000	34-26(4a)
	Motor vehicle to $2,000	34-26(8)
	Personal injury causes of action & recoveries	34-28.1
	Pets	34-26(5)
	Prepaid tuition contracts	23-38.81(E)
	Wedding & engagement rings	34-26(1a)
public benefits	Aid to blind, aged, disabled; general relief	63.2-506
	Crime victims' compensation unless seeking to discharge debt for treatment of injury incurred during crime	19.2-368.12
	Payments to tobacco farmers	3.1-1111.1
	Unemployment compensation	60.2-600
	Workers' compensation	65.2-531
tools of trade	For farmer, pair of horses, or mules with gear; one wagon or cart, one tractor to $3,000; 2 plows & wedges; one drag, harvest cradle, pitchfork, rake; fertilizer to $1,000	34-27
	Tools, books, & instruments of trade, including motor vehicles, to $10,000, needed in your occupation or education	34-26(7)
	Uniforms, arms, equipment of military member	44-96
wages	Minimum 75% of weekly disposable earnings or 40 times the federal minimum hourly wage, whichever is greater; bankruptcy judge may authorize more for low-income debtors	34-29
wildcard	Unused portion of homestead or personal property exemption	34-13
	$10,000 of any property for disabled veterans	34-4.1

Washington

Federal bankruptcy exemptions available. All law references are to Revised Code of Washington Annotated unless otherwise noted.

ASSET	EXEMPTION	LAW
homestead	Must record homestead declaration before sale of home if property unimproved or home unoccupied	6.15.040
	Real property or manufactured home to $125,000; unimproved property intended for residence to $15,000 (spouses may not double)	6.13.010; 6.13.030
insurance	Annuity contract proceeds to $2,500 per month	48.18.430
	Disability proceeds, avails, or benefits	48.36A.180
	Fraternal benefit society benefits	48.18.400

insurance (continued)	Group life insurance policy or proceeds	48.18.420
	Life insurance proceeds or avails if beneficiary is not the insured	48.18.410
miscellaneous	Child support payments	6.15.010(3)(d)
pensions	Tax-exempt retirement accounts, including 401(k)s, 403(b)s, profit-sharing and money purchase plans, SEP and SIMPLE IRAs, and defined-benefit plans	11 U.S.C. § 522(b)(3)(C)
	Traditional and Roth IRAs to $1,171,650 per person	11 U.S.C. § 522(b)(3)(C); (n)
	City employees	41.28.200; 41.44.240
	ERISA-qualified benefits, IRAs, Roth IRAs, & Keoghs	6.15.020
	Judges	2.10.180; 2.12.090
	Law enforcement officials & firefighters	41.26.053
	Police officers	41.20.180
	Public & state employees	41.40.052
	State patrol officers	43.43.310
	Teachers	41.32.052
	Volunteer firefighters	41.24.240
personal property	Appliances, furniture, household goods, home & yard equipment to $2,700 total for individual ($5,400 for community)	6.15.010(3)(a)
	Books to $1,500	6.15.010(2)
	Burial ground	68.24.220
	Burial plots sold by nonprofit cemetery association	68.20.120
	Clothing, no more than $1,000 in furs, jewelry, ornaments	6.15.010(1)
	Fire insurance proceeds for lost, stolen, or destroyed exempt property	6.15.030
	Food & fuel for comfortable maintenance	6.15.010(3)(a)
	Health aids prescribed	6.15.010(3)(e)
	Keepsakes & family pictures	6.15.010(2)
	Motor vehicle to $2,500 total for individual (two vehicles to $5,000 for community)	6.15.010(3)(c)
	Personal injury recoveries to $16,150	6.15.010(3)(f)
	Tuition units purchased more than 2 years before	6.15.010(5)
public benefits	Child welfare	74.13.070
	Crime victims' compensation	7.68.070(10)
	General assistance	74.04.280
	Industrial insurance (workers' compensation)	51.32.040
	Old age assistance	74.08.210
	Unemployment compensation	50.40.020
tools of trade	Farmer's trucks, stock, tools, seed, equipment, & supplies to $5,000 total	6.15.010(4)(a)
	Library, office furniture, office equipment, & supplies of physician, surgeon, attorney, clergy, or other professional to $5,000 total	6.15.010(4)(b)
	Tools & materials used in any other trade to $5,000	6.15.010(4)(c)
wages	Minimum 75% of weekly disposable earnings or 30 times the federal minimum hourly wage, whichever is greater; bankruptcy judge may authorize more for low-income debtors	6.27.150
wildcard	$2,000 of any personal property (no more than $200 in cash, bank deposits, bonds, stocks, & securities)	6.15.010(3)(b)

West Virginia

Federal bankruptcy exemptions not available. All law references are to West Virginia Code unless otherwise noted.

Some of the exemptions in this table may not be available to you in some bankruptcy courts. Before filing bankruptcy, check with a bankruptcy attorney to find out which exemptions are acceptable in your court. See, "Some courts might not allow 'bankruptcy specific' exemptions," at the beginning of this appendix for more information.

ASSET	EXEMPTION	LAW
homestead	Real or personal property used as residence to $25,000; unused portion of homestead may be applied to any property	38-10-4(a)
insurance	Fraternal benefit society benefits	33-23-21
	Group life insurance policy or proceeds	33-6-28
	Health or disability benefits	38-10-4(j)(3)
	Life insurance payments from policy for person you depended on, needed for support	38-10-4(k)(3)
	Unmatured life insurance contract, except credit insurance policy	38-10-4(g)
	Unmatured life insurance contract's accrued dividend, interest, or loan value to $8,000, if debtor owns contract & insured is either debtor or a person on whom debtor is dependent	38-10-4(h)
miscellaneous	Alimony, child support needed for support	38-10-4(j)(4)
pensions	Tax-exempt retirement accounts, including 401(k)s, 403(b)s, profit-sharing and money purchase plans, SEP and SIMPLE IRAs, and defined-benefit plans	11 U.S.C. § 522(b)(3)(C)
	Traditional and Roth IRAs to $1,171,650 per person	11 U.S.C. § 522(b)(3)(C); (n)
	ERISA-qualified benefits, IRAs needed for support	38-10-4(j)(5)
	Public employees	5-10-46
	Teachers	18-7A-30
personal property	Animals, crops, clothing, appliances, books, household goods, furnishings, musical instruments to $400 per item, $8,000 total	38-10-4(c)
	Burial plot to $25,000, in lieu of homestead	38-10-4(a)
	Health aids	38-10-4(i)
	Jewelry to $1,000	38-10-4(d)
	Lost earnings payments needed for support	38-10-4(k)(5)
	Motor vehicle to $2,400	38-10-4(b)
	Personal injury recoveries to $15,000	38-10-4(k)(4)
	Prepaid higher education tuition trust fund & savings plan payments	38-10-4(k)(6)
	Wrongful death recoveries for person you depended on, needed for support	38-10-4(k)(2)
public benefits	Aid to blind, aged, disabled; general assistance	9-5-1
	Crime victims' compensation	38-10-4(k)(1)
	Social Security	38-10-4(j)(1)
	Unemployment compensation	38-10-4(j)(1)
	Veterans' benefits	38-10-4(j)(2)
	Workers' compensation	23-4-18
tools of trade	Implements, books, & tools of trade to $1,500	38-10-4(f)
wages	Minimum 30 times the federal minimum hourly wage per week; bankruptcy judge may authorize more for low-income debtors	38-5A-3
wildcard	$800 plus unused portion of homestead or burial exemption, of any property	38-10-4(e)

Wisconsin

Federal bankruptcy exemptions available. All law references are to Wisconsin Statutes Annotated unless otherwise noted.

ASSET	EXEMPTION	LAW
homestead	Property you occupy or intend to occupy to $75,000; $150,000 for married couples filing jointly; sale proceeds exempt for 2 years if you intend to purchase another home (spouses may not double)	815.20
insurance	Federal disability insurance benefits	815.18(3)(ds)
	Fraternal benefit society benefits	614.96
	Life insurance proceeds for someone debtor depended on, needed for support	815.18(3)(i)(a)
	Life insurance proceeds held in trust by insurer, if clause prohibits proceeds from being used to pay beneficiary's creditors	632.42
	Unmatured life insurance contract (except credit insurance contract) if debtor owns contract & insured is debtor or dependents, or someone debtor is dependent on	815.18(3)(f)
	Unmatured life insurance contract's accrued dividends, interest, or loan value to $4,000 total, if debtor owns contract & insured is debtor or dependents, or someone debtor is dependent on	815.18(3)(f)
miscellaneous	Alimony, child support needed for support	815.18(3)(c)
	Property of business partnership	178.21(3)(c)
pensions	Tax-exempt retirement accounts, including 401(k)s, 403(b)s, profit-sharing and money purchase plans, SEP and SIMPLE IRAs, and defined-benefit plans	11 U.S.C. § 522(b)(3)(C)
	Traditional and Roth IRAs to $1,171,650 per person	11 U.S.C. § 522(b)(3)(C); (n)
	Certain municipal employees	62.63(4)
	Firefighters, police officers who worked in city with population over 100,000	815.18(3)(ef)
	Military pensions	815.18(3)(n)
	Private or public retirement benefits	815.18(3)(j)
	Public employees	40.08(1)
personal property	Burial plot, tombstone, coffin	815.18(3)(a)
	College savings account or tuition trust fund	14.64(7); 14.63(8)
	Deposit accounts to $5,000	815.18(3)(k)
	Fire & casualty proceeds for destroyed exempt property for 2 years from receiving	815.18(3)(e)
	Household goods & furnishings, clothing, keepsakes, jewelry, appliances, books, musical instruments, firearms, sporting goods, animals, & other tangible personal property to $12,000 total	815.18(3)(d)
	Lost future earnings recoveries, needed for support	815.18(3)(i)(d)
	Motor vehicles to $4,000; unused portion of $12,000 personal property exemption may be added	815.18(3)(g)
	Personal injury recoveries to $50,000	815.18(3)(i)(c)
	Tenant's lease or stock interest in housing co-op, to homestead amount	182.004(6)
	Wages used to purchase savings bonds	20.921(1)(e)
	Wrongful death recoveries, needed for support	815.18(3)(i)(b)
public benefits	Crime victims' compensation	949.07
	Social services payments	49.96
	Unemployment compensation	108.13
	Veterans' benefits	45.03(8)(b)
	Workers' compensation	102.27

tools of trade	Equipment, inventory, farm products, books, & tools of trade to $15,000 total	815.18(3)(b)
wages	75% of weekly net income or 30 times the greater of the federal or state minimum hourly wage; bankruptcy judge may authorize more for low-income debtors	815.18(3)(h)
	Wages of county jail prisoners	303.08(3)
	Wages of county work camp prisoners	303.10(7)
	Wages of inmates under work-release plan	303.065(4)(b)
wildcard	None	

Wyoming

Federal bankruptcy exemptions not available. All law references are to Wyoming Statutes Annotated unless otherwise noted.

ASSET	EXEMPTION	LAW
homestead	Property held as tenancy by the entirety may be exempt against debts owed by only one spouse	*In re Anselmi*, 52 B.R. 479 (D. Wy. 1985)
	Real property you occupy to $10,000 or house trailer you occupy to $6,000	1-20-101; 102; 104
	Spouse or child of deceased owner may claim homestead exemption	1-20-103
insurance	Annuity contract proceeds to $350 per month	26-15-132
	Disability benefits if clause prohibits proceeds from being used to pay beneficiary's creditors	26-15-130
	Fraternal benefit society benefits	26-29-218
	Group life or disability policy or proceeds, cash surrender & loan values, premiums waived, & dividends	26-15-131
	Individual life insurance policy proceeds, cash surrender & loan values, premiums waived, & dividends	26-15-129
	Life insurance proceeds held by insurer, if clause prohibits proceeds from being used to pay beneficiary's creditors	26-15-133
miscellaneous	Liquor licenses & malt beverage permits	12-4-604
pensions	Tax-exempt retirement accounts, including 401(k)s, 403(b)s, profit-sharing and money purchase plans, SEP and SIMPLE IRAs, and defined-benefit plans	11 U.S.C. § 522(b)(3)(C)
	Traditional and Roth IRAs to $1,171,650 per person	11 U.S.C. § 522(b)(3)(C); (n)
	Criminal investigators, highway officers	9-3-620
	Firefighters' death benefits	15-5-209
	Game & fish wardens	9-3-620
	Police officers	15-5-313(c)
	Private or public retirement funds & accounts	1-20-110
	Public employees	9-3-426
personal property	Bedding, furniture, household articles, & food to $2,000 per person in the home	1-20-106(a)(iii)
	Bible, schoolbooks, & pictures	1-20-106(a)(i)
	Burial plot	1-20-106(a)(ii)
	Clothing & wedding rings to $1,000	1-20-105
	Medical savings account contributions	1-20-111
	Motor vehicle to $2,400	1-20-106(a)(iv)
	Prepaid funeral contracts	26-32-102

public benefits	Crime victims' compensation	1-40-113
	General assistance	42-2-113(b)
	Unemployment compensation	27-3-319
	Workers' compensation	27-14-702
tools of trade	Library & implements of profession to $2,000 or tools, motor vehicle, implements, team & stock in trade to $2,000	1-20-106(b)
wages	Earnings of National Guard members	19-9-401
	Minimum 75% of disposable weekly earnings or 30 times the federal hourly minimum wage, whichever is more	1-15-511
	Wages of inmates in adult community corrections program	7-18-114
	Wages of inmates in correctional industries program	25-13-107
	Wages of inmates on work release	7-16-308
wildcard	None	

Federal Bankruptcy Exemptions

Spouses filing jointly may double all exemptions. All references are to 11 U.S.C. § 522. These exemptions were last adjusted in 2010. Every three years ending on April 1, these amounts will be adjusted to reflect changes in the Consumer Price Index. Debtors in the following states may select the federal bankruptcy exemptions:

Arkansas	Massachusetts	New Jersey	Texas
Connecticut	Michigan	New Mexico	Vermont
District of Columbia	Minnesota	Pennsylvania	Washington
Hawaii	New Hampshire	Rhode Island	Wisconsin
Kentucky			

ASSET	EXEMPTION	SUBSECTION
homestead	Real property, including co-op or mobile home, or burial plot to $21,625; unused portion of homestead to $10,825 may be applied to any property	(d)(1); (d)(5)
insurance	Disability, illness, or unemployment benefits	(d)(10)(C)
	Life insurance payments from policy for person you depended on, needed for support	(d)(11)(C)
	Life insurance policy with loan value, in accrued dividends or interest, to $11,525	(d)(8)
	Unmatured life insurance contract, except credit insurance policy	(d)(7)
miscellaneous	Alimony, child support needed for support	(d)(10)(D)
pensions	Tax exempt retirement accounts (including 401(k)s, 403(b)s, profit-sharing and money purchase plans, SEP and SIMPLE IRAs, and defined-benefit plans	(b)(3)(C)
	IRAs and Roth IRAs to $1,171,650 per person	(b)(3)(C)(n)
personal property	Animals, crops, clothing, appliances, books, furnishings, household goods, musical instruments to $550 per item, $11,525 total	(d)(3)
	Health aids	(d)(9)
	Jewelry to $1,450	(d)(4)
	Lost earnings payments	(d)(11)(E)
	Motor vehicle to $3,450	(d)(2)
	Personal injury recoveries to $21,625 (not to include pain & suffering or pecuniary loss)	(d)(11)(D)
	Wrongful death recoveries for person you depended on	(d)(11)(B)

public benefits	Crime victims' compensation	(d)(11)(A)
	Public assistance	(d)(10)(A)
	Social Security	(d)(10)(A)
	Unemployment compensation	(d)(10)(A)
	Veterans' benefits	(d)(10)(A)
tools of trade	Implements, books, & tools of trade to $2,175	(d)(6)
wages	None	
wildcard	$1,150 of any property	(d)(5)
	Up to $10,825 of unused homestead exemption amount, for any property	(d)(5)

Federal Nonbankruptcy Exemptions

These exemptions are available only if you select your state exemptions. You may use them for any exemptions in addition to those allowed by your state, but they cannot be claimed if you file using federal bankruptcy exemptions. All law references are to the United States Code.

ASSET	EXEMPTION	LAW
death & disability benefits	Government employees	5 § 8130
	Longshoremen & harbor workers	33 § 916
	War risk, hazard, death, or injury compensation	42 § 1717
miscellaneous	Debts of seaman incurred while on a voyage	46 § 11111
	Indian lands or homestead sales or lease proceeds	25 § 410; 412a
	Klamath Indian tribe benefits for Indians residing in Oregon; agricultural or grazing lands to $5,000	25 §§ 543; 545
	Life insurance benefits for Serviceman's Group Life Ins. or Veteran's Group Life Ins.	38 § 1970(g)
	Military deposits in savings accounts while on permanent duty outside U.S.	10 § 1035
	Military group life insurance	38 § 1970(g)
	Railroad workers' unemployment insurance	45 § 352(e)
	Seamen's clothing	46 § 11110
	Seamen's wages (except for spousal and child support)	46 § 11109
	Minimum 75% of disposable weekly earnings or 30 times the federal minimum hourly wage, whichever is more; bankruptcy judge may authorize more for low-income debtors	15 § 1673
retirement	CIA employees	50 § 403
	Civil service employees	5 § 8346
	Foreign Service employees	22 § 4060
	Military Medal of Honor Roll pensions	38 § 1562(c)
	Military service employees	10 § 1440
	Railroad workers	45 § 231m
	Social Security	42 § 407
	Veterans' benefits	38 § 5301
survivor's benefits	Judges, U.S. court & judicial center directors, administrative assistants to U.S. Supreme Court Chief Justice	28 § 376
	Lighthouse workers	33 § 775
	Military service	10 § 1450

Charts and Worksheets

Median Family Income Chart (Effective March 15, 2011)			
	Family Size		
State	1 Earner	2 People	3 People	4 People *
Alabama	$38,642	$46,900	$52,460	$64,016
Alaska	$51,950	$75,460	$81,447	$85,964
Arizona	$42,603	$55,404	$59,659	$67,113
Arkansas	$32,834	$44,081	$49,599	$54,401
California	$48,009	$62,970	$68,670	$78,869
Colorado	$48,598	$64,679	$70,861	$83,976
Connecticut	$57,863	$71,961	$83,655	$103,314
Delaware	$48,415	$62,432	$68,518	$85,305
DC	$48,822	$80,172	$80,172	$80,172
Florida	$40,029	$50,130	$54,594	$65,135
Georgia	$39,384	$52,024	$56,682	$69,239
Hawaii	$50,664	$64,179	$75,670	$86,587
Idaho	$39,050	$48,648	$55,453	$61,480
Illinois	$46,355	$60,073	$69,910	$81,097
Indiana	$40,135	$51,104	$59,028	$69,226
Iowa	$40,456	$56,036	$63,510	$75,569
Kansas	$41,654	$57,174	$64,863	$69,272
Kentucky	$37,606	$45,001	$51,883	$63,768
Louisiana	$38,108	$48,704	$55,699	$67,239
Maine	$39,497	$51,600	$59,050	$68,466
Maryland	$55,774	$74,493	$87,152	$103,361
Massachusetts	$55,049	$68,243	$83,736	$102,110
Michigan	$42,562	$50,738	$60,161	$71,758
Minnesota	$45,760	$61,690	$74,082	$85,146
Mississippi	$32,658	$41,579	$47,058	$55,711
Missouri	$39,332	$51,120	$58,610	$69,832

* Add $7,500 for each individual in excess of 4.

Median Family Income Chart (Effective March 15, 2011) (cont'd)

State	Family Size			
	1 Earner	2 People	3 People	4 People *
Montana	$38,577	$52,412	$56,265	$67,921
Nebraska	$38,915	$54,124	$65,486	$71,097
Nevada	$43,041	$57,541	$60,783	$70,509
New Hampshire	$51,460	$63,534	$82,465	$89,990
New Jersey	$59,060	$70,680	$85,573	$101,106
New Mexico	$37,274	$51,855	$52,303	$53,709
New York	$46,295	$57,777	$68,396	$83,942
North Carolina	$37,781	$50,630	$55,468	$67,578
North Dakota	$41,443	$56,411	$69,328	$79,637
Ohio	$40,749	$51,319	$60,247	$72,625
Oklahoma	$36,884	$49,711	$54,135	$64,037
Oregon	$44,707	$55,553	$60,523	$72,767
Pennsylvania	$44,897	$53,706	$67,113	$79,916
Rhode Island	$46,136	$58,511	$72,184	$88,593
South Carolina	$37,055	$50,500	$52,738	$63,074
South Dakota	$35,582	$53,443	$58,794	$68,016
Tennessee	$38,144	$47,194	$53,227	$63,217
Texas	$38,294	$55,178	$56,445	$65,477
Utah	$50,635	$56,126	$61,944	$69,834
Vermont	$43,042	$57,948	$65,829	$78,392
Virginia	$50,296	$63,613	$73,260	$86,990
Washington	$49,930	$63,224	$72,524	$82,602
West Virginia	$39,750	$42,607	$51,350	$60,280
Wisconsin	$41,150	$56,080	$66,256	$77,438
Wyoming	$46,172	$60,829	$69,677	$76,361

* Add $7,500 for each individual in excess of 4.

Worksheet A: Current Monthly Income

Use this worksheet to calculate your current monthly income; use figures for you and your spouse if you plan to file jointly.

Line 1. Calculate your total income over the last six months from wages, salary, tips, bonuses, overtime, and so on.

    A.   Month 1 $ _____

    B.   Month 2   _____

    C.   Month 3   _____

    D.   Month 4   _____

    E.   Month 5   _____

    F.   Month 6   _____

    G.   TOTAL WAGES (add Lines 1A–1F) $ _____

Line 2. Add up all other income for the last six months.

    A.   Net business, profession, or farm income   _____

    B.   Interest, dividends, and royalties   _____

    C.   Net income from rents and real property   _____

    D.   Pension and retirement income   _____

    E.   Alimony or family support   _____

    F.   Spousal contributions (if not filing jointly)   _____

    G.   Unemployment compensation   _____

    H.   Workers' compensation   _____

    I.   State disability insurance   _____

    J.   Annuity payments   _____

    K.   Other   _____

    L.   TOTAL OTHER INCOME (add Lines 2A–2K) $ _____

Line 3. Calculate total income over the six months prior to filing.

    A.   Enter total wages (Line 1G)   _____

    B.   Enter total other income (Line 2L)   _____

    C.   TOTAL INCOME OVER THE SIX MONTHS PRIOR TO FILING. Add Lines 3A and 3B together. $ _____

Line 4. Average monthly income over the six months prior to filing. This is called your "current monthly income."

    A.   Enter total six-month income (Line 3C).   _____

    B.   CURRENT MONTHLY INCOME. Divide Line 4A by six. $ _____

Worksheet B: Allowable Monthly Expenses

Use this worksheet to calculate the monthly expenses allowed by the IRS.

Calculate total allowable monthly expenses.

A.	Food, clothing, and so on	$ _____
B.	Transportation	_____
C.	Housing & utilities	_____
D.	Domestic violence	_____
E.	Dependent care	_____
F.	Education	_____
G.	Taxes	_____
H.	Mandatory payroll deductions	_____
I.	Insurance	_____
J.	Court-ordered payments	_____
K.	Charitable contributions	_____
L.	Child care	_____
M.	Health care	_____
N.	Communications	_____
O.	Total allowable monthly expenses. Add lines A–N together	$ _____

Current Monthly Income (from Worksheet A, Line 4B). $ _____

Total Allowable Monthly Expenses (from Line O above).   _____

Net monthly income. $ _____

● If net monthly income is less than $110, you have passed the means test and you do not need to continue.

● If net monthly income is $110 or more, complete Worksheet C.

Worksheet C: Monthly Disposable Income

Use this worksheet to find out how much income you would have left over, after paying the IRS expenses calculated in Worksheet B, your secured and priority debts, any arrearages on your secured debts, and the administrative costs associated with a Chapter 13 bankruptcy, to devote to your unsecured, nonpriority debts.

Line 1. Figure out what you would have to pay each month over the next five years on your secured debts.

A. Total amount due over the next five years for a mortgage or second deed of trust $ _____

B. Total amount due over the next five years on a car note _____

C. Total amount due over the next five years on all other secured debts _____

D. Add Lines 1A–1C together to figure out the total amount you owe on all secured debts for the next five years. _____

E. Divide Line 1D by 60 to determine how much you would have to pay each month on these debts for the next five years. _____

Line 2. Figure out what you would have to pay each month over the next five years to make up your arrearages (missed payments) on secured debts.

A. Total arrearage on mortgage or second deed of trust $ _____

B. Total arrearage on car note _____

C. Total arrearage on all other secured debts _____

D. Add Lines 2A–2C together to figure out your total arrearage on secured debts. _____

E. Divide Line 2D by 60 to determine how much you would have to pay each month to pay off these arrearages over the next five years. _____

Line 3. Figure out how much you will owe on your priority debts for the next five years.

A. Back child support and alimony you owe $ _____

B. Priority income taxes you owe _____

C. Other priority debts you owe _____

D. Add Lines 3A–3C together to figure out the total priority debt you owe. _____

E. Divide Line 3D by 60 to determine how much you would have to pay each month to pay off these priority debts over the next five years. _____

Line 4. Calculate the total amount you would have left over each month after paying allowable expenses and the debts you would have to pay in full in a Chapter 13 plan.

A. Enter your current monthly income (from Line 4B on Worksheet A). $ _____

B. Enter your allowable monthly expenses (from Line O) on Worksheet B). _____

C. Subtract Line 4B from Line 4A to calculate your net income, after allowable expenses. _____

D. Enter your total monthly payments for secured debts, arrearages on secured debts, and priority debts (the sum of Lines 1E, 2E, and 3E, above). _____

E. Subtract Line 4D from Line 4C to calculate how much you would have left over each month, after paying your allowable expenses and your monthly payments on the debts you would have to pay in full in a Chapter 13 plan. _____

Line 5. Calculate your monthly disposable income.

A. Enter your leftover monthly income from Line 4E, above. $ _____

B. Multiply Line 5A by the administrative expense multiplier for your judicial district to calculate how much you would have to pay each month for administrative costs. _____

C. MONTHLY DISPOSABLE INCOME. Subtract Line 5B from Line 5A. $ _____

● If your monthly disposable income (Line 5C) is less than $110, you have passed the means test and you do not need to continue.

● If your monthly disposable income (Line 5C) is $110 or more, complete Worksheet D.

Worksheet D: The Means Test

Use this worksheet to figure out whether you will be allowed to file for Chapter 7 bankruptcy, or whether you will be limited to Chapter 13.

Line 1. Figure out how much disposable income you will have over the next five years.

    A.   Enter your monthly disposable income (from Line 5C of Worksheet C). $ _____

    B.   Multiply Line 1A by 60 to calculate your monthly disposable income for the next five years. $ _____

● If Line 1B is more than $10,950, you have failed the means test. Do not continue.

● If Line 1B is less than $6,575, you have passed the means test. Do not continue.

● If Line 1B at least $6,575 but not more than $10,950, continue to Line 2.

Line 2. Add up your unsecured, nonpriority debts.

    A.   Back rent $ _____

    B.   Medical bills   _____

    C.   Alimony and child support   _____

    D.   Student loans   _____

    E.   Utility bills   _____

    F.   Loans from friends or relatives   _____

    G.   Health club dues   _____

    H.   Lawyer and accountant bills   _____

    I.   Union dues   _____

    J.   Church or synagogue dues   _____

    K.   Money judgments arising out of contract disputes   _____

    L.   Money judgments arising out of negligent behavior   _____

M. Deficiency judgments from secured loans _____

N. Credit and charge card purchases and cash advances _____

O. Department store credit card purchases _____

P. Other _____

Q. TOTAL UNSECURED, NONPRIORITY DEBT.
    Add Lines 2A–2P. _____

R. Divide Line 2Q by four to calculate 25% of your total unsecured,
    nonpriority debt. $ _____

- If Line 2R is larger than Line 1B, you have passed the means test and you do not need to continue.

- If Line 1B is equal or larger than Line 2R, you have failed the means test unless you can prove special circumstances.

Worksheet E: Personal Property Checklist

Cash on hand (include sources)

- ☐ In your home
- ☐ In your wallet
- ☐ Under your mattress

Deposits of money (include sources)

- ☐ Bank account
- ☐ Brokerage account (with stockbroker)
- ☐ Certificates of deposit (CDs)
- ☐ Credit union deposit
- ☐ Escrow account
- ☐ Money market account
- ☐ Money in a safe deposit box
- ☐ Savings and loan deposit

Security deposits

- ☐ Electric
- ☐ Gas
- ☐ Heating oil
- ☐ Security deposit on a rental unit
- ☐ Prepaid rent
- ☐ Rented furniture or equipment
- ☐ Telephone
- ☐ Water

Household goods, supplies, and furnishings

- ☐ Antiques
- ☐ Appliances
- ☐ Carpentry tools
- ☐ China and crystal
- ☐ Clocks
- ☐ Dishes
- ☐ Food (total value)

- ☐ Furniture (list every item; go from room to room so you don't miss anything)
- ☐ Gardening tools
- ☐ Home computer (for personal use)
- ☐ Iron and ironing board
- ☐ Lamps
- ☐ Lawn mower or tractor
- ☐ Microwave oven
- ☐ Patio or outdoor furniture
- ☐ Radios
- ☐ Rugs
- ☐ Sewing machine
- ☐ Silverware and utensils
- ☐ Small appliances
- ☐ Snow blower
- ☐ Stereo system
- ☐ Telephone and answering machines
- ☐ Televisions
- ☐ Vacuum cleaner
- ☐ Video equipment (VCR, camcorder)

Books, pictures, and other art objects; stamp, coin, and other collections

- ☐ Art prints
- ☐ Bibles
- ☐ Books
- ☐ Coins
- ☐ Collectibles (such as political buttons, baseball cards)
- ☐ Family portraits
- ☐ Figurines
- ☐ Original artworks

- [ ] Photographs
- [ ] Records, CDs, and audiotapes
- [ ] Stamps
- [ ] Videotapes, DVDs

Apparel

- [ ] Clothing
- [ ] Furs

Jewelry

- [ ] Engagement and wedding rings
- [ ] Gems
- [ ] Precious metals
- [ ] Watches

Firearms, sports equipment, and other hobby equipment

- [ ] Board games
- [ ] Bicycle
- [ ] Camera equipment
- [ ] Electronic musical equipment
- [ ] Exercise machine
- [ ] Fishing gear
- [ ] Guns (rifles, pistols, shotguns, and muskets)
- [ ] Model or remote-controlled cars or planes
- [ ] Musical instruments
- [ ] Scuba diving equipment
- [ ] Ski equipment
- [ ] Other sports equipment
- [ ] Other weapons (swords and knives)

Interests in insurance policies

- [ ] Credit insurance
- [ ] Disability insurance
- [ ] Health insurance

- [ ] Homeowners' or renters' insurance
- [ ] Term life insurance
- [ ] Whole life insurance

Annuities

Pension or profit-sharing plans

- [ ] IRA
- [ ] Keogh
- [ ] Pension or retirement plan
- [ ] 401(k) plan

Stock and interests in incorporated and unincorporated companies

Interests in partnerships

- [ ] Limited partnership interest
- [ ] General partnership interest

Government and corporate bonds and other investment instruments

- [ ] Corporate bonds
- [ ] Municipal bonds
- [ ] Promissory notes
- [ ] U.S. savings bonds

Accounts receivable

- [ ] Accounts receivable from business
- [ ] Commissions already earned

Family support

- [ ] Alimony (spousal support, and maintenance) due under court order
- [ ] Child support payments due under court order
- [ ] Payments due under divorce property settlement

Other debts for which the amount owed is known and definite

☐ Disability benefits due

☐ Disability insurance due

☐ Judgments obtained against third parties you haven't yet collected

☐ Sick pay earned

☐ Social Security benefits due

☐ Tax refund due under returns already filed

☐ Vacation pay earned

☐ Wages due

☐ Workers' compensation due

Any special powers that you or another person can exercise for your benefit, other than those listed under "real estate"

☐ A right to receive, at some future time, cash, stock, or other personal property placed in an irrevocable trust

☐ Current payments of interest or principal from a trust

☐ General power of appointment over personal property

An interest in property due to another person's death

☐ Any interest as the beneficiary of a living trust, if the trustor has died

☐ Expected proceeds from a life insurance policy where the insured has died

☐ Inheritance from an existing estate in probate (the owner has died and the court is overseeing the distribution of the property), even if the final amount is not yet known

☐ Inheritance under a will that is contingent on one or more events occurring, but only if the owner has died

All other contingent claims and claims where the amount owed you is not known, including tax refunds, counterclaims, and rights to setoff claims (claims you think you have against a person, government, or corporation, but you haven't yet sued on)

☐ Claims against a corporation, government entity, or individual

☐ Potential tax refund on a return that is not yet filed

Patents, copyrights, and other intellectual property

☐ Copyrights

☐ Patents

☐ Trade secrets

☐ Trademarks

☐ Trade names

Licenses, franchises, and other general intangibles

☐ Building permits

☐ Cooperative association holdings

☐ Exclusive licenses

☐ Liquor licenses

☐ Nonexclusive licenses

☐ Patent licenses

☐ Professional licenses

Automobiles and other vehicles

☐ Car

☐ Minibike or motor scooter

☐ Mobile or motor home, if on wheels

☐ Motorcycle

☐ Recreational vehicle (RV)

☐ Trailer

☐ Truck

☐ Van

Boats, motors, and accessories

- ☐ Boat (canoe, kayak, rowboat, shell, sailboat, pontoon, and yacht)
- ☐ Boat radar, radio, or telephone
- ☐ Outboard motor

Aircraft and accessories

- ☐ Aircraft
- ☐ Aircraft radar, radio, and other accessories

Office equipment, furnishings, and supplies

- ☐ Artwork in your office
- ☐ Computers, software, modems, and printers
- ☐ Copier
- ☐ Fax machine
- ☐ Furniture
- ☐ Rugs
- ☐ Supplies
- ☐ Telephones
- ☐ Typewriters

Machinery, fixtures, equipment, and supplies used in business

- ☐ Military uniforms and accoutrements
- ☐ Tools of your trade

Business inventory

Livestock, poultry, and other animals

- ☐ Birds
- ☐ Cats
- ☐ Dogs
- ☐ Fish and aquarium equipment
- ☐ Horses
- ☐ Other pets
- ☐ Livestock and poultry

Crops—growing or harvested

Farming equipment and implements

Farm supplies, chemicals, and feed

Other personal property of any kind not already listed

- ☐ Church pew
- ☐ Health aids (such as a wheelchair or crutches)
- ☐ Hot tub or portable spa
- ☐ Season tickets

Worksheet F: Property Value Schedule

List the total replacement value of each item in your Personal Property Checklist.

Item	Replacement Value
1. Cash	$ _____
2. Bank accounts	_____
3. Security deposits	_____
4. Household goods and furniture	_____
5. Books, pictures, etc.	_____
6. Clothing	_____
7. Furs and jewelry	_____
8. Sports and hobby equipment	_____
9. Interest in insurance	_____
10. Annuities	_____
11. Pensions and profit-sharing plans	_____
12. Stock and interest in business	_____
13. Interest in partnership and ventures	_____
14. Bonds	_____
15. Accounts receivable	_____
16. Alimony and family support	_____
17. Other liquidated debts, tax refund	_____
18. Future interests and life estates	_____
19. Interests due to another's death	_____
20. Other contingent claims	_____
21. Intellectual property rights	_____
22. Licenses and franchises	_____
23. Vehicles	_____
24. Boats, motors, and accessories	_____
25. Aircraft and accessories	_____
26. Office equipment, furniture, and supplies	_____
27. Machinery, fixtures, etc.	_____
28. Inventory	_____
29. Animals	_____
30. Crops—growing or harvested	_____
31. Farm equipment	_____
32. Farm supplies, chemicals, and feed	_____
33. Anything not listed above	_____
TOTAL	$ _____

Sample Bankruptcy Forms

B1 (Official Form 1)(4/10)

United States Bankruptcy Court Northern District of California	Voluntary Petition

Name of Debtor (if individual, enter Last, First, Middle): **Edwards, Carrie Anne**	Name of Joint Debtor (Spouse) (Last, First, Middle):

All Other Names used by the Debtor in the last 8 years (include married, maiden, and trade names):	All Other Names used by the Joint Debtor in the last 8 years (include married, maiden, and trade names):

Last four digits of Soc. Sec. or Individual-Taxpayer I.D. (ITIN) No./Complete EIN (if more than one, state all) **xxx-xx-6287**	Last four digits of Soc. Sec. or Individual-Taxpayer I.D. (ITIN) No./Complete EIN (if more than one, state all)

Street Address of Debtor (No. and Street, City, and State): **3045 Berwick St** **Lakeport, CA** ZIP Code **95453**	Street Address of Joint Debtor (No. and Street, City, and State): ZIP Code

County of Residence or of the Principal Place of Business: **Lake**	County of Residence or of the Principal Place of Business:

Mailing Address of Debtor (if different from street address): **PO Box 1437** **Lakeport, CA** ZIP Code **95453**	Mailing Address of Joint Debtor (if different from street address): ZIP Code

Location of Principal Assets of Business Debtor (if different from street address above):	

Type of Debtor
(Form of Organization)
(Check one box.)

- ■ Individual (includes Joint Debtors)
  See Exhibit D on page 2 of this form.
- ☐ Corporation (includes LLC and LLP)
- ☐ Partnership
- ☐ Other (If debtor is not one of the above entities, check this box and state type of entity below.)

Nature of Business
(Check one box)

- ☐ Health Care Business
- ☐ Single Asset Real Estate as defined in 11 U.S.C. § 101 (51B)
- ☐ Railroad
- ☐ Stockbroker
- ☐ Commodity Broker
- ☐ Clearing Bank
- ☐ Other

Tax-Exempt Entity
(Check box, if applicable)

- ☐ Debtor is a tax-exempt organization under Title 26 of the United States Code (the Internal Revenue Code).

Chapter of Bankruptcy Code Under Which the Petition is Filed (Check one box)

- ■ Chapter 7
- ☐ Chapter 9
- ☐ Chapter 11
- ☐ Chapter 12
- ☐ Chapter 13
- ☐ Chapter 15 Petition for Recognition of a Foreign Main Proceeding
- ☐ Chapter 15 Petition for Recognition of a Foreign Nonmain Proceeding

Nature of Debts
(Check one box)

- ■ Debts are primarily consumer debts, defined in 11 U.S.C. § 101(8) as "incurred by an individual primarily for a personal, family, or household purpose."
- ☐ Debts are primarily business debts.

Filing Fee (Check one box)

- ■ Full Filing Fee attached
- ☐ Filing Fee to be paid in installments (applicable to individuals only). Must attach signed application for the court's consideration certifying that the debtor is unable to pay fee except in installments. Rule 1006(b). See Official Form 3A.
- ☐ Filing Fee waiver requested (applicable to chapter 7 individuals only). Must attach signed application for the court's consideration. See Official Form 3B.

Chapter 11 Debtors

Check one box:
- ☐ Debtor is a small business debtor as defined in 11 U.S.C. § 101(51D).
- ☐ Debtor is not a small business debtor as defined in 11 U.S.C. § 101(51D).

Check if:
- ☐ Debtor's aggregate noncontingent liquidated debts (excluding debts owed to insiders or affiliates) are less than $2,343,300 (amount subject to adjustment on 4/01/13 and every three years thereafter).

Check all applicable boxes:
- ☐ A plan is being filed with this petition.
- ☐ Acceptances of the plan were solicited prepetition from one or more classes of creditors, in accordance with 11 U.S.C. § 1126(b).

Statistical/Administrative Information

- ☐ Debtor estimates that funds will be available for distribution to unsecured creditors.
- ■ Debtor estimates that, after any exempt property is excluded and administrative expenses paid, there will be no funds available for distribution to unsecured creditors.

THIS SPACE IS FOR COURT USE ONLY

Estimated Number of Creditors

■	☐	☐	☐	☐	☐	☐	☐	☐	☐
1-49	50-99	100-199	200-999	1,000-5,000	5,001-10,000	10,001-25,000	25,001-50,000	50,001-100,000	OVER 100,000

Estimated Assets

☐	☐	■	☐	☐	☐	☐	☐	☐	☐
$0 to $50,000	$50,001 to $100,000	$100,001 to $500,000	$500,001 to $1 million	$1,000,001 to $10 million	$10,000,001 to $50 million	$50,000,001 to $100 million	$100,000,001 to $500 million	$500,000,001 to $1 billion	More than $1 billion

Estimated Liabilities

☐	☐	■	☐	☐	☐	☐	☐	☐	☐
$0 to $50,000	$50,001 to $100,000	$100,001 to $500,000	$500,001 to $1 million	$1,000,001 to $10 million	$10,000,001 to $50 million	$50,000,001 to $100 million	$100,000,001 to $500 million	$500,000,001 to $1 billion	More than $1 billion

B1 (Official Form 1)(4/10)   Page 2

Voluntary Petition	Name of Debtor(s):
(This page must be completed and filed in every case)	**Edwards, Carrie Anne**

All Prior Bankruptcy Cases Filed Within Last 8 Years (If more than two, attach additional sheet)		
Location Where Filed: **- None -**	Case Number:	Date Filed:
Location Where Filed:	Case Number:	Date Filed:

Pending Bankruptcy Case Filed by any Spouse, Partner, or Affiliate of this Debtor (If more than one, attach additional sheet)		
Name of Debtor: **- None -**	Case Number:	Date Filed:
District:	Relationship:	Judge:

Exhibit A	**Exhibit B**
	(To be completed if debtor is an individual whose debts are primarily consumer debts.)
(To be completed if debtor is required to file periodic reports (e.g., forms 10K and 10Q) with the Securities and Exchange Commission pursuant to Section 13 or 15(d) of the Securities Exchange Act of 1934 and is requesting relief under chapter 11.)	I, the attorney for the petitioner named in the foregoing petition, declare that I have informed the petitioner that [he or she] may proceed under chapter 7, 11, 12, or 13 of title 11, United States Code, and have explained the relief available under each such chapter. I further certify that I delivered to the debtor the notice required by 11 U.S.C. §342(b).
☐ Exhibit A is attached and made a part of this petition.	X _____ Signature of Attorney for Debtor(s) (Date)

Exhibit C

Does the debtor own or have possession of any property that poses or is alleged to pose a threat of imminent and identifiable harm to public health or safety?

☐ Yes, and Exhibit C is attached and made a part of this petition.

■ No.

Exhibit D

(To be completed by every individual debtor. If a joint petition is filed, each spouse must complete and attach a separate Exhibit D.)

■ Exhibit D completed and signed by the debtor is attached and made a part of this petition.

If this is a joint petition:

☐ Exhibit D also completed and signed by the joint debtor is attached and made a part of this petition.

Information Regarding the Debtor - Venue
(Check any applicable box)
■　Debtor has been domiciled or has had a residence, principal place of business, or principal assets in this District for 180 days immediately preceding the date of this petition or for a longer part of such 180 days than in any other District.
☐　There is a bankruptcy case concerning debtor's affiliate, general partner, or partnership pending in this District.
☐　Debtor is a debtor in a foreign proceeding and has its principal place of business or principal assets in the United States in this District, or has no principal place of business or assets in the United States but is a defendant in an action or proceeding [in a federal or state court] in this District, or the interests of the parties will be served in regard to the relief sought in this District.

Certification by a Debtor Who Resides as a Tenant of Residential Property
(Check all applicable boxes)
☐　Landlord has a judgment against the debtor for possession of debtor's residence. (If box checked, complete the following.)

_____
(Name of landlord that obtained judgment)

_____
(Address of landlord)

☐　Debtor claims that under applicable nonbankruptcy law, there are circumstances under which the debtor would be permitted to cure the entire monetary default that gave rise to the judgment for possession, after the judgment for possession was entered, and

☐　Debtor has included in this petition the deposit with the court of any rent that would become due during the 30-day period after the filing of the petition.

☐　Debtor certifies that he/she has served the Landlord with this certification. (11 U.S.C. § 362(l)).

B1 (Official Form 1)(4/10)   Page 3

Voluntary Petition

(This page must be completed and filed in every case)

Name of Debtor(s):
Edwards, Carrie Anne

Signatures

Signature(s) of Debtor(s) (Individual/Joint)

I declare under penalty of perjury that the information provided in this petition is true and correct.
[If petitioner is an individual whose debts are primarily consumer debts and has chosen to file under chapter 7] I am aware that I may proceed under chapter 7, 11, 12, or 13 of title 11, United States Code, understand the relief available under each such chapter, and choose to proceed under chapter 7.
[If no attorney represents me and no bankruptcy petition preparer signs the petition] I have obtained and read the notice required by 11 U.S.C. §342(b).

I request relief in accordance with the chapter of title 11, United States Code, specified in this petition.

X **/s/ Carrie Anne Edwards**
Signature of Debtor **Carrie Anne Edwards**

X
Signature of Joint Debtor

(707) 274 1234
Telephone Number (If not represented by attorney)

Date

Signature of Attorney*

X **Debtor not represented by attorney**
Signature of Attorney for Debtor(s)

Printed Name of Attorney for Debtor(s)

Firm Name

Address

Telephone Number

Date
*In a case in which § 707(b)(4)(D) applies, this signature also constitutes a certification that the attorney has no knowledge after an inquiry that the information in the schedules is incorrect.

Signature of Debtor (Corporation/Partnership)

I declare under penalty of perjury that the information provided in this petition is true and correct, and that I have been authorized to file this petition on behalf of the debtor.

The debtor requests relief in accordance with the chapter of title 11, United States Code, specified in this petition.

X
Signature of Authorized Individual

Printed Name of Authorized Individual

Title of Authorized Individual

Date

Signature of a Foreign Representative

I declare under penalty of perjury that the information provided in this petition is true and correct, that I am the foreign representative of a debtor in a foreign proceeding, and that I am authorized to file this petition.

(Check only one box.)

☐ I request relief in accordance with chapter 15 of title 11, United States Code. Certified copies of the documents required by 11 U.S.C. §1515 are attached.

☐ Pursuant to 11 U.S.C. §1511, I request relief in accordance with the chapter of title 11 specified in this petition. A certified copy of the order granting recognition of the foreign main proceeding is attached.

X
Signature of Foreign Representative

Printed Name of Foreign Representative

Date

Signature of Non-Attorney Bankruptcy Petition Preparer

I declare under penalty of perjury that: (1) I am a bankruptcy petition preparer as defined in 11 U.S.C. § 110; (2) I prepared this document for compensation and have provided the debtor with a copy of this document and the notices and information required under 11 U.S.C. §§ 110(b), 110(h), and 342(b); and, (3) if rules or guidelines have been promulgated pursuant to 11 U.S.C. § 110(h) setting a maximum fee for services chargeable by bankruptcy petition preparers, I have given the debtor notice of the maximum amount before preparing any document for filing for a debtor or accepting any fee from the debtor, as required in that section. Official Form 19 is attached.

Printed Name and title, if any, of Bankruptcy Petition Preparer

Social-Security number (If the bankruptcy petition preparer is not an individual, state the Social Security number of the officer, principal, responsible person or partner of the bankruptcy petition preparer.)(Required by 11 U.S.C. § 110.)

Address

X

Date

Signature of Bankruptcy Petition Preparer or officer, principal, responsible person, or partner whose Social Security number is provided above.

Names and Social-Security numbers of all other individuals who prepared or assisted in preparing this document unless the bankruptcy petition preparer is not an individual:

If more than one person prepared this document, attach additional sheets conforming to the appropriate official form for each person.

A bankruptcy petition preparer's failure to comply with the provisions of title 11 and the Federal Rules of Bankruptcy Procedure may result in fines or imprisonment or both 11 U.S.C. §110; 18 U.S.C. §156.

B 1D (Official Form 1, Exhibit D) (12/09)

United States Bankruptcy Court
Northern District of California

In re   **Carrie Anne Edwards**   Case No. _____

                                               Debtor(s)   Chapter   **7**

EXHIBIT D - INDIVIDUAL DEBTOR'S STATEMENT OF COMPLIANCE WITH CREDIT COUNSELING REQUIREMENT

Warning: You must be able to check truthfully one of the five statements regarding credit counseling listed below. If you cannot do so, you are not eligible to file a bankruptcy case, and the court can dismiss any case you do file. If that happens, you will lose whatever filing fee you paid, and your creditors will be able to resume collection activities against you. If your case is dismissed and you file another bankruptcy case later, you may be required to pay a second filing fee and you may have to take extra steps to stop creditors' collection activities.

Every individual debtor must file this Exhibit D. If a joint petition is filed, each spouse must complete and file a separate Exhibit D. Check one of the five statements below and attach any documents as directed.

■ 1. Within the 180 days **before the filing of my bankruptcy case**, I received a briefing from a credit counseling agency approved by the United States trustee or bankruptcy administrator that outlined the opportunities for available credit counseling and assisted me in performing a related budget analysis, and I have a certificate from the agency describing the services provided to me. *Attach a copy of the certificate and a copy of any debt repayment plan developed through the agency.*

☐ 2. Within the 180 days **before the filing of my bankruptcy case**, I received a briefing from a credit counseling agency approved by the United States trustee or bankruptcy administrator that outlined the opportunities for available credit counseling and assisted me in performing a related budget analysis, but I do not have a certificate from the agency describing the services provided to me. *You must file a copy of a certificate from the agency describing the services provided to you and a copy of any debt repayment plan developed through the agency no later than 14 days after your bankruptcy case is filed.*

☐ 3. I certify that I requested credit counseling services from an approved agency but was unable to obtain the services during the seven days from the time I made my request, and the following exigent circumstances merit a temporary waiver of the credit counseling requirement so I can file my bankruptcy case now. *[Summarize exigent circumstances here.]* ____

If your certification is satisfactory to the court, you must still obtain the credit counseling briefing within the first 30 days after you file your bankruptcy petition and promptly file a certificate from the agency that provided the counseling, together with a copy of any debt management plan developed through the agency. Failure to fulfill these requirements may result in dismissal of your case. Any extension of the 30-day deadline can be granted only for cause and is limited to a maximum of 15 days. Your case may also be dismissed if the court is not satisfied with your reasons for filing your bankruptcy case without first receiving a credit counseling briefing.

☐ 4. I am not required to receive a credit counseling briefing because of: *[Check the applicable statement.] [Must be accompanied by a motion for determination by the court.]*

B 1D (Official Form 1, Exhibit D) (12/09) - Cont.

☐ Incapacity. (Defined in 11 U.S.C. § 109(h)(4) as impaired by reason of mental illness or mental deficiency so as to be incapable of realizing and making rational decisions with respect to financial responsibilities.);

☐ Disability. (Defined in 11 U.S.C. § 109(h)(4) as physically impaired to the extent of being unable, after reasonable effort, to participate in a credit counseling briefing in person, by telephone, or through the Internet.);

☐ Active military duty in a military combat zone.

☐ 5. The United States trustee or bankruptcy administrator has determined that the credit counseling requirement of 11 U.S.C. § 109(h) does not apply in this district.

I certify under penalty of perjury that the information provided above is true and correct.

Signature of Debtor: /s/ **Carrie Anne Edwards**
                        Carrie Anne Edwards

Date: _____

B6A (Official Form 6A) (12/07)

In re   **Carrie Anne Edwards**   ,   Case No. _____

                                   Debtor

SCHEDULE A - REAL PROPERTY

    Except as directed below, list all real property in which the debtor has any legal, equitable, or future interest, including all property owned as a cotenant, community property, or in which the debtor has a life estate. Include any property in which the debtor holds rights and powers exercisable for the debtor's own benefit. If the debtor is married, state whether husband, wife, both, or the marital community own the property by placing an "H," "W," "J," or "C" in the column labeled "Husband, Wife, Joint, or Community." If the debtor holds no interest in real property, write "None" under "Description and Location of Property."

    Do not include interests in executory contracts and unexpired leases on this schedule. List them in Schedule G - Executory Contracts and Unexpired Leases.

    If an entity claims to have a lien or hold a secured interest in any property, state the amount of the secured claim. See Schedule D. If no entity claims to hold a secured interest in the property, write "None" in the column labeled "Amount of Secured Claim." If the debtor is an individual or if a joint petition is filed, state the amount of any exemption claimed in the property only in Schedule C - Property Claimed as Exempt.

Description and Location of Property	Nature of Debtor's Interest in Property	Husband, Wife, Joint, or Community	Current Value of Debtor's Interest in Property, without Deducting any Secured Claim or Exemption	Amount of Secured Claim
Residence **Location: 3045 Berwick St, Lakeport CA** **Residence is in foreclosure. Sale of property has been scheduled for Jan 19, 2011. I am still living in the house but am no longer making payments on either the first or the second mortgage.**	**Fee Simple**	-	**130,000.00**	**153,000.00**
		Sub-Total >	**130,000.00**	(Total of this page)
		Total >	**130,000.00**	

  0   continuation sheets attached to the Schedule of Real Property   (Report also on Summary of Schedules)

B6B (Official Form 6B) (12/07)

In re **Carrie Anne Edwards**   Case No. _____
                                                    ,
                                    Debtor

SCHEDULE B - PERSONAL PROPERTY

Except as directed below, list all personal property of the debtor of whatever kind. If the debtor has no property in one or more of the categories, place an "x" in the appropriate position in the column labeled "None." If additional space is needed in any category, attach a separate sheet properly identified with the case name, case number, and the number of the category. If the debtor is married, state whether husband, wife, both, or the marital community own the property by placing an "H," "W," "J," or "C" in the column labeled "Husband, Wife, Joint, or Community." If the debtor is an individual or a joint petition is filed, state the amount of any exemptions claimed only in Schedule C - Property Claimed as Exempt.

Do not list interests in executory contracts and unexpired leases on this schedule. List them in Schedule G - Executory Contracts and Unexpired Leases.

If the property is being held for the debtor by someone else, state that person's name and address under "Description and Location of Property."
If the property is being held for a minor child, simply state the child's initials and the name and address of the child's parent or guardian, such as "A.B., a minor child, by John Doe, guardian." Do not disclose the child's name. See, 11 U.S.C. §112 and Fed. R. Bankr. P. 1007(m).

	Type of Property	N O N E	Description and Location of Property	Husband, Wife, Joint, or Community	Current Value of Debtor's Interest in Property, without Deducting any Secured Claim or Exemption
1.	Cash on hand		**Cash in wallet**	-	50.00
2.	Checking, savings or other financial accounts, certificates of deposit, or shares in banks, savings and loan, thrift, building and loan, and homestead associations, or credit unions, brokerage houses, or cooperatives.		**Bank of America Checking Account #12345 Lakeport California**	-	150.00
			from wages		
			WestAmerica Bank, Lakeport CA Savings Account	-	300.00
3.	Security deposits with public utilities, telephone companies, landlords, and others.	X			
4.	Household goods and furnishings, including audio, video, and computer equipment.		**All items at replacement value**	-	2,450.00
			Stereo system ($300), washer dryer set (200), refrigerator (400), electric stove (250), misc furniture (couch, 2 chairs) (450) minor appliances (blender, toaster, mixer) (125), vacuum (50), 20 inch tv (75), lawnmower (200), swing set, childrens toys (240), snowblower (160) Location: 3045 Berwick St, Lakeport CA		
			2 end tables (500), roll top desk (700), bed and bedding (800), oriental rug (2500)	-	4,500.00
5.	Books, pictures and other art objects, antiques, stamp, coin, record, tape, compact disc, and other collections or collectibles.		**250 books at used book store prices Location: 3045 Berwick St, Lakeport CA**	-	1,250.00
6.	Wearing apparel.		**normal clothing at used clothing store prices Location: 3045 Berwick St, Lakeport CA**		800.00
7.	Furs and jewelry.		**diamond necklace at used jewelry store price (800), watch at flea market price (75) Location: 3045 Berwick St, Lakeport CA**	-	875.00

Sub-Total >   10,375.00
(Total of this page)

3 continuation sheets attached to the Schedule of Personal Property

B6B (Official Form 6B) (12/07) - Cont.

In re **Carrie Anne Edwards** _____, Case No. _____
                          Debtor

SCHEDULE B - PERSONAL PROPERTY
(Continuation Sheet)

Type of Property	N O N E	Description and Location of Property	Husband, Wife, Joint, or Community	Current Value of Debtor's Interest in Property, without Deducting any Secured Claim or Exemption
8. Firearms and sports, photographic, and other hobby equipment.		**Mountain bike at used bicycle store price (250), Digital camera priced at ebay (200), sword collection priced at antique store (800) Location: 3045 Berwick St, Lakeport CA**	-	1,250.00
9. Interests in insurance policies. Name insurance company of each policy and itemize surrender or refund value of each.	X			
10. Annuities. Itemize and name each issuer.	X			
11. Interests in an education IRA as defined in 26 U.S.C. § 530(b)(1) or under a qualified State tuition plan as defined in 26 U.S.C. § 529(b)(1). Give particulars. (File separately the record(s) of any such interest(s). 11 U.S.C. § 521(c).)	X			
12. Interests in IRA, ERISA, Keogh, or other pension or profit sharing plans. Give particulars.		**TIAA/CREF (ERISA Qualified Pension), not in bankruptcy estate**	-	Undetermined
		IRA, Bank of America, Lakeport CA (25,000), not in bankruptcy estate	-	0.00
13. Stock and interests in incorporated and unincorporated businesses. Itemize.		**5,000 shares in BLP Bankruptcy Services, Inc, a close corporation Location of certificates: 3045 Berwick St, Lakeport CA (valued at $.10 a share**	-	500.00
14. Interests in partnerships or joint ventures. Itemize.	X			
15. Government and corporate bonds and other negotiable and nonnegotiable instruments.		**Negotiable promissory note from Jonathan Edwards, Carrie's brother, dated 11/3/XX Location: 3045 Berwick St, Lakeport CA**	-	500.00
16. Accounts receivable.	X			
17. Alimony, maintenance, support, and property settlements to which the debtor is or may be entitled. Give particulars.	X			
18. Other liquidated debts owed to debtor including tax refunds. Give particulars.		**Refund for 2009 Taxes (expected but not yet received)**	-	600.00

                                                          Sub-Total >   2,850.00
                                                      (Total of this page)

Sheet __1__ of __3__ continuation sheets attached
to the Schedule of Personal Property

B6B (Official Form 6B) (12/07) - Cont.

In re **Carrie Anne Edwards**   ,   Case No. _____

Debtor

SCHEDULE B - PERSONAL PROPERTY
(Continuation Sheet)

Type of Property	N O N E	Description and Location of Property	Husband, Wife, Joint, or Community	Current Value of Debtor's Interest in Property, without Deducting any Secured Claim or Exemption
19. Equitable or future interests, life estates, and rights or powers exercisable for the benefit of the debtor other than those listed in Schedule A - Real Property.	X			
20. Contingent and noncontingent interests in estate of a decedent, death benefit plan, life insurance policy, or trust.	X			
21. Other contingent and unliquidated claims of every nature, including tax refunds, counterclaims of the debtor, and rights to setoff claims. Give estimated value of each.	X			
22. Patents, copyrights, and other intellectual property. Give particulars.		**Copyright in book published by Nolo Press (Independent Paralegal's Handbook)**	-	Undetermined
23. Licenses, franchises, and other general intangibles. Give particulars.	X			
24. Customer lists or other compilations containing personally identifiable information (as defined in 11 U.S.C. § 101(41A)) provided to the debtor by individuals in connection with obtaining a product or service from the debtor primarily for personal, family, or household purposes.	X			
25. Automobiles, trucks, trailers, and other vehicles and accessories.		**2006 Buick LeSabre fully loaded in good condition (replacement value from nada.com)**	-	8,000.00
		2001 23 foot Travel Trailer Location: 3045 Berwick St, Lakeport CA	-	11,000.00
26. Boats, motors, and accessories.	X			
27. Aircraft and accessories.	X			
28. Office equipment, furnishings, and supplies.		**Used computer valued at Ebay price, used in business**	-	800.00
		Copier (used Xerox) no known market for replacement value	-	Undetermined

Sub-Total >   19,800.00
(Total of this page)

Sheet __2__ of __3__ continuation sheets attached
to the Schedule of Personal Property

B6B (Official Form 6B) (12/07) - Cont.

In re   **Carrie Anne Edwards**   ,   Case No._____

                                                  Debtor

SCHEDULE B - PERSONAL PROPERTY
(Continuation Sheet)

Type of Property	N O N E	Description and Location of Property	Husband, Wife, Joint, or Community	Current Value of Debtor's Interest in Property, without Deducting any Secured Claim or Exemption
29. Machinery, fixtures, equipment, and supplies used in business.	X			
30. Inventory.	X			
31. Animals.	X			
32. Crops - growing or harvested. Give particulars.	X			
33. Farming equipment and implements.	X			
34. Farm supplies, chemicals, and feed.	X			
35. Other personal property of any kind not already listed. Itemize.	X			

Sub-Total >	0.00
(Total of this page)	
Total >	33,025.00

Sheet __3__ of __3__ continuation sheets attached
to the Schedule of Personal Property

(Report also on Summary of Schedules)

B6C (Official Form 6C) (4/10)

In re   **Carrie Anne Edwards** _____,   Case No. _____

                             Debtor

SCHEDULE C - PROPERTY CLAIMED AS EXEMPT

Debtor claims the exemptions to which debtor is entitled under: ☐ Check if debtor claims a homestead exemption that exceeds
(Check one box) $146,450. *(Amount subject to adjustment on 4/1/13, and every three years thereafter*
☐ 11 U.S.C. §522(b)(2)   *with respect to cases commenced on or after the date of adjustment.)*
■ 11 U.S.C. §522(b)(3)

Description of Property	Specify Law Providing Each Exemption	Value of Claimed Exemption	Current Value of Property Without Deducting Exemption
Cash on Hand Cash in wallet	C.C.P. § 703.140(b)(5)	50.00	50.00
Checking, Savings, or Other Financial Accounts, Certificates of Deposit Bank of America Checking Account #12345 Lakeport California from wages	C.C.P. § 703.140(b)(5)	150.00	150.00
WestAmerica Bank, Lakeport CA Savings Account	C.C.P. § 703.140(b)(5)	300.00	300.00
Household Goods and Furnishings All items at replacement value	C.C.P. § 703.140(b)(3)	2,450.00	2,450.00
Stereo system ($300), washer dryer set (200), refrigerator (400), electric stove (250), misc furniture (couch, 2 chairs) (450) minor appliances (blender, toaster, mixer) (125), vacuum (50), 20 inch tv (75), lawnmower (200), swing set, childrens toys (240), snowblower (160) Location: 3045 Berwick St, Lakeport CA			
2 end tables (500), roll top desk (700), bed and bedding (800), oriental rug (2500)	C.C.P. § 703.140(b)(5)	4,500.00	4,500.00
Books, Pictures and Other Art Objects; Collectibles 250 books at used book store prices Location: 3045 Berwick St, Lakeport CA	C.C.P. § 703.140(b)(5)	1,250.00	1,250.00
Wearing Apparel normal clothing at used clothing store prices Location: 3045 Berwick St, Lakeport CA	C.C.P. § 703.140(b)(3)	800.00	800.00
Furs and Jewelry diamond necklace at used jewelry store price (800), watch at flea market price (75) Location: 3045 Berwick St, Lakeport CA	C.C.P. § 703.140(b)(4)	875.00	875.00
Firearms and Sports, Photographic and Other Hobby Equipment Mountain bike at used bicycle store price (250), Digital camera priced at ebay (200), sword collection priced at antique store (800) Location: 3045 Berwick St, Lakeport CA	C.C.P. § 703.140(b)(5)	1,250.00	1,250.00
Stock and Interests in Businesses 5,000 shares in BLP Bankruptcy Services, Inc, a close corporation Location of certificates: 3045 Berwick St, Lakeport CA (valued at $.10 a share	C.C.P. § 703.140(b)(5)	500.00	500.00

    __1__   continuation sheets attached to Schedule of Property Claimed as Exempt

B6C (Official Form 6C) (4/10) -- Cont.

In re   **Carrie Anne Edwards**   ,   Case No._____

Debtor

SCHEDULE C - PROPERTY CLAIMED AS EXEMPT
(Continuation Sheet)

Description of Property	Specify Law Providing Each Exemption	Value of Claimed Exemption	Current Value of Property Without Deducting Exemption
Government & Corporate Bonds, Other Negotiable & Non-negotiable Inst. Negotiable promissory note from Jonathan Edwards, Carrie's brother, dated 11/3/XX Location: 3045 Berwick St, Lakeport CA	C.C.P. § 703.140(b)(5)	500.00	500.00
Other Liquidated Debts Owing Debtor Including Tax Refund Refund for 2009 Taxes (expected but not yet received)	C.C.P. § 703.140(b)(5)	600.00	600.00
Automobiles, Trucks, Trailers, and Other Vehicles 2001 23 foot Travel Trailer Location: 3045 Berwick St, Lakeport CA	C.C.P. § 703.140(b)(5)	11,000.00	11,000.00
Office Equipment, Furnishings and Supplies Used computer valued at Ebay price, used in business	C.C.P. § 703.140(b)(6)	800.00	800.00
Total:		25,025.00	25,025.00

Sheet __1__ of __1__ continuation sheets attached to the Schedule of Property Claimed as Exempt

B6D (Official Form 6D) (12/07)

In re   **Carrie Anne Edwards**   Case No. _____
                                                              ,
                                    Debtor

SCHEDULE D - CREDITORS HOLDING SECURED CLAIMS

State the name, mailing address, including zip code, and last four digits of any account number of all entities holding claims secured by property of the debtor as of the date of filing of the petition. The complete account number of any account the debtor has with the creditor is useful to the trustee and the creditor and may be provided if the debtor chooses to do so. List creditors holding all types of secured interests such as judgment liens, garnishments, statutory liens, mortgages, deeds of trust, and other security interests.

List creditors in alphabetical order to the extent practicable. If a minor child is a creditor, the child's initials and the name and address of the child's parent or guardian, such as "A.B., a minor child, by John Doe, guardian." Do not disclose the child's name. See, 11 U.S.C. §112 and Fed. R. Bankr. P. 1007(m). If all secured creditors will not fit on this page, use the continuation sheet provided.

If any entity other than a spouse in a joint case may be jointly liable on a claim, place an "X" in the column labeled "Codebtor" ,include the entity on the appropriate schedule of creditors, and complete Schedule H - Codebtors. If a joint petition is filed, state whether the husband, wife, both of them, or the marital community may be liable on each claim by placing an "H", "W", "J", or "C" in the column labeled "Husband, Wife, Joint, or Community".

If the claim is contingent, place an "X" in the column labeled "Contingent". If the claim is unliquidated, place an "X" in the column labeled "Unliquidated". If the claim is disputed, place an "X" in the column labeled "Disputed". (You may need to place an "X" in more than one of these three columns.)

Total the columns labeled "Amount of Claim Without Deducting Value of Collateral" and "Unsecured Portion, if Any" in the boxes labeled "Total(s)" on the last sheet of the completed schedule. Report the total from the column labeled "Amount of Claim" also on the Summary of Schedules and, if the debtor is an individual with primarily consumer debts, report the total from the column labeled "Unsecured Portion" on the Statistical Summary of Certain Liabilities and Related Data.

☐   Check this box if debtor has no creditors holding secured claims to report on this Schedule D.

CREDITOR'S NAME AND MAILING ADDRESS INCLUDING ZIP CODE, AND ACCOUNT NUMBER (See instructions above.)	CODEBTOR	Husband, Wife, Joint, or Community H W J C	DATE CLAIM WAS INCURRED, NATURE OF LIEN, AND DESCRIPTION AND VALUE OF PROPERTY SUBJECT TO LIEN	CONTINGENT	UNLIQUIDATED	DISPUTED	AMOUNT OF CLAIM WITHOUT DEDUCTING VALUE OF COLLATERAL	UNSECURED PORTION, IF ANY
Account No. **444555666777** **GMAC** **PO Box 23567** **Duchesne, UT 84021**	-		November, 2003 **Purchase Money Security** **2003 Buick LeSabre fully loaded in good condition (replacement value from nada.com)**			X		
			Value $ 8,000.00				15,000.00	7,000.00
Account No. **64-112-1861** **Grand Junction Mortgage** **3456 Eight St.** **Clearlake, CA 95422**	-		12/XX **First Mortgage** **Residence** **Location: 3045 Berwick St, Lakeport CA Residence is in foreclosure. Sale of property has been scheduled for July 19, 2010. I am still living in the house and hoping to modify the mortgage.**					
			Value $ 130,000.00				135,000.00	5,000.00
Account No. **55555555555** Lending Tree **PO Box 3333** Palo Alto, CA 94310	-		12/xx **Second Mortgage** **Residence** Location: 3045 Berwick St, Lakeport CA Residence is in foreclosure. Sale of property has been scheduled for July 19, 2010. I am still living in the house and hoping to modify the mortgage					
			Value $ 130,000.00				18,000.00	18,000.00
Account No.								
			Value $					

0   continuation sheets attached

	Subtotal (Total of this page)	168,000.00	30,000.00
	Total (Report on Summary of Schedules)	168,000.00	30,000.00

B6E (Official Form 6E) (4/10)

In re   **Carrie Anne Edwards**

_____ ,   Case No. _____

Debtor

SCHEDULE E - CREDITORS HOLDING UNSECURED PRIORITY CLAIMS

A complete list of claims entitled to priority, listed separately by type of priority, is to be set forth on the sheets provided. Only holders of unsecured claims entitled to priority should be listed in this schedule. In the boxes provided on the attached sheets, state the name, mailing address, including zip code, and last four digits of the account number, if any, of all entities holding priority claims against the debtor or the property of the debtor, as of the date of the filing of the petition. Use a separate continuation sheet for each type of priority and label each with the type of priority.

The complete account number of any account the debtor has with the creditor is useful to the trustee and the creditor and may be provided if the debtor chooses to do so. If a minor child is a creditor, state the child's initials and the name and address of the child's parent or guardian, such as "A.B., a minor child, by John Doe, guardian." Do not disclose the child's name. See, 11 U.S.C. §112 and Fed. R. Bankr. P. 1007(m).

If any entity other than a spouse in a joint case may be jointly liable on a claim, place an "X" in the column labeled "Codebtor," include the entity on the appropriate schedule of creditors, and complete Schedule H-Codebtors. If a joint petition is filed, state whether the husband, wife, both of them, or the marital community may be liable on each claim by placing an "H," "W," "J," or "C" in the column labeled "Husband, Wife, Joint, or Community." If the claim is contingent, place an "X" in the column labeled "Contingent." If the claim is unliquidated, place an "X" in the column labeled "Unliquidated." If the claim is disputed, place an "X" in the column labeled "Disputed." (You may need to place an "X" in more than one of these three columns.)

Report the total of claims listed on each sheet in the box labeled "Subtotals" on each sheet. Report the total of all claims listed on this Schedule E in the box labeled "Total" on the last sheet of the completed schedule. Report this total also on the Summary of Schedules.

Report the total of amounts entitled to priority listed on each sheet in the box labeled "Subtotals" on each sheet. Report the total of all amounts entitled to priority listed on this Schedule E in the box labeled "Totals" on the last sheet of the completed schedule. Individual debtors with primarily consumer debts report this total also on the Statistical Summary of Certain Liabilities and Related Data.

Report the total of amounts <u>not</u> entitled to priority listed on each sheet in the box labeled "Subtotals" on each sheet. Report the total of all amounts not entitled to priority listed on this Schedule E in the box labeled "Totals" on the last sheet of the completed schedule. Individual debtors with primarily consumer debts report this total also on the Statistical Summary of Certain Liabilities and Related Data.

☐ Check this box if debtor has no creditors holding unsecured priority claims to report on this Schedule E.

TYPES OF PRIORITY CLAIMS (Check the appropriate box(es) below if claims in that category are listed on the attached sheets)

■ **Domestic support obligations**

Claims for domestic support that are owed to or recoverable by a spouse, former spouse, or child of the debtor, or the parent, legal guardian, or responsible relative of such a child, or a governmental unit to whom such a domestic support claim has been assigned to the extent provided in 11 U.S.C. § 507(a)(1).

☐ **Extensions of credit in an involuntary case**

Claims arising in the ordinary course of the debtor's business or financial affairs after the commencement of the case but before the earlier of the appointment of a trustee or the order for relief. 11 U.S.C. § 507(a)(3).

☐ **Wages, salaries, and commissions**

Wages, salaries, and commissions, including vacation, severance, and sick leave pay owing to employees and commissions owing to qualifying independent sales representatives up to $11,725* per person earned within 180 days immediately preceding the filing of the original petition, or the cessation of business, whichever occurred first, to the extent provided in 11 U.S.C. § 507(a)(4).

☐ **Contributions to employee benefit plans**

Money owed to employee benefit plans for services rendered within 180 days immediately preceding the filing of the original petition, or the cessation of business, whichever occurred first, to the extent provided in 11 U.S.C. § 507(a)(5).

☐ **Certain farmers and fishermen**

Claims of certain farmers and fishermen, up to $5,775* per farmer or fisherman, against the debtor, as provided in 11 U.S.C. § 507(a)(6).

☐ **Deposits by individuals**

Claims of individuals up to $2,600* for deposits for the purchase, lease, or rental of property or services for personal, family, or household use, that were not delivered or provided. 11 U.S.C. § 507(a)(7).

■ **Taxes and certain other debts owed to governmental units**

Taxes, customs duties, and penalties owing to federal, state, and local governmental units as set forth in 11 U.S.C. § 507(a)(8).

☐ **Commitments to maintain the capital of an insured depository institution**

Claims based on commitments to the FDIC, RTC, Director of the Office of Thrift Supervision, Comptroller of the Currency, or Board of Governors of the Federal Reserve System, or their predecessors or successors, to maintain the capital of an insured depository institution. 11 U.S.C. § 507 (a)(9).

☐ **Claims for death or personal injury while debtor was intoxicated**

Claims for death or personal injury resulting from the operation of a motor vehicle or vessel while the debtor was intoxicated from using alcohol, a drug, or another substance. 11 U.S.C. § 507(a)(10).

* Amount subject to adjustment on 4/01/13, and every three years thereafter with respect to cases commenced on or after the date of adjustment.

2____ continuation sheets attached

B6E (Official Form 6E) (4/10) - Cont.

In re **Carrie Anne Edwards** , Case No. _____

_____ Debtor

SCHEDULE E - CREDITORS HOLDING UNSECURED PRIORITY CLAIMS
(Continuation Sheet)

Domestic Support Obligations

TYPE OF PRIORITY

CREDITOR'S NAME, AND MAILING ADDRESS INCLUDING ZIP CODE, AND ACCOUNT NUMBER (See instructions.)	CODEBTOR	Husband, Wife, Joint, or Community		DATE CLAIM WAS INCURRED AND CONSIDERATION FOR CLAIM	CONTINGENT	UNLIQUIDATED	DISPUTED	AMOUNT OF CLAIM	AMOUNT NOT ENTITLED TO PRIORITY, IF ANY / AMOUNT ENTITLED TO PRIORITY
		H W	J C						
Account No. 2005									
Jon Edwards 900 Grand View Jackson, WY 83001	-			Child support				0.00	
								4,500.00	4,500.00
Account No.									
Account No.									
Account No.									
Account No.									

Sheet **1** of **2** continuation sheets attached to Schedule of Creditors Holding Unsecured Priority Claims

Subtotal (Total of this page)

0.00		
4,500.00	4,500.00	

B6E (Official Form 6E) (4/10) - Cont.

In re **Carrie Anne Edwards** Case No. _____

_____,

Debtor

SCHEDULE E - CREDITORS HOLDING UNSECURED PRIORITY CLAIMS
(Continuation Sheet)

**Taxes and Certain Other Debts
Owed to Governmental Units**

TYPE OF PRIORITY

CREDITOR'S NAME, AND MAILING ADDRESS INCLUDING ZIP CODE, AND ACCOUNT NUMBER (See instructions.)	CODEBTOR	Husband, Wife, Joint, or Community H / W / J / C	DATE CLAIM WAS INCURRED AND CONSIDERATION FOR CLAIM	CONTINGENT	UNLIQUIDATED	DISPUTED	AMOUNT OF CLAIM	AMOUNT NOT ENTITLED TO PRIORITY, IF ANY	AMOUNT ENTITLED TO PRIORITY
Account No. **IRS** **Columbus, OH 43266**	-		**April 15, 20XX tax liability and interest**				3,000.00	0.00	3,000.00
Account No.									
Account No.									
Account No.									
Account No.									

Sheet __2__ of __2__ continuation sheets attached to
Schedule of Creditors Holding Unsecured Priority Claims

Subtotal (Total of this page)	3,000.00	0.00 / 3,000.00
Total (Report on Summary of Schedules)	7,500.00	0.00 / 7,500.00

B6F (Official Form 6F) (12/07)

In re **Carrie Anne Edwards**   Case No. _____
_____,
                                     Debtor

SCHEDULE F - CREDITORS HOLDING UNSECURED NONPRIORITY CLAIMS

State the name, mailing address, including zip code, and last four digits of any account number, of all entities holding unsecured claims without priority against the debtor or the property of the debtor, as of the date of filing of the petition. The complete account number of any account the debtor has with the creditor is useful to the trustee and the creditor and may be provided if the debtor chooses to do so. If a minor child is a creditor, state the child's initials and the name and address of the child's parent or guardian, such as "A.B., a minor child, by John Doe, guardian." Do not disclose the child's name. See, 11 U.S.C. §112 and Fed. R. Bankr. P. 1007(m). Do not include claims listed in Schedules D and E. If all creditors will not fit on this page, use the continuation sheet provided.

If any entity other than a spouse in a joint case may be jointly liable on a claim, place an "X" in the column labeled "Codebtor," include the entity on the appropriate schedule of creditors, and complete Schedule H - Codebtors. If a joint petition is filed, state whether the husband, wife, both of them, or the marital community may be liable on each claim by placing an "H," "W," "J," or "C" in the column labeled "Husband, Wife, Joint, or Community."

If the claim is contingent, place an "X" in the column labeled "Contingent." If the claim is unliquidated, place an "X" in the column labeled "Unliquidated." If the claim is disputed, place an "X" in the column labeled "Disputed." (You may need to place an "X" in more than one of these three columns.)

Report the total of all claims listed on this schedule in the box labeled "Total" on the last sheet of the completed schedule. Report this total also on the Summary of Schedules and, if the debtor is an individual with primarily consumer debts, report this total also on the Statistical Summary of Certain Liabilities and Related Data.

☐   Check this box if debtor has no creditors holding unsecured claims to report on this Schedule F.

CREDITOR'S NAME, MAILING ADDRESS INCLUDING ZIP CODE, AND ACCOUNT NUMBER (See instructions above.)	CODEBTOR	Husband, Wife, Joint, or Community H / W / J / C	DATE CLAIM WAS INCURRED AND CONSIDERATION FOR CLAIM. IF CLAIM IS SUBJECT TO SETOFF, SO STATE.	CONTINGENT	UNLIQUIDATED	DISPUTED	AMOUNT OF CLAIM
Account No. Alan Accountant 5 Green St. Cleveland, OH 44118		-	4 /XX Tax preparation				500.00
Account No. 41 89-0000-2613-5556 American Allowance PO Box 1 New York, NY 10001		-	1/xx to 4/xx credit card charges				5,600.00
Account No. Angel of Mercy Hospital 4444 Elevator St Belmont, CA 94003		-	12/xx uninsured surgery and medical treatment				34,000.00
Account No. Bob Jones III 4566 Fifth Ave. New York, NY 10020		-	5/xx Auto accident--negligence claim				75,000.00

__2__ continuation sheets attached

Subtotal
(Total of this page)   115,100.00

B6F (Official Form 6F) (12/07) - Cont.

In re   **Carrie Anne Edwards**   ,   Case No. _____
                                                    Debtor

SCHEDULE F - CREDITORS HOLDING UNSECURED NONPRIORITY CLAIMS
(Continuation Sheet)

CREDITOR'S NAME, MAILING ADDRESS INCLUDING ZIP CODE, AND ACCOUNT NUMBER (See instructions above.)	CODEBTOR	HWJC	DATE CLAIM WAS INCURRED AND CONSIDERATION FOR CLAIM. IF CLAIM IS SUBJECT TO SETOFF, SO STATE.	CONTINGENT	UNLIQUIDATED	DISPUTED	AMOUNT OF CLAIM
Account No. Bonnie Johnson 3335 Irving St Clearlake, CA 95422		-	8/xx Personal loan				5,500.00
Account No. 3434 4567 1234 2345 Cal State Central Credit Union 1205 N. Dutton Ave Santa Rosa, CA 95401		-	January 2004 to present Misc charges				8,765.00
Account No. 845061-86-3 Citibank 200 East North St Columbus, OH 43266		-	20xx Student loan				10,000.00
Account No. 4401 Dr. Dennis Dentist 45 Superior Way Cleveland, OH 44118		-	12/xx to 6/xx dental work				1,050.00
Account No. 555671 Dr. Helen Jones 443 First St. Soledad, CA 94750		-	4/xx to 8/xx Pediatric Care				5,000.00

Sheet no. __1__ of __2__ sheets attached to Schedule of
Creditors Holding Unsecured Nonpriority Claims

Subtotal
(Total of this page)   30,315.00

B6F (Official Form 6F) (12/07) - Cont.

In re   **Carrie Anne Edwards** _____ ,   Case No. _____

                                 Debtor

SCHEDULE F - CREDITORS HOLDING UNSECURED NONPRIORITY CLAIMS
(Continuation Sheet)

CREDITOR'S NAME, MAILING ADDRESS INCLUDING ZIP CODE, AND ACCOUNT NUMBER (See instructions above.)	CODEBTOR	HWJC Husband, Wife, Joint, or Community	DATE CLAIM WAS INCURRED AND CONSIDERATION FOR CLAIM. IF CLAIM IS SUBJECT TO SETOFF, SO STATE.	CONTINGENT	UNLIQUIDATED	DISPUTED	AMOUNT OF CLAIM
Account No. Fannie's Furniture 55544 Grove St. Berkeley, CA 94710	X	-	12/xx used bedroomset				1,300.00
Account No. 222387941 Illuminating Co. 20245 Old Hwy 53 Clearlake, CA 95422		-	3/xx to 7/xx electrical work on house				750.00
Account No. John White Esq. PO Box 401 Finley, CA 95435		-	2/xx to 8/xx Legal representation in lawsuit against neighbor for incursion on property				3,450.00
Account No. 11210550 PG&E 215 North Forbes St. Lakeport, CA 95453		-	12/xx to 6/xx gas and electric service				1,200.00
Account No. 487310097 Sears PO Box 11 Chicago, IL 60619		-	20xx to 200xy Dept store and catalog charges				3,800.00

Sheet no. __2__ of __2__ sheets attached to Schedule of
Creditors Holding Unsecured Nonpriority Claims

Subtotal
(Total of this page)   **10,500.00**

Total
(Report on Summary of Schedules)   **155,915.00**

B6G (Official Form 6G) (12/07)

In re   **Carrie Anne Edwards**   Case No. _____

                                          Debtor

SCHEDULE G - EXECUTORY CONTRACTS AND UNEXPIRED LEASES

Describe all executory contracts of any nature and all unexpired leases of real or personal property. Include any timeshare interests. State nature of debtor's interest in contract, i.e., "Purchaser", "Agent", etc. State whether debtor is the lessor or lessee of a lease. Provide the names and complete mailing addresses of all other parties to each lease or contract described. If a minor child is a party to one of the leases or contracts, state the child's initials and the name and address of the child's parent or guardian, such as "A.B., a minor child, by John Doe, guardian." Do not disclose the child's name. See, 11 U.S.C. §112 and Fed. R. Bankr. P. 1007(m).

☐ Check this box if debtor has no executory contracts or unexpired leases.

Name and Mailing Address, Including Zip Code, of Other Parties to Lease or Contract	Description of Contract or Lease and Nature of Debtor's Interest. State whether lease is for nonresidential real property. State contract number of any government contract.
Beauty Products Leasing Co. **44332 Eighth St.** **Geismar, LA 70734**	**Laser skin treatment machine. Lease for 5 year period that expires on 2012**
Herman Jones **45543 Woodleigh Court** **Smith River, CA 95567**	**Sales contract for debtor's home entered into between debtor and Herman Jones on 2 /1/XX**

0

____ continuation sheets attached to Schedule of Executory Contracts and Unexpired Leases

B6H (Official Form 6H) (12/07)

In re   **Carrie Anne Edwards**   ,   Case No._____

Debtor

SCHEDULE H - CODEBTORS

    Provide the information requested concerning any person or entity, other than a spouse in a joint case, that is also liable on any debts listed by debtor in the schedules of creditors. Include all guarantors and co-signers. If the debtor resides or resided in a community property state, commonwealth, or territory (including Alaska, Arizona, California, Idaho, Louisiana, Nevada, New Mexico, Puerto Rico, Texas, Washington, or Wisconsin) within the eight year period immediately preceding the commencement of the case, identify the name of the debtor's spouse and of any former spouse who resides or resided with the debtor in the community property state, commonwealth, or territory. Include all names used by the nondebtor spouse during the eight years immediately preceding the commencement of this case. If a minor child is a codebtor or a creditor, state the child's initials and the name and address of the child's parent or guardian, such as "A.B., a minor child, by John Doe, guardian." Do not disclose the child's name. See, 11 U.S.C. §112 and Fed. R. Bankr. P. 1007(m).

☐ Check this box if debtor has no codebtors.

NAME AND ADDRESS OF CODEBTOR	NAME AND ADDRESS OF CREDITOR
Bonnie Johnson **3335 Irving St.** **Clearlake, CA 95422**	**Fannie's Furniture** **55544 Grove St.** **Berkeley, CA 94710**

0

_____ continuation sheets attached to Schedule of Codebtors

B6I (Official Form 6I) (12/07)

In re   **Carrie Anne Edwards**   Case No. _____

                                        Debtor(s)

SCHEDULE I - CURRENT INCOME OF INDIVIDUAL DEBTOR(S)

The column labeled "Spouse" must be completed in all cases filed by joint debtors and by every married debtor, whether or not a joint petition is filed, unless the spouses are separated and a joint petition is not filed. Do not state the name of any minor child. The average monthly income calculated on this form may differ from the current monthly income calculated on Form 22A, 22B, or 22C.

Debtor's Marital Status:	DEPENDENTS OF DEBTOR AND SPOUSE	
	RELATIONSHIP(S):	AGE(S):
Divorced	**Daughter**	**12**
	Son	**14**

Employment:	DEBTOR	SPOUSE
Occupation	**Retail**	
Name of Employer	**Macy's**	
How long employed	**2 months**	
Address of Employer	**2356 Cleveland Ave.** **Santa Rosa, CA 95402**	

INCOME: (Estimate of average or projected monthly income at time case filed)	DEBTOR	SPOUSE
1. Monthly gross wages, salary, and commissions (Prorate if not paid monthly)	$ 4,950.67	$ N/A
2. Estimate monthly overtime	$ 0.00	$ N/A
3. SUBTOTAL	$ 4,950.67	$ N/A
4. LESS PAYROLL DEDUCTIONS		
a. Payroll taxes and social security	$ 541.67	$ N/A
b. Insurance	$ 0.00	$ N/A
c. Union dues	$ 0.00	$ N/A
d. Other (Specify): _____	$ 0.00	$ N/A
	$ 0.00	$ N/A
5. SUBTOTAL OF PAYROLL DEDUCTIONS	$ 541.67	$ N/A
6. TOTAL NET MONTHLY TAKE HOME PAY	$ 4,409.00	$ N/A
7. Regular income from operation of business or profession or farm (Attach detailed statement)	$ 0.00	$ N/A
8. Income from real property	$ 0.00	$ N/A
9. Interest and dividends	$ 0.00	$ N/A
10. Alimony, maintenance or support payments payable to the debtor for the debtor's use or that of dependents listed above	$ 400.00	$ N/A
11. Social security or government assistance (Specify): _____	$ 0.00	$ N/A
	$ 0.00	$ N/A
12. Pension or retirement income	$ 0.00	$ N/A
13. Other monthly income (Specify): _____	$ 0.00	$ N/A
	$ 0.00	$ N/A
14. SUBTOTAL OF LINES 7 THROUGH 13	$ 400.00	$ N/A
15. AVERAGE MONTHLY INCOME (Add amounts shown on lines 6 and 14)	$ 4,809.00	$ N/A
16. COMBINED AVERAGE MONTHLY INCOME: (Combine column totals from line 15)		$ 4,809.00

                        (Report also on Summary of Schedules and, if applicable, on
                        Statistical Summary of Certain Liabilities and Related Data)

17. Describe any increase or decrease in income reasonably anticipated to occur within the year following the filing of this document:
     Wages are being reduced and I will probably be making $100 a month less than is currently the case.

B6J (Official Form 6J) (12/07)

In re **Carrie Anne Edwards**   Case No. _____
                               Debtor(s)

SCHEDULE J - CURRENT EXPENDITURES OF INDIVIDUAL DEBTOR(S)

Complete this schedule by estimating the average or projected monthly expenses of the debtor and the debtor's family at time case filed. Prorate any payments made bi-weekly, quarterly, semi-annually, or annually to show monthly rate. The average monthly expenses calculated on this form may differ from the deductions from income allowed on Form 22A or 22C.

☐   Check this box if a joint petition is filed and debtor's spouse maintains a separate household. Complete a separate schedule of expenditures labeled "Spouse."

1. Rent or home mortgage payment (include lot rented for mobile home)	$	900.00
a. Are real estate taxes included? Yes **X** No ___		
b. Is property insurance included? Yes ___ No **X**		
2. Utilities: a. Electricity and heating fuel	$	150.00
b. Water and sewer	$	150.00
c. Telephone	$	200.00
d. Other **See Detailed Expense Attachment**	$	130.00
3. Home maintenance (repairs and upkeep)	$	75.00
4. Food	$	500.00
5. Clothing	$	125.00
6. Laundry and dry cleaning	$	40.00
7. Medical and dental expenses	$	300.00
8. Transportation (not including car payments)	$	400.00
9. Recreation, clubs and entertainment, newspapers, magazines, etc.	$	100.00
10. Charitable contributions	$	300.00
11. Insurance (not deducted from wages or included in home mortgage payments)		
a. Homeowner's or renter's	$	100.00
b. Life	$	0.00
c. Health	$	200.00
d. Auto	$	200.00
e. Other	$	0.00
12. Taxes (not deducted from wages or included in home mortgage payments)		
(Specify)	$	0.00
13. Installment payments: (In chapter 11, 12, and 13 cases, do not list payments to be included in the plan)		
a. Auto	$	450.00
b. Other	$	0.00
c. Other	$	0.00
14. Alimony, maintenance, and support paid to others	$	0.00
15. Payments for support of additional dependents not living at your home	$	0.00
16. Regular expenses from operation of business, profession, or farm (attach detailed statement)	$	0.00
17. Other **Child care**	$	400.00
Other	$	0.00

18. AVERAGE MONTHLY EXPENSES (Total lines 1-17. Report also on Summary of Schedules and, if applicable, on the Statistical Summary of Certain Liabilities and Related Data.) $ **4,720.00**

19. Describe any increase or decrease in expenditures reasonably anticipated to occur within the year following the filing of this document:
_____

20. STATEMENT OF MONTHLY NET INCOME		
a. Average monthly income from Line 15 of Schedule I	$	4,809.00
b. Average monthly expenses from Line 18 above	$	4,720.00
c. Monthly net income (a. minus b.)	$	89.00

B6J (Official Form 6J) (12/07)

In re   **Carrie Anne Edwards**   Case No. _____

                                                                    Debtor(s)

SCHEDULE J - CURRENT EXPENDITURES OF INDIVIDUAL DEBTOR(S)
Detailed Expense Attachment

Other Utility Expenditures:

Satellite TV	$	90.00
DSL	$	40.00
Total Other Utility Expenditures	$	130.00

B6 Summary (Official Form 6 - Summary) (12/07)

United States Bankruptcy Court
Northern District of California

In re   **Carrie Anne Edwards**

Case No. _____

Debtor

Chapter _____ 7 _____

SUMMARY OF SCHEDULES

Indicate as to each schedule whether that schedule is attached and state the number of pages in each. Report the totals from Schedules A, B, D, E, F, I, and J in the boxes provided. Add the amounts from Schedules A and B to determine the total amount of the debtor's assets. Add the amounts of all claims from Schedules D, E, and F to determine the total amount of the debtor's liabilities. Individual debtors must also complete the "Statistical Summary of Certain Liabilities and Related Data" if they file a case under chapter 7, 11, or 13.

NAME OF SCHEDULE	ATTACHED (YES/NO)	NO. OF SHEETS	ASSETS	LIABILITIES	OTHER
A - Real Property	Yes	1	130,000.00		
B - Personal Property	Yes	4	33,025.00		
C - Property Claimed as Exempt	Yes	2			
D - Creditors Holding Secured Claims	Yes	1		168,000.00	
E - Creditors Holding Unsecured Priority Claims (Total of Claims on Schedule E)	Yes	3		7,500.00	
F - Creditors Holding Unsecured Nonpriority Claims	Yes	3		155,915.00	
G - Executory Contracts and Unexpired Leases	Yes	1			
H - Codebtors	Yes	1			
I - Current Income of Individual Debtor(s)	Yes	1			4,809.00
J - Current Expenditures of Individual Debtor(s)	Yes	2			4,720.00
Total Number of Sheets of ALL Schedules		10			
Total Assets			163,025.00		
Total Liabilities				331,415.00	

Form 6 - Statistical Summary (12/07)

United States Bankruptcy Court
Northern District of California

In re   **Carrie Anne Edwards**   Case No._____

                                  Debtor

                                        Chapter_____ 7 _____

STATISTICAL SUMMARY OF CERTAIN LIABILITIES AND RELATED DATA (28 U.S.C. § 159)

If you are an individual debtor whose debts are primarily consumer debts, as defined in § 101(8) of the Bankruptcy Code (11 U.S.C.§ 101(8)), filing a case under chapter 7, 11 or 13, you must report all information requested below.

☐   Check this box if you are an individual debtor whose debts are NOT primarily consumer debts. You are not required to report any information here.

This information is for statistical purposes only under 28 U.S.C. § 159.

Summarize the following types of liabilities, as reported in the Schedules, and total them.

Type of Liability	Amount
Domestic Support Obligations (from Schedule E)	4,500.00
Taxes and Certain Other Debts Owed to Governmental Units (from Schedule E)	3,000.00
Claims for Death or Personal Injury While Debtor Was Intoxicated (from Schedule E) (whether disputed or undisputed)	0.00
Student Loan Obligations (from Schedule F)	0.00
Domestic Support, Separation Agreement, and Divorce Decree Obligations Not Reported on Schedule E	0.00
Obligations to Pension or Profit-Sharing, and Other Similar Obligations (from Schedule F)	0.00
TOTAL	7,500.00

State the following:

Average Income (from Schedule I, Line 16)	4,809.00
Average Expenses (from Schedule J, Line 18)	4,720.00
Current Monthly Income (from Form 22A Line 12; OR, Form 22B Line 11; OR, Form 22C Line 20)	5,350.67

State the following:

1. Total from Schedule D, "UNSECURED PORTION, IF ANY" column		30,000.00
2. Total from Schedule E, "AMOUNT ENTITLED TO PRIORITY" column	7,500.00	
3. Total from Schedule E, "AMOUNT NOT ENTITLED TO PRIORITY, IF ANY" column		0.00
4. Total from Schedule F		155,915.00
5. Total of non-priority unsecured debt (sum of 1, 3, and 4)		185,915.00

B6 Declaration (Official Form 6 - Declaration). (12/07)

United States Bankruptcy Court
Northern District of California

In re **Carrie Anne Edwards**

Debtor(s)

Case No.

Chapter   **7**

DECLARATION CONCERNING DEBTOR'S SCHEDULES

DECLARATION UNDER PENALTY OF PERJURY BY INDIVIDUAL DEBTOR

    I declare under penalty of perjury that I have read the foregoing summary and schedules, consisting of **21** sheets, and that they are true and correct to the best of my knowledge, information, and belief.

Date _____

Signature **/s/ Carrie Anne Edwards**

              Carrie Anne Edwards

              Debtor

Penalty for making a false statement or concealing property: Fine of up to $500,000 or imprisonment for up to 5 years or both. 18 U.S.C. §§ 152 and 3571.

B7 (Official Form 7) (04/10)

United States Bankruptcy Court
Northern District of California

In re   **Carrie Anne Edwards**   Case No. _____

                                          Debtor(s)   Chapter   **7**   _____

STATEMENT OF FINANCIAL AFFAIRS

       This statement is to be completed by every debtor. Spouses filing a joint petition may file a single statement on which the information for both spouses is combined. If the case is filed under chapter 12 or chapter 13, a married debtor must furnish information for both spouses whether or not a joint petition is filed, unless the spouses are separated and a joint petition is not filed. An individual debtor engaged in business as a sole proprietor, partner, family farmer, or self-employed professional, should provide the information requested on this statement concerning all such activities as well as the individual's personal affairs. To indicate payments, transfers and the like to minor children, state the child's initials and the name and address of the child's parent or guardian, such as "A.B., a minor child, by John Doe, guardian." Do not disclose the child's name. See, 11 U.S.C. § 112; Fed. R. Bankr. P. 1007(m).

       Questions 1 - 18 are to be completed by all debtors. Debtors that are or have been in business, as defined below, also must complete Questions 19 - 25. **If the answer to an applicable question is "None," mark the box labeled "None."** If additional space is needed for the answer to any question, use and attach a separate sheet properly identified with the case name, case number (if known), and the number of the question.

DEFINITIONS

       "In business." A debtor is "in business" for the purpose of this form if the debtor is a corporation or partnership. An individual debtor is "in business" for the purpose of this form if the debtor is or has been, within six years immediately preceding the filing of this bankruptcy case, any of the following: an officer, director, managing executive, or owner of 5 percent or more of the voting or equity securities of a corporation; a partner, other than a limited partner, of a partnership; a sole proprietor or self-employed full-time or part-time. An individual debtor also may be "in business" for the purpose of this form if the debtor engages in a trade, business, or other activity, other than as an employee, to supplement income from the debtor's primary employment.

       "Insider." The term "insider" includes but is not limited to: relatives of the debtor; general partners of the debtor and their relatives; corporations of which the debtor is an officer, director, or person in control; officers, directors, and any owner of 5 percent or more of the voting or equity securities of a corporate debtor and their relatives; affiliates of the debtor and insiders of such affiliates; any managing agent of the debtor. 11 U.S.C. § 101.

---

1. Income from employment or operation of business

None
☐

       State the gross amount of income the debtor has received from employment, trade, or profession, or from operation of the debtor's business, including part-time activities either as an employee or in independent trade or business, from the beginning of this calendar year to the date this case was commenced. State also the gross amounts received during the **two years** immediately preceding this calendar year. (A debtor that maintains, or has maintained, financial records on the basis of a fiscal rather than a calendar year may report fiscal year income. Identify the beginning and ending dates of the debtor's fiscal year.) If a joint petition is filed, state income for each spouse separately. (Married debtors filing under chapter 12 or chapter 13 must state income of both spouses whether or not a joint petition is filed, unless the spouses are separated and a joint petition is not filed.)

             AMOUNT   SOURCE
             $114,200.00   **2009 ($60,100) (employment at Microsoft as software engineer**
                                          2010 ($54,100) (employment at Microsoft and Macy's retail)
                                          None yet earned in 2011

2. Income other than from employment or operation of business

None ☐   State the amount of income received by the debtor other than from employment, trade, profession, or operation of the debtor's business during the **two years** immediately preceding the commencement of this case. Give particulars. If a joint petition is filed, state income for each spouse separately. (Married debtors filing under chapter 12 or chapter 13 must state income for each spouse whether or not a joint petition is filed, unless the spouses are separated and a joint petition is not filed.)

AMOUNT	SOURCE
$28,800.00	Jan 10-Jan 11 (9600 royalties, 4800 child support)
	Jan 09-Jan 10 (9600 royalties, 4800 child support)

3. Payments to creditors

None ☐   *Complete a. or b., as appropriate, and c.*

a.   *Individual or joint debtor(s) with primarily consumer debts.* List all payments on loans, installment purchases of goods or services, and other debts to any creditor made within **90 days** immediately preceding the commencement of this case unless the aggregate value of all property that constitutes or is affected by such transfer is less than $600. Indicate with an (*) any payments that were made to a creditor on account of a domestic support obligation or as part of an alternative repayment schedule under a plan by an approved nonprofit budgeting and credit counseling agency. (Married debtors filing under chapter 12 or chapter 13 must include payments by either or both spouses whether or not a joint petition is filed, unless the spouses are separated and a joint petition is not filed.)

NAME AND ADDRESS OF CREDITOR	DATES OF PAYMENTS	AMOUNT PAID	AMOUNT STILL OWING
Loantree PO Box 305 Lucerne, CA 95458	12/xx	$800.00	$0.00

None ■   b.   *Debtor whose debts are not primarily consumer debts:* List each payment or other transfer to any creditor made within **90 days** immediately preceding the commencement of the case unless the aggregate value of all property that constitutes or is affected by such transfer is less than $5,850*. If the debtor is an individual, indicate with an asterisk (*) any payments that were made to a creditor on account of a domestic support obligation or as part of an alternative repayment schedule under a plan by an approved nonprofit budgeting and credit counseling agency. (Married debtors filing under chapter 12 or chapter 13 must include payments and other transfers by either or both spouses whether or not a joint petition is filed, unless the spouses are separated and a joint petition is not filed.)

NAME AND ADDRESS OF CREDITOR	DATES OF PAYMENTS/ TRANSFERS	AMOUNT PAID OR VALUE OF TRANSFERS	AMOUNT STILL OWING

None ■   c.   *All debtors:* List all payments made within **one year** immediately preceding the commencement of this case to or for the benefit of creditors who are or were insiders. (Married debtors filing under chapter 12 or chapter 13 must include payments by either or both spouses whether or not a joint petition is filed, unless the spouses are separated and a joint petition is not filed.)

NAME AND ADDRESS OF CREDITOR AND RELATIONSHIP TO DEBTOR	DATE OF PAYMENT	AMOUNT PAID	AMOUNT STILL OWING

4. Suits and administrative proceedings, executions, garnishments and attachments

None ☐   a. List all suits and administrative proceedings to which the debtor is or was a party within **one year** immediately preceding the filing of this bankruptcy case. (Married debtors filing under chapter 12 or chapter 13 must include information concerning either or both spouses whether or not a joint petition is filed, unless the spouses are separated and a joint petition is not filed.)

CAPTION OF SUIT AND CASE NUMBER	NATURE OF PROCEEDING	COURT OR AGENCY AND LOCATION	STATUS OR DISPOSITION
Bob Jones III v. Carrie Edwards Case # cv34457	Negligence action for auto accident	Lake County Superior Court 255 N. Forbes St. Lakeport, CA 95453	Trial pending

* Amount subject to adjustment on 4/01/13, and every three years thereafter with respect to cases commenced on or after the date of adjustment.

3

None ☐ b. Describe all property that has been attached, garnished or seized under any legal or equitable process within **one year** immediately preceding the commencement of this case. (Married debtors filing under chapter 12 or chapter 13 must include information concerning property of either or both spouses whether or not a joint petition is filed, unless the spouses are separated and a joint petition is not filed.)

NAME AND ADDRESS OF PERSON FOR WHOSE BENEFIT PROPERTY WAS SEIZED	DATE OF SEIZURE	DESCRIPTION AND VALUE OF PROPERTY
JNR Adjustment Co. PO Box 27070 Minneapolis, MN 55427	**4/XX**	**wage garnishment for two months totaling $510 for judgment on debt owed to DVD club.**

5. Repossessions, foreclosures and returns

None ☐ List all property that has been repossessed by a creditor, sold at a foreclosure sale, transferred through a deed in lieu of foreclosure or returned to the seller, within **one year** immediately preceding the commencement of this case. (Married debtors filing under chapter 12 or chapter 13 must include information concerning property of either or both spouses whether or not a joint petition is filed, unless the spouses are separated and a joint petition is not filed.)

NAME AND ADDRESS OF CREDITOR OR SELLER	DATE OF REPOSSESSION, FORECLOSURE SALE, TRANSFER OR RETURN	DESCRIPTION AND VALUE OF PROPERTY
Eskanos & Adler 2325 Clayton Rd. Concord, CA 94520	**4/XX**	**Repossessed furniture worth $800**
Grand Junction Mortgage 3456 Eighth St. Clearlake, CA 95422	**Notice of Default Sent March 20, 20XX**	**Home described in Schedule A. Sale is scheduled but hasn't happened yet.**

6. Assignments and receiverships

None ■ a. Describe any assignment of property for the benefit of creditors made within **120 days** immediately preceding the commencement of this case. (Married debtors filing under chapter 12 or chapter 13 must include any assignment by either or both spouses whether or not a joint petition is filed, unless the spouses are separated and a joint petition is not filed.)

NAME AND ADDRESS OF ASSIGNEE	DATE OF ASSIGNMENT	TERMS OF ASSIGNMENT OR SETTLEMENT

None ■ b. List all property which has been in the hands of a custodian, receiver, or court-appointed official within **one year** immediately preceding the commencement of this case. (Married debtors filing under chapter 12 or chapter 13 must include information concerning property of either or both spouses whether or not a joint petition is filed, unless the spouses are separated and a joint petition is not filed.)

NAME AND ADDRESS OF CUSTODIAN	NAME AND LOCATION OF COURT CASE TITLE & NUMBER	DATE OF ORDER	DESCRIPTION AND VALUE OF PROPERTY

7. Gifts

None ☐ List all gifts or charitable contributions made within **one year** immediately preceding the commencement of this case except ordinary and usual gifts to family members aggregating less than $200 in value per individual family member and charitable contributions aggregating less than $100 per recipient. (Married debtors filing under chapter 12 or chapter 13 must include gifts or contributions by either or both spouses whether or not a joint petition is filed, unless the spouses are separated and a joint petition is not filed.)

NAME AND ADDRESS OF PERSON OR ORGANIZATION	RELATIONSHIP TO DEBTOR, IF ANY	DATE OF GIFT	DESCRIPTION AND VALUE OF GIFT
Universal Life Church 43322 First St. Lakeport, CA 95453	**None**	**Monthly**	**charitible contributions of $300 per month**

4

8. Losses

None ■

List all losses from fire, theft, other casualty or gambling within **one year** immediately preceding the commencement of this case **or since the commencement of this case.** (Married debtors filing under chapter 12 or chapter 13 must include losses by either or both spouses whether or not a joint petition is filed, unless the spouses are separated and a joint petition is not filed.)

DESCRIPTION AND VALUE OF PROPERTY	DESCRIPTION OF CIRCUMSTANCES AND, IF LOSS WAS COVERED IN WHOLE OR IN PART BY INSURANCE, GIVE PARTICULARS	DATE OF LOSS

9. Payments related to debt counseling or bankruptcy

None ☐

List all payments made or property transferred by or on behalf of the debtor to any persons, including attorneys, for consultation concerning debt consolidation, relief under the bankruptcy law or preparation of the petition in bankruptcy within **one year** immediately preceding the commencement of this case.

NAME AND ADDRESS OF PAYEE	DATE OF PAYMENT, NAME OF PAYOR IF OTHER THAN DEBTOR	AMOUNT OF MONEY OR DESCRIPTION AND VALUE OF PROPERTY
Jim McDonald Esq. 444 State St. Ukiah, CA	7/xx	$100 for bankruptcy telephone advice

10. Other transfers

None ☐

a. List all other property, other than property transferred in the ordinary course of the business or financial affairs of the debtor, transferred either absolutely or as security within **two years** immediately preceding the commencement of this case. (Married debtors filing under chapter 12 or chapter 13 must include transfers by either or both spouses whether or not a joint petition is filed, unless the spouses are separated and a joint petition is not filed.)

NAME AND ADDRESS OF TRANSFEREE, RELATIONSHIP TO DEBTOR	DATE	DESCRIBE PROPERTY TRANSFERRED AND VALUE RECEIVED
Robert James 5554 15th St. Lakeport, CA 95453 Arms length	03/23/XX	02 Infinity XX, sold for $8,000, fair market value according to KBB, money spent on house payment, car payment and bills.

None ■

b. List all property transferred by the debtor within **ten years** immediately preceding the commencement of this case to a self-settled trust or similar device of which the debtor is a beneficiary.

NAME OF TRUST OR OTHER DEVICE	DATE(S) OF TRANSFER(S)	AMOUNT OF MONEY OR DESCRIPTION AND VALUE OF PROPERTY OR DEBTOR'S INTEREST IN PROPERTY

11. Closed financial accounts

None ☐

List all financial accounts and instruments held in the name of the debtor or for the benefit of the debtor which were closed, sold, or otherwise transferred within **one year** immediately preceding the commencement of this case. Include checking, savings, or other financial accounts, certificates of deposit, or other instruments; shares and share accounts held in banks, credit unions, pension funds, cooperatives, associations, brokerage houses and other financial institutions. (Married debtors filing under chapter 12 or chapter 13 must include information concerning accounts or instruments held by or for either or both spouses whether or not a joint petition is filed, unless the spouses are separated and a joint petition is not filed.)

NAME AND ADDRESS OF INSTITUTION	TYPE OF ACCOUNT, LAST FOUR DIGITS OF ACCOUNT NUMBER, AND AMOUNT OF FINAL BALANCE	AMOUNT AND DATE OF SALE OR CLOSING
WestAmerica Bank 444 North Main St. Lakeport, CA 95453	Checking Acct #4444444 Final balance ($50)	July, XX, XXXX

5

12. Safe deposit boxes

None ■ List each safe deposit or other box or depository in which the debtor has or had securities, cash, or other valuables within **one year** immediately preceding the commencement of this case. (Married debtors filing under chapter 12 or chapter 13 must include boxes or depositories of either or both spouses whether or not a joint petition is filed, unless the spouses are separated and a joint petition is not filed.)

NAME AND ADDRESS OF BANK OR OTHER DEPOSITORY	NAMES AND ADDRESSES OF THOSE WITH ACCESS TO BOX OR DEPOSITORY	DESCRIPTION OF CONTENTS	DATE OF TRANSFER OR SURRENDER, IF ANY

13. Setoffs

None ■ List all setoffs made by any creditor, including a bank, against a debt or deposit of the debtor within **90 days** preceding the commencement of this case. (Married debtors filing under chapter 12 or chapter 13 must include information concerning either or both spouses whether or not a joint petition is filed, unless the spouses are separated and a joint petition is not filed.)

NAME AND ADDRESS OF CREDITOR	DATE OF SETOFF	AMOUNT OF SETOFF

14. Property held for another person

None ☐ List all property owned by another person that the debtor holds or controls.

NAME AND ADDRESS OF OWNER	DESCRIPTION AND VALUE OF PROPERTY	LOCATION OF PROPERTY
Bonnie Johnson 3335 Irving St Clearlake, CA 95422	Poodle (Binkie) $300	Edwards residence
Vannie Edwards 4444 Cleveland Ave. Pope Valley, CA 94567	$50,000 savings account owned by my grandmother. I am on the account as an informal trustee to help her manage her expenses. I am operating under a fiduciary duty to only withdraw funds for my grandmother's benefit.	Bank of America, 5555 Cleveland Ave. Pope Valley CA 94567

15. Prior address of debtor

None ☐ If the debtor has moved within **three years** immediately preceding the commencement of this case, list all premises which the debtor occupied during that period and vacated prior to the commencement of this case. If a joint petition is filed, report also any separate address of either spouse.

ADDRESS	NAME USED	DATES OF OCCUPANCY
21 Scarborough Rd. South Cleveland Heights OH 41118	Carrie Edwards	1/1/XX-- 5/1/XX

16. Spouses and Former Spouses

None ☐ If the debtor resides or resided in a community property state, commonwealth, or territory (including Alaska, Arizona, California, Idaho, Louisiana, Nevada, New Mexico, Puerto Rico, Texas, Washington, or Wisconsin) within **eight years** immediately preceding the commencement of the case, identify the name of the debtor's spouse and of any former spouse who resides or resided with the debtor in the community property state.

NAME
Torrey Edwards

6

17. Environmental Information.

For the purpose of this question, the following definitions apply:

"Environmental Law" means any federal, state, or local statute or regulation regulating pollution, contamination, releases of hazardous or toxic substances, wastes or material into the air, land, soil, surface water, groundwater, or other medium, including, but not limited to, statutes or regulations regulating the cleanup of these substances, wastes, or material.

"Site" means any location, facility, or property as defined under any Environmental Law, whether or not presently or formerly owned or operated by the debtor, including, but not limited to, disposal sites.

"Hazardous Material" means anything defined as a hazardous waste, hazardous substance, toxic substance, hazardous material, pollutant, or contaminant or similar term under an Environmental Law

None
■   a. List the name and address of every site for which the debtor has received notice in writing by a governmental unit that it may be liable or potentially liable under or in violation of an Environmental Law. Indicate the governmental unit, the date of the notice, and, if known, the Environmental Law:

SITE NAME AND ADDRESS	NAME AND ADDRESS OF GOVERNMENTAL UNIT	DATE OF NOTICE	ENVIRONMENTAL LAW

None
■   b. List the name and address of every site for which the debtor provided notice to a governmental unit of a release of Hazardous Material. Indicate the governmental unit to which the notice was sent and the date of the notice.

SITE NAME AND ADDRESS	NAME AND ADDRESS OF GOVERNMENTAL UNIT	DATE OF NOTICE	ENVIRONMENTAL LAW

None
■   c. List all judicial or administrative proceedings, including settlements or orders, under any Environmental Law with respect to which the debtor is or was a party. Indicate the name and address of the governmental unit that is or was a party to the proceeding, and the docket number.

NAME AND ADDRESS OF GOVERNMENTAL UNIT	DOCKET NUMBER	STATUS OR DISPOSITION

18 . Nature, location and name of business

None
■   a. *If the debtor is an individual*, list the names, addresses, taxpayer identification numbers, nature of the businesses, and beginning and ending dates of all businesses in which the debtor was an officer, director, partner, or managing executive of a corporation, partner in a partnership, sole proprietor, or was self-employed in a trade, profession, or other activity either full- or part-time within **six years** immediately preceding the commencement of this case, or in which the debtor owned 5 percent or more of the voting or equity securities within **six years** immediately preceding the commencement of this case.

If the debtor is a partnership, list the names, addresses, taxpayer identification numbers, nature of the businesses, and beginning and ending dates of all businesses in which the debtor was a partner or owned 5 percent or more of the voting or equity securities, within **six years** immediately preceding the commencement of this case.

If the debtor is a corporation, list the names, addresses, taxpayer identification numbers, nature of the businesses, and beginning and ending dates of all businesses in which the debtor was a partner or owned 5 percent or more of the voting or equity securities within **six years** immediately preceding the commencement of this case.

NAME	LAST FOUR DIGITS OF SOCIAL-SECURITY OR OTHER INDIVIDUAL TAXPAYER-I.D. NO. (ITIN)/ COMPLETE EIN	ADDRESS	NATURE OF BUSINESS	BEGINNING AND ENDING DATES

None
■   b. Identify any business listed in response to subdivision a., above, that is "single asset real estate" as defined in 11 U.S.C. § 101.

NAME	ADDRESS

7

The following questions are to be completed by every debtor that is a corporation or partnership and by any individual debtor who is or has been, within **six years** immediately preceding the commencement of this case, any of the following: an officer, director, managing executive, or owner of more than 5 percent of the voting or equity securities of a corporation; a partner, other than a limited partner, of a partnership, a sole proprietor, or self-employed in a trade, profession, or other activity, either full- or part-time.

*(An individual or joint debtor should complete this portion of the statement **only** if the debtor is or has been in business, as defined above, within six years immediately preceding the commencement of this case. A debtor who has not been in business within those six years should go directly to the signature page.)*

19. Books, records and financial statements

None
■ a. List all bookkeepers and accountants who within **two years** immediately preceding the filing of this bankruptcy case kept or supervised the keeping of books of account and records of the debtor.

NAME AND ADDRESS   DATES SERVICES RENDERED

None
■ b. List all firms or individuals who within the **two years** immediately preceding the filing of this bankruptcy case have audited the books of account and records, or prepared a financial statement of the debtor.

NAME   ADDRESS   DATES SERVICES RENDERED

None
■ c. List all firms or individuals who at the time of the commencement of this case were in possession of the books of account and records of the debtor. If any of the books of account and records are not available, explain.

NAME   ADDRESS

None
■ d. List all financial institutions, creditors and other parties, including mercantile and trade agencies, to whom a financial statement was issued by the debtor within **two years** immediately preceding the commencement of this case.

NAME AND ADDRESS   DATE ISSUED

20. Inventories

None
■ a. List the dates of the last two inventories taken of your property, the name of the person who supervised the taking of each inventory, and the dollar amount and basis of each inventory.

DATE OF INVENTORY   INVENTORY SUPERVISOR   DOLLAR AMOUNT OF INVENTORY
                                                        (Specify cost, market or other basis)

None
■ b. List the name and address of the person having possession of the records of each of the two inventories reported in a., above.

DATE OF INVENTORY   NAME AND ADDRESSES OF CUSTODIAN OF INVENTORY
                                          RECORDS

21 . Current Partners, Officers, Directors and Shareholders

None
■ a. If the debtor is a partnership, list the nature and percentage of partnership interest of each member of the partnership.

NAME AND ADDRESS   NATURE OF INTEREST   PERCENTAGE OF INTEREST

None
■ b. If the debtor is a corporation, list all officers and directors of the corporation, and each stockholder who directly or indirectly owns, controls, or holds 5 percent or more of the voting or equity securities of the corporation.

NAME AND ADDRESS   TITLE   NATURE AND PERCENTAGE
                                                           OF STOCK OWNERSHIP

22 . Former partners, officers, directors and shareholders

None ■ a. If the debtor is a partnership, list each member who withdrew from the partnership within **one year** immediately preceding the commencement of this case.

NAME   ADDRESS   DATE OF WITHDRAWAL

None ■ b. If the debtor is a corporation, list all officers, or directors whose relationship with the corporation terminated within **one year** immediately preceding the commencement of this case.

NAME AND ADDRESS   TITLE   DATE OF TERMINATION

23 . Withdrawals from a partnership or distributions by a corporation

None ■ If the debtor is a partnership or corporation, list all withdrawals or distributions credited or given to an insider, including compensation in any form, bonuses, loans, stock redemptions, options exercised and any other perquisite during **one year** immediately preceding the commencement of this case.

NAME & ADDRESS OF RECIPIENT, RELATIONSHIP TO DEBTOR	DATE AND PURPOSE OF WITHDRAWAL	AMOUNT OF MONEY OR DESCRIPTION AND VALUE OF PROPERTY

24. Tax Consolidation Group.

None ■ If the debtor is a corporation, list the name and federal taxpayer identification number of the parent corporation of any consolidated group for tax purposes of which the debtor has been a member at any time within **six years** immediately preceding the commencement of the case.

NAME OF PARENT CORPORATION   TAXPAYER IDENTIFICATION NUMBER (EIN)

25. Pension Funds.

None ■ If the debtor is not an individual, list the name and federal taxpayer-identification number of any pension fund to which the debtor, as an employer, has been responsible for contributing at any time within **six years** immediately preceding the commencement of the case.

NAME OF PENSION FUND   TAXPAYER IDENTIFICATION NUMBER (EIN)

DECLARATION UNDER PENALTY OF PERJURY BY INDIVIDUAL DEBTOR

I declare under penalty of perjury that I have read the answers contained in the foregoing statement of financial affairs and any attachments thereto and that they are true and correct.

Date _____ Signature **/s/ Carrie Anne Edwards**
                                        Carrie Anne Edwards
                                        Debtor

Penalty for making a false statement: Fine of up to $500,000 or imprisonment for up to 5 years, or both. 18 U.S.C. §§ 152 and 3571

B8 (Form 8) (12/08)

United States Bankruptcy Court
Northern District of California

In re   **Carrie Anne Edwards**   Case No. _____

                                          Debtor(s)   Chapter   **7**

CHAPTER 7 INDIVIDUAL DEBTOR'S STATEMENT OF INTENTION

PART A - Debts secured by property of the estate. (Part A must be fully completed for **EACH** debt which is secured by property of the estate. Attach additional pages if necessary.)

Property No. 1

Creditor's Name: **GMAC**	**Describe Property Securing Debt:** **2003 Buick LeSabre fully loaded in good condition** **(replacement value from nada.com)**

Property will be (check one):

☐ Surrendered   ■ Retained

If retaining the property, I intend to (check at least one):
   ☐ Redeem the property
   ■ Reaffirm the debt
   ☐ Other. Explain _____ (for example, avoid lien using 11 U.S.C. § 522(f)).

Property is (check one):
   ☐ Claimed as Exempt   ■ Not claimed as exempt

Property No. 2

Creditor's Name: **Grand Junction Mortgage**	**Describe Property Securing Debt:** **Residence** **Location: 3045 Berwick St, Lakeport CA** **Residence is in foreclosure. Sale of property has been scheduled for July 19, 2010. I am still living in the house and hoping to modify the mortgage.**

Property will be (check one):

☐ Surrendered   ■ Retained

If retaining the property, I intend to (check at least one):
   ☐ Redeem the property
   ☐ Reaffirm the debt
   ■ Other. Explain   **Debtor will retain collateral and continue to make regular payments.**   (for example, avoid lien using 11 U.S.C. § 522(f)).

Property is (check one):
   ☐ Claimed as Exempt   ■ Not claimed as exempt

B8 (Form 8) (12/08)   Page 1

Property No. 3	
Creditor's Name: **Lending Tree**	**Describe Property Securing Debt:** **Residence** **Location: 3045 Berwick St, Lakeport CA** **Residence is in foreclosure. Sale of property has been scheduled for July 19, 2010. I am still living in the house and hoping to modify the mortgage**

Property will be (check one):
  ☐ Surrendered   ■ Retained

If retaining the property, I intend to (check at least one):
  ☐ Redeem the property
  ☐ Reaffirm the debt
  ■ Other. Explain **Debtor will retain collateral and continue to make regular payments.** (for example, avoid lien using 11 U.S.C. § 522(f)).

Property is (check one):
  ☐ Claimed as Exempt   ■ Not claimed as exempt

PART B - Personal property subject to unexpired leases. (All three columns of Part B must be completed for each unexpired lease. Attach additional pages if necessary.)

Property No. 1		
Lessor's Name: **Beauty Products Leasing Co.**	**Describe Leased Property:** **Laser skin treatment machine. Lease for 5 year period that expires on 2012**	Lease will be Assumed pursuant to 11 U.S.C. § 365(p)(2): ■ YES ☐ NO

I declare under penalty of perjury that the above indicates my intention as to any property of my estate securing a debt and/or personal property subject to an unexpired lease.

Date _____   Signature **/s/ Carrie Anne Edwards** _____
                                                    Carrie Anne Edwards
                                                    Debtor

B 201A (Form 201A) (12/09)

WARNING: Effective December 1, 2009, the 15-day deadline to file schedules and certain other documents under Bankruptcy Rule 1007(c) is shortened to 14 days. For further information, see note at bottom of page 2

UNITED STATES BANKRUPTCY COURT
NORTHERN DISTRICT OF CALIFORNIA

NOTICE TO CONSUMER DEBTOR(S) UNDER § 342(b)
OF THE BANKRUPTCY CODE

In accordance with § 342(b) of the Bankruptcy Code, this notice to individuals with primarily consumer debts: (1) Describes briefly the services available from credit counseling services; (2) Describes briefly the purposes, benefits and costs of the four types of bankruptcy proceedings you may commence; and (3) Informs you about bankruptcy crimes and notifies you that the Attorney General may examine all information you supply in connection with a bankruptcy case.

You are cautioned that bankruptcy law is complicated and not easily described. Thus, you may wish to seek the advice of an attorney to learn of your rights and responsibilities should you decide to file a petition. Court employees cannot give you legal advice.

Notices from the bankruptcy court are sent to the mailing address you list on your bankruptcy petition. In order to ensure that you receive information about events concerning your case, Bankruptcy Rule 4002 requires that you notify the court of any changes in your address. If you are filing a **joint case** (a single bankruptcy case for two individuals married to each other), and each spouse lists the same mailing address on the bankruptcy petition, you and your spouse will generally receive a single copy of each notice mailed from the bankruptcy court in a jointly-addressed envelope, unless you file a statement with the court requesting that each spouse receive a separate copy of all notices.

1. Services Available from Credit Counseling Agencies

With limited exceptions, § 109(h) of the Bankruptcy Code requires that all individual debtors who file for bankruptcy relief on or after October 17, 2005, receive a briefing that outlines the available opportunities for credit counseling and provides assistance in performing a budget analysis. The briefing must be given within 180 days **before** the bankruptcy filing. The briefing may be provided individually or in a group (including briefings conducted by telephone or on the Internet) and must be provided by a nonprofit budget and credit counseling agency approved by the United States trustee or bankruptcy administrator. The clerk of the bankruptcy court has a list that you may consult of the approved budget and credit counseling agencies. Each debtor in a joint case must complete the briefing.

In addition, after filing a bankruptcy case, an individual debtor generally must complete a financial management instructional course before he or she can receive a discharge. The clerk also has a list of approved financial management instructional courses. Each debtor in a joint case must complete the course.

2. The Four Chapters of the Bankruptcy Code Available to Individual Consumer Debtors

Chapter 7: Liquidation ($245 filing fee, $39 administrative fee, $15 trustee surcharge: Total Fee $299)

Chapter 7 is designed for debtors in financial difficulty who do not have the ability to pay their existing debts. Debtors whose debts are primarily consumer debts are subject to a "means test" designed to determine whether the case should be permitted to proceed under chapter 7. If your income is greater than the median income for your state of residence and family size, in some cases, the United States trustee (or bankruptcy administrator), the trustee, or creditors have the right to file a motion requesting that the court dismiss your case under § 707(b) of the Code. It is up to the court to decide whether the case should be dismissed.

Under chapter 7, you may claim certain of your property as exempt under governing law. A trustee may have the right to take possession of and sell the remaining property that is not exempt and use the sale proceeds to pay your creditors.

The purpose of filing a chapter 7 case is to obtain a discharge of your existing debts. If, however, you are found to have committed certain kinds of improper conduct described in the Bankruptcy Code, the court may deny your discharge and, if it does, the purpose for which you filed the bankruptcy petition will be defeated.

Even if you receive a general discharge, some particular debts are not discharged under the law. Therefore, you may still be responsible for most taxes and student loans; debts incurred to pay nondischargeable taxes; domestic support and property settlement obligations; most fines, penalties, forfeitures, and criminal restitution obligations; certain debts which are not properly listed in your bankruptcy papers; and debts for death or personal injury caused by operating a motor vehicle, vessel, or aircraft while intoxicated from alcohol or drugs. Also, if a creditor can prove that a debt arose from fraud, breach of fiduciary duty, or theft, or from a willful and malicious injury, the bankruptcy court may determine that the debt is not discharged.

Chapter 13: Repayment of All or Part of the Debts of an Individual with Regular Income ($235 filing fee, $39 administrative fee: Total fee $274)

Chapter 13 is designed for individuals with regular income who would like to pay all or part of their debts in installments over a period of time. You are only eligible for chapter 13 if your debts do not exceed certain dollar amounts set forth in the Bankruptcy Code.

Under chapter 13, you must file with the court a plan to repay your creditors all or part of the money that you owe them, using your future earnings. The period allowed by the court to repay your debts may be three years or five years, depending upon your income and other factors. The court must approve your plan before it can take effect.

After completing the payments under your plan, your debts are generally discharged except for domestic support obligations; most student loans; certain taxes; most criminal fines and restitution obligations; certain debts which are not properly listed in your bankruptcy papers; certain debts for acts that caused death or personal injury; and certain long term secured obligations.

Chapter 11: Reorganization ($1000 filing fee, $39 administrative fee: Total fee $1039)

Chapter 11 is designed for the reorganization of a business but is also available to consumer debtors. Its provisions are quite complicated, and any decision by an individual to file a chapter 11 petition should be reviewed with an attorney.

Chapter 12: Family Farmer or Fisherman ($200 filing fee, $39 administrative fee: Total fee $239)

Chapter 12 is designed to permit family farmers and fishermen to repay their debts over a period of time from future earnings and is similar to chapter 13. The eligibility requirements are restrictive, limiting its use to those whose income arises primarily from a family-owned farm or commercial fishing operation.

3. <u>Bankruptcy Crimes and Availability of Bankruptcy Papers to Law Enforcement Officials</u>

A person who knowingly and fraudulently conceals assets or makes a false oath or statement under penalty of perjury, either orally or in writing, in connection with a bankruptcy case is subject to a fine, imprisonment, or both. All information supplied by a debtor in connection with a bankruptcy case is subject to examination by the Attorney General acting through the Office of the United States Trustee, the Office of the United States Attorney, and other components and employees of the Department of Justice.

WARNING: Section 521(a)(1) of the Bankruptcy Code requires that you promptly file detailed information regarding your creditors, assets, liabilities, income, expenses and general financial condition. Your bankruptcy case may be dismissed if this information is not filed with the court within the time deadlines set by the Bankruptcy Code, the Bankruptcy Rules, and the local rules of the court. The documents and the deadlines for filing them are listed on Form B200, which is posted at http://www.uscourts.gov/bkforms/bankruptcy_forms.html#procedure.

Many filing deadlines change on December 1, 2009. Of special note, 12 rules that set 15 days to act are amended to require action within 14 days, including Rule 1007(c), filing the initial case papers; Rule 3015(b), filing a chapter 13 plan; Rule 8009(a), filing appellate briefs; and Rules 1019, 1020, 2015, 2015.1, 2016, 4001, 4002, 6004, and 6007.

B 201B (Form 201B) (12/09)

United States Bankruptcy Court
Northern District of California

In re   **Carrie Anne Edwards**   Case No. _____

                                   Debtor(s)   Chapter   **7** _____

CERTIFICATION OF NOTICE TO CONSUMER DEBTOR(S)
UNDER § 342(b) OF THE BANKRUPTCY CODE

Certification of Debtor

     I (We), the debtor(s), affirm that I (we) have received and read the attached notice, as required by § 342(b) of the Bankruptcy Code.

Carrie Anne Edwards _____   X **/s/ Carrie Anne Edwards** _____

Printed Name(s) of Debtor(s)   Signature of Debtor   Date

Case No. (if known) _____   X _____

                                         Signature of Joint Debtor (if any)   Date

---

Instructions: Attach a copy of Form B 201 A, Notice to Consumer Debtor(s) Under § 342(b) of the Bankruptcy Code.

Use this form to certify that the debtor has received the notice required by 11 U.S.C. § 342(b) **only** if the certification has **NOT** been made on the Voluntary Petition, Official Form B1. Exhibit B on page 2 of Form B1 contains a certification by the debtor's attorney that the attorney has given the notice to the debtor. The Declarations made by debtors and bankruptcy petition preparers on page 3 of Form B1 also include this certification.

United States Bankruptcy Court
Northern District of California

In re   **Carrie Anne Edwards**   Case No. _____

                             Debtor(s)   Chapter   **7** _____

CREDITOR MATRIX COVER SHEET

      I declare that the attached Creditor Mailing Matrix, consisting of __**4**__ sheets, contains the correct, complete and current names and addresses of all priority, secured and unsecured creditors listed in debtor's filing and that this matrix conforms with the Clerk's promulgated requirements.

Date: _____   _____

                                  Signature of Attorney

Creditor Mailing Matrix

In re ___Carrie Ann Edwards___   Case No. _____
         Debtor(s)   Chapter ___7___

Alan Accountant   Chasum and Grabit Law Firm
5 Green St.   4444 Park Ave.
Cleveland, OH 44118   Lexington, KY 40567

American Allowance   Citibank
PO Box 1   200 East North St
New York, NY 10001   Columbus, OH 43266

Angel of Mercy Hospital   Dr. Dennis Dentist
4444 Elevisior St.   45 Superior Way
Belmont, CA 94003   Cleveland, OH 44118

Beauty Products Leasing Co.   Dr. Helen Jones
44332   443 First St.
Geismar, LA 70734   Soledad, CA 94750

Bob Jones III   Fannie's Furniture
4566 Fifth Ave.   55544 Grove St.
New York, NY 10020   Berkeley, CA 94710

Bonnie Johnson   Forbes and Jones Law Firm
3335 Irving St   3436 State St.
Clearlake, CA 95422   Karlstad, MN 56732

Cal State Central Credit Union   GMAC
1205 N. Dutton Ave   PO Box 23567
Santa Rosa, CA 95401   Duchesne, UT 84021

                                        Grand Junction Mortgage
                                        3456 Eight St.
                                        Clearlake, CA 95422

Creditor Mailing Matrix

In re ___Carrie Ann Edwards___   Case No. _____
Debtor(s)   Chapter _____7_____

Herman Jones   PG&E
45543 Woodleigh Court   315 North Forbes St.
Smith River, CA 95567   Lakeport, CA 95453

Illuminating Co.   Sears
20245 Old Hwy 53   PO Box 11
Clearlake, CA 95422   Chicago, IL 60619

IRS   XYZ Collections
Columbus, OH 43266   9812 First Ave.
                                  Clearlake, CA 95422

John White Esq.
PO Box 401
Finley, CA 95435

Jon Edwards
900 Grand View
Jackson, WY 83001

Lending Tree
PO Box 3333
Palo Alto, CA 94310

Loan Shark Collections
PO Box 666
Clearlake, CA 95422

Loan Shark Collections
4568 Main St.
Fortuna, CA, CA 90543

In re ___Carrie Ann Edwards___   Creditor Matrix   Page 2 of 2
Debtor(s)

B21 (Official Form 21) (12/07)

STATEMENT OF SOCIAL-SECURITY NUMBER OR
INDIVIDUAL TAXPAYER-IDENTIFICATION NUMBER (ITIN)

United States Bankruptcy Court
Northern District of California

In re   **Carrie Anne Edwards**
                                                                    Debtor   Case No. _____

         3045 Berwick St
Address **Lakeport, CA 95453**   Chapter   **7**
Employer's Tax Identification (EIN) No(s). [if any]: _____
Last four digits of Social Security No(s).:   **xxx-xx-6287**

STATEMENT OF SOCIAL-SECURITY NUMBER(S)
(or other Individual Taxpayer-Identification Number(s) (ITIN(s)))

1. Name of Debtor (enter Last, First, Middle): **Edwards, Carrie Anne**
(Check the appropriate box and, if applicable, provide the required information.)

   ■ Debtor has a Social Security Number and it is: ___**573-55-6287**___
                 (If more than one, state all.)
   ☐ Debtor does not have a Social Security Number but has an Individual Taxpayer-Identification Number (ITIN),
       and it is: __.
       (If more than one, state all.)
   ☐ Debtor does not have either a Social-Security Number or an Individual Taxpayer-Identification Number (ITIN).

2. Name of Joint Debtor (enter Last, First, Middle): _____
(Check the appropriate box and, if applicable, provide the required information.)

   ☐ Joint Debtor has a Social Security Number and it is: __
                 (If more than one, state all.)
   ☐ Joint Debtor does not have a Social Security Number but has an Individual Taxpayer-Identification Number and
       it is: __.
                 (If more than one, state all.)
   ☐ Joint Debtor does not have a Social Security Number or an Individual Taxpayer Identification Number (ITIN).

I declare under penalty of perjury that the foregoing is true and correct.

   X   **/s/ Carrie Anne Edwards**_____
       Carrie Anne Edwards   Date
       Signature of Debtor

   X   _____
       Signature of Joint Debtor   Date

Joint debtors must provide information for both spouses.
Penalty for making a false statement: Fine of up to $250,000 or up to 5 years imprisonment or both. 18 U.S.C. §§ 152 and 3571.
Software Copyright (c) 1996-2010 Best Case Solutions - Evanston, IL - bestcase.com   Best Case Bankruptcy

B22A (Official Form 22A) (Chapter 7) (04/10)

In re   **Carrie Anne Edwards** _____

                    Debtor(s)

Case Number: _____
                   (If known)

According to the information required to be entered on this statement (check one box as directed in Part I, III, or VI of this statement):

☐ **The presumption arises.**

■ **The presumption does not arise.**

☐ **The presumption is temporarily inapplicable.**

CHAPTER 7 STATEMENT OF CURRENT MONTHLY INCOME AND MEANS-TEST CALCULATION

In addition to Schedules I and J, this statement must be completed by every individual chapter 7 debtor, whether or not filing jointly. Unless the exclusion in Line 1C applies, joint debtors may complete a single statement. If the exclusion in Line 1C applies, each joint filer must complete a separate statement.

	Part I. MILITARY AND NON-CONSUMER DEBTORS
1A	**Disabled Veterans.** If you are a disabled veteran described in the Declaration in this Part 1A, (1) check the box at the beginning of the Declaration, (2) check the box for "The presumption does not arise" at the top of this statement, and (3) complete the verification in Part VIII. Do not complete any of the remaining parts of this statement. ☐ **Declaration of Disabled Veteran.** By checking this box, I declare under penalty of perjury that I am a disabled veteran (as defined in 38 U.S.C. § 3741(1)) whose indebtedness occurred primarily during a period in which I was on active duty (as defined in 10 U.S.C. § 101(d)(1)) or while I was performing a homeland defense activity (as defined in 32 U.S.C. §901(1)).
1B	**Non-consumer Debtors.** If your debts are not primarily consumer debts, check the box below and complete the verification in Part VIII. Do not complete any of the remaining parts of this statement. ☐ **Declaration of non-consumer debts.** By checking this box, I declare that my debts are not primarily consumer debts.

1C	**Reservists and National Guard Members; active duty or homeland defense activity.** Members of a reserve component of the Armed Forces and members of the National Guard who were called to active duty (as defined in 10 U.S.C. § 101(d)(1)) after September 11, 2001, for a period of at least 90 days, or who have performed homeland defense activity (as defined in 32 U.S.C. § 901(1)) for a period of at least 90 days, are excluded from all forms of means testing during the time of active duty or homeland defense activity and for 540 days thereafter (the "exclusion period"). If you qualify for this temporary exclusion, (1) check the appropriate boxes and complete any required information in the Declaration of Reservists and National Guard Members below, (2) check the box for "The presumption is temporarily inapplicable" at the top of this statement, and (3) complete the verification in Part VIII. **During your exclusion period you are not required to complete the balance of this form, but you must complete the form no later than 14 days after the date on which your exclusion period ends, unless the time for filing a motion raising the means test presumption expires in your case before your exclusion period ends.**
	
	☐ **Declaration of Reservists and National Guard Members.** By checking this box and making the appropriate entries below, I declare that I am eligible for a temporary exclusion from means testing because, as a member of a reserve component of the Armed Forces or the National Guard
	
	        a. ☐ I was called to active duty after September 11, 2001, for a period of at least 90 days and
	                ☐ I remain on active duty /or/
	                ☐ I was released from active duty on _____, which is less than 540 days before this bankruptcy case was filed,
	
	        OR
	
	        b. ☐ I am performing homeland defense activity for a period of at least 90 days /or/
	                ☐ I performed homeland defense activity for a period of at least 90 days terminating on _____, which is less than 540 days before this bankruptcy case was filed.

B22A (Official Form 22A) (Chapter 7) (04/10)   2

	Part II. CALCULATION OF MONTHLY INCOME FOR § 707(b)(7) EXCLUSION		
2	**Marital/filing status.** Check the box that applies and complete the balance of this part of this statement as directed. a. ■ **Unmarried. Complete only Column A ("Debtor's Income") for Lines 3-11.** b. ☐ Married, not filing jointly, with declaration of separate households. By checking this box, debtor declares under penalty of perjury: "My spouse and I are legally separated under applicable non-bankruptcy law or my spouse and I are living apart other than for the purpose of evading the requirements of § 707(b)(2)(A) of the Bankruptcy Code." **Complete only column A ("Debtor's Income") for Lines 3-11.** c. ☐ Married, not filing jointly, without the declaration of separate households set out in Line 2.b above. **Complete both Column A ("Debtor's Income") and Column B ("Spouse's Income") for Lines 3-11.** d. ☐ Married, filing jointly. **Complete both Column A ("Debtor's Income") and Column B ("Spouse's Income") for Lines 3-11.**		

	All figures must reflect average monthly income received from all sources, derived during the six calendar months prior to filing the bankruptcy case, ending on the last day of the month before the filing. If the amount of monthly income varied during the six months, you must divide the six-month total by six, and enter the result on the appropriate line.	**Column A** Debtor's Income	**Column B** Spouse's Income
3	**Gross wages, salary, tips, bonuses, overtime, commissions.**	$ 4,950.67	$
4	**Income from the operation of a business, profession or farm.** Subtract Line b from Line a and enter the difference in the appropriate column(s) of Line 4. If you operate more than one business, profession or farm, enter aggregate numbers and provide details on an attachment. Do not enter a number less than zero. **Do not include any part of the business expenses entered on Line b as a deduction in Part V.** a. Gross receipts — Debtor $ 0.00 Spouse $ b. Ordinary and necessary business expenses — Debtor $ 0.00 Spouse $ c. Business income — Subtract Line b from Line a	$ 0.00	$
5	**Rents and other real property income.** Subtract Line b from Line a and enter the difference in the appropriate column(s) of Line 5. Do not enter a number less than zero. **Do not include any part of the operating expenses entered on Line b as a deduction in Part V.** a. Gross receipts — Debtor $ 0.00 Spouse $ b. Ordinary and necessary operating expenses — Debtor $ 0.00 Spouse $ c. Rent and other real property income — Subtract Line b from Line a	$ 0.00	$
6	**Interest, dividends, and royalties.**	$ 0.00	$
7	**Pension and retirement income.**	$ 0.00	$
8	**Any amounts paid by another person or entity, on a regular basis, for the household expenses of the debtor or the debtor's dependents, including child support paid for that purpose.** Do not include alimony or separate maintenance payments or amounts paid by your spouse if Column B is completed.	$ 400.00	$
9	**Unemployment compensation.** Enter the amount in the appropriate column(s) of Line 9. However, if you contend that unemployment compensation received by you or your spouse was a benefit under the Social Security Act, do not list the amount of such compensation in Column A or B, but instead state the amount in the space below: Unemployment compensation claimed to be a benefit under the Social Security Act — Debtor $ 0.00 Spouse $	$ 0.00	$
10	**Income from all other sources.** Specify source and amount. If necessary, list additional sources on a separate page. **Do not include alimony or separate maintenance payments paid by your spouse if Column B is completed, but include all other payments of alimony or separate maintenance.** Do not include any benefits received under the Social Security Act or payments received as a victim of a war crime, crime against humanity, or as a victim of international or domestic terrorism. a. — Debtor $ Spouse $ b. — Debtor $ Spouse $ Total and enter on Line 10	$ 0.00	$
11	**Subtotal of Current Monthly Income for § 707(b)(7).** Add Lines 3 thru 10 in Column A, and, if Column B is completed, add Lines 3 through 10 in Column B. Enter the total(s).	$ 5,350.67	$

B22A (Official Form 22A) (Chapter 7) (04/10)

| 12 | **Total Current Monthly Income for § 707(b)(7).** If Column B has been completed, add Line 11, Column A to Line 11, Column B, and enter the total. If Column B has not been completed, enter the amount from Line 11, Column A. | $ | **5,350.67** |

Part III. APPLICATION OF § 707(b)(7) EXCLUSION

13	**Annualized Current Monthly Income for § 707(b)(7).** Multiply the amount from Line 12 by the number 12 and enter the result.	$	**64,208.04**
14	**Applicable median family income.** Enter the median family income for the applicable state and household size. (This information is available by family size at www.usdoj.gov/ust/ or from the clerk of the bankruptcy court.)		
	a. Enter debtor's state of residence: **CA** b. Enter debtor's household size: **3**	$	**67,562.00**
15	**Application of Section 707(b)(7).** Check the applicable box and proceed as directed.
	■ **The amount on Line 13 is less than or equal to the amount on Line 14.** Check the box for "The presumption does not arise" at the top of page 1 of this statement, and complete Part VIII; do not complete Parts IV, V, VI or VII.
	☐ **The amount on Line 13 is more than the amount on Line 14.** Complete the remaining parts of this statement.

Complete Parts IV, V, VI, and VII of this statement only if required. (See Line 15.)

Part IV. CALCULATION OF CURRENT MONTHLY INCOME FOR § 707(b)(2)

| 16 | **Enter the amount from Line 12.** | | $ | |
| 17 | **Marital adjustment.** If you checked the box at Line 2.c, enter on Line 17 the total of any income listed in Line 11, Column B that was NOT paid on a regular basis for the household expenses of the debtor or the debtor's dependents. Specify in the lines below the basis for excluding the Column B income (such as payment of the spouse's tax liability or the spouse's support of persons other than the debtor or the debtor's dependents) and the amount of income devoted to each purpose. If necessary, list additional adjustments on a separate page. If you did not check box at Line 2.c, enter zero. | | |

a.		$
b.		$
c.		$
d.		$

| Total and enter on Line 17 | | $ | |

| 18 | **Current monthly income for § 707(b)(2).** Subtract Line 17 from Line 16 and enter the result. | | $ | |

Part V. CALCULATION OF DEDUCTIONS FROM INCOME

Subpart A: Deductions under Standards of the Internal Revenue Service (IRS)

| 19A | **National Standards: food, clothing and other items.** Enter in Line 19A the "Total" amount from IRS National Standards for Food, Clothing and Other Items for the applicable household size. (This information is available at www.usdoj.gov/ust/ or from the clerk of the bankruptcy court.) | | $ | |
| 19B | **National Standards: health care.** Enter in Line a1 below the amount from IRS National Standards for Out-of-Pocket Health Care for persons under 65 years of age, and in Line a2 the IRS National Standards for Out of Pocket Health Care for persons 65 years of age or older. (This information is available at www.usdoj.gov/ust/ or from the clerk of the bankruptcy court.) Enter in Line b1 the number of members of your household who are under 65 years of age, and enter in Line b2 the number of members of your household who are 65 years of age or older. (The total number of household members must be the same as the number stated in Line 14b.) Multiply Line a1 by Line b1 to obtain a total amount for household members under 65, and enter the result in Line c1. Multiply Line a2 by Line b2 to obtain a total amount for household members 65 and older, and enter the result in Line c2. Add Lines c1 and c2 to obtain a total health care amount, and enter the result in Line 19B. | | |

Household members under 65 years of age		Household members 65 years of age or older		
a1.	Allowance per member		a2.	Allowance per member	
b1.	Number of members		b2.	Number of members	
c1.	Subtotal		c2.	Subtotal		$

| 20A | **Local Standards: housing and utilities; non-mortgage expenses.** Enter the amount of the IRS Housing and Utilities Standards; non-mortgage expenses for the applicable county and household size. (This information is available at www.usdoj.gov/ust/ or from the clerk of the bankruptcy court.) | | $ | |

B22A (Official Form 22A) (Chapter 7) (04/10)   4

20B	**Local Standards: housing and utilities; mortgage/rent expense.** Enter, in Line a below, the amount of the IRS Housing and Utilities Standards; mortgage/rent expense for your county and household size (this information is available at www.usdoj.gov/ust/ or from the clerk of the bankruptcy court); enter on Line b the total of the Average Monthly Payments for any debts secured by your home, as stated in Line 42; subtract Line b from Line a and enter the result in Line 20B. **Do not enter an amount less than zero.**	

	a.	IRS Housing and Utilities Standards; mortgage/rental expense	$
	b.	Average Monthly Payment for any debts secured by your home, if any, as stated in Line 42	$
	c.	Net mortgage/rental expense	Subtract Line b from Line a. $

21	**Local Standards: housing and utilities; adjustment.** If you contend that the process set out in Lines 20A and 20B does not accurately compute the allowance to which you are entitled under the IRS Housing and Utilities Standards, enter any additional amount to which you contend you are entitled, and state the basis for your contention in the space below: _____	$

22A	**Local Standards: transportation; vehicle operation/public transportation expense.** You are entitled to an expense allowance in this category regardless of whether you pay the expenses of operating a vehicle and regardless of whether you use public transportation. Check the number of vehicles for which you pay the operating expenses or for which the operating expenses are included as a contribution to your household expenses in Line 8. ☐ 0 ☐ 1 ☐ 2 or more. If you checked 0, enter on Line 22A the "Public Transportation" amount from IRS Local Standards: Transportation. If you checked 1 or 2 or more, enter on Line 22A the "Operating Costs" amount from IRS Local Standards: Transportation for the applicable number of vehicles in the applicable Metropolitan Statistical Area or Census Region. (These amounts are available at www.usdoj.gov/ust/ or from the clerk of the bankruptcy court.)	$

22B	**Local Standards: transportation; additional public transportation expense.** If you pay the operating expenses for a vehicle and also use public transportation, and you contend that you are entitled to an additional deduction for you public transportation expenses, enter on Line 22B the "Public Transportation" amount from IRS Local Standards: Transportation. (This amount is available at www.usdoj.gov/ust/ or from the clerk of the bankruptcy court.)	$

23	**Local Standards: transportation ownership/lease expense; Vehicle 1.** Check the number of vehicles for which you claim an ownership/lease expense. (You may not claim an ownership/lease expense for more than two vehicles.) ☐ 1 ☐ 2 or more. Enter, in Line a below, the "Ownership Costs" for "One Car" from the IRS Local Standards: Transportation (available at www.usdoj.gov/ust/ or from the clerk of the bankruptcy court); enter in Line b the total of the Average Monthly Payments for any debts secured by Vehicle 1, as stated in Line 42; subtract Line b from Line a and enter the result in Line 23. **Do not enter an amount less than zero.**	

	a.	IRS Transportation Standards, Ownership Costs	$
	b.	Average Monthly Payment for any debts secured by Vehicle 1, as stated in Line 42	$
	c.	Net ownership/lease expense for Vehicle 1	Subtract Line b from Line a. $

24	**Local Standards: transportation ownership/lease expense; Vehicle 2.** Complete this Line only if you checked the "2 or more" Box in Line 23. Enter, in Line a below, the "Ownership Costs" for "One Car" from the IRS Local Standards: Transportation (available at www.usdoj.gov/ust/ or from the clerk of the bankruptcy court); enter in Line b the total of the Average Monthly Payments for any debts secured by Vehicle 2, as stated in Line 42; subtract Line b from Line a and enter the result in Line 24. **Do not enter an amount less than zero.**	

	a.	IRS Transportation Standards, Ownership Costs	$
	b.	Average Monthly Payment for any debts secured by Vehicle 2, as stated in Line 42	$
	c.	Net ownership/lease expense for Vehicle 2	Subtract Line b from Line a. $

25	**Other Necessary Expenses: taxes.** Enter the total average monthly expense that you actually incur for all federal, state and local taxes, other than real estate and sales taxes, such as income taxes, self employment taxes, social security taxes, and Medicare taxes. **Do not include real estate or sales taxes.**	$

26	**Other Necessary Expenses: involuntary deductions for employment.** Enter the total average monthly payroll deductions that are required for your employment, such as retirement contributions, union dues, and uniform costs. **Do not include discretionary amounts, such as voluntary 401(k) contributions.**	$

B22A (Official Form 22A) (Chapter 7) (04/10)   7

27	**Other Necessary Expenses: life insurance.** Enter total average monthly premiums that you actually pay for term life insurance for yourself. **Do not include premiums for insurance on your dependents, for whole life or for any other form of insurance.**	$
28	**Other Necessary Expenses: court-ordered payments.** Enter the total monthly amount that you are required to pay pursuant to the order of a court or administrative agency, such as spousal or child support payments. **Do not include payments on past due obligations included in Line 44.**	$
29	**Other Necessary Expenses: education for employment or for a physically or mentally challenged child.** Enter the total average monthly amount that you actually expend for education that is a condition of employment and for education that is required for a physically or mentally challenged dependent child for whom no public education providing similar services is available.	$
30	**Other Necessary Expenses: childcare.** Enter the total average monthly amount that you actually expend on childcare - such as baby-sitting, day care, nursery and preschool. **Do not include other educational payments.**	$
31	**Other Necessary Expenses: health care.** Enter the total average monthly amount that you actually expend on health care that is required for the health and welfare of yourself or your dependents, that is not reimbursed by insurance or paid by a health savings account, and that is in excess of the amount entered in Line 19B. **Do not include payments for health insurance or health savings accounts listed in Line 34.**	$
32	**Other Necessary Expenses: telecommunication services.** Enter the total average monthly amount that you actually pay for telecommunication services other than your basic home telephone and cell phone service - such as pagers, call waiting, caller id, special long distance, or internet service - to the extent necessary for your health and welfare or that of your dependents. **Do not include any amount previously deducted.**	$
33	**Total Expenses Allowed under IRS Standards.** Enter the total of Lines 19 through 32.	$

<table>
<tr><td colspan="3" align="center">Subpart B: Additional Living Expense Deductions
Note: Do not include any expenses that you have listed in Lines 19-32</td></tr>
<tr><td>34</td><td>
Health Insurance, Disability Insurance, and Health Savings Account Expenses. List the monthly expenses in the categories set out in lines a-c below that are reasonably necessary for yourself, your spouse, or your dependents.

a.	Health Insurance	$
b.	Disability Insurance	$
c.	Health Savings Account	$

Total and enter on Line 34.

If you do not actually expend this total amount, state your actual total average monthly expenditures in the space below:

$ _____
</td><td>$</td></tr>
<tr><td>35</td><td>Continued contributions to the care of household or family members. Enter the total average actual monthly expenses that you will continue to pay for the reasonable and necessary care and support of an elderly, chronically ill, or disabled member of your household or member of your immediate family who is unable to pay for such expenses.</td><td>$</td></tr>
<tr><td>36</td><td>Protection against family violence. Enter the total average reasonably necessary monthly expenses that you actually incurred to maintain the safety of your family under the Family Violence Prevention and Services Act or other applicable federal law. The nature of these expenses is required to be kept confidential by the court.</td><td>$</td></tr>
<tr><td>37</td><td>Home energy costs. Enter the total average monthly amount, in excess of the allowance specified by IRS Local Standards for Housing and Utilities, that you actually expend for home energy costs. You must provide your case trustee with documentation of your actual expenses, and you must demonstrate that the additional amount claimed is reasonable and necessary.</td><td>$</td></tr>
<tr><td>38</td><td>Education expenses for dependent children less than 18. Enter the total average monthly expenses that you actually incur, not to exceed $147.92* per child, for attendance at a private or public elementary or secondary school by your dependent children less than 18 years of age. <strong>You must provide your case trustee with documentation of your actual expenses, and you must explain why the amount claimed is reasonable and necessary and not already accounted for in the IRS Standards.</strong></td><td>$</td></tr>
</table>

* Amount subject to adjustment on 4/01/13, and every three years thereafter with respect to cases commenced on or after the date of adjustment.

B22A (Official Form 22A) (Chapter 7) (04/10)   6

39	**Additional food and clothing expense.** Enter the total average monthly amount by which your food and clothing expenses exceed the combined allowances for food and clothing (apparel and services) in the IRS National Standards, not to exceed 5% of those combined allowances. (This information is available at www.usdoj.gov/ust/ or from the clerk of the bankruptcy court.) **You must demonstrate that the additional amount claimed is reasonable and necessary.**	$
40	**Continued charitable contributions.** Enter the amount that you will continue to contribute in the form of cash or financial instruments to a charitable organization as defined in 26 U.S.C. § 170(c)(1)-(2).	$
41	**Total Additional Expense Deductions under § 707(b).** Enter the total of Lines 34 through 40	$

Subpart C: Deductions for Debt Payment

42	**Future payments on secured claims.** For each of your debts that is secured by an interest in property that you own, list the name of the creditor, identify the property securing the debt, and state the Average Monthly Payment, and check whether the payment includes taxes or insurance. The Average Monthly Payment is the total of all amounts scheduled as contractually due to each Secured Creditor in the 60 months following the filing of the bankruptcy case, divided by 60. If necessary, list additional entries on a separate page. Enter the total of the Average Monthly Payments on Line 42.	

	Name of Creditor	Property Securing the Debt	Average Monthly Payment	Does payment include taxes or insurance?	
a.			$	☐yes ☐no	
			Total: Add Lines		$

43	**Other payments on secured claims.** If any of debts listed in Line 42 are secured by your primary residence, a motor vehicle, or other property necessary for your support or the support of your dependents, you may include in your deduction 1/60th of any amount (the "cure amount") that you must pay the creditor in addition to the payments listed in Line 42, in order to maintain possession of the property. The cure amount would include any sums in default that must be paid in order to avoid repossession or foreclosure. List and total any such amounts in the following chart. If necessary, list additional entries on a separate page.	

	Name of Creditor	Property Securing the Debt	1/60th of the Cure Amount	
a.			$	
			Total: Add Lines	$

44	**Payments on prepetition priority claims.** Enter the total amount, divided by 60, of all priority claims, such as priority tax, child support and alimony claims, for which you were liable at the time of your bankruptcy filing. **Do not include current obligations, such as those set out in Line 28.**	$
45	**Chapter 13 administrative expenses.** If you are eligible to file a case under Chapter 13, complete the following chart, multiply the amount in line a by the amount in line b, and enter the resulting administrative expense.	

a.	Projected average monthly Chapter 13 plan payment.	$
b.	Current multiplier for your district as determined under schedules issued by the Executive Office for United States Trustees. (This information is available at www.usdoj.gov/ust/ or from the clerk of the bankruptcy court.)	x
c.	Average monthly administrative expense of Chapter 13 case	Total: Multiply Lines a and b

		$
46	**Total Deductions for Debt Payment.** Enter the total of Lines 42 through 45.	$

Subpart D: Total Deductions from Income

47	**Total of all deductions allowed under § 707(b)(2).** Enter the total of Lines 33, 41, and 46.	$

Part VI. DETERMINATION OF § 707(b)(2) PRESUMPTION

48	**Enter the amount from Line 18 (Current monthly income for § 707(b)(2))**	$
49	**Enter the amount from Line 47 (Total of all deductions allowed under § 707(b)(2))**	$
50	**Monthly disposable income under § 707(b)(2).** Subtract Line 49 from Line 48 and enter the result.	$
51	**60-month disposable income under § 707(b)(2).** Multiply the amount in Line 50 by the number 60 and enter the result.	$

B22A (Official Form 22A) (Chapter 7) (04/10)   7

52	**Initial presumption determination.** Check the applicable box and proceed as directed. ☐ **The amount on Line 51 is less than $7,025*.** Check the box for "The presumption does not arise" at the top of page 1 of this statement, and complete the verification in Part VIII. Do not complete the remainder of Part VI. ☐ **The amount set forth on Line 51 is more than $11,725*** Check the box for "The presumption arises" at the top of page 1 of this statement, and complete the verification in Part VIII. You may also complete Part VII. Do not complete the remainder of Part VI. ☐ **The amount on Line 51 is at least $7,025*, but not more than $11,725*.** Complete the remainder of Part VI (Lines 53 through 55).

53	Enter the amount of your total non-priority unsecured debt	$
54	**Threshold debt payment amount.** Multiply the amount in Line 53 by the number 0.25 and enter the result.	$

55	**Secondary presumption determination.** Check the applicable box and proceed as directed. ☐ **The amount on Line 51 is less than the amount on Line 54.** Check the box for "The presumption does not arise" at the top of page 1 of this statement, and complete the verification in Part VIII. ☐ **The amount on Line 51 is equal to or greater than the amount on Line 54.** Check the box for "The presumption arises" at the top of page 1 of this statement, and complete the verification in Part VIII. You may also complete Part VII.

Part VII. ADDITIONAL EXPENSE CLAIMS

56	**Other Expenses.** List and describe any monthly expenses, not otherwise stated in this form, that are required for the health and welfare of you and your family and that you contend should be an additional deduction from your current monthly income under § 707(b)(2)(A)(ii)(I). If necessary, list additional sources on a separate page. All figures should reflect your average monthly expense for each item. Total the expenses.

	Expense Description	Monthly Amount
a.		$
b.		$
c.		$
d.		$
	Total: Add Lines a, b, c, and d	$

Part VIII. VERIFICATION

57	I declare under penalty of perjury that the information provided in this statement is true and correct. *(If this is a joint case, both debtors must sign.)*
	
	Date: _____ Signature: **/s/ Carrie Anne Edwards**
	
	                                                              Carrie Anne Edwards
	                                                                    (Debtor)

* Amounts are subject to adjustment on 4/01/13, and every three years thereafter with respect to cases commenced on or after the date of adjustment.

B23 (Official Form 23) (12/08)

United States Bankruptcy Court
Northern District of California

In re   **Carrie Anne Edwards** _____   Case No. _____

Debtor(s)   Chapter   **7** _____

DEBTOR'S CERTIFICATION OF COMPLETION OF POSTPETITION INSTRUCTIONAL COURSE CONCERNING PERSONAL FINANCIAL MANAGEMENT

Every individual debtor in a chapter 7, chapter 11 in which § 1141(d)(3) applies, or chapter 13 case must file this certification. If a joint petition is filed, each spouse must complete and file a separate certification. Complete one of the following statements and file by the deadline stated below:

■ I, **Carrie Anne Edwards** , the debtor in the above-styled case, hereby certify that on **01/01/20XX** , I completed an instructional course in personal financial management provided by **Consumer Credit Counseling Service** , an approved personal financial management provider.

Certificate No. (if any): **4565433** .

☐ I, _____ , the debtor in the above-styled case, hereby certify that no personal financial management course is required because of *[Check the appropriate box.]*:
    ☐ Incapacity or disability, as defined in 11 U.S.C.§ 109(h);
    ☐ Active military duty in a military combat zone; or
    ☐ Residence in a district in which the United States trustee (or bankruptcy administrator) has determined that the approved instructional courses are not adequate at this time to serve the additional individuals who would otherwise be required to complete such courses.

Signature of Debtor: **/s/ Carrie Anne Edwards** _____
                         Carrie Anne Edwards

Date: _____

Instructions: Use this form only to certify whether you completed a course in personal financial management. (Fed. R. Bankr. P. 1007(b)(7).) Do NOT use this form to file the certificate given to you by your prepetition credit counseling provider and do NOT include with the petition when filing your case.

Filing Deadlines: In a chapter 7 case, file within 45 days of the first date set for the meeting of creditors under § 341 of the Bankruptcy Code. In a chapter 11 or 13 case, file no later than the last payment made by the debtor as required by the plan or the filing of a motion for a discharge under § 1141(d)(5)(B) or § 1328(b) of the Code. (See Fed. R. Bankr. P. 1007(c).)

United States Bankruptcy Court
Northern District of California

In re   **Carrie Anne Edwards**   Case No. _____

                                  Debtor(s)   Chapter   **7** _____

STATEMENT PURSUANT TO RULE 2016(B)

The undersigned, pursuant to Rule 2016(b), Bankruptcy Rules, states that:

1.   The undersigned is the attorney for the debtor(s) in this case.

2.   The compensation paid or agreed to be paid by the debtor(s), to the undersigned is:

      a)   For legal services rendered or to be rendered in contemplation of and in connection with this case $ _____ **0.00**

      b)   Prior to the filing of this statement, debtor(s) have paid $ _____ **0.00**

      c)   The unpaid balance due and payable is $ _____ **0.00**

3. $ **0.00** of the filing fee in this case has been paid.

4.   The Services rendered or to be rendered include the following:

      a.   Analysis of the financial situation, and rendering advice and assistance to the debtor(s) in determining whether to file a petition under title 11 of the United States Code.

      b.   Preparation and filing of the petition, schedules, statement of affairs and other documents required by the court.

      c.   Representation of the debtor(s) at the meeting of creditors.

5.   The source of payments made by the debtor(s) to the undersigned was from earnings, wages and compensation for services performed, and

6.   The source of payments to be made by the debtor(s) to the undersigned for the unpaid balance remaining, if any, will be from earnings, wages and compensation for services performed, and

7.   The undersigned has received no transfer, assignment or pledge of property from debtor(s) except the following for the value stated:

8.   The undersigned has not shared or agreed to share with any other entity, other than with members of undersigned's law firm, any compensation paid or to be paid except as follows:

Dated: _____   Respectfully submitted,

                                         Attorney for Debtor.

B27 (Official Form 27) (12/09)

United States Bankruptcy Court
NORTHERN DISTRICT OF CALIFORNIA

In re **Carrie Anne Edwards**

Debtor   Case No. _____

                                                Chapter   **7**

REAFFIRMATION AGREEMENT COVER SHEET

This form must be completed in its entirety and filed, with the reaffirmation agreement attached, within the time set under Rule 4008. It may be filed by any party to the reaffirmation agreement.

1.   Creditor's Name: __**GMAC**__

2.   Amount of the debt subject to this reaffirmation agreement:
      $ **15,000**   on the date of bankruptcy $ **15,000**   to be paid under reaffirmation agreement

3.   Annual percentage rate of interest: **8** % prior to bankruptcy
      8 % under reaffirmation agreement (**X** Fixed Rate ___ Adjustable Rate)

4.   Repayment terms (if fixed rate): $ **450** per month for **36** months

5.   Collateral, if any, securing the debt: Current market value: $**7000**
      Description: **Buick LeSabre**

6.   Does the creditor assert that the debt is nondischargeable? ___Yes **X** No
(If yes, attach a declaration setting forth the nature of the debt and basis for the contention that the debt is nondischargeable.)

Debtor's Schedule I and J Entries   Debtor's Income and Expenses
                                                 as Stated on Reaffirmation Agreement

7A.   Total monthly income from $ **4,809.00**   7B.   Monthly income from all $ **4809**
      Schedule I, line 16   sources after payroll deductions

8A.   Total monthly expenses $ **4,720.00**   8B.   Monthly expenses $ **4,720**
      from Schedule J, line 18

9A.   Total monthly payments on $ **0**   9B.   Total monthly payments on $ **0**
      reaffirmed debts not listed on   reaffirmed debts not included in
      Schedule J   monthly expenses

                                                     10B.   Net monthly income $ **89**
                                                            (Subtract sum of lines 8B and 9B from
                                                            line 7B. If total is less than zero, put the
                                                            number in brackets.)

11.   Explain with specificity any difference between the income amounts (7A and 7B):
      _____
      _____

12.   Explain with specificity any difference between the expense amounts (8A and 8B):
      _____
      _____

B27 (Official Form 27) (12/09)   2

     If line 11 or 12 is completed, the undersigned debtor, and joint debtor if applicable, certifies that any explanation contained on those lines is true and correct.

_____   _____
Carrie Anne Edwards
Signature of Debtor (only required if   Signature of Joint Debtor (if applicable, and only
line 11 or 12 is completed)   required if line 11 or 12 is completed)

<u>Other Information</u>

[ ]   Check this box if the total on line 10B is less than zero. If that number is less than zero, a presumption of undue hardship arises (unless the creditor is a credit union) and you must explain with specificity the sources of funds available to the Debtor to make the monthly payments on the reaffirmed debt: _____
_____

Was debtor represented by counsel during the course of negotiating this reaffirmation agreement?
    ___ Yes   **X** No

If debtor was represented by counsel during the course of negotiating this reaffirmation agreement, has counsel executed a certification (affidavit or declaration) in support of the reaffirmation agreement?
    ___ Yes   ___ No

FILER'S CERTIFICATION

     I hereby certify that the attached agreement is a true and correct copy of the reaffirmation agreement between the parties identified on this Reaffirmation Agreement Cover Sheet.

_____
Signature

Attorney for Debtor
_____
Print/Type Name & Signer's Relation to Case

B240B (Form B240B) (12/09)

United States Bankruptcy Court
Northern District of California

In re   **Carrie Anne Edwards** _____   Case No. _____

                                              Debtor(s)   Chapter   **7** _____

MOTION FOR APPROVAL OF REAFFIRMATION AGREEMENT

I (we), the debtor(s), affirm the following to be true and correct:

I am not represented by an attorney in connection with this reaffirmation agreement.

I believe this reaffirmation agreement is in my best interest based on the income and expenses I have disclosed in my Statement in Support of Reaffirmation Agreement, and because (provide any additional relevant reasons the court should consider):

Therefore, I ask the court for an order approving this reaffirmation agreement under the following provisions *(check all applicable boxes)*:

         ☒ 11 U.S.C. § 524(c)(6) (debtor is not represented by an attorney during the course of the negotiation of the reaffirmation agreement)

         ☐ 11 U.S.C. § 524(m) (presumption of undue hardship has arisen because monthly expenses exceed monthly income, as explained in Part II of Form B240A, Reaffirmation Documents)

Signed: _____

             Carrie Edwards

            _____

             (Joint Debtor, if any)

Date: _____

B240A (Form B240A) (04/10)

Check one.

☐ **Presumption of Undue Hardship**

☒ **No Presumption of Undue Hardship**

See Debtor's Statement in Support of Reaffirmation, Part II below, to determine which box to check

United States Bankruptcy Court
Northern District of California

In re **Carrie Anne Edwards**

Debtor(s)

Case No. _____

Chapter **7**

REAFFIRMATION DOCUMENTS

Name of Creditor: **GMAC** _____

☐ Check this box if Creditor is a Credit Union

PART I. REAFFIRMATION AGREEMENT

Reaffirming a debt is a serious financial decision. Before entering into this Reaffirmation Agreement, you must review the important disclosures, instructions, and definitions found in Part V of this form.

A. Brief description of the original agreement being reaffirmed: _____
Auto loan

For example, auto loan

B. *AMOUNT REAFFIRMED:* $ _____ **15,000**

The Amount Reaffirmed is the entire amount that you are agreeing to pay. This may include unpaid principal, interest, and fees and costs (if any) arising on or before **1/1/XXXX** , which is the date of the Disclosure Statement portion of this form (Part V).

See the definition of "Amount Reaffirmed" in Part V, Section C below.

C. The *ANNUAL PERCENTAGE RATE* applicable to the Amount Reaffirmed is **8** %.

See definition of "Annual Percentage Rate" in Part V, Section C below.

This is a *(check one)* ☒ Fixed rate ☐ Variable rate

If the loan has a variable rate, the future interest rate may increase or decrease from the Annual Percentage Rate disclosed here.

D. Reaffirmation Agreement Repayment Terms *(check and complete one)*:

☒ $ **450** per month for **36** months starting on **1/1/XXXX** .

☒ Describe repayment terms, including whether future payment amount(s) may be different from the initial payment amount. **Eqeal monthly payments** .

E. Describe the collateral, if any, securing the debt:

B240A, Reaffirmation Documents   Page 2

Description: 06 **Buick Le Sabre**
Current Market Value $ _____**8000**_____

F. Did the debt that is being reaffirmed arise from the purchase of the collateral described above?

☒ Yes   What was the purchase price for the collateral? $ _____**27,000**_____
☐ No   What was the amount of the original loan? $ _____

G. Specify the changes made by this Reaffirmation Agreement to the most recent credit terms on the reaffirmed debt and any related agreement:

	Terms as of the Date of Bankruptcy	Terms After Reaffirmation
Balance due (including fees and costs)	$ _____	$ _____**No Changes**_____
Annual Percentage Rate	_____ %	_____ %
Monthly Payment	$ _____	$ _____

H. ☐ Check this box if the creditor is agreeing to provide you with additional future credit in connection with this Reaffirmation Agreement. Describe the credit limit, the Annual Percentage Rate that applies to future credit and any other terms on future purchases and advances using such credit:

_____

PART II. DEBTOR'S STATEMENT IN SUPPORT OF REAFFIRMATION AGREEMENT

A. Were you represented by an attorney during the course of negotiating this agreement?

Check one. ☐ Yes   ☒ No

B. Is the creditor a credit union?

Check one. ☐ Yes   ☒ No

C. If your answer to EITHER question A. or B. above is "No" complete 1. and 2. below.

1. Your present monthly income and expenses are:

a. Monthly income from all sources after payroll deductions
(take-home pay plus any other income) $ _____**4809**

b. Monthly expenses (including all reaffirmed debts except this one) $ _____**4270**

c. Amount available to pay this reaffirmed debt (subtract b. from a.) $ _____**539**

d. Amount of monthly payment required for this reaffirmed debt $ _____**450**

*If the monthly payment on this reaffirmed debt (line d.) **is greater than** the amount you have available to pay this reaffirmed debt (line c.), you must check the box at the top of page one that says "Presumption of Undue Hardship." Otherwise, you must check the box at the top of page one that says "No Presumption of Undue Hardship."*

2. You believe this reaffirmation agreement will not impose an undue hardship on you or your dependents because:

Check one of the two statements below, if applicable:

☒ You can afford to make the payments on the reaffirmed debt because your monthly income is greater than your monthly expenses even after you include in your expenses the monthly payments on all debts your are reaffirming, including this one.

☐ You can afford to make the payments on the reaffirmed debt even though your monthly income is less than your monthly expenses after you include in your expenses the monthly payments on all debts you are reaffirming, including this one, because:

_____

Use an additional page if needed for a full explanation.

D. If your answers to BOTH question A. or B. above were "Yes," check the following statement, if applicable:

☒ You believe this Reaffirmation Agreement is in your financial interest and you can afford to make the payments on the reaffirmed debt.

Also, check the box at the top of page one that says "No Presumption of Undue Hardship."

B240A, Reaffirmation Documents   Page 4

PART III. CERTIFICATION BY DEBTOR(S) AND SIGNATURES OF PARTIES

I hereby certify that:

    (1)   I agree to reaffirm the debt described above.

    (2)   Before signing this Reaffirmation Agreement, I read the terms disclosed in this Reaffirmation Agreement (Part I) and the Disclosure Statement, Instructions and Definitions included in Part V below;

    (3)   The Debtor's Statement in Support of Reaffirmation Agreement (Part II above) is true and complete;

    (4)   I am entering into this agreement voluntarily and fully informed of my rights and responsibilities; and

    (5)   I have received a copy of this completed and signed Reaffirmation Documents form.

SIGNATURE(S) (If a joint Reaffirmation Agreement, both debtors must sign.):

Date   _____   Signature _____

                                         Carrie Anne Edwards

                                                         Debtor

Date   _____   Signature _____

                                                       Joint Debtor, if any

Reaffirmation Agreement Terms Accepted by Creditor:

Creditor   **GMAC** _____   **PO Box 23567**
                                                   Duchesne, UT 84021

                  Print Name   Address

_____   _____   _____

  Print Name of Representative   Signature   Date

PART IV. CERTIFICATION BY DEBTOR'S ATTORNEY (IF ANY)

To be filed only if the attorney represented the debtor during the course of negotiating this agreement.

I hereby certify that: (1) this agreement represents a fully informed and voluntary agreement by the debtor; (2) this agreement does not impose an undue hardship on the debtor or any dependent of the debtor; and (3) I have fully advised the debtor of the legal effect and consequences of this agreement and any default under this agreement.

☐ A presumption of undue hardship has been established with respect to this agreement. In my opinion, however, the debtor is able to make the required payment.

Check box, if the presumption of undue hardship box is checked on page 1 and the creditor is not a Credit Union.

Date   _____   Signature of Debtor's Attorney   _____

                                            Print Name of Debtor's Attorney   _____

PART V. DISCLOSURE STATEMENT AND INSTRUCTIONS TO DEBTOR(S)

Before agreeing to reaffirm a debt, review the terms disclosed in the Reaffirmation Agreement (Part I above) and these additional important disclosures and instructions.

Reaffirming a debt is a serious financial decision. The law requires you to take certain steps to make sure the decision is in your best interest. If these steps, which are detailed in the Instructions provided in Part V, Section B below, are not completed, the Reaffirmation Agreement is not effective, even though you have signed it.

A. DISCLOSURE STATEMENT

1. **What are your obligations if you reaffirm a debt?** A reaffirmed debt remains your personal legal obligation to pay. Your reaffirmed debt is not discharged in your bankruptcy case. That means that if you default on your reaffirmed debt after your bankruptcy case is over, your creditor may be able to take your property or your wages. Your obligations will be determined by the Reaffirmation Agreement, which may have changed the terms of the original agreement. If you are reaffirming an open end credit agreement, that agreement or applicable law may permit the creditor to change the terms of that agreement in the future under certain conditions.

2. **Are you required to enter into a reaffirmation agreement by any law?** No, you are not required to reaffirm a debt by any law. Only agree to reaffirm a debt if it is in your best interest. Be sure you can afford the payments that you agree to make.

3. **What if your creditor has a security interest or lien?** Your bankruptcy discharge does not eliminate any lien on your property. A ''lien'' is often referred to as a security interest, deed of trust, mortgage, or security deed. The property subject to a lien is often referred to as collateral. Even if you do not reaffirm and your personal liability on the debt is discharged, your creditor may still have a right under the lien to take the collateral if you do not pay or default on the debt. If the collateral is personal property that is exempt or that the trustee has abandoned, you may be able to redeem the item rather than reaffirm the debt. To redeem, you make a single payment to the creditor equal to the current value of the collateral, as the parties agree or the court determines.

4. **How soon do you need to enter into and file a reaffirmation agreement?** If you decide to enter into a reaffirmation agreement, you must do so before you receive your discharge. After you have entered into a reaffirmation agreement and all parts of this form that require a signature have been signed, either you or the creditor should file it as soon as possible. The signed agreement must be filed with the court no later than 60 days after the first date set for the meeting of creditors, so that the court will have time to schedule a hearing to approve the agreement if approval is required. However, the court may extend the time for filing, even after the 60-day period has ended.

5. **Can you cancel the agreement?** You may rescind (cancel) your Reaffirmation Agreement at any time before the bankruptcy court enters your discharge, or during the 60-day period that begins on the date your Reaffirmation Agreement is filed with the court, whichever occurs later. To rescind (cancel) your Reaffirmation Agreement, you must notify the creditor that your Reaffirmation Agreement is rescinded (or canceled). Remember that you can rescind the agreement, even if the court approves it, as long as you rescind within the time allowed.

6. **When will this reaffirmation agreement be effective?**

   a. **If you** *were* **represented by an attorney during the negotiation of your reaffirmation agreement**

   i. **if the creditor is not a Credit Union,** your Reaffirmation Agreement becomes effective when it is filed with the court unless the reaffirmation is presumed to be an undue hardship. If the Reaffirmation Agreement is presumed to be an undue hardship, the court must review it and may set a hearing to determine whether you have rebutted the presumption of undue hardship.

         ii. **if the creditor is a Credit Union**, your Reaffirmation Agreement becomes effective when it is filed with the court.

      b. If you *were not* **represented by an attorney during the negotiation of your Reaffirmation Agreement,** the Reaffirmation Agreement will not be effective unless the court approves it. To have the court approve your agreement, you must file a motion. See Instruction 5, below. The court will notify you and the creditor of the hearing on your Reaffirmation Agreement. You must attend this hearing, at which time the judge will review your Reaffirmation Agreement. If the judge decides that the Reaffirmation Agreement is in your best interest, the agreement will be approved and will become effective. However, if your Reaffirmation Agreement is for a consumer debt secured by a mortgage, deed of trust, security deed, or other lien on your real property, like your home, you do not need to file a motion or get court approval of your Reaffirmation Agreement.

   7.   **What if you have questions about what a creditor can do?** If you have questions about reaffirming a debt or what the law requires, consult with the attorney who helped you negotiate this agreement. If you do not have an attorney helping you, you may ask the judge to explain the effect of this agreement to you at the hearing to approve the Reaffirmation Agreement. When this disclosure refers to what a creditor "may" do, it is not giving any creditor permission to do anything. The word "may" is used to tell you what might occur if the law permits the creditor to take the action.

B.   INSTRUCTIONS

   1.   Review these Disclosures and carefully consider the decision to reaffirm. If you want to reaffirm, review and complete the information contained in the Reaffirmation Agreement (Part I above). If your case is a joint case, both spouses must sign the agreement if both are reaffirming the debt.

   2.   Complete the Debtor's Statement in Support of Reaffirmation Agreement (Part II above). Be sure that you can afford to make the payments that you are agreeing to make and that you have received a copy of the Disclosure Statement and a completed and signed Reaffirmation Agreement.

   3.   If you were represented by an attorney during the negotiation of your Reaffirmation Agreement, your attorney must sign and date the Certification By Debtor's Attorney section (Part IV above).

   4.   You or your creditor must file with the court the original of this Reaffirmation Documents packet and a completed Reaffirmation Agreement Cover Sheet (Official Bankruptcy Form 27).

   5.   *If you are not represented by an attorney, you must also complete and file with the court a separate document entitled "Motion for Court Approval of Reaffirmation Agreement" unless your Reaffirmation Agreement is for a consumer debt secured by a lien on your real property, such as your home.* You can use Form B240B to do this.

C.   DEFINITIONS

   1.   **"Amount Reaffirmed"** means the total amount of debt that you are agreeing to pay (reaffirm) by entering into this agreement. The total amount of debt includes any unpaid fees and costs that you are agreeing to pay that arose on or before the date of disclosure, which is the date specified in the Reaffirmation Agreement (Part I, Section B above). Your credit agreement may obligate you to pay additional amounts that arise after the date of this disclosure. You should consult your credit agreement to determine whether you are obligated to pay additional amounts that may arise after the date of this disclosure.

   2.   **"Annual Percentage Rate"** means the interest rate on a loan expressed under the rules required by federal law. The annual percentage rate (as opposed to the "stated interest rate") tells you the full cost of your credit including many of the creditor's fees and charges. You will find the annual percentage rate for your original

agreement on the disclosure statement that was given to you when the loan papers were signed or on the monthly statements sent to you for an open end credit account such as a credit card.

3. **"Credit Union"** means a financial institution as defined in 12 U.S.C. § 461(b)(1)(A)(iv). It is owned and controlled by and provides financial services to its members and typically uses words like "Credit Union" or initials like "C.U." or "F.C.U." in its name.

B240C ALT (Form B240C ALT) (4/10)

United States Bankruptcy Court
Northern District of California

In re **Carrie Anne Edwards** _____   Case No. _____
                                                      Debtor(s)   Chapter   **7** _____

ORDER ON REAFFIRMATION AGREEMENT

The debtor(s) **Carrie Anne Edwards** ___ has (have) filed a motion for approval of the reaffirmation agreement dated _____ made between the debtor(s) and creditor _____. The court held the hearing required by 11 U.S.C. § 524(d) on notice to the debtor(s) and the creditor on _____ (date).

COURT ORDER: ☐   The court grants the debtor's motion under 11 U.S.C. § 524(c)(6)(A) and approves the reaffirmation agreement described above as not imposing an undue hardship on the debtor(s) or a dependent of the debtor(s) and as being in the best interest of the debtor(s).

                        ☐   The court grants the debtor's motion under 11 U.S.C. § 524(k)(8) and approves the reaffirmation agreement described above.

                        ☐   The court does not disapprove the reaffirmation agreement under 11 U.S.C. § 524(m).

                        ☐   The court disapproves the reaffirmation agreement under 11 U.S.C. § 524(m).

                        ☐   The court does not approve the reaffirmation agreement.

BY THE COURT

Date: _____   _____
                                       United States Bankruptcy Judge

Index

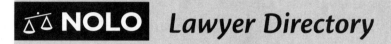